W9-AST-387

683.82 E85ki

Ettlinger, Steve.

The kitchenware book

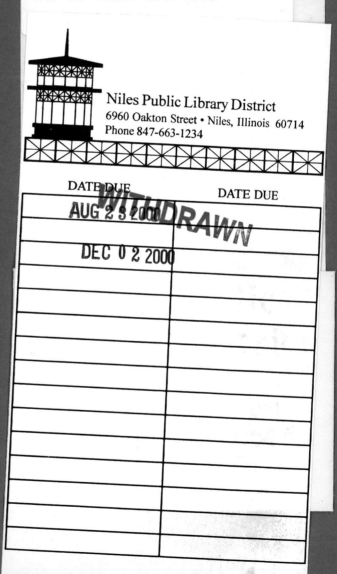

Niles Public Library District
6960 Oakton Street • Niles, Illinois 60714
Phone 847-663-1234

WITHDRAWN

DATE DUE	DATE DUE
AUG 2 3 2000	
DEC 0 2 2000	

THE KITCHENWARE BOOK

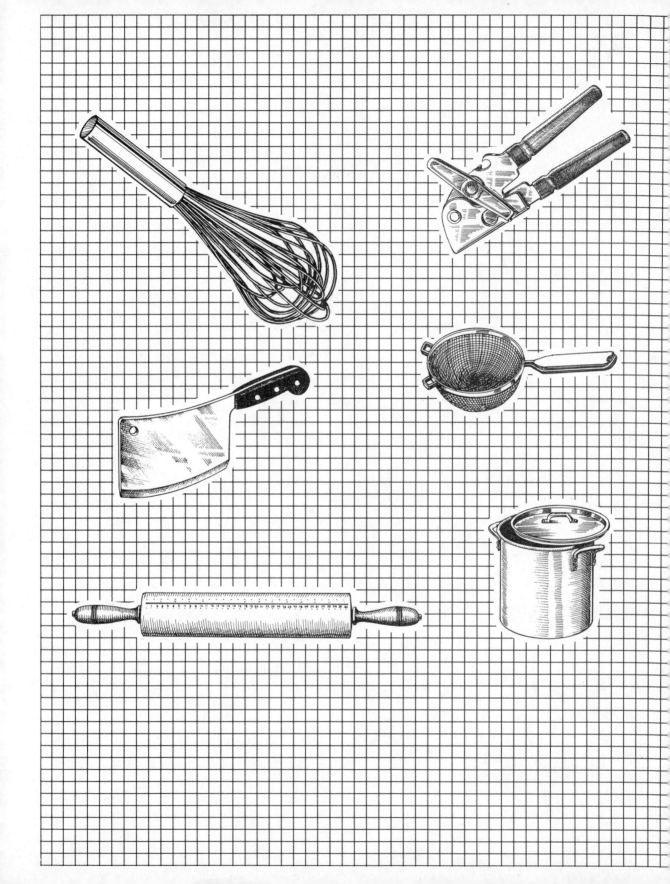

The Kitchenware Book

Steve Ettlinger

research consultant: Irena Chalmers
illustrations by Robert Strimban
conceived, written, and edited by Ettlinger Editorial Projects

Macmillan Publishing Company
NEW YORK

Maxwell Macmillan Canada
TORONTO

Maxwell Macmillan International
NEW YORK   OXFORD   SINGAPORE   SYDNEY

Copyright © 1992 by Stephen R. Ettlinger

All rights reserved. No part of this book may be reproduced or transmitted in any form or by any means, electronic or mechanical, including photocopying, recording, or by any information storage and retrieval system, without permission in writing from the Publisher.

Macmillan Publishing Company	Maxwell Macmillan Canada, Inc.
866 Third Avenue	1200 Eglinton Avenue East
New York, NY 10022	Don Mills, Ontario M3C 3N1

Macmillan Publishing Company is part of the Maxwell Communication Group of Companies.

Library of Congress Cataloging-in-Publication Data
Ettlinger, Steve.
The kitchenware book / Steve Ettlinger ; illustrations by Robert Strimban ; conceived and edited by Ettlinger Editorial Projects.
p.   cm.
ISBN 0-02-536302-6
1. Kitchen utensils.   I. Stephen R. Ettlinger Editorial Projects.
II. Title.
TX656.E88   1993
683′.82—dc20   92-28847   CIP

This book is intended only to orient the consumer to the various categories of products available. It is by no means intended to be a buying guide to specific products, and neither the author nor the publisher recommends the purchase or avoidance of any items listed here, nor do they recommend avoiding any products not listed here. Sample brand names appear from time to time but do not imply any endorsement of any kind.

Furthermore, neither the author nor the publisher can be held responsible for the use of any items noted within. Use tips are by their very nature incomplete and not intended to be fully instructive.

Macmillan books are available at special discounts for bulk purchases for sales promotions, premiums, fund-raising, or educational use. For details, contact:

Special Sales Director
Macmillan Publishing Company
866 Third Avenue
New York, NY 10022

10 9 8 7 6 5 4 3 2 1

PRINTED IN THE UNITED STATES OF AMERICA

This book is dedicated to all of us who have spent time in kitchenware stores wondering what all those little gadgets are really for.

Contents

Part III: Beverage, Garnishing, and Serving Items

Part IV: Kitchen Accessories

Appendixes

Acknowledgments

It was a great pleasure to work with Irena Chalmers, one of the world's leading cooking experts and most prolific cookbook authors, who provided numerous tips and details as well as many extremely helpful suggestions and resources that helped make the book complete.

Carol Murashige became my editorial assistant halfway through this project and took it on as if it were her own. She has made an invaluable contribution to the book and in general made this huge project run much more smoothly than it might have without her. I am very lucky that she appeared in my office and look forward to doing many more books with her. Marc Medoff and Mary Ellen O'Neill helped with the preliminary research.

Besides his delightfully detailed drawings, Bob Stimban, along with his wife, Irma, has contributed a general spirit of goodwill and inspiration to this project. He worked full time for many months to do all these beautiful illustrations, and his hard work, dedication, and good humor are much appreciated.

Finally, though it may be getting boring for readers of my previous, similar, big guides (*The Complete Illustrated Guide to Everything Sold in Hardware Stores* and *The Complete Illustrated Guide to Everything Sold in Garden Centers*), I must thank my parents once again for their assistance with the research. This is not just self-serving praise—my mother, Margery, is a serious cook, editor, and co-hostess of a cable TV cooking show, "Culinary Delights." My father, Ralph, who is far better at gourmet eating than cooking (alas, an inherited trait!), contributed to those sections where he had expertise as well. I am very grateful that my parents share my professional concerns.

Thanks go out to the hundreds of manufacturers who responded to our requests for catalogs. I would like to acknowledge some who were particularly helpful and spent time searching out answers to our detailed questions.

Peter Baer, Progressus Company; Janet Bergman, Fox Run Craftsmen; Mick Freeman, Griffo Grill; Bud Haley, Hoan Products, Ltd.; Zella Junkin, Wilton Enterprises; Anita Levor, Better Houseware Corp.; Jeff Merrifield, Best Manufacturers; Hans Rathsack, Wüsthof-Trident of America, Inc.; Louis Richardone, Charles Lamalle; Charles Rosner, Robinson Design Group; Norman Schoenfeld, Meyer Corp., U.S.; Bill Travers and Julie Mazer, Rowoco; Michel Scheinmann, Bourgeat USA, Inc.; Mike

Sullivan, The Wine Enthusiast; Louis Van Leeuwen, Cuisine de France, Ltd.

Certain other kitchenware experts provided answers at times that were assuredly inconvenient to them, and I wish to extend my thanks to:

Barbara Bloch, cookbook author; Todd Johnson, Kitchen Bazaar; Jean Kozar, General Mills; Peter Kump, Peter Kump's NY Cooking School; Nadia Linsalata; Marshall Marcovitz, Chef's Catalog; Arlene Marvin, the Cookery Dock, Southampton and Greenport, New York; Doris and John Mason; Alex Miles, grand pastry chef; Veronica Murashige; Paul Murphy, metalurgy expert; Anne Nuebling, California Kitchens; Roark O'Flennikan, chef, Park Avenue Gourmandises; Elizabeth Patterson, 2nd Avenue Bazaar; Anne Willan, La Varenne Cooking School.

I'd like to make a general and apologetic thanks to the various kitchenware stores where I shopped and bothered the staff with research questions, especially Williams-Sonoma and Broadway Panhandler, both in New York City. Also a thanks to those many restaurants where chefs tolerated my seemingly bizarre questions that no one had ever asked them before. I'm sure they all wondered why I was asking such details.

Thanks are due to my editors, Pam Hoenig and Justin Schwartz, and publishers, Barry Lippman and Bill Rosen, for their support of this and my previous two books with Macmillan.

This book is further dedicated in gratitude to my mother-in-law, Jean Lange, and my wife, Gusty, whose continuous support and encouragement throughout this long and immense project made it all possible.

STEVE ETTLINGER

Preface

Cooking at home should be a simple task, but for many of us it is rather intimidating. There are plenty of cookbooks and recipes in magazines and newspapers which tell you how to cook, but they so often mention the utensils to use only in passing—and often by unfamiliar names. Furthermore, when they call for ingredients that must be prepared there is often no suggestion as to what to prepare them with. For example, an apple pie calls for cored and sliced apples, but rarely do you see explained that one of the fastest ways to do this is with an inexpensive tool designed expressly for the job.

Some of you may have inherited a kitchen drawer full of exotic-looking gadgets you never could figure out or use only rarely. Others would like to broaden their cooking repertoire but are hampered by a lack of tools. You may suspect that you are hampering yourself by just using whatever utensils you happen to have on hand and not seeking out the right tool for the job. Many beginners do not even recognize the value of having at least one really good knife. Finally, few of us have the family training to cook that used to be so common. All this can be very daunting, especially to the beginner.

Even more frustrating is the huge number of gadgets and utensils for sale in any given kitchenware store or department. Those large displays are intimidating, and all the labels seem to claim the same thing. These are not items you buy every day, but more likely things you buy only once, and so you are quite unfamiliar with them. Few knowledgeable salespeople are available to help. The stakes are high if you are trying to make an expensive, once-in-a-lifetime cookware or cutlery set purchase, usually when you are just setting up housekeeping or making a gift to someone who is. Where can you seek help?

The answers to all of these problems are contained in this book. As with its predecessors in this series, *The Complete Illustrated Guide to Everything Sold in Hardware Stores* and *The Complete Illustrated Guide to Everything Sold in Garden Centers,* I've searched out every manufacturer possible, combed hundreds of catalogs, talked to chefs, consultants, cooking teachers, and home cooks of all stripes in order to find out what all those whatchamacallits and thingamajigs are. After all, its inspiration was the same: my daunting weekend forays to these vast emporiums in the search for these strange items.

Kitchenware stores are like hardware stores or garden centers: You don't go into one often enough to learn your way around. Now, after reading any of these books you can enter these stores on better terms with the salespeople and make an informed choice. You'll no longer have to buy something you don't really understand. Or, if you are like me, you may want just to browse through the illustrations for pure pleasure. Maybe you'll even discover an item that inspires you to attempt something new. I sure hope you will. This book puts you back in charge.

Although it may seem odd to say this at the beginning of a book that lists over 1,000 cooking tools, most professional chefs and cooking teachers will say that the three most important cook's tools are a good chef's knife (page 12), a good whisk (page 78), and the cook's hands—the point being that while there is much room for personal preference in choosing many other tools, you can't do too well without these. I agree.

I always like to hear from readers with a new AKA (Also Known As) or an item that I may have overlooked. Suggestions for use tips and buying tips are welcome, too. Please write to me c/o Macmillan Publishing Company, 866 Third Avenue, New York, NY 10022.

STEVE ETTLINGER

Introduction

How This Book Is Organized

Cooking meals is a well-defined process and this book is organized to follow that process logically. The first items are those used in basic preparation, such as chopping and grating, and the others follow in a similar manner for the actual cooking and serving. Notable accessories for cleaning and storage are listed in a final section, followed by some useful appendixes on stoves and mail-order catalogs.

You should be able to find any item listed here in your local kitchenware store or from a national mail-order catalog such as those listed in Appendix B (see pages 453–56). Antique or extraordinarily rare international items are not listed here, and though some cleaning, storage, and convenience items are listed in Part IV, items that are really general houseware products are not included. On the other hand, the line between houseware and kitchenware is a blurry one, so this is one area where there is some overlap or you may perceive a gap. No supplies or consumable items are listed.

How to Use This Book

While examining catalog after catalog, all of us doing research got both hungry and inspired. How can you read hundreds of details about cake pans without wanting to eat or even make a cake, after all? Browsing through this book may encourage you. The specialized items sections should be especially inspirational, as you may want to try your hand at some dishes that must be cooked with a particular item described here. Others are noteworthy because they solve a particular problem you may have. So please just sit down and really *read* this book, and don't limit your use of it to looking up specific things.

Terms Used

The names used for items are the ones that most experts use and not what you might see on some packages. You may be surprised to find that a familiar item is listed under a strange name. That is why each item has an *Also Known*

As line for manufacturer, regional, or personal names that actually may not be correct. No brand names are included.

In cookware especially, item names suffer badly from mangled or wildly imaginative catalog copy and bad translations from foreign languages. Many manufacturers seem to have picked up foreign names because they sound authentic but then they use the terms incorrectly, confusing everyone with their apparent authenticity.

Another problem is creatively designed tools that combine features of several basic tools, such as a colander/grater. These are hard to classify, so cross-references are made wherever possible to ease any confusion.

One of the most interesting aspects of researching a book like this is seeing how various experts react to the same question. Nowhere was this more intriguing than in the area of pots and pans, particularly with the supposedly definitive French terms. Almost everyone was quite sure of themselves when they gave totally different answers to the same basic question, such as "What is a sauté pan?" Even a dictionary of culinary terms gave different names and descriptions to the same item on the same page. And certain pans are called pots and certain pots called pans by almost everyone, further confusing the issue.

Gadgets suffer from another problem—multiple names. More than one manufacturer lists the same item in more than one place under different names. In one catalog, an item was listed twice on the same page, with one name referring to its use ("nut chopper") and another to its material ("glass chopper"). With that kind of stuff going on, you need a book like this to straighten things out.

General Buying Tips

Throughout the book buying tips have been included wherever possible. You will note that sometimes they encourage and other times they discourage the purchase of a particular item. This is based on general consensus. Inclusion in this book is not an endorsement, and even the ones that are described as being of little use may be of interest to somebody, somewhere. Much of consumer satisfaction is personal preference, and that is why the buying tips are not as absolute as some readers might wish.

One of the nicest recent developments in the kitchenware industry is the evidence of more attention to ergonometric design. This shows up especially in the arrival of large and soft-handled gadgets that are easy to grip for all of us, especially those of us who have weak grips due to arthritis, for example. Another is the arrival of professional-quality cookware in mainstream consumer lines. And many manufacturers of utensils with rosewood or teak in them have identified their sources as being renewable or from conservation forests. Be sure to examine any item of exotic wood to determine if its source is environmentally correct.

Probably the most important buying advice in the tips or short section introductions is the occasional suggestion to spring for the best quality in a given item or group of items, such as knives. The introductory section on materials is detailed so that you can sort out exaggerated claims from meaningful ones, something that is rampant among the cutlery and cookware manufacturers. Items that are truly handy and good for most cooks to have are noted as such in the individual *Buying Tips* sections.

Preparation Items

Cutting Tools and Accessories

About Cutting Tools and Accessories

Perhaps more basic than a pot or pan, knives and related tools come to mind as the simplest utensils in the kitchen. However, in this simplicity there is much need for perfection and refinement: in design, in construction, and in usage.

About Cutting Tool Design

All cutting tools must be designed so that they are easy to hold securely. Sharp cutting edges are essential to good cutting jobs, but if the knife or gadget doesn't feel good in your hand, don't buy it. The shape of the handle should be comfortable (some soft, wide-handled gadgets are now made for those of us who have trouble gripping small handles) and the whole tool should be well balanced. Before buying an inexpensive knife you should try some top-of-the-line models just to see the difference in balance and feel (they all cut the same at first, more or less), especially for a chef's knife. More about this is discussed in the section on construction, below.

Note that the basic types of knives listed below indicate what the knife is to be used for. Of course, one can use any knife for a multitude of purposes, but if not designed for that purpose it may be awkward or inefficient to use. Worse, you might ruin a good piece of meat or fish. Beware of claims made for "multiple-purpose" knives and gadgets. All too often they turn out to be less effective than those designed for one purpose. The same goes for those serrated-edge knives that "never need

3

sharpening." According to one manufacturer, that is true only in the sense that you cannot sharpen them because they have a sawtooth edge, and once they get dull, you throw them out instead of sharpening them. There is strong mass market consumer demand for this type of knife nonetheless because of its "miracle" labor-saving appeal. Better to buy a more costly model that needs sharpening but lasts forever.

On the other hand, the names each manufacturer uses for its knives overlap quite often, blurring the real use. For example, some call their paring knife a parer/boner, or a tomato knife becomes a tomato/utility knife, whereas all four categories are listed separately here. The best way out of this confusion is to consider your needs and the knife's function: When you need a narrow knife for boning, just look for a narrow knife and don't worry if it is called something else. Let function dictate.

Knife sizes generally refer to the length of the blade.

About Knife Construction

The best-quality knives are works of art and worth purchasing, especially chef's knives. They have beautiful, comfortable handles that are sealed and seamless with the end and tang of the blade. The *tang,* the flat, wide tail end of the metal piece from which the blade is made, should go through the entire handle, especially on heavier duty models, and be riveted (usually with three brass or stainless steel rivets) in the case of wooden handles or permanently bonded inside a plastic handle.

Full tang means the tang goes all the way through the handle, like a sandwich (side to side and to the end), and *partial tang* (also called *half* or *canoe tang*) means it goes only part way, which is more common on smaller knives. In order to reduce the weight of some knives, a narrow, rod-shaped tang, sometimes called a *rattail tang* (also called a *whittle tang*), is used inside the handle of a visible, flat, handle-wide tang. A *pin tang* goes all the way through the handle and is secured with a pin at the end.

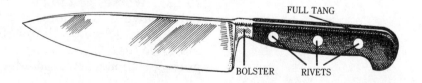

FULL TANG

BOLSTER   RIVETS

KNIFE HANDLES

The handle of a knife is almost as important as the blade. Avoid knives with handles that have gaps between the blade or tang and the handle material, because food and water can get into that space and cause deterioration. A good handle is extremely smooth and sealed against the blade for maximum resistance; the best plastic ones, usually polypropylene, are "over-molded" and then ground back even with the blade material.

So-called top-quality wooden handles are plastic-impregnated compressed wood, seasoned and dried for resistance to heat and water as well as bacteria formation from decomposing bits of food. If it has rivets, they should be ground smooth. A smooth, ergonomically designed, comfortable handle makes the knife that much safer to use. Look for one that feels good in your hand. Try before you buy.

KNIFE BLADES

The blade is the essence of the knife, of course, and the two general categories of knife construction are defined by the way the blade is made. Most models of the traditional, standard-setting, top-quality German and French knives are *forged,* or hammered out of a thick piece of steel, an expensive process that takes something like thirty-eight steps, mostly done by skilled craftsmen. Forging actually affects the molecular structure of the steel. All others are *stamped* or *blanked,* actually die-cut from a sheet of steel, in a process that is more automated and less expensive. Many specialized knives are only available stamped, but the most common models are made in both styles.

Although steel is made from a blend of alloys that varies from manufacturer to manufacturer, it is generally accepted that forged steel blades are stronger and hold an edge better than stamped steel blades. A stamped blade can be welded onto a forged handle, and at least one major manufacturer does this. A manufacturer may call this "forged technology" in order to disguise the fact that it contains a stamped blade (this is easy to do because the forged handle has a bolster just like fully forged knives). On the other hand, all manufacturers claim that their type of steel is less breakable, easier to sharpen, and better in general, no matter how they are made. If you handle a knife with care and use it only sporadically, it is very hard to tell what type is better. If you use a knife often and compare types, you will find that it is worth it to buy the best—it will be easier to use, will take a sharper edge, hold it longer, and will last forever.

The most distinctive feature of forged blades is a thick midsection just in front of the handle, called the *bolster, choil,* or *guard.* A stamped blade cannot, by definition, have an integral bolster (that is why it is frustrating for some people to see stamped blades welded to the bolster of a forged handle). Stamped blades have a top edge that is basically the same thickness from tip to tail, though all are ground thin near the point. The thick integral bolster of forged blades provides strength but above all it provides balance. The balance point on the best forged chef's and paring knives, for example, is behind the bolster, at the start of the handle. This makes for more comfortable use over time. It also causes the knife to drop handle-first if you knock it off the countertop. Stamped blades generally do not offer this balance point, though some have weighted handles for this reason.

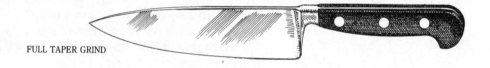

FULL TAPER GRIND

CUTTING EDGES

Another difference is the way the blade is shaped and the edge created. Knife edges are either *flat ground,* with a basic V-shaped bevel edge, or *hollow ground,* in which a slight concave curve is ground into the sides of the knife. There is more steel behind the flat sides of the beveled flat ground edge, so it holds longer. It is usually ground by hand and then honed and polished. The better knives, made from thick steel whether forged or stamped, are ground to a taper at the point and edge, making a distinctive wedge shape. This is sometimes called a *full taper grind.* It gives a front to rear flexibility with strength and aids in balance, and makes for a strong knife. A plain, inexpensive, stamped blade is beveled only at the cutting edge and is flat and even elsewhere.

The shape of the hollow-ground edge leaves less steel in the thickness of the blade (it is cut in from both sides)

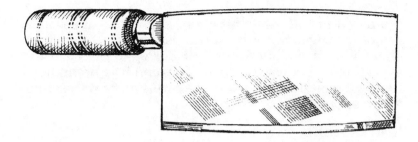

FLAT GROUND BLADE

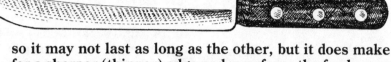

HOLLOW GROUND BLADE

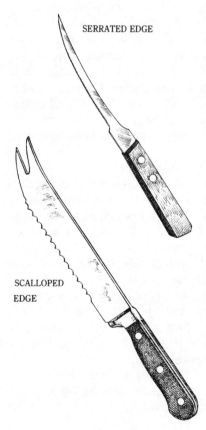

SERRATED EDGE

SCALLOPED
EDGE

so it may not last as long as the other, but it does make for a sharper (thinner) edge and may force the food away as you slice it. After repeated sharpenings, however, the thinner edge wears away faster. Hollow-ground blades are generally not as flexible as flat-ground blades.

Other knife edges are less common but lend themselves to specialized knives. Serrated edges have extremely small square-ended sawteeth. Wavy or scalloped edges (often called *serrated* too) are sharpened only on one side. Both are used to saw through something with either a hard crust (French bread) or a hard surface (fruit and vegetables) as well as to slice soft food (roast meat, smoked salmon) with a sawing motion. Plain-edged knives are used for slicing too, but more often for chopping and straight downward cutting.

Wavy-edged blades can be sharpened, though the points of the scallops will eventually wear down faster if you do—but the alternative is a dull knife that gets thrown out. Knives labeled "never needs sharpening" are usually inexpensive and just not sharpened—they are disposed of or used dull, making them no bargain.

Some fine Japanese knives are made with a very thick blade that is beveled only on one side. Made of laminated alternating layers of different types of steel with varied hardnesses, they can be sharpened to a degree not possible with conventional steel blades. The absolute extreme of sharpness requires extremely brittle and thin material. Some ceramic-edged blades are found, but they are so delicate that they are impractical for use as cooking tools.

Honing and *stropping* are polishing actions which knock off small burrs and align the microscopic fibers of the metal in the same direction, making for a sharper, smoother edge. Sometimes this is done in the factory, along with a well-polished full blade, to enhance the overall effectiveness of the knife when it is brand new. The best hand-finishing leaves a satiny grain rather than a mirror polish.

KNIFE STEEL

A final difference from knife to knife is the steel. For years, all knives were made of *carbon steel,* also called *low carbon* or just *plain steel.* This material could be sharpened extremely well and did not break easily due to its relative softness (measured on the Rockwell steel hardness scale it is rated low, at about 52 degrees). However, it stained and rusted easily and had to be resharpened between uses. Professionals often sharpened their frequently used knives between each cut. It is virtually impossible to find carbon steel knives anymore except from specialized European importers, made available for those few die-hard traditionalists who demand them.

The consumer welcomed the development of *stainless steel,* which did not have the problems associated with carbon steel knives. However, when first introduced, stainless steel was so hard that it was difficult to sharpen due to its molecular structure. People tended not to sharpen their knives because of this difficulty, used them after they became dull, and stainless steel got a bad name, though some inexpensive knives are still made of this.

Recently a formula for stainless steel with more carbon in it, *high-carbon stainless steel,* was developed in order to solve this problem (it is called *no-stain steel* by some top manufacturers to further differentiate it from the older variety of stainless steel). It contains carbon, molybdenum, chromium, and nickel in varying amounts, has a Rockwell hardness of about 56–57 degrees, and seems to have properties that respond to the criteria set by all users. The qualities (and ingredients) that help it keep a sharp edge are balanced by others that keep it from being too brittle. All better-quality knives are now made of this steel.

Recipes for the various mixes of chromium, molybdenum, vanadium, carbon, and nickel in stainless steel vary with each manufacturer, and confusing claims abound. For example, some manufacturers boast that their knives are made of *surgical steel*—it sounds high-tech but it ultimately is meaningless to the consumer because any stainless steels containing more than 5 percent carbon can be called surgical steel, and most do (they have from 15 to 80 percent carbon). The mix and manufacturing processes are what count. Similarly, another brand might call their stainless steel *molybedenum vanadium steel*. That's a little like claiming your food contains salt: a little, in just the right amount, makes the whole product right. Just claiming that it is there does not make the product any better, though it may sound nice.

About the Use and Care of Knives

KNIFE BLOCK

Knives really should never be put into the dishwasher as the hot and cold cycles of the dishwasher can change the temper of the steel and harm the handle. Nor should they be dropped into a utensil drawer where the edges can be banged and nicked and dulled—especially scalloped or serrated edges.

Store knives in a *knife block* (see page 52), or on a *magnetic bar* (see page 54). Even "stainless" steel will stain when certain acids are left on them or water on the edge, so wipe knives dry after every use. Lay the knife on a flat surface and wipe one side at a time for increased safety.

You should treat your knives with the respect a surgeon has for his or her tools. Above all, keep knives as sharp as possible. It is not only easier to use a sharp knife, but safer, too. Sharpen and hone regularly with any of the devices noted in this chapter. Test the sharpness of a knife by seeing if it will pierce a paper towel or slice through a tomato with minimal pressure.

Commonly Used Knives

About Commonly Used Knives

Most of us use these, not the specialized knives listed further on, and they are usually acquired as a set. This is an excellent time to shop for top quality and to buy a name brand—or to wish for the same as a gift.

Because of the vast array of cutting tools available, the choice is sometimes a little complicated. In general, you can get by with a chef's knife, a paring knife, and a tomato knife—the three most frequently used knives.

Later on you can match the knife or gadget to the specific task you do most often, but when starting out, keep to the basic three. In all cases, get the best you can afford. Always buy top-of-the-line cutlery to the extent possible. Good knives last forever and bad knives can be hard to use and dangerous.

BONING KNIFE

DESCRIPTION: A 4- to 6-inch-long, very pointed, narrow blade—about ½ inch wide—with a wooden or plastic handle. The handle may have a pronounced "grip" design for maximum control. The blade usually curves up toward the top ridge a bit toward the handle so it curves down slightly to the bolster. Available in both rigid and slightly flexible styles.

USE: Removing meat from bones (especially leg of lamb or chicken), where control and precise placement of the blade is important. Flexible models are used on fish.

USE TIPS: The point of the blade is inserted into the meat while fingertips of the opposite hand feel the bone to give direction and a sense of depth. Be careful when cutting near the other hand.

BUYING TIPS: Very handy and much easier to use for this purpose than any other knife. Flexible models are rare and a question of personal preference.

BONING KNIFE

BREAD KNIFE

ALSO KNOWN AS: French bread knife

DESCRIPTION: 8- to 10-inch-long blade, usually just over an inch wide, with a deeply scalloped or serrated edge and a tip that is curved down toward the cutting edge rather than up, as with most knives. Handle made of wood or plastic. Some brands offer a left-handed version. A very rare version is the *fiddle bow bread knife,* which has a wavy 10-inch-long, serrated blade held by a 16-inch-long wooden frame, much like a violin bow (the blade is the "string"). Usually made of fine cherry, the fiddle bow comes in either a right-handed or left-handed version.

USE: Slicing bread. Provides a cleaner slice with less crumbling than other knives that are not specifically designed for cutting bread. The scalloped edge gives some "bite" to the slicing motion and avoids squishing soft loaves as you slice. Deeply scalloped blades may also be used for slicing roast meats. The fiddle bow model is used to cut thick slices evenly.

USE TIPS: Works best on firm-textured loaves with fairly thick crust.

BUYING TIPS: Look for a bevel on both sides of the blade; if it is beveled on the right side only, it may not cut as well for a left-handed cook as it does for a right-handed one.

BREAD KNIFE

 FIDDLE BOW KNIFE

BUTCHER CLEAVER

ALSO KNOWN AS: Meat cleaver, cleaver, kitchen cleaver

DESCRIPTION: Widest and heaviest knife in the chef's arsenal, as much as 4 inches wide and usually no longer than about 7 inches. Heavy, but not necessarily very sharp. Not to be confused with the *Chinese cleaver* (see page 13).

USE: Flattening slices of meats such as veal (for veal scallopine) and to break down muscle of tougher cuts such as flank steak, rather than as a cutting or slicing knife. Used for major butchering when cutting bones apart at the joint or even splitting them in the middle.

USE TIPS: Let the weight of the blade work for you; swing hearty.

BUYING TIPS: Buy the best. Cheap ones really won't work as well.

BUTCHER CLEAVER

BUTCHER KNIFE

DESCRIPTION: Large knife with a long blade with a slightly wide, bulbous tip. Some manufacturers make a plain model that looks like a heavy-duty *chef's knife* (see next entry).

USE: Cutting or slicing large pieces of meat; may be particularly useful for cutting cubes for stewing.

USE TIPS: Let the weight of the blade work for you.

BUYING TIPS: More of a professional item; popular in delis.

BUTCHER KNIFE

CHEF'S KNIFE

ALSO KNOWN AS: Cook's knife, French chef's knife, chef knife, French chef knife, French knife

DESCRIPTION: A wide, rigid, triangular blade, typically 1½ to 2 inches wide, about 8 to 10 inches long (with 6- and 12-inch models available; the 6- to 8-inch models may be called a *utility knife*), with a large, comfortable handle. The cutting edge has a slight curve, or belly, to it in most models (especially German ones), but some are available which are almost straight (especially French ones). Also available in an extra-wide version, sometimes, at the extreme, called an *oriental knife* (see page 17).

CHEF'S KNIFE

THUMB AND FOREFINGER
STRADDLING THE BLADE

HOLDING A KNIFE FOR MAXIMUM CONTROL

Found in a wide range of styles and qualities, including plain carbon steel (very difficult to find), soft stainless steel, and the harder high-carbon stainless ("no stain") steel; hollow or bevel ground, forged or stamped, with wooden or plastic handles.

USE: General purpose knife for cutting, carving, and chopping most foods. Wider blades are most useful for dicing vegetables. Most common, basic chef's tool.

USE TIPS: Hold the food you are cutting with your fingertips curled under your knuckles, almost like making a fist, to avoid cutting them off. Hold the knife with your thumb and forefinger on either side of the blade at the tail end, or bolster, for more control. Cut between bones rather than through them to avoid damaging the blade, which is always kept very sharp.

BUYING TIPS: The essential chef's tool; you should consider it a lifetime investment and your first purchase. In this case, price is a good indicator of quality, so buy a well-known brand with the traditional design. Ask friends for suggested brands. The 8-inch model is the most popular, for both men and women, though those with very large hands may prefer a 10-inch blade. Often sold in sets with two or more sizes as well as other knives, such as *paring knives* (see page 18). Generally the 100 percent forged, high-carbon stainless steel, top-of-the-line models are the most popular. The stamped models are lighter and therefore may be harder to use. The balance point should be just behind the bolster, in the handle.

CHINESE CLEAVER

ALSO KNOWN AS: All-in-one knife, Chinese-style chef's knife, Chinese cleaver, oriental cleaver

DESCRIPTION: Heavy, wide knife with a thick rectangular steel blade, about 8 inches long and about 3 inches wide, with a short wooden handle, and either a straight or ever-so-slightly curved cutting edge. The cutting edge is extremely sharp. So well-engineered and beautifully balanced, no one has been able to improve on the design in thousands of years. Available in carbon and stainless steel. Some may refer to this, incorrectly, as an *oriental chef's knife* (see page 17).

USE: All-purpose: cutting, chopping, shredding, slicing, mincing of all foods.

USE TIPS: Unless you are an expert, don't try to move as fast as chefs in Chinese restaurants. The art of using these knives with speed has been passed down through the generations. Still, the wide blade allows you great control and enables you to scoop up large quantities of chopped food. Keep this knife absolutely as sharp as possible. Especially good on small things like herbs and garlic.

BUYING TIPS: This can replace many other knives, so it is worth the investment to get a good, name-brand one. Now sold everywhere.

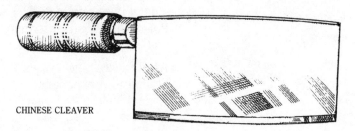

CHINESE CLEAVER

CIMETER KNIFE

ALSO KNOWN AS: Scimitar knife

DESCRIPTION: Large, wide, threatening-looking knife that curves up to a point. Usually 10 or 12 inches long.

USE: Making large slices of meat.

USE TIPS: Keep extraordinarily sharp. Start cutting with the point first and rock down in one motion.

BUYING TIPS: Not a handy knife.

CIMETER KNIFE

DEBA KNIFE

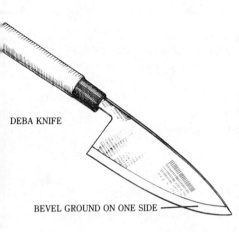

DEBA KNIFE

BEVEL GROUND ON ONE SIDE

DESCRIPTION: Thick-backed, cleaver-type knife with a long triangular shape, ground sharp on one side only in left- and right-handed versions, and may be hollow ground on the nonbeveled side. Blades are 6 to 8 inches long. A *Japanese decorating knife* is similar, but with only 3½-inch blade. The bevel, on one side only, is very shallow—only about 14 degrees. Available in stainless, laminated alternating stainless and carbon steel, or all carbon steel.

USE: Cutting or chopping large pieces of meat, poultry, or fish, and filleting fish.

USE TIPS: Keep extra-sharp and treat carefully. The edge is very delicate.

BUYING TIPS: Carried only by the most serious catalogs and stores.

ELECTRIC KNIFE

ELECTRIC KNIFE

ALSO KNOWN AS: Electric carving knife, electric slicing knife.

DESCRIPTION: Two long, serrated, stainless steel blades that are linked loosely together so that they slide back and forth next to each other, held by a large plastic handle which houses a motor. Available in cordless and plug-in versions. Typical length is 9 inches, though 6¾-inch paring/trimming blades are offered. Some are slender and weigh just over one pound, but most are bulky and weigh more. May come with a wall-mounted storage rack. Blades are released by a button for cleaning and replacement.

USE: Slicing roasted meat and poultry.

USE TIPS: Cordless model is useful at an outdoor barbecue.

BUYING TIPS: Not for most cooks, but handy for arthritic or elderly people who have trouble gripping a knife. No more effective than a regular knife. Blades must be replaced when dull as they are not sharpenable.

FRUIT KNIFE

ALSO KNOWN AS: Fruit-bar knife, bar knife, bar/fruit knife

DESCRIPTION: Any smallish knife, but usually a 4-inch-long, wavy-edged serrated or plain, narrow, pointed blade with wooden or plastic handle. The blade edge usually has a slight curve up to the point. Another common version has a short, thick, triangular blade. Stainless steel as a rule. This is one item that is hard to define, as manufacturers label a wide variety of knives "fruit knives" because any small, sharp knife can do the job.

USE: Cutting lemons and limes into wedges or slices for drinks, or other small slicing chores.

USE TIPS: Do not use a dull knife here, as it is likely to slip.

BUYING TIPS: Use only stainless steel; the citric acid will stain a plain carbon steel blade. Any sharp knife will do—a *utility knife* (see page 21) is really the same thing.

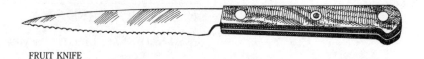

FRUIT KNIFE

FRUIT/VEGETABLE SLICER

ALSO KNOWN AS: Fruit knife, vegetable slicer

DESCRIPTION: Long, narrow, microserrated blade that curves up in a slight scimitar shape, with a wooden or plastic handle. Blade is stainless steel and about 5 inches long (8 inches overall). The *Japanese fruit/vegetable slicer*, a *usuba knife* (see page 21), is a quite different looking item though it serves the same purpose.

USE: Slicing fruits and vegetables.

USE TIPS: Dull slicers do not work well at all.

BUYING TIPS: There are many inexpensive versions of this knife, so search out one you really like to use.

FRUIT/VEGETABLE SLICER

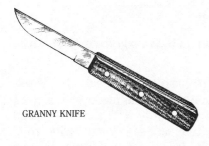

GRANNY KNIFE

GRANNY KNIFE

ALSO KNOWN AS: Grandma's parer, granny parer

DESCRIPTION: Long-handled paring knife with short, 1½-inch blade slightly narrower than the handle. Often has an angled tip. Available in both carbon and stainless steel. For some manufacturers, this is just another name for a utility or paring knife.

USE: Chopping, trimming, peeling, and cutting small items where control and convenience matters.

USE TIPS: Keep this sharp or it may be dangerous to use.

BUYING TIPS: Basically just another general-use knife, or slight variation on the *paring knife* (see page 18). Not a necessary item if you have the other basic knives.

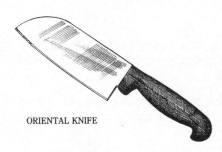

ORIENTAL KNIFE

ORIENTAL KNIFE

ALSO KNOWN AS: Oriental chef's knife, oriental cook's knife, Japanese cook's knife, santucko knife

DESCRIPTION: Boxy-shaped stainless steel or high carbon special cutlery steel knife—a wider and shorter version of the classic *chef's knife* (see page 12)—that comes with either a wood or plastic handle. The entire knife is usually about 6 inches long, with a snub-tipped blade of about 3 inches by 1½ inches. The tip of the blade may be serrated. The back edge curves down to meet the straight or only slightly curved cutting edge. Lighter in weight than a *butcher cleaver* (see page 11) or a *Chinese cleaver* (see page 13), but heavier than a *chef's knife* (see page 12).

USE: Slicing thin pieces of meat, fish, or vegetables, and dicing. The wide blade allows you to scoop up vegetables as you slice them and move them away from the cutting area.

USE TIPS: This is an all-purpose knife useful for all kitchen cutting chores including chopping herbs and mushrooms.

BUYING TIPS: The lighter the knife, the better and easier for you. Do not confuse this knife with the heavier *Chinese cleaver* (see page 13).

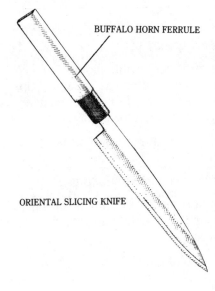

BUFFALO HORN FERRULE

ORIENTAL SLICING KNIFE

ORIENTAL SLICING KNIFE

ALSO KNOWN AS: Pointed sashimi knife, yanagi knife (Ja.), sushi knife

DESCRIPTION: 10- or 12-inch-long, narrow, thin blade that is extremely sharp and pointed. Traditionally it is made with a thick wooden handle (made from Japanese hardwood) usually secured by a buffalo horn ferrule. Most often made in Japan of high carbon steel, and highly polished. Thick blade is ground sharp only on one side for either right-handed or left-handed use. Also available in a square-end version, called a *takohiki*. The very thin cutting edge is honed from sword steel that is alloyed to a harder steel back for stiffness. May be sold as a smaller version with a wooden sheath for portability, and called a *bento knife*, meaning "take away" in Japanese.

USE: Cutting extraordinarily thin or accurately trimmed pieces of raw fish or other foods for sashimi or sushi. Of course, it may be used on other foods, too.

USE TIPS: Take care not to let it jostle against other utensils in a drawer or the blade may be nicked. Very delicate, but capable of holding an extremely sharp edge.

BUYING TIPS: Here again let price be your guide to quality. A fine knife worth its price. Note the left- and right-handed versions.

SPEARPOINT
PARING KNIFE

PARING KNIFE

ALSO KNOWN AS: Utility knife, parer, kitchen knife, couteau d'office (Fr.)

DESCRIPTION: Most frequently used, small, hand-sized knife. Usually the 2- to 4-inch blade has a basically triangular, spear shape ("spearpoint"), though many other designs are available, such as narrow or wide, or with a convex or concave curve. Made of stainless or high-carbon steel with wooden or plastic handles. Many manufacturers call their various models of paring knives by different names, a confusing practice which makes it seem like they have more models instead of just different sizes, such as a *utility parer* as well as a plain *parer*. Others are miniature and/or specialized knives, such as a thin paring knife called a *miniature boning knife* (see page 10).

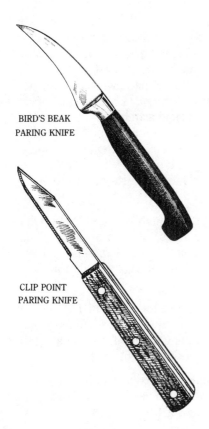

BIRD'S BEAK
PARING KNIFE

CLIP POINT
PARING KNIFE

TYPES: *Bird's beak* (Also Known As *vegetable knife, curved vegetable knife, turning knife* [for "turned" or carved, rounded, vegetables], *peeling knife*): Has a pronounced concave curve used on garnishes and removing potato eyes.

Chef's paring knife (Also Known As *spearpoint paring knife*): Has a slight belly to the cutting edge instead of being flat or having a concave curve.

Clip-point parer: Short, with an angular point.

Food processor-bladed paring knife: The absolutely sharpest style that has a blade made with a pronounced double bevel, ground on one side like a food processor blade. Available in three shapes: bird's beak, chef's, and sheep's foot.

Parer/peeler: Combined with a peeling blade along the back edge.

Sheep's foot: Straight cutting edge with a top edge that curves outward down to the point.

Slim jim: Very narrow blade.

USE: Peeling fruit or vegetables, or cutting, trimming, or even slicing any small pieces of food where close control is essential.

USE TIPS: More specialized, similar knives are listed in Chapter 13, Garnishing Items (see pages 339 to 349).

BUYING TIPS: The balance point should be behind the bolster, about 1 to 1½ inches into the handle. This is one of the most frequently used knives, along with the *chef's knife* (see page 12) and the *tomato knife* (see page 30). Get a good one. The more control you need for precise work, the smaller the knife to get.

SLICER

ALSO KNOWN AS: Carver, slicing knife, roast slicer, meat carver

DESCRIPTION: Long, narrow blade that may have a scalloped edge and may come to a rounded or pointed tip; from 5 to 12 inches long. Made of high-carbon or stainless steel with a plastic, bone (for the fanciest tableside carving knives), or wood handle. Generally a shorter, 8-inch plain model is considered a *carving knife* and the longer, 10-inch narrower model is called a *slicing knife*. This knife is distinguished from the *chef's knife* (see page 12), and *bread knife* (see page 10) by its narrower, thinner, and more flexible blade.

One model has the scallops ground into the side of the blade, not the edge, and it may be called a *scallop(ed) carver* or *slicer* or a *ham* or a *roast beef slicer*. This style is known as *hollow ground vacuum* or *Granton edge* (named after the Englishman who developed this process). The longest and narrowest model, at a minimum of 9 inches, may be called a *narrow slicer* or *ham slicer*.

An *adjustable slicing knife* has a rigid arm parallel to the blade that is adjusted to various distances from the blade. The distance sets the thickness of the slice desired. A simpler version, a *stripper knife,* is a *paring knife* (see page 18) with a long wire clip stuck onto the cutting edge (the blade is inserted into the spring coils on either end of the wire).

USE: Short models are for slicing raw vegetables and fruits, while longer ones are for meat (roasts, hams), and large poultry such as turkeys. Also handy for deboning large fish. The longest, narrowest, and most flexible are usually specially made for slicing smoked salmon into paper-thin slices.

USE TIPS: Longer knives are easier to use for slicing in that they can produce a slice in a single stroke. The hollows of a hollow-ground slicer reduce the blade surface touching the food, thus helping the knife move smoothly through the food without sticking.

BUYING TIPS: The thinner the knife the easier it is to use. Get a good, thin, flexible one if that is what you need. The balance point of a carving knife should be at the bolster.

CARVING KNIFE

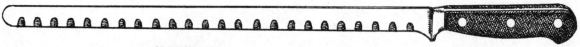

GRANTON EDGE

SCALLOPED CARVER

USUBA KNIFE

ALSO KNOWN AS: The little Chinese knife, vegetable/fruit slicer

DESCRIPTION: Rectangular, 2-inch-wide blade about 8 inches long. Available with either a square tip or rounded on one corner (sheep's-foot tip). Ground on one side, and available in stainless and more commonly carbon steel.

USE: Vegetable chopper, useful for light chopping, mincing, slicing, and dicing.

USE TIPS: Flat "back side" allows you to make garnish cuts, such as spirals, and the beveled front side forces the food away from the blade as it is cut.

BUYING TIPS: Found only in your more serious stores and catalogs.

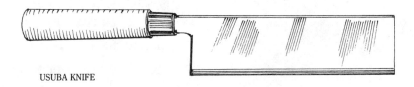

USUBA KNIFE

UTILITY KNIFE

ALSO KNOWN AS: All-purpose knife, kitchen knife, salad knife

DESCRIPTION: A small knife with about a 5-inch blade in the traditional shape with a wooden or plastic handle. Often has a wavy serrated edge, and also called a *vegetable knife, tomato knife, fruit knife, sausage knife,* or *sandwich knife,* depending on the brand (the latter two are usually 6 or 8 inches long). Longer, wider versions are more often called *kitchen knives.*

USE: General purpose knife for cutting vegetables, fruit, and small pieces of meat, sausage, or cheese.

USE TIPS: Many people become inordinately attached to one utility knife that is beloved over all others.

BUYING TIPS: Handy to have a comfortable one, but not necessary and maybe redundant if you have other specialized knives. A 4-inch blade is most useful size.

Specialized Knives

About Specialized Knives

Most cooks do not need these, as the rare occasions where a special knife is needed do not quite offset their expense. After all, with care and skill, you can use even a pocketknife for most jobs. However, if you find yourself performing any of these operations a few times, you will be happier with a knife that makes your job easier through its special design. Or if you know someone with a special interest, one of these can make a particularly good gift.

BLOODING KNIFE

BLOODING KNIFE

ALSO KNOWN AS: Sticking knife, butcher knife

DESCRIPTION: 6- to 8-inch-long pointed blade with rigid, straight back and cutting edge that slopes gently up toward the tip.

USE: Making the initial cuts in carcasses to drain them of blood.

USE TIPS: Used wherever tight control of a large knife is called for.

BUYING TIPS: Very useful to butchers or hunters, but also makes a good steak knife or all-purpose knife.

BUTCHER SAW

DESCRIPTION: Stainless steel bowlike saw frame with a narrow stainless blade and metal or wooden handle, just like a regular hack saw.

USE: Cutting large pieces of raw meat and bone.

USE TIPS: Clean raw meat off very carefully after use.

BUYING TIPS: Generally useful only to butchers.

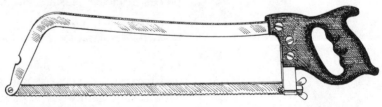

BUTCHER SAW

CHEESE KNIFE

DESCRIPTION: 4½- to 10-inch-long, offset, straight-edge blade.

USE: Cutting servings of all kinds of cheeses.

BUYING TIPS: This specialized offset design makes it easier to cut off a clean slice of cheese because you can cut straight down without hitting your knuckles on the cutting board.

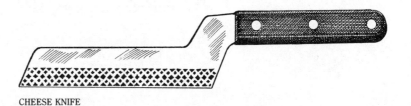

CHEESE KNIFE

CHESTNUT KNIFE

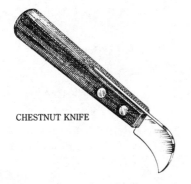

CHESTNUT KNIFE

DESCRIPTION: 4-inch straight handle with an inch-long, wide blade that is curved downward in a flat, bird's beak form. Blades are plain or stainless steel.

USE: Slitting and shelling chestnuts.

USE TIPS: Be careful not to slip when holding a chestnut. Use a glove for protection if necessary. Slitting is done prior to roasting.

BUYING TIPS: Good gift item if you can find it.

CLAM KNIFE

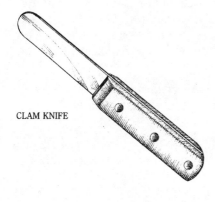

CLAM KNIFE

DESCRIPTION: Small, stumpy-looking, sturdy knife with a wide, thick blade about 3 inches long and a thick handle. Tip is usually rounded. A narrow version is available too. Though some manufacturers claim their knife is good for both clams and oysters, usually the one sharp side design is unique for opening clams. (See page 27 for *oyster knives.*) A *clam and oyster knife* is likely to have a pointed end as well as a sharp side.

USE: Opening clams. Sturdiness of blade and handle is essential for prying open recalcitrant clams.

USE TIPS: Get 'em while they're sleeping! Leave them alone for a while, and stay quiet—vibrations wake them up. You can easily insert a knife into a clam if it is calm—often they open partially. Once you disturb a clam, it clamps shut very tightly (it clams up?), making the use of extreme force necessary. Never use a clam that is wide open or opens with no resistance—it is probably dead. Wear at least one glove, on the clam-holding hand, for safety reasons.

BUYING TIPS: Get a well-made knife that feels really comfortable in your hand, because you'll be applying lots of pressure.

CLAM OPENER

ALSO KNOWN AS: Shell shucker

DESCRIPTION: Scissorlike device with one concave jaw and one straight, stiff-bladed jaw. Some models come apart so you can use one blade as a knife. Basically the curved jaw holds a clam against the blade.

USE: Opening clams with steady mechanical pressure.

USE TIPS: Also works on mussels and oysters.

BUYING TIPS: Once you learn to use a clam knife well, this is less appealing.

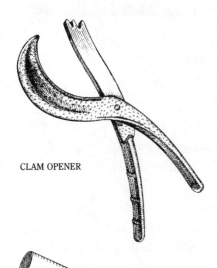

CLAM OPENER

CLAM SHUCKER

CLAM SHUCKER/OYSTER SHUCKER

DESCRIPTION: Small, rectangular, wooden base with a steel post a few inches high at one end. A knife blade about 5 inches long is hinged to the post and has a wooden handle. Midway out on the blade is an inch-wide wedge, in the case of the clam shucker, and a small wedge point, in the case of the oyster shucker. The wooden base has a small indentation in the middle to hold the edge of the shell.

USE: Opening clams or oysters with mechanical advantage. The blade is raised and lowered like a lever, forcing the wedge into the shell and splitting it open.

USE TIPS: Place the clam accurately or this will not work. Note that this also slices the clam or oyster, making it good only for chowder and the like.

BUYING TIPS: Helpful if you have a large quantity of shellfish to open.

CRAB KNIFE

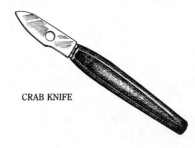

CRAB KNIFE

DESCRIPTION: Short, flat, pointed, wide stainless knife with a thin handle, sometimes forged of one piece. Overall length is only 6 inches. Sometimes the blade has a small hole in the base, and the cutting edge is at a slight angle.

USE: Removing meat from boiled crabs. Heavy metal handle can be used to crack shells.

BUYING TIPS: Short blade and long handle provide the control necessary for all the maneuvering associated with the joy of crab eating.

DOUGH KNIFE

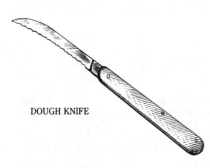

DOUGH KNIFE

DESCRIPTION: Small, hooked, wavy-edged blade, about 3 inches long, with a metal handle. Separate blades of various similar shapes are also available.

USE: Cutting hunks of raw dough.

USE TIPS: Be careful not to cut the hand holding the dough when working.

BUYING TIPS: Not necessary unless you do a lot of baking in large quantities.

FISH FILLETING KNIFE

ALSO KNOWN AS: Filleting knife

DESCRIPTION: Comes in two lengths, either 3 or 7 inches long. The pointed blade is narrow, about ½ or ¾ inch wide (some are just over an inch), thin, and flexible, with a handle of either plastic or wood. May be slightly upturned toward the tip.

USE: Filleting fish by cutting the bones from the meat.

USE TIPS: The long, slim shape allows you to cut cleanly and close to the bone, eliminating waste. Usually the blade is placed at a 15-degree angle to the bone for best results.

BUYING TIPS: Consider the size of fish you usually fillet. The smaller knife is used for smaller fish, the longer one for larger fish.

FRENCH FRY KNIFE

ALSO KNOWN AS: Potato chipper

DESCRIPTION: Small knife, about the size of a regular *paring knife* (see page 18), but with eight small blades at a right angle to the cutting blade at about ¼-inch intervals.

USE: Cutting thick strips of raw potatoes for French fries, one slice at a time.

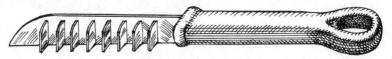

FRENCH FRY KNIFE

FROZEN FOOD KNIFE

ALSO KNOWN AS: Freezer saw

DESCRIPTION: Certainly the most dramatic-looking knife in the cook's arsenal, this is about 16 inches long and has deep, sharp saw teeth set apart by wide gaps along one edge. The other edge is scalloped. Usually has a forked tip and a large plastic handle, and is made of stainless steel. An even larger version is made as a *frozen food saw,* with a saw handle.

USE: Cutting frozen food with the sawtooth edge, and slicing cooked food with the scalloped edge.

USE TIPS: Works on plain ice as well—the sawtooth edge is a crosscut saw.

GRAPEFRUIT KNIFE

GRAPEFRUIT KNIFE

DESCRIPTION: Short stainless steel knife about 3½ inches long, with serrated edges on two sides that come to a point. The point is slightly upturned from the flat side. Handles made of wood or plastic, and the latter are available in various colors. Also made in a decorative, very thin version with two business ends of different widths and curves; one is scalloped-edged, the other serrated.

USE: Cutting membranes from pulp of the fruit, section by section, either by the cook in the kitchen or by the diner at the table in an informal situation. Also handy for scooping the entire grapefruit out of the shell; the empty shell can be used as a bowl for fruit, berries, sorbet, or ice cream.

USE TIPS: A regular *paring knife* (see page 18) can be used to cut the vertical membranes.

BUYING TIPS: Nothing else works as well as this inexpensive item.

OYSTER KNIFE

ALSO KNOWN AS: Oyster opener

DESCRIPTION: Small, hand-sized knife made in two different styles, both approximately 3 inches long.

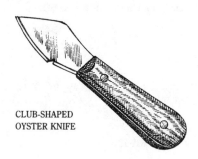

CLUB-SHAPED
OYSTER KNIFE

TYPES: *Club-shaped:* Sometimes with one serrated edge or sharp on both sides; about 1½ inches wide at the "shoulder" coming to approximately ½ inch wide at the base, with a sharp point at the head. Circular plastic or steel guard, about ½ inch wide, protects hand where blade meets handle on most models. Some have a small notch at the base for breaking off the edge of the shell for a starting cut.

Straight: About ½ inch wide, flat blade with angular (New Haven type) or blunt, rounded (Providence type) tips. The New Haven type is slightly curved; the Providence type is sharpened with bevels on both sides. May have an oblong guard at the base of the blade to protect fingers.

USE: Opening oyster shells by cutting the muscles and membranes loose from the shell.

USE TIPS: Even the pros wear gloves when shucking large numbers of oysters. Between the cold and the wet, your skin can get quite raw. And of course the oyster shell is sharp, not to mention the knife. So wear at least one glove.

BUYING TIPS: This is no time to economize. Choose a well-constructed knife; a lightweight flimsy knife may break in your hand.

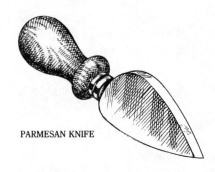

PARMESAN KNIFE

PARMESAN KNIFE

ALSO KNOWN AS: Cheese knife, cheese gouger, cheese scraper and gouger, Italian cheese cutter

DESCRIPTION: Rounded triangular stainless steel blade, about 5 inches long, with a short, thick wooden handle.

USE: Chipping chunks of parmesan or other extremely hard cheese from a large block. Designed to pierce the rind and break off pieces.

BUYING TIPS: Extremely specialized and rarely used knife.

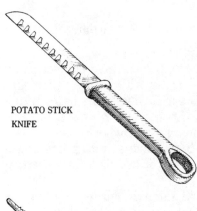

POTATO STICK KNIFE

POTATO STICK KNIFE

DESCRIPTION: Small knife, the size of a regular *paring knife* (see page 18), but with about ten small blades sticking out from the side of the regular cutting edge.

USE: Cutting potato sticks from raw potatoes.

USE TIPS: This cuts smaller pieces than the *french fry knife* (see page 26).

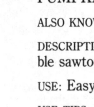

PUMPKIN KNIFE

PUMPKIN KNIFE

ALSO KNOWN AS: Safety pumpkin knife

DESCRIPTION: Small, plastic-handled knife with a short, stiff, double sawtooth-edged blade. Teeth are not very sharp.

USE: Easy and safe carving of pumpkins for Halloween.

USE TIPS: Intended for use by children.

BUYING TIPS: A good, safe alternative to regular knives.

RACLETTE KNIFE

DESCRIPTION: Wide, double- and wavy-edged blade, with a thick wooden handle. Slightly thicker along the center with a gentle taper to the edges. Usually about 10 inches long overall.

USE: Slicing servings of partially melted cheese off a large piece for the Swiss dish, raclette.

SANDWICH KNIFE

DESCRIPTION: Medium-sized 2½- to 5-inch-long serrated stainless steel blade with a straight cutting edge that does not turn up, as a steak knife does. Handle is about 2 inches long, and made of wood or plastic.

USE: Ostensibly designed for making and cutting sandwiches, but actually just a handy, general-use knife.

USE TIPS: As you might guess, you can use absolutely any knife to cut a sandwich, though the serrated edge helps.

BUYING TIPS: This is just a very slight refinement of the standard kitchen knife design. You can probably find a knife from your collection that suffices without having to purchase a specially designated sandwich knife.

SAUSAGE KNIFE

ALSO KNOWN AS: Salami knife

DESCRIPTION: 6- or 8-inch-long knife with an offset, serrated or wavy-edge blade. Wooden or plastic handle.

USE: Slicing smoked sausage, salami, or other hard food that comes in small sizes.

USE TIPS: Do not use a dull sausage knife—it may slip.

BUYING TIPS: Any sharp, scallop-bladed knife will do here.

SAUSAGE KNIFE

SKELETON CHEESE KNIFE

SKELETON CHEESE KNIFE

ALSO KNOWN AS: Soft cheese knife

DESCRIPTION: Wide-bladed knife, about 6 inches long, usually made of stainless steel with a plastic handle. The blade is hollowed out in three places, and has a forked point and a wavy or micro-serrated edge.

USE: Cutting soft cheese, hard cheese, fudge, cake, or tomatoes.

BUYING TIPS: Very good idea—soft foods are hard to slice, and this helps.

SKINNING KNIFE

SKINNING KNIFE

DESCRIPTION: Upturned, teardrop-shaped blade, typically 6 or 7 inches long. Sharp mainly near the tip.

USE: Skinning meat.

BUYING TIPS: This difficult job is much easier with such a knife.

TOMATO KNIFE

ALSO KNOWN AS: Tomato sharpie

DESCRIPTION: Small knife with extremely sharp, scalloped-edged blade 4½ to 6 inches long. Commonly made of stainless steel, usually with plastic or wooden handle. Blade may be straight, slightly curved, or even offset from handle. Some tomato knives have a forked tip. One manufacturer calls its model a *tomato/bagel knife.*

USE: Easy and clean slicing of tomatoes or other things with hard outsides. Scalloped edge cuts better than a plain edge in this case, as it goes through the skin better. Forked tip can be used to pierce tomato skins or to pick up slices.

USE TIPS: Cut super-ripe tomatoes with a sawing motion so the juice will stay in the slice and not go all over the cutting board. Also useful for cutting citrus fruits.

BUYING TIPS: Buy only a stainless steel blade as tomato acid will stain carbon steel. Look for a bevel on both sides of the blade; if it is beveled on the right side only, it may not cut as well for a left-handed cook as it does for a right-handed one, though it can be found in a left-handed version.

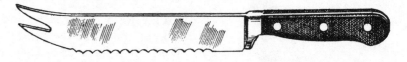

TOMATO KNIFE

TWO-HANDLED CHEESE KNIFE

ALSO KNOWN AS: Double-handled cheese cutter

DESCRIPTION: Wide stainless steel blade with two wood handles, one on each end. 12 or 14 inches long.

USE: Cutting portions of hard cheese from larger pieces, such as wheels.

USE TIPS: Lean into it, putting your weight on the handles.

BUYING TIPS: More appropriate to a cheese store than to the average home.

Choppers, Cutters, and Slicers

About Choppers, Cutters, and Slicers

This is the inventor's arena, where the search for the perfect gadget has come to full evolution. These highly specialized items can find their way into a cook's kitchen, but some still resist them, preferring an old and worn but familiar knife—maybe a chef's knife, maybe a lowly paring or utility knife—to anything else. In any case, they often are used in conjunction with a knife (the food must be cut down to workable size, or the ends must be cut off, and the like). So you end up with two things to wash instead of one. But if you have a great quantity of food to prepare, these items can make a particular recipe simpler by their sheer efficiency. And don't forget that despite the specialized names, like *pasta wheel* or *parsley mincer,* they can often be used on a wide variety of foods.

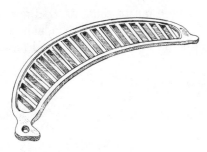

BANANA SLICER

BANANA SLICER

DESCRIPTION: 11-inch-long, banana-shaped piece of flat yellow plastic, with ladder-runglike plastic cutting blades in its entire length.

USE: Pressed down onto a banana to make up to nineteen perfectly even slices at once.

BUYING TIPS: Helpful if you have lots of bananas to slice. Otherwise use a knife.

BEAN SLICER

BEAN SLICER

ALSO KNOWN AS: French-style bean slicer, bean stringer and slicer, green bean slicer, bean Frencher

DESCRIPTION: Hand-sized, plastic-and-stainless-steel device with two cutting blade sets: One is a small hole near one end that contains cutting blades for snapping off the end of the bean; the other is a cross hairs of wire that cuts the bean into four pieces. A smaller version is just a small plastic square with half a dozen blades in a small opening (similar to the design found on the end of some vegetable peelers (see page 61). In both cases, beans are pushed through the opening. Also available as a hand-cranked rotary machine that clamps onto a table or countertop.

USE: Cutting green beans lengthwise; also removes strings.

USE TIPS: Only works well with crisp beans.

BUYING TIPS: Beans can be cooked and eaten whole, so this is only necessary if you choose to slice them as a matter of taste.

BUTTER SLICER

ALSO KNOWN AS: Butter/cheese slicer

DESCRIPTION: Chrome plated steel or cast aluminum item, roughly the shape and size of a *butter tray* (see page 372) but with a set of ladder-runglike wire cutting blades instead of a solid surface.

BUTTER SLICER

USE: Cutting fifteen pats of butter simultaneously from ¼-pound sticks. Also used to cut pats of hard cheese.

USE TIPS: For precise, clean slices, the butter must be cold and the slicer must be wet. Pats can be frozen for easier handling in certain recipes, such as sticking them between the skin and the meat of chicken breasts.

BUYING TIPS: Not an expensive item.

CARROT STICK CUTTER

CARROT STICK CUTTER

ALSO KNOWN AS: Carrot stick maker

DESCRIPTION: Flat, lightweight stamped aluminum, about 4 inches long and 2 inches wide, with a hole in the center which houses a crosspiece of two stainless steel cutting blades.

USE: Cutting carrot sticks into quarters, lengthwise.

BUYING TIPS: For most cooks it is probably easier to use a knife.

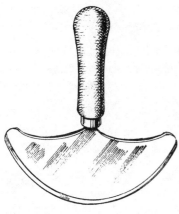

CURVED CHOPPER

CURVED CHOPPER

ALSO KNOWN AS: Bowl chopper, hachoir

DESCRIPTION: Sort of the heavier, French version of the two-handled *mezzaluna* (see page 41), this is one or two flat, thin, crescent-shaped blades with a single handle in or over the middle, basically a knife with the handle on top of the blade instead of at the end, sold with a shallow wooden (hard maple or yellow birch) or high density plastic *chopping bowl* (see page 50) that has the same curve as the blade and an extra-thick bottom. Other versions include:

TYPES: *All-purpose chopper:* Has a long, wide blade, similar to a chef's knife, but with a handle built in over the cutting edge.

Chopper (Also Known As a *double chopper* [two blades] or *multi-chopper*): Short, wavy (corrugated) or flat blade with a handle directly above it—basically a knife with the handle on top of the blade instead of at the end. Similar to the *fluted knife,* a garnishing tool (see page 342). Also called a *serrator* and on occasion, a *meat tenderizer* if used for that purpose. Wavy blades have more cutting edge for chopping efficiency, and can be used for decorative cuts.

Flat chopper (Also Known As *flat cutter*): Merely a plain, flat, rectangular piece of stainless steel with a handle along one edge, in this case, the top side. It doubles as a *scraper* or *dough scraper* (see page 248) and in a heavier version as a *knife* for cutting large pieces of very hard cheese.

Mincer/chopper (Also Known As *food chopper* or *four blade chopper*): The most complex version, with perpendicular blades arching back from a center point, like an upside-down mushroom.

USE: Chopping small quantities of pecans and walnuts, as well as garlic, onions, shallots, or parsley, in a chopping bowl or on a cutting board, with an up-and-down chopping motion. Used with one hand. Flat or straight version can be used as a scraper.

USE TIPS: Similar to a traditional design used by native Alaskans.

BUYING TIPS: Good gift item. Very useful if you are often chopping small quantities of these foods and dislike using a regular knife. Often sold with the bowl as a *chopping bowl* set.

DUMPLING MAKER

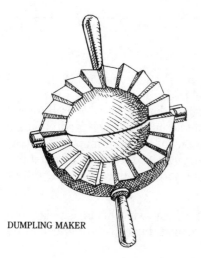

DUMPLING MAKER

ALSO KNOWN AS: Pot-sticker press, dough press

DESCRIPTION: Small, plastic bowl, split in two and hinged, with handles on either side and a wide, corrugated edge. One half folds over the other. Another version, a *pierogi maker,* consists of two plaques with this same pattern and sharp ridges in the middle of each circle. The pierogis are assembled on top of one plaque and the other is pressed down on them to seal and cut them apart. Available in single and triple sizes. And there is a bell-shaped version, misnamed a *tartmaker,* which sits over an assembled dumpling, and when pressed down, cuts, crimps, and seals the dumpling in one motion.

USE: Forming dumplings such as pierogis, wontons, empanadas, ravioli, kreplach, and the like.

BUYING TIPS: Some cooks prefer the pleasure of making dumplings by hand.

EGG PIERCER

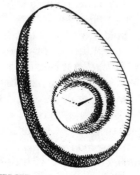

EGG PIERCER

ALSO KNOWN AS: Egg pricker

DESCRIPTION: Small, ½-inch thick, oval-shaped, solid plastic device with a deep hole in one side. In the middle of the hole is a sharp pin which ends below the surface. The edges of the hole are slightly beveled.

USE: Piercing the shell of raw eggs with a pinprick prior to boiling. This prevents the eggs from cracking or bursting while being cooked in the shell by allowing the pressure inside to dissipate.

USE TIPS: A small amount of egg white will usually escape from the hole, but this is easily wiped off when the egg is removed from the water. Pierce the *wide* end of the egg only.

BUYING TIPS: A heavy sewing needle can be used in place of this gadget.

EGG TOPPER

EGG TOPPER

ALSO KNOWN AS: Egg cutter, eggshell cutter

DESCRIPTION: Wide metal flange forming a ring a few inches across with a pair of built-in scissor handles. A circular set of jagged teeth open to width of ring and close in just enough to pierce an eggshell. Another version is the *egg slicer,* which is essentially a pair of extremely wide-bladed scissors; one blade has an open ring in it (to hold an egg top) and the other slides neatly across it. Made of chrome-plated or stainless steel, but also available in fancy, gold-plated, decorative versions.

USE: Neatly slicing off the ends of soft-cooked eggs.

USE TIPS: The topper only cuts the shell; the slicer cuts off the entire top.

EGG WEDGER

EGG WEDGER

ALSO KNOWN AS: Egg sectioner

DESCRIPTION: Hand-sized cast-aluminum or plastic tool with two arms joined by a hinge at one end; the business end of one arm has a small cup with slitted sides suitable for holding the narrow end of a hard-boiled egg, and the other end has a small open ring crisscrossed by three stainless steel wires forming six sections. This same open ring is found in a double model which has an egg slicer (see above) built in next to it. Sometimes supplied with a small metal tool with a curved triangular blade for making rosettes.

USE: Slices hard-boiled eggs from the tip to the base, creating six wedges, when the two arms are squeezed together.

USE TIPS: A knife is easily used for this job except when preparing quantities of hard-boiled eggs for a large group. Dip the blade in cold water to keep the yolk from sticking to the blade.

BUYING TIPS: A fairly nonessential gadget.

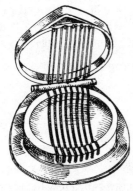

EGG/MUSHROOM SLICER

EGG/MUSHROOM SLICER

ALSO KNOWN AS: Egg slicer, mushroom slicer, egg, mushroom, and tomato slicer, dual slicer

DESCRIPTION: Flat stainless steel, chrome-plated steel, plastic, or cast-aluminum device, a little larger than an egg, with hinged door made of six stainless steel wires and a frame that closes into the base. The wires go into slots in the base, which has a curved depression to hold an egg. Some models have a mushroom- (T-) shaped depression and are called *mushroom slicers*. One brand has a version with slots for an egg slicer on one end and for an *egg wedger* (see previous entry) on the other, with the blades hinged in the middle, called an *egg machine*.

USE: Neatly slicing very fresh, firm mushrooms or hard-boiled eggs into as many as nine slices, depending on the size of the item being cut and the number of wires.

USE TIPS: In general, a slicer will give you neater slices than a knife. One cut through gives neat slices, but turning the cut egg 90 degrees and cutting again allows you to cut the slices into small pieces, which is useful for making egg salad.

BUYING TIPS: In this case the least-expensive supermarket model is the one to get.

ELECTRIC SLICER-SHREDDER

DESCRIPTION: A type of hand-held *food processor* without a work-bowl (see page 73) or an *electric rotograter* (see page 117), this large plastic-covered electric motor has a feed tube with a round opening at the bottom which contains various cutting blades in the form of cones or drums. Whole pieces of cheese, fruit, or vegetables are pushed down the tube with one hand while the hand holds the machine over a salad or workbowl.

USE: Rapid slicing or shredding of foods, depending on the blades inserted into the opening.

USE TIPS: Accessories make ripple cut as well as regular thick and thin slices. Others can grate chocolate, chop nuts, and crumb crackers. Some cooks make thin-sliced fruit for tarts or pies with this tool.

BUYING TIPS: Available in a regular or professional (large) style. Look for a model with several interchangeable slicing and shredding blades.

FOOD CHOPPER

FOOD CHOPPER

ALSO KNOWN AS: Vegetable chopper

DESCRIPTION: Small plastic cylinder with an open bottom and a plunger-type handle coming out the center top. The plunger, which is on a spring, controls a set of stainless steel blades which stay in the top part of the cylinder when not being pushed down onto food. A simple and easy-to-clean device.

USE: Chopping small pieces of food, like nuts and mushrooms. Larger models are good for chopping onions while minimizing eye irritation.

BUYING TIPS: An inexpensive gadget for those who dislike using knives. This is a rather specialized piece of equipment and unless you collect such things as a hobby, a chef's knife can be used just as effectively.

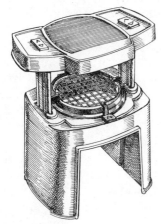

FOOD CUTTER

FOOD CUTTER

DESCRIPTION: Large, multifaceted gadget made of two parts: an inverted U-shaped base that holds a cutting screen in a rotating turret at the top, and a large plunger handle. Made of plastic.

USE: Rapidly makes thin or thick slices, julienne slices, French fries, and dices vegetables through the use of interchangeable and repositionable screens.

USE TIPS: Particularly handy if you have large quantities of food to cut in this manner.

BUYING TIPS: There are numerous versions of this around, most of which combine features found in the other, more specialized items noted in this chapter. Get the most versatile model you can find.

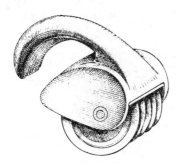

FOOD MINCER

FOOD MINCER

ALSO KNOWN AS: Rolling mincer, gourmet mincer, parsley mincer, rotary mincer, vegetable dicer, vegetable cutter

DESCRIPTION: Small hand-sized device consisting of a handle with a wide, flat blade area containing five to ten small stainless steel cutting disks on an axle. Handle is usually made of plastic. A slightly larger version called a *tenderizer/mincer/slicer* comes with two sets of disks, or blades: one for mincing or slicing, as with the smaller model, and a set of crenulated, toothed discs for tenderizing.

USE: Mincing (fine cutting or chopping) or slicing onions and other soft vegetables into small pieces by simply rolling this over the food repeatedly.

USE TIPS: Especially good for chopping parsley and other herbs; not advised for chopping garlic—it just doesn't work well.

BUYING TIPS: This is not an essential kitchen tool. More experienced chefs prefer using a regular chopping knife for this task.

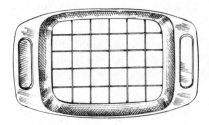

FRENCH FRY CUTTER

FRENCH FRY CUTTER

ALSO KNOWN AS: French fry slicer, potato cutter

DESCRIPTION: Grid of stainless steel cutting wires which is contained in either of two types of cutters:

TYPES: *Hand:* Small, potato-sized rectangular cast-aluminum frame 3½ inches wide and 5 inches long, holding a grid of nine stainless steel wires cutting twenty strips.
Mechanical: Rectangular box-shaped device, about 8 inches long and 4 inches high, with a large lever-type handle and a stainless steel grid of cutting edges at one end. When the handle is raised, the opening is large enough for a potato; when it is pushed down, the potato is pressed through the grid. Often sold with two grids, one for thick and one for thin fries, usually thirty-six and sixty-four pieces, respectively. Some come with a grid that makes home fry, vegetable, or cheese slices, with thin rectangular openings, and another grid similar to a *fruit slicer* (see page 62) called an *apple slicer/corer,* which removes cores and cuts fruit into wedges.

MECHANICAL FRENCH FRY CUTTER

USE: Automatic cutting of French fries from raw potato.

USE TIPS: This works quickly, but it may waste some potato around the edges. Small pieces should be discarded because they will burn before the thicker ones are cooked.

BUYING TIPS: Only for those cooks who make French fries regularly.

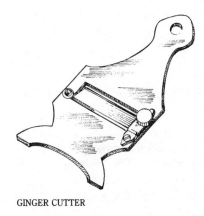

GINGER CUTTER

GINGER CUTTER

ALSO KNOWN AS: Chocolate cutter, truffle cutter, chocolate shaver, shaver, truffle mandoline

DESCRIPTION: Flat piece of stainless steel, about 6 inches long and 4 inches wide, with a violin shape and one wide, adjustable blade in the center. Quite similar to a *mandoline* (see page 40) but much smaller and less adjustable. Another version of a *truffle cutter* is a small metal band in a decorative shape, much like a *cookie cutter* (see page 234).

USE: Making extremely thin slices from whole ginger root, large pieces of chocolate, or truffles. The cookie-cutter model is for cutting thin slices of truffle into decorative shapes, such as clovers or fleurs de lis, for use in aspics, glazes, or other decorative dishes.

BUYING TIPS: It seems unlikely that most cooks need to slice truffles, but this works quite well on any hard food such as chocolate or ginger root.

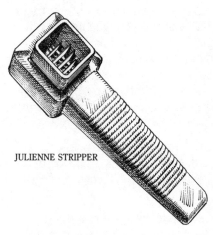

JULIENNE STRIPPER

JULIENNE STRIPPER

ALSO KNOWN AS: Julienne cutter, julienne strips

DESCRIPTION: 5-inch-long plastic device with a 1-inch-square funnel at one end. A matrix of eight stainless steel cutting blades is inside the funnel.

USE: Cutting hard, long vegetables into matchstick-thin julienne strips for cooking or garnishing.

USE TIPS: Insert the thick end of the vegetable into the thin end of the funnel, toward the cutting edge of the blades. Push with short, sharp strokes. Lay cuttings parallel and chop with a knife for garnishes. Soak cuttings in ice water to get them to curl up.

BUYING TIPS: Faster than using a knife, especially for the uninitiated.

GUARD

STAINLESS STEEL MANDOLINE

MANDOLINE

ALSO KNOWN AS: Slaw cutter, slicer, universal grater, vegetable slicer

DESCRIPTION: A flat, stationary cutter that is available in two styles.

TYPES: *Hand-held* (Also Known As *vegetable slicer*): Wooden, metal, or plastic ramp that has an interchangeable stainless steel blade mounted within it. The cutting edge is often at an angle or in a V shape (it can be called a *V-slicer*). Blades are somewhat adjustable for the thickness of the cut and are either straight or corrugated. Interchangeable blades provide for slicing or cutting julienne strips in various thicknesses, as well as grating and shredding. May be offered with a bowl that fits underneath to catch the cuttings. Ranges in design from complex plastic to a simple, triangular metal stand with a blade at the top and a little platform that slides up and down the angled stand. A smaller version of this is the *ginger cutter* (see page 39).

Mountable, stainless steel: A multibladed cutter, made up of a ramp that contains various changeable blades, a device called a *guard* or *protector* for holding the food to be cut that slides on this ramp, and a folding leg mechanism that may be screwable to a countertop. Ramp is approximately 4½ inches wide and well over a foot long. The largest, stainless models are considered professional tools.

USE: Fast, convenient, and consistent slicing of potatoes and other firm vegetables. Can be adjusted for thick, thin, or decorative cuts such as shoestring, julienne, French fry, waffle, or other miscellaneous cuts.

USE TIPS: The larger, mountable model is easier and safer to use—the food holder protects your fingers. However, it is bulky in storage and quite expensive.

BUYING TIPS: Many gadget-oriented manufacturers have clever variations on this traditional design, so shop around until you find one that pleases you. They all have different features such as many interchangeable blades, storage bins, colors, and so on.

MEAT SLICER

ALSO KNOWN AS: Slicing machine

DESCRIPTION: Movable tray that glides on a base and has a side wall that holds a protected circular blade powered by hand crank or an electric motor. A slim opening between the blade and a guard can be adjusted to the desired thickness of the slice, and a clamp of sorts holds the meat or cheese to be cut. The base of the slicer has suction cups or a clamp to hold it steady. The blade angle may be adjustable up to 45 degrees. Electric models are usually made entirely of stainless steel, or stainless with a plastic base. Hand-cranked models are made of all stainless steel, enameled cast aluminum, chromed steel, or plastic. Commonly just over a foot long.

USE: Slicing meat or hard cheeses. The meat is held firm and steady against the blade with the clamp device and one hand.

USE TIPS: Keep your hands away from the blade. The back and forth motion can be very distracting. Put blade at an angle for larger slices. Wash thoroughly and completely after use. Typical range of cuts is from paper thin to as thick as 1½ inches.

BUYING TIPS: Unless you regularly plan big parties, you can probably skip this very expensive item. Any butcher or deli will happily slice specialty meats for you.

MEZZALUNA

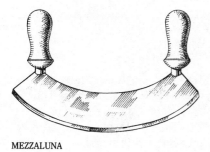

MEZZALUNA

ALSO KNOWN AS: Crescent cutter, rocking mincer, half-moon, mincing knife

DESCRIPTION: One or two parallel, crescent-shaped steel blades, spaced about an inch apart in the case of the double models, with short bulbous handles attached to each end. Lighter than the *curved chopper* (see page 33), a similar item. Mezzaluna means "half-moon" in Italian, which describes the crescent-shaped blades.

USE: Quick and thorough chopping and dicing. Use on a wooden cutting board. Works with a rocking motion, with two hands.

USE TIPS: A mezzaluna is a sophisticated substitute for the *chef's knife* (see page 12), which is more commonly used for chopping and dicing. It can be safer, however, and quicker and easier to work with.

BUYING TIPS: Recommended for chefs who use a lot of fresh vegetables in their recipes.

MUFFIN SPLITTER

DESCRIPTION: Short, wide plastic fork with thick, flat tines.

USE: Splitting open English muffins while preserving their distinct texture.

USE TIPS: Insert carefully, in the exact middle.

BUYING TIPS: Better than a regular fork. Worth it if you are a perfectionist.

ONION SLICER

ONION SLICER

DESCRIPTION: Cast-aluminum device made of two levers hinged together at one end. One has a large hopper, sort of a square funnel, with several rows of cutting blades near the open bottom. The other serves as a plunger. When squeezed together, they force an onion (up to 2 inches wide) over the blades. A similar item is a *vegetable slicer.*

USE: Convenient and quick slicing of onions into ⅛-inch slices.

USE TIPS: Be sure onion is well-peeled and not too big.

BUYING TIPS: One way to avoid tears when slicing onions.

PARSLEY MINCER

PARSLEY MINCER

ALSO KNOWN AS: Herb mill, rotary herb chopper

DESCRIPTION: Available in two steel and plastic versions, one is hand-held, with a little squarish, open-ended funnel-shaped chamber called a hopper on the end and a crank on the side. The crank turns a set of sharp cutting teeth at the bottom of the hopper. The other version is called a *food mincer* (see page 37). The hopper model is available in a left-handed version.

USE: Fine, quick, and thorough chopping of parsley.

USE TIPS: Make sure the cutting edges are very sharp or you may bruise the parsley instead of cutting it, making the tool more trouble than it is worth. Keep parsley dry prior to chopping. Refrigerate in a covered jar after chopping.

BUYING TIPS: Not essential. It may be easier to chop parsley with a chef's knife, or, if you have much to do, in a food processor.

PASTA WHEEL

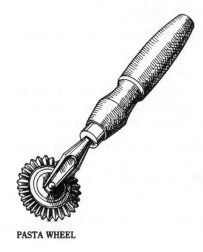

PASTA WHEEL

ALSO KNOWN AS: Ravioli crimper, ravioli cutter, jagger, jagging wheel, pastry jagger, fluted pastry wheel, pasta/pastry wheel, pasta cutter, pastry crimper, pie crimper

DESCRIPTION: Small stainless steel wheel with fluted or corrugated edge, usually about 2 inches in diameter, axle-mounted on a short handle made of wood or cast aluminum. Very often confused with the similar *pastry wheel* (see below), which does not have a wavy edge. Also available as half of a combination model called either a *dual pastry wheel* or a *crimper/cutter*, when the other blade is a flat pastry-wheel blade.

USE: Cutting wide pasta into decorative, jagged-edged strips for ravioli or lattice crusts or for making other decorative cuts in any kind of pastry or cookie dough.

USE TIPS: Practice making raviolis before attempting large-scale production, as it takes some getting used to.

PASTRY CRIMPER AND SEALER

PASTRY CRIMPER AND SEALER

ALSO KNOWN AS: Pastry crimper, crimper/sealer/cutter, cutter/sealer, pastry crimp

DESCRIPTION: Two small, ¼-inch-thick cast-aluminum disks axle-mounted on the end of a hand-sized handle. Their edges are made of regular, small square openings which give a crenulated effect. A sharp cutting edge is between the two sides. Some crimpers are made with one sharp edge and one crenulated edge.

USE: Crimping and sealing pastry or ravioli dough. The wheel is rolled around the pastry as needed.

USE TIPS: Typically used on dumplinglike dishes.

BUYING TIPS: Another version seals only and has no cutting wheel (see page 251).

PASTRY WHEEL

ALSO KNOWN AS: Pastry cutter, straight-edged pastry wheel

DESCRIPTION: Small, flat, stainless steel disc, axle-mounted on a short wooden or plastic handle. Often confused with the wavy-edged *pasta wheel* (see page 43). Also available as half of a combination model, called either a *dual pastry wheel* or a *crimper/cutter,* when the other blade is a corrugated, or fluted, *pasta wheel* blade.

USE: Cutting or marking strips of cookie or pastry dough, especially for crisscross open patterns, and for cutting sheets of homemade pasta with straight edges for items such as lasagna.

USE TIPS: Because this is a lightweight item, do not use on pizza; use a heavier constructed *pizza wheel* (see below) instead. Remember, this cuts a straight edge; a *pasta wheel* (see page 43) cuts a distinctive corrugated edge for ravioli.

BUYING TIPS: Handy item for all kinds of pastry cutting.

PIZZA POPPER

DESCRIPTION: 17- to 43-inch-long stainless steel wire rod with a wooden handle and a sharp point bent at a right angle.

USE: Popping cheese blisters on pizzas which are still in the oven.

BUYING TIPS: Only necessary if you make lots of pizza in large ovens.

PIZZA WHEEL

ALSO KNOWN AS: Pizza cutter

DESCRIPTION: Round stainless steel, chromed steel, or brass wheel with blade-sharp edge, from 2½ to 4 inches in diameter, axle-mounted on a short handle made of wood or cast aluminum. Most models have solid thumbguards and large, comfortable handles. A smaller, lighter version without the thumbguards is called a *pastry wheel* (see page 43).

USE: Cutting pizza into serving pieces. Yields a sharper, cleaner cut than a knife edge; easier and quicker than scissors.

USE TIPS: This can move fast, so watch out for your other hand. Bearing down to get through a thick crust means that when you do cut through, you will also be cutting into the pizza pan or the counter underneath. Practice to get the feel for how much pressure to use. Also good for pies and quiches.

BUYING TIPS: Beware of cheap models here. Get a good, solid, comfortable model with a big thumbguard.

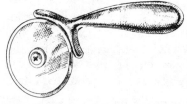

PIZZA WHEEL

RAVIOLI FORM

ALSO KNOWN AS: Ravioli pan, ravioli maker

DESCRIPTION: Cast-aluminum mold with either twelve or sixteen round or square holes or cups for ravioli, with a jagged edge that surrounds each hole; sold either with a plastic sheet, a *press,* with small domes that correspond to the openings in the form, or just a small wooden rolling pin. The press's domes are pressed into the sheet of pasta and the filling placed in the depressions made. After the lower layer is filled, the top layer is forced down with either the press or the roller so that the toothed edge surrounding each mold or hole makes the traditional jagged-edge cut and forms individual pieces of ravioli.

USE: Making ravioli twelve or sixteen pieces at a time.

BUYING TIPS: Most efficient of the hand-operated ravioli cutters.

RAVIOLI FORM

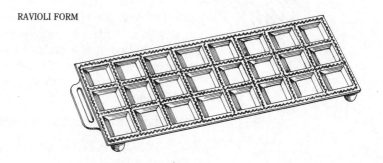

RAVIOLI ROLLING PIN

DESCRIPTION: 23-inch-long, narrow rolling pin made of ten sections and three ridges that run the length of the pin.

USE: Cutting small pieces of pasta dough from one large sheet for making ravioli.

USE TIPS: The raviolis must still be assembled one at a time.

RAVIOLI ROLLING PIN

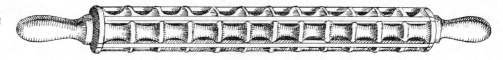

RAVIOLI STAMP

RAVIOLI STAMP

DESCRIPTION: Round or square cast-aluminum cutter with a short wooden handle that resembles an open rubber stamp with a slightly jagged edge. Either 2 or 2½ inches across or square. Another version is an ingenious *rolling ravioli cutter* that is made of two small axle-mounted cutting wheels and a flat blade mounted between them. The axle is mounted on a short wooden handle. When the tool is rolled along, the blade rotates and comes down to cut across the panel of dough every 2 inches.

USE: Cutting squares of ravioli from sheets of pasta, one at a time.

USE TIPS: The raviolis must still be assembled one at a time.

BUYING TIPS: This is inexpensive but slow.

TOMATO SLICER

TOMATO SLICER

DESCRIPTION: Rectangular wire frame about 4 inches long and 3 inches wide with a set of ten thin sawtooth cutting blades suspended between the ends. Plastic handle. May be sold with a square plastic block with many points on it, called a *pusher*. This is used to push the tomato onto the blades without risk of cutting your fingers.

USE: Slicing tomatoes into eleven slices all at once.

USE TIPS: Use a gentle sawing motion, especially on very soft, ripe tomatoes.

BUYING TIPS: Handy item if you are not good at delicate slicing jobs.

TOMATO WEDGER

DESCRIPTION: Round plastic device a few inches in diameter with four cutting blades in a star pattern. The cutting blades have jagged edges.

USE: Cutting tomatoes into eight wedges simultaneously.

USE TIPS: Be extra careful with very ripe tomatoes.

BUYING TIPS: Cutting a tomato with a knife is not very hard and poses less risk at failure than using this device does.

Scissors, Shears, and Snips

About Scissors, Shears, and Snips

The best scissors and shears are generally easy to spot: they are cleanly designed with comfortable grips and, above all, blades of stainless steel. Shears, which usually are spring-loaded, are intended for bigger and tougher jobs than scissors, while snips tend to be specialized. All are more efficient in certain jobs than knives, such as cutting types of pastry or poultry joints. When you buy any of these, be sure your grip is large enough to reach the finger holes when the device is fully opened.

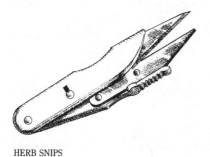

HERB SNIPS

HERB SNIPS

ALSO KNOWN AS: Kitchen snips

DESCRIPTION: Tiny scissors with short, thick, straight blades embedded in plastic handles that are spring-loaded.

USE: Cutting up fresh herbs.

USE TIPS: Add a drop of oil onto the hinge or spring from time to time.

BUYING TIPS: These do a much better job than regular scissors.

KITCHEN SCISSORS

ALSO KNOWN AS: Kitchen shears

DESCRIPTION: Short, tapered stainless or chrome-plated steel-bladed scissors which only rarely have one serrated edge. Many different makes and models available. Models with particularly sturdy or shorter, slightly curved and wider blades, usually about 8 inches long overall, may be called *all-purpose shears*. Available in a left-handed version and even with soft handles. *Pizza shears* have extra-wide blades; *grape shears* extra-short ones. Most kitchen shears have a notched, inner curve on the handles.

USE: General cutting chores, such as string, butcher's twine, pizza, artichoke leaves, etc. The curved, notched inner handle edges can be used like a *jar wrench* (see page 430) to remove jar lids or bottle tops. The notched inside edge is for cutting poultry bones. Pizza shears are useful when a pizza is in a nonstick pan, the surface of which would be damaged by using a *pizza wheel* (see page 44); their width makes them easier to use on thick pizza.

USE TIPS: You may want to separate shears used for food from those used for nonfood items for reasons of sanitation or convenience. Nonplastic models can go in the dishwasher; always wash thoroughly after they are used on food.

BUYING TIPS: These are an essential kitchen item. It's worth the extra cost to buy sturdy, long-lasting ones, always of stainless steel.

POULTRY SHEARS

ALSO KNOWN AS: Curved shears

DESCRIPTION: Large scissors, typically 9½ inches long, with scimitar-shaped (curved) blades and serrated edges. Made of chromed or stainless steel and often spring-loaded (the spring forces the blades apart). The lower blade usually has a notch near the hinge for cutting bones.

USE: Cutting all types of poultry instead of using a knife. Especially useful for quartering ducks (cutting them into four sections).

USE TIPS: Be sure to wash in hot, soapy water or in dishwasher after use on raw poultry to avoid any possibility of salmonella contamination. The high heat of an automatic dishwasher is necessary to prevent the development of salmonella bacteria.

BUYING TIPS: Chickens used to be larger—over 4 pounds—and older, making the bones tougher. Today's chickens are smaller and younger so regular shears or knives can suffice, and poultry shears are not needed as much.

— NOTCH

POULTRY SHEARS

SHELLFISH SHEARS

DESCRIPTION: Stainless-steel scissors, about 8½ inches long, with short, angled cutting edges, much like surgical scissors. Top cutting edge has small notches to cut around joints, bottom edge has forked tip for extracting meat. Another version is a straight set of heavy-duty scissors, called *lobster shears,* or *lobster pincers,* which are short, narrow, pointed blades with long, spring-loaded straight handles.

USE: Easy and precise opening of shellfish shells. Also intended for cutting ribs and poultry.

SHELLFISH SHEARS

USE TIPS: Especially good on king crab legs; lobster shears are handy when you have many lobsters to prepare for stew.

BUYING TIPS: A good substitute for nutcrackers and lobster forks if you are dealing with large quantities of shellfish.

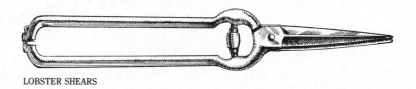

LOBSTER SHEARS

Cutting Accessories

CARVING FORK

ALSO KNOWN AS: Roast fork

DESCRIPTION: Large, long, two-prong fork with knife-type handle. Made of stainless steel with plastic, wood, bone, or metal handle. Usually straight or only slightly curved. Usually sold as part of a carving set, with a *carving knife* (see page 19) and *sharpening steel* (see page 55). Generally fine, decorative style and finish, but also available as a plain, workaday *utility fork*.

USE: Holding a roast while carving.

USE TIPS: The straightness allows you to slice right next to the fork, while using a curved fork creates a gap. However, a curved fork may be easier to use while cooking for moving large pieces of meat.

BUYING TIPS: Look for a fork made by the same company as your fine carving knife, and with the same construction quality: full tang (see page 4), forged steel, strong design. Personal preference dictates whether you should use straight or curved models, but a good compromise is one that is only slightly curved.

CARVING FORK

CHOPPING BOWL

ALSO KNOWN AS: Salad bowl, salad/chopping bowl

DESCRIPTION: Large, shallow, thick, wooden bowl carved out of hard maple or yellow birch. Very few manufacturers still make these; most bowls are made in Vermont, cut from tree trunks as thick as the diameter of these bowls. Available in 9-, 11-, 13-, and 15-inch diameters.

USE: Contains food as it is chopped by a *curved chopper* (see page 33), though more commonly used to serve salad. Better than a flat cutting board for items like walnuts, as the bowl keeps the pieces in place.

USE TIPS: Wipe with salad oil from time to time to prevent drying out, unless used for salads, in which case just wipe dry and let the remaining trace of salad oil remain. Never place in dishwasher.

BUYING TIPS: Curve of chopper should fit the curve of the bowl.

CITRUS SLICE GUIDE

DESCRIPTION: Plastic cone made of flexible slats with a flat base made of two horizontal disks about an inch apart. An orange or lemon is placed in the top and forces the slats slightly apart so a knife can fit between them.

USE: Holding an orange or a lemon for slicing into halves, quarters, or eighths.

BUYING TIPS: Slicing a citrus fruit into wedges is not so difficult that you really need a guide.

CITRUS SLICE GUIDE

CUTTING BOARD

ALSO KNOWN AS: Utility board, chopping board, trencher board

DESCRIPTION: Flat board of various shapes and materials, typically about ¾ inch thick and a foot or so long by a little less wide, though available in a wide range of sizes and shapes. Commonly made of hardwood, whether solid or of strips glued together, but also made of semirigid white polyethylene, clear acrylic plastic, and even marble or tempered glass. Some models have small nonskid feet and others are designed to be used on both sides, perhaps with grooves on one side to catch juices. One cutting

GRAVY GROOVE

CARVING BOARD

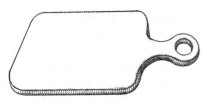

PADDLE BOARD

board has angled sides which form a chute for the food to be scraped out of.

TYPES: *Bread board:* May be quite small and decoratively shaped or rectangular, and used primarily for bread.

Carving board (Also Known As *au jus carver*): Usually with spikes for holding meat and cups or channels, sometimes called *gravy grooves,* for juices.

Chopping block: Extra-thick, solid wooden board for serious chopping. Surface is end grain of wood.

Crumb box: Wooden box with a platform of wooden slats that fits on top. When bread is cut on the slats, crumbs fall into the box for later recovery.

Over-the-sink board: Wide handles that fit over the edges of a sink.

Paddle board (Also Known As a *slicing board*): Small, with a handle, making it look like a paddle. Hole in handle is for hanging on a rack.

Pizza cutting board: 14-inch-diameter wooden cutting board with slots forming eight wedges. Makes cutting a pizza easier and neater.

USE: Provides a soft surface to cut on and protects your counter surface from cuts. Soft materials like polyethylene will not dull the blades of knives that cut through the food and touch the board.

USE TIPS: It is essential to keep this very clean. Scrub it immediately after each use with hot soapy water and a hot rinse. Any board in regular use is a target for microbial infection, so give it a weekly cleaning with a bleach solution of two teaspoons to one gallon of water. Hard, high-density, plastic boards are best for use with raw poultry, fish, and meats, because they are nonporous and can be put in the dishwasher for sanitizing, but they tend to dull knives. Wooden cutting boards are fine for all other foods, such as cheese, bread, and vegetables; do not use them for raw poultry. Treat wood with mineral oil, not vegetable oils, which can turn rancid. Wash wooden boards in warm soapy water and dry immediately; never put in the dishwasher.

BUYING TIPS: The advantage of a smaller, plastic board is that it can go in the dishwasher, but many cooks have a personal preference for wood. Get the largest one you have room for, both in the sink or dishwasher and in storage. The pebbly surface of the hard, acrylic boards assists in drainage and makes them a bit less slippery, but they accumulate unsightly scratches and scars. Soft polyethylene is probably easiest on knife edges, but some wooden cutting board manufacturers claim otherwise. None of the plastic boards should warp, splinter, or chip, and they should be nonporous, nontoxic, and odor- and bacteria-proof. Wooden boards should be made of the best hardwood, such as hard maple. Get one big enough to cut all your food on but that is small enough to fit your counter space. Glass and marble are not good for cutting except as serving or presentation items because they dull the edges of knives more quickly than the softer boards.

KNIFE BLOCK

KNIFE BLOCK

ALSO KNOWN AS: Counter block, slant block, blade block, knife rack, knife case

DESCRIPTION: Any one of a number of designs with slots that knives fit into. The most common one is a wood *knife holder,* made of hardwood (ash, mahogany, etc.) with horizontal or vertical slots for each type of knife (long, short, wide, thick, etc.). Holds from six to twelve knives. One kind has a mysterious, hidden sharpener in each slot, so that the knives are honed every time they are removed for use.

USE: Holding knives while preserving their cutting edges. Prevents them from touching one another and getting dull.

BUYING TIPS: Mahogany, with its deep, dark patterns, is considered the nicest wood for this item.

KNIFE SHEATH

DESCRIPTION: One flat piece of thick, somewhat flexible plastic that is folded over. Spring tension holds it firmly in place on a knife blade. Available in various lengths and widths but always rectangular in shape.

USE: Protecting knife edges in drawers and fingers from being cut by same. Also suitable for transportation on picnics or trips.

USE TIPS: Dishwasher safe.

BUYING TIPS: Good substitute for a *knife block* (see previous entry) in small kitchens.

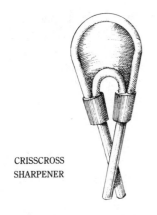

CRISSCROSS
SHARPENER

RING SHARPENER

ROLLING KNIFE SHARPENER

KNIFE SHARPENER

DESCRIPTION: Abrasive material held in various designs ranging from the simplest stone to complex electric models. Most fall into these categories:

TYPES: *Crisscross sharpener:* Two short, rough steel or ceramic arms crossed to form a V through which a knife blade is dragged. 3 to 4 inches long overall.

Electric knife sharpener: Rectangular device around 7 or 8 inches long, 4 inches high, and 3½ inches deep, with two or three large slots on top. The slots contain various grades of abrasive stones (industrial diamonds on the better models) and magnets that hold the knife in the exact, correct position for accurate sharpening, honing, and polishing, in that order. Usually the on/off switch is a large, flat button right in the middle of the top, or it may go on automatically when a knife is inserted. Some models have an "overload" feature which prevents damage to a blade that is pressed too hard against the stone; the best models require you to merely drag the knife through without applying pressure.

Ring-type sharpener: Small housing for several hardened steel rings; the knife blade is dragged through the spot where the rings meet. The curve of the rings forms the proper angle for the edge.

Rolling knife sharpener: Small plastic wheels, each about the size of a quarter, which form a 2-inch-thick sandwich for an abrasive disc. The wheels' inside edges are angled in such a way that when a knife is drawn through causing the sharpener to roll along a countertop, the knife is held at precisely the correct angle for sharpening.

USE: Sharpening and honing knives with traditional, plain blades.

USE TIPS: Not normally for knives with scalloped or serrated edges (though some specialized versions can sharpen scalloped edges, they will wear down the points over time). Granton-edged *slicing knives* (see page 19) can be sharpened without this problem because they have a straight cutting edge. Don't use too much pressure or you'll wear the knives down.

BUYING TIPS: Each type is easier or harder to use depending on your preferences—all strive to do the same job. Look for the one that meets your standards of performance but also ease of storage. No doubt the automatic one can do the best and most complete job (it sharpens knives just like some factories do), but it takes up much counter space and costs quite a bit. Look for a model with diamond wheels which won't heat up and detemper your blades. Some of the other models take less than an inch of drawer space and cost next to nothing, but are harder to use—and all are for the same basic job. A good alternative is the sharpening steel (see opposite).

MAGNETIC BAR

ALSO KNOWN AS: Magnetic organizer, magnetic utensil rack, cutlery rack, magnetic knife bar

DESCRIPTION: Double row of magnetic strips embedded in a plastic or wooden base 8, 12, 18, and 24 inches long (single strip on the shortest model). Usually designed to be wall-mounted, though some come with powerful magnets on the back for attachment to large appliances (refrigerators, range hoods, etc.) instead of the wall.

USE: Convenient storage of knives or other steel utensils near a workspace.

BUYING TIPS: Utensils can be removed and replaced very easily from these devices, and their visibility makes the choice of utensil that much quicker.

ONION HOLDER

ONION HOLDER

ALSO KNOWN AS: English muffin breaker, onion fork, vegetable holder

DESCRIPTION: Square, flat wooden or plastic handle with about 10 or 20 stainless-steel wire prongs 2 to 3 inches long, about ¼ inch apart. Similar to a hair pick.

USE: Making evenly sized onion slices. You hold the handle with one hand, plunge it into an onion, and use the prongs as a guide for your slicing knife. Also used for cutting an English muffin in half without ruining the nooks and crannies that are distinctive to this item, and as a guide when slicing soft items like tomatoes or even giblets.

USE TIPS: Slice through every other slot for thicker slices. Can be used just to hold the vegetable at one end while you slice it normally, too.

BUYING TIPS: Too many specialized tools will clutter your drawer, so consider whether or not you really need an onion holder when a little practice with a good, sharp knife (or with a fork on an English muffin) will do the same job.

SHARPENING STEEL

ALSO KNOWN AS: Sharpener, butcher's steel, steel, straightening steel

DESCRIPTION: Long, narrow, hardened steel rod, about 8 to 12 inches long, with a rough texture or longitudinal grooves and a wooden or plastic handle with a hanging ring on the end. Rod is tapered a little bit to a blunt point. Available in oval as well as round shapes. Generally the steel is magnetized. A similar model, often called by its brand-name, Zip-Zap™, is available with a 6-inch-long ceramic rod instead of steel.

USE: Sharpening knives by running the blade up and down and across the rough-patterned steel at a 15- or 20-degree angle about six to ten times on each side. Do the opposite for the ceramic rod: hold knife still and move rod against it. Intended for routine use on sharp knives that just need a little freshening up, or honing, before each day's use—not for extremely dull knives.

USE TIPS: Always keep the blade at the same shallow angle (15 or 20 degrees, per knife-manufacturer's instructions). This kind of movement should be smooth and rhythmic, and is very hard for some people to do right, while others seem to have an innate ability to do it well. The steel is not meant to be washed, but rather brushed off with a brass-bristled brush. The ceramic rod is cleaned with soapy water. Clean knife after sharpening, though. Have knives professionally ground periodically. Store the ceramic model carefully to avoid breaking it.

BUYING TIPS: Get the thickest, longest one you can afford. Thicker rods present more sharpening surface to the knife and so last longer and work faster (oval models present the most surface but wear out faster because only two sides are used, making this more popular with professionals, who can afford new ones, than with amateurs). Look for magnetized models so that the small metal pieces will not fall on the table or counter, and for handles with good guard shoulders that will block any upstrokes that are too vigorous. The ceramic model is better for people who fear using the larger steel. It is also much less expensive than the steel. These have been largely replaced by *electric sharpeners* (see page 53), but many skilled cooks (it doesn't take much, really) still prefer the sharpening steel.

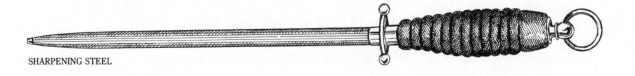

SHARPENING STEEL

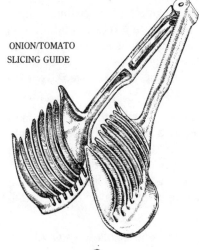

ONION/TOMATO
SLICING GUIDE

SLICING GUIDE

ALSO KNOWN AS: Carving guide, tomato slicer, onion/tomato slicing guide, slicing aid, roast slicing tongs

DESCRIPTION: Long, spring-loaded, cast-aluminum or stainless steel tongs with very wide, slotted gripping ends of various sizes and designs. The smallest, also called an *onion/tomato slicing guide,* has curved tines forming a 2-inch-wide cup at a right angle to the handles. The midsized model has curved claws with wider slots. The largest model has flat slotted claws.

USE: Cutting uniformly thin slices of onion, tomato (small model), French or Italian bread (intermediate model), and melon or canned ham (large model).

USE TIPS: Use every other slot for thicker slices.

BUYING TIPS: Sharp knives and a little practice allow most cooks to get by without these gadgets, though perhaps one could be of some use for making extremely thin slices of French bread.

SLICING GUIDE—
LARGE MODEL

WHETSTONE

ALSO KNOWN AS: Hone stone, honing stone

DESCRIPTION: A block of stone or Carborundum, housed in a wooden case. May have one fine side and one extra-fine side.

USE: Sharpening dull knives. The knife is drawn across the stone at an angle of about 20 degrees, about five or six times for each side of the blade.

USE TIPS: These are recommended over electric sharpeners if you have the ability to use them easily. Most people do not, though they are not hard to use. When properly used, they'll keep the edge of the blade in excellent working order. Not for use on serrated edges.

BUYING TIPS: Stones can sharpen more than a *sharpening steel* (see page 55), but fine-grained stones can be used for honing or touch up, too.

Peelers, Pitters, Strippers, and Corers

About Peelers, Pitters, Strippers, and Corers

This is definitely an area where the simplest knife can handle almost any of the jobs these implements have been designed to do. In fact, some knives are designed especially for these jobs, except for pitters and corers, as these merely imitate what a knife would do, but with guides and designs to make it an easier task. Some models combine several functions, too.

APPLE CORER

APPLE CORER

ALSO KNOWN AS: Fruit corer, core-all

DESCRIPTION: Small, hand-sized, straight utensil with a half hollow stainless-steel blade about 6 inches long that has a ½-inch-long cylinder at the end (some are just a full cylinder); the end's edges are sharp and scalloped, plain, or serrated. Also comes in larger sizes. Some larger models have a two-part cylindrical handle with a small inner part that slides down to eject the fruit core. One pointed, half-cylindrical type, a *corer and peeler* (see page 61), has a peeler-style blade along one side and a jagged cutting edge on the other.

USE: Coring apples. Just plunge this into an apple from the stem side and the core is sliced out in a neat, long, round piece. Larger models can be used on a wide variety of fruits such as grapefruit and pineapples.

USE TIPS: A definite timesaver if you use many apples.

BUYING TIPS: Get the larger size—you only need to go in once, and a small one may miss some seeds or part of the core. Some of the larger ones may be called by names relating to larger fruit, such as a *grapefruit corer* (see page 63). The *fruit slicer and corer* model (see page 62) is probably more useful for making pies and the like.

BLADE EDGE

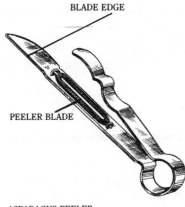

PEELER BLADE

ASPARAGUS PEELER

ASPARAGUS PEELER

DESCRIPTION: U-shaped, chrome-plated steel device, about 7 inches long, with one straight and one slightly rippled finger. The rippled side holds an asparagus stalk in place against the other side, which has a small double, swivel peeler embedded in it; the end is a knife blade. Another version, the *asparagus peeling knife*, also known as a *special peeling knife*, consists of a flat blade a few inches long with a little bracket about 2 inches long attached to it.

USE: Removing thin layers from the base of asparagus stalks carefully and accurately.

USE TIPS: Do not remove too much. Experiment until you get it right.

BUYING TIPS: Removing the tough skin at the base improves asparagus tenderness.

AVOCADO SKINNER

DESCRIPTION: A small knife with a wide, blunt-ended blade that ends in a short curve to the side. Not very sharp on the end or the sides. Usually has a plastic handle.

USE: Quick and efficient removal of skin from the meat of avocados.

USE TIPS: Also useful for removing the seed.

BUYING TIPS: Good gift item.

AVOCADO SKINNER

CITRUS FRUIT PEELER

CITRUS FRUIT PEELER

ALSO KNOWN AS: Citrus peeler, orange peeler

DESCRIPTION: Small plastic device that is found with various designs all of which incorporate a small point for slicing the skin and a curved blade for separating it from the fruit. One type looks like the outline of a snail, with a ring-sized loop over a curved, flat, pointed part. A small dorsal fin projects from the bottom. Another kind is about 6 inches long, ¼ inch wide, and flat, with a fishhook-shaped tip. Also made as a stainless steel knife with a wide, curved, serrated blade and a sharkfinlike starter blade protruding from the side.

USE: Zipping open and removing citrus fruit peels easily.

USE TIPS: Works better on thick-skinned types of fruit. Try first to be sure you have a suitable type of fruit before you attempt to impress your friends.

BUYING TIPS: Excellent inexpensive gift item; very handy.

CORN SLITTER

ALSO KNOWN AS: Scraper/slitter

DESCRIPTION: Small stainless steel paddle with several holes punched through that form teeth on one side. As the teeth are dragged over the kernels on an ear of corn, they are slit open, and pushing the curved blade removes the opened kernels completely.

USE: Removing the corn kernels from the ear for corn chowder, corn relish, or creamed corn–type dishes.

USE TIPS: The slitting process releases the maximum amount of juice.

BUYING TIPS: A knife will do for small quantities, but it does not expose the meat inside the kernels. For removing kernels without slitting, try a *corn stripper* (see next entry).

CORN STRIPPER

ALSO KNOWN AS: Kernel stripper, corn cutter, corn cutter/stripper

DESCRIPTION: U-shaped metal bar with a small cylindrical blade in the center. It is placed over an ear of corn held vertically, and pushed down. The ring is made of spring steel and spreads open to fit any size cob. A more serious style is a half-cylindrical strip of wood or stainless steel with a blade in the middle against which the cob is pushed, sometimes called a *corn cutter/creamer*. The latter model also slits the kernels if desired ("cream style").

USE: Stripping corn kernels off ears of corn in large quantities for canning, creamed corn, or making relish.

USE TIPS: Adjusts to any size ear. Very easy to use.

BUYING TIPS: Inexpensive item. For slitting, also see the previous entry.

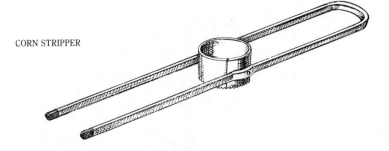

CORN STRIPPER

ELECTRIC PEELER

DESCRIPTION: Flashlight-sized, plug-in, 12-volt gadget with a cupped end that contains revolving stainless steel blades. Cupped shield reverses for use by left- or right-handers.

USE: Power-peeling all kinds of vegetables and fruits.

USE TIPS: Follow directions rigorously and practice. This is not easy to use at first but eventually it becomes comfortable.

BUYING TIPS: This may be a good way to peel enormous quantities of vegetables with less effort than a manual peeler, but it is not necessarily faster. Makes good citrus zests and peels tomatoes well.

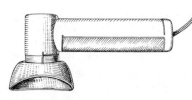

ELECTRIC PEELER

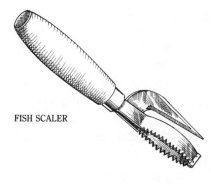

FISH SCALER

FISH SCALER

DESCRIPTION: Double-bladed and double-function small knife made of aluminum or stainless steel. The open, curved, jagged-edged part is for scaling, and the sharp, pointed, flat blade that goes off to one side is for gutting. Other versions have rough-textured surfaces instead of scaling blades, or are flat, U-shaped blades with crenulated edges.

USE: Scaling and gutting fish.

BUYING TIPS: Better than a plain knife. Fish stores will usually remove scales at no charge.

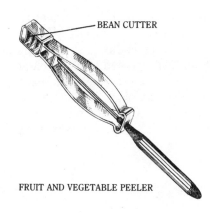

BEAN CUTTER

FRUIT AND VEGETABLE PEELER

FRUIT AND VEGETABLE PEELER

ALSO KNOWN AS: Potato peeler, vegetable peeler, peeler

DESCRIPTION: Many variations on the basic design of this simple, common tool are available. Usually it is a short, hand-sized, knife-like utensil with a narrow, curved, pointed carbon or stainless steel blade with a sharp-edged slot down its middle for the peelings to slip through. Some have a small triangle or blade on the back side for removing potato buds, called, not surprisingly, a *potato bud remover*. A *floating peeler* has a thick, hollow handle, and some have wide, plastic handles shaped like fanciful whales or hippos. Often combined with other cutting or grating tools.

TYPES: *Corer and peeler:* Fixed blade, with a large, half cylinder.

Harp peeler: Has a large loop for a handle (a "harp frame") instead of the usual small knifelike grip.

Parer/peeler: Combined with a *paring knife* (see page 18).

Peeler/bean slicer: Traditional peeler design with a small rectangle on the end that contains three small blades; green beans can be forced through it to be sliced into small strips.

Peeler brush: Peeler with some brush bristles on one side for cleaning peeling debris away.

Peeler/fish scaler: Flat, U-shaped blade with a crenulated edge for scaling fish on the side opposite the swivel peeler blade.

Spray peeler: Has a hose that connects to the kitchen sink faucet—the water washes the peels away as you cut them.

Swivel peeler (Also Known As *swivel-action peeler*): Very common and inexpensive item, considered traditional design. Just a frame that holds a slotted blade which swivels on an axle, with stainless steel, aluminum, or nylon handles.

USE: Peeling vegetables, especially potatoes, as well as apples, firm peaches, carrots, and the lower end of firm, fresh, asparagus. Not used for removing the skins from tomatoes or other soft fruits and vegetables.

USE TIPS: Use the point of the peeler, or else a special pointed device on the side of the peeler, to remove potato buds. Be sure to keep plain carbon steel blades dry to prevent rust.

BUYING TIPS: An indispensable basic kitchen tool. Experiment to find the model that suits you best. The harp or any wide frame may offer the most control. The swivel type is the most efficient, conforming to the shape of the food being peeled, but the fixed type offers more control even if sometimes it does cut more meat. Most are designed to be used either way, but some are specifically designed for left-handed use. Carbon steel blades cost less and stay sharper longer, but rust more easily than stainless steel blades.

FRUIT AND VEGETABLE PITTER

ALSO KNOWN AS: Tomato spoon, peach pitter

DESCRIPTION: Short, thick-handled knife with a pointed, cupped, leaflike carbon steel blade only about 1½ inches long and ¾ inch wide. It is sharpened on both sides.

USE: Scooping pits out of peaches, eyes out of pineapples, pulp out of tomatoes, and coring many different fruits or vegetables.

BUYING TIPS: Much more effective than any nonspecialized knife.

FRUIT AND VEGETABLE PITTER

FRUIT SLICER AND CORER

ALSO KNOWN AS: Fruit slicer/corer, fruit wedger, apple wedge slicer, fruit slicer, apple corer and slicer, corer/sectioner, apple divider, apple and pear slicer, apple and pear divider, fruit divider/corer

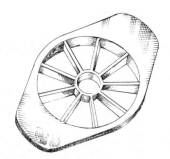

FRUIT SLICER AND CORER

DESCRIPTION: 3- or 4-inch-diameter round, flat plastic or metal device with spokes radiating from a ½-inch-diameter center cylinder. The bottom edges of the spokes are sharp, and there is a flange formed into handles on the top edge.

USE: Cutting apples or other similarly shaped, solid fruit, such as pears, into neat, evenly sized wedges with one motion. The core is cut out by the central cylinder.

USE TIPS: Makes convenient serving sizes. Do not use on fruit such as peaches with large seeds or pits that cannot fit through the core cutter part. Use a pineapple corer (see page 64) if you need a larger corer section—this one is often too small.

BUYING TIPS: Handy item if you must wedge a lot of apples, such as when baking apple pies or for serious snacking. Get a good-quality, sharp one.

GRAPEFRUIT CORER

GRAPEFRUIT CORER

DESCRIPTION: Short, stainless-steel cylinder with a two-pronged handle extending from one end by a few inches. A wooden dowel joins the two prongs to form the grip.

USE: Coring grapefruit by plunging down inside it.

USE TIPS: Very difficult to use; wastes a lot of juice.

BUYING TIPS: Not a necessary item except for very specialized garnishing.

PEAR CORER

PEAR CORER

ALSO KNOWN AS: Pear corer/stemmer

DESCRIPTION: 4-inch-long wooden handle with a squished oval wire band loop about an inch wide and deep at one end. The edges of the band are sharp, and one end is pointed while the other end is rounded.

USE: Removing the core from pear halves.

USE TIPS: Cut the pear in half first. Practice a bit and it will be easy.

PEELER/SLICER/CORER

ALSO KNOWN AS: Apple machine, apple parer, corer and slicer, potato peeler, apple/potato peeler

DESCRIPTION: Cast metal or enameled steel and stainless steel lathe that clamps onto the edge of a counter or table or sticks via a suction-cup base, with a hand crank on one end and two blades on the other. The shaft is rotated by the hand crank, turning the apple and pushing it against the two cutting blades. An electric version is available which holds the fruit or vegetable in an upright position but otherwise works the same, *sans* the crank. A smaller and rarer version is a *turning vegetable slicer.*

USE: Simultaneously peeling, slicing, and coring apples at the rate of up to seven per minute. Most machines can be adjusted to do only one of these actions at a time if so desired. Most can be adjusted to peel potatoes or other vegetables or fruits as well. The turning vegetable slicer can be adjusted to cut long "angel hair" strands of extremely delicate curls.

BUYING TIPS: Only worth the effort if you have hundreds of apples to prepare for large-scale canning or baking projects.

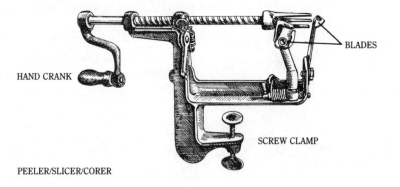

HAND CRANK

BLADES

SCREW CLAMP

PEELER/SLICER/CORER

PINEAPPLE CORER

DESCRIPTION: Two circular blades, one small and one large, held one inside the other by a stainless steel handle structure about a foot high. Another version, a *pineapple peeler,* consists of a small flat, plastic pineapple-shaped piece with a handle on one side and a cutting blade that folds out perpendicularly on the other. A spike on one end pierces the center of a pineapple after its top

PINEAPPLE CORER

has been cut off, and the blade pierces the meat just inside of the skin; it is then rotated around to cut out the core.

USE: Coring and/or peeling a pineapple neatly after the top and bottom have been sliced off.

BUYING TIPS: Only useful if you serve a lot of pineapples.

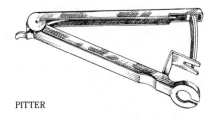

PITTER

PITTER

ALSO KNOWN AS: Cherry pitter, olive pitter, olive/cherry pitter, cherry stoner

DESCRIPTION: Any one of a variety of designs that usually employs two levers, hinged together at one end. One variation is a wire syringelike construction, with an L-shaped end that a plunger pushes against. Another is a plierlike tool hinged in the middle, with a ring or prongs that hold a piece of food at the end of one lever and a perpendicular prong at the end of the other. Made of aluminum or stainless steel. A quite different version is the *automatic cherry stoner,* a large plastic container with a plastic bowl-like hopper on top. The hopper has a plunger handle projecting out at an angle, and a spout below that. When the plunger is raised, a cherry falls into a slot; lowering the plunger pushes the pit out of the cherry and into the bottom chamber, and the cherry falls out of the spout into a waiting container.

USE: Removing the pits of cherries or olives cleanly, leaving behind an almost perfect fruit. Works like a leather punch and prevents staining and breaking fingernails.

USE TIPS: Works better on cherries than on olives. Olives are often served with the pit left in, or it can be removed with a *paring knife* (see page 18). Also, both olives and cherries are sold without pits.

BUYING TIPS: A giant metal hairpin substitutes nicely for a cherry pitter. Very useful if you pick your own cherries.

PLUM PITTER

ALSO KNOWN AS: Plum stoner

DESCRIPTION: Hand-sized, two-levered tool, hinged at one end. One open end has a small cup to hold a plum, and the other has an angled, 4-bladed tip made of stainless steel. Also made in a

PLUM PITTER

larger, box version with a plunger on top, similar to the *cherry pitter* (see previous entry).

USE: When squeezed together, quarters and pits a plum in one move.

BUYING TIPS: Handy for large-scale operations.

POTATO/ONION CUTTER

ALSO KNOWN AS: Curleque cutter

DESCRIPTION: Almost exactly similar to the *peeler/slicer/corer* (see page 64), this is an enameled steel lathe with a hand crank and a spiked plate that holds an onion or a potato against a metal plate with a cutting blade in it. The lathe clamps onto a table or countertop. As the crank is turned, the blade cuts long spirals of vegetable. Recently electric cutters have been introduced with blades for this kind of cut. The potato or onion is held vertically in an enclosed cylinder and spun around. The motor is in the base.

USE: Cutting spirals for French fried potatoes or onions.

BUYING TIPS: This is useful for cooks who make large quantities of French fried potatoes or onion rings.

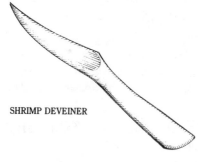

SHRIMP DEVEINER

SHRIMP DEVEINER

ALSO KNOWN AS: Shrimp cleaner and deveiner, shrimp cleaner, shrimper, shrimp peeler, shrimp peeler and deveiner

DESCRIPTION: Small knifelike tool made of cast aluminum with a pointed and slight scallop shape to the thick blade, which does not have a sharp edge. Other versions have flat stainless steel blades with a bird's beak tip that angles down, or are of scissorlike design with a very short lower "jaw" and an upper jaw that resembles the knife version. When they are opened inside a shrimp, they force the shell off the body. Yet another version is a small scimitar-shaped knife with a large notch at the base that has a small winglike piece across it. And one make is just a long, thin, pointed piece of plastic, wider at the handle end, or bent into a hook shape.

USE: Removing shrimp shells and intestinal veins in one move. Most are just placed on the vein and then pushed out.

USE TIPS: Keep shrimp cool while working on them. Return them to refrigeration or move them on to be cooked just as soon as possible. Very small shrimp do not need to be deveined. Larger ones need to have the vein removed for both taste and cosmetic reasons.

BUYING TIPS: Slightly more convenient than using your fingers and a small knife.

STRAWBERRY HULLER

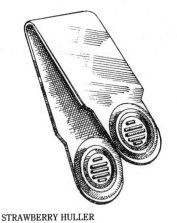

STRAWBERRY HULLER

DESCRIPTION: Small, wide piece of metal, either tin-plated or stainless steel, folded into a V-shape, with textured gripping surfaces on its two ends. Finger-sized, it holds its opening to about an inch thanks to a spring tension in the metal.

USE: Pulling the green stem and core—the hull—out of strawberries.

USE TIPS: Particularly useful when you have a large quantity of strawberries to prepare such as when making jam or preserves—saves your fingertips from wear and tear. Also sold as a *chicken plucker,* and as a sort of heavy-duty, wide tweezer, useful even on hard-to-hold chicken innards.

BUYING TIPS: Highly recommended and inexpensive item good for plucking feathers or stems.

TOMATO/STRAWBERRY CORER

TOMATO/STRAWBERRY CORER

ALSO KNOWN AS: Tomato corer, tomato shark

DESCRIPTION: Hand-sized, knifelike utensil with a ¾-inch-diameter round stainless steel blade that is cupped and has a jagged edge.

USE: Removing the stems from tomatoes or strawberries, coring tomatoes, removing apple and pear seeds, potato eyes, and vegetable blemishes.

USE TIPS: Works best on tomatoes—this is a little big for strawberries.

BUYING TIPS: Handy, inexpensive gadget.

ZUCCHINI CORER

DESCRIPTION: Long stainless steel blade, in an open, half-round shape, with a sharp point and wooden or plastic handle.

USE: Removing the core of seeds from zucchini for stuffing.

USE TIPS: Cut all your zucchini into similar lengths for easier coring.

BUYING TIPS: Nothing else similar.

ZUCCHINI CORER

Mixing and Mashing Utensils

Mixing, Blending, and Beating Utensils

About Mixing, Blending, and Beating Utensils

Nothing is standard in this area, where the cook's personal preferences, kitchen space, and budget dominate the choice of utensils. Some prefer the most high-tech and streamlined designs, while others are satisfied with hand-me-downs from previous generations. On that note, it is interesting that many designs are time-tested (the mortar and pestle, the garlic press, the egg beater), and only a few items are relatively new to this scene (the food processor, the immersion blender). And great beauty is to be found in the simplest of items, the mixing bowl, in which traditional earthenware styles are treasured by many cooks.

BATTER BOWL

ALSO KNOWN AS: Mix-and-measure bowl

DESCRIPTION: Essentially a very large *liquid measuring cup* (see page 95). Usually holds about two quarts, with a handle, a pouring spout, and measurements imprinted on the side. Available in glass, plastic, or earthenware. Also found in larger, deeper models that are sold in sets of three or four graduated sizes.

BATTER BOWL

USE: Mixing both wet and dry ingredients, especially when using an electric beater—the sides do not slope, so there is less spatter.

USE TIPS: Particularly good for whipping cream.

BUYING TIPS: The better plastic models have rubber nonskid bottoms.

BLENDER

ALSO KNOWN AS: Jug blender, liquifier

DESCRIPTION: Small, heavy steel or plastic-covered base, housing an electric motor, with a small drive shaft in the shape of flat gear on top. A large, slightly conical plastic, glass, or metal container —three to four pints is not uncommon—fits on top of this, and has a special, small propellerlike device in the bottom, usually with four blades. The base has the controls for the motor, which may include more than a dozen speed options, or only a few.

Few models have attachments, but one is a beater device for making mayonnaise. One blender is now made as an attachment for a *food processor* (see page 73). A portable, lightweight version is a battery-operated model mounted in the top of a 20-ounce container. A *bar blender* is a heavy-duty model with only two speeds.

USE: Liquefying, aerating, and blending foods and mixing drinks. Also grinds ice cubes.

USE TIPS: Blenders are particularly good at liquefying foods, so be careful not to keep the motor running too long or you may liquefy something that you intended to puree.

BUYING TIPS: Get a simple but powerful model. Complements a food processor because it can handle larger volumes of liquid, though otherwise it is not as versatile.

CHOCOLATE FROTHER

ALSO KNOWN AS: Chocolate swizzle, molinillo (Sp.), chocolate beater, swizzle stick

DESCRIPTION: Foot-long carved wooden item that looks something like a sophisticated baby rattle. A fluted, hollow tip about 2 inches deep has a notched collar and two floating rings above that, followed by a long, tapered handle.

CHOCOLATE FROTHER

USE: Spun between your palms to whip hot chocolate and milk into a froth.

USE TIPS: Store in spot where it can be easily seen, as it is bound to inspire entertaining questions.

BUYING TIPS: Unless you make traditional, pure hot chocolate, this is more decorative than useful. If you do, then it is perfect.

EGG BEATER

ALSO KNOWN AS: Beater/mixer, rotary egg beater, hand mixer, rotary beater

EGG BEATER

DESCRIPTION: A fairly complex assembly that includes two inverted, cone-shaped metal beaters a few inches long made of flat, ¼-inch-wide metal strips which balloon out to a base of about 2 inches in diameter. They intermesh at the base and are connected by gears at the top, just below a handle and hand-crank mechanism. The whole item is about a foot long and a few inches across. The handle varies from model to model, sometimes on top, sometimes offset at an angle, and sometimes on the side. The framework is made of either aluminum or plastic, the gears of metal or nylon, and the whipping heads of stainless or chromed steel. A *one hand mixer/twirler* has no crank. Instead it has a spiral shaft and twirls when the handle is pushed down.

USE: Beating eggs, whipping cream and other light liquids to incorporate air.

USE TIPS: It is easier to sustain a long beating action with this than with a *whisk* (see page 78).

BUYING TIPS: Make sure the rotary action is smooth. Inexpensive beaters with ill-fitting parts can be very frustrating to use as they jam frequently. The best quality models are made of stainless steel with nylon gears. Better yet is the motorized version, the *hand-held mixer* (see page 74).

ELECTRIC MIXER

ALSO KNOWN AS: Stand mixer, table mixer

DESCRIPTION: Large, 14-inch-high, heavy-duty electric machine consisting of a stand with a flat base, an upright on one side, and a motor housing across the top. The tip of the motor housing

ELECTRIC MIXER

holds one or two beaters of various kinds, and a removable work-bowl, usually made of stainless steel, sits underneath it on the base of the stand. The part that holds the bowl may rotate slowly when the mixer is on.

Accessories include mixing paddles of various designs, such as a *dough hook, wire whip,* and a *flat beater,* which can be inserted into the tip of the motor housing. Some models have *pouring shields* or covers for the bowls to prevent splatter and aid in pouring. Common, powerful, large models (300-watt motor, ten speeds) usually come with 3- or 4½-quart bowls that can handle 2- or even 3½-pound batches of bread dough, for example, though serious bakers may want a 5- or 7-quart model. Copper-lined bowls or copper bowls that serve as liners are available for mixing egg whites, and quilted dustcovers are sometimes offered, too. Some models detach for use as *hand mixers* (see page 74).

USE: Heavy, slow, hard work such as mixing cake batters, whipping large amounts of cream, making homemade mayonnaise or mashed potatoes, kneading bread dough, and literally hundreds of other uses.

USE TIPS: Better at some delicate mixing tasks than the *food processor* (see next entry). Experiment with the pouring shield—some are difficult to use.

BUYING TIPS: Choose a heavy mixer for greater versatility—look for bowls with at least a 4½-quart capacity and a motor of about 300 watts. Make sure the beaters reach the bottom of the bowl for thorough mixing. Some are quite noisy, so listen before you buy. Buy extra bowls and beaters for use with complicated cake recipes. Look for one that either rotates the bowl or oscillates the beaters from center to side, or both, and has many adjustable speeds. And see if it has optional accessories, such as a *food grinder* (doubles as a *pasta maker* and *sausage stuffer*), *grain mill, citrus juicer, juice extractor, can opener, slicer/shredder/grater, potato peeler, coffee or spice grinder, blender, bean and citrus peel slicer, cream maker, food mill,* and *fruit/vegetable strainer* (see the index for entries for most of these functions). One brand even offers a *water jacket,* a larger bowl for the workbowl to sit inside of, which is then filled with ice or hot water to keep the workbowl cool or warm. To get all of these accessories would be absurd, but if you have special needs, by all means look into one that can help you.

FOOD PROCESSOR

ALSO KNOWN AS: Cuisinart® (brand name that has become almost generic)

DESCRIPTION: Large, heavy electric machine with many attachments. Basic design is a boxy motor housing on the bottom, a straight-sided strong, clear plastic workbowl in the middle, and a clear plastic feeder tube and cover on top. A central shaft in the workbowl takes various blades that are supplied with the processor. The feeder tube is for the addition of ingredients while the machine is in operation.

The standard size processor may stand a total of 12 inches high with feeder attached. A large model can knead 5 pounds of dough, 4 cups of liquid, or 6½ cups of dry food; a small one can knead 2½ pounds of dough. An *electric slicer-shredder* (see page 36) is a hand-held food processor that dispenses with the workbowl and has instead a chute for the sliced food. Also available in mini-sizes, called a *mini-processor* or *mini-chopper,* with a 3½-ounce workbowl, about 5 inches in diameter and 7½ inches high. Accessories include racks and containers for the various blades. A hybrid model with 19- and 27-ounce jars and both chopping and whipping blades is also available.

Different machines come with different attachments. Pasta is usually made with a large, heavy, boxy mechanism, a *pasta attachment,* that has a powerful worm gear which forces the pasta dough through various disks to make a variety of pasta shapes, but the other attachments are more often just cutting blades in the form of disks.

USE: Pureeing, chopping, dicing, slicing, shredding, grating, kneading dough, making pasta, and more. A mini-processor is better for use with small recipes, like fresh baby food, or dicing garlic, onions, parsley, or grinding chocolate, nuts, or coffee beans (check directions). They are used most often as grinders, choppers, and mincers.

USE TIPS: These machines do a lot, but they still are not designed to do everything—most can't whip cream, egg whites, or cake batters, for example, though one model does have a whisk attachment. Some brands can hold a good deal of liquid and others cannot—a blender is better at this. Ice cubes might damage the blade or bowl. Be sure to experiment before attempting a recipe with a lot of liquid in it, strain the liquid out if necessary, and puree the solids separately. Some cooks find that they get better results from chopping onions by hand, because the processor forces much moisture out, and they enjoy kneading dough by hand enough to avoid using the processor for these tasks. Note that many "mini" models do not have feeder tubes and must be turned off to be filled, which can make preparing a mayonnaise difficult or impossible.

BUYING TIPS: Even traditional chefs agree that at times the food processor seems to take its place alongside the knife or whisk as an indispensable kitchen tool. The primary reason is that it reduces the amount of time needed to puree or mix many items. A secondary reason is that it permits the amateur to make some recipes—mousses and pâtés come to mind—that they might not attempt otherwise. Note that a variety of sizes are available, so you can get one to fit your kitchen. Get a second workbowl for the miniature version so that you can process two different foods in quick succession (some are supplied with a second bowl and cover, some aren't). And always make sure you get a flat-bladed *bowl scraper* with your processor.

HAND-HELD MIXER

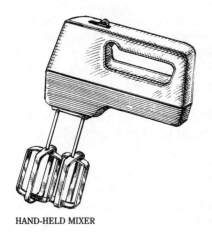

HAND-HELD MIXER

ALSO KNOWN AS: Hand mixer, mixer, electric beater, power mixer

DESCRIPTION: Portable electric device, about 6 inches long, a few inches deep and less than 2 inches wide, with two removable metal beater heads. Cordless models are available, as are some with small stands for bowls. Some may come with a flat, clear plastic cover that you can slide the beaters through in order to avoid splatter. Some are designed with a beveled rear end so that they can be set down on a countertop with the beaters in place. Another has a spatula attachment which scrapes the sides of the mixing bowl continuously as it is being used. Most have a "beater eject" button for easy removal of beaters, and some have convenient clips for storing them on the mixer itself.

USE: Whipping cream, egg whites, sauces, mixing cookie and cake batters, and other light kitchen work in any small or medium bowl.

USE TIPS: Do not operate with beaters outside of bowl or you will splatter the kitchen with whatever you were mixing.

BUYING TIPS: Look for a lightweight but high-quality model and check to see that it is comfortable to hold. Those with the weight forward of the grip tend to be easier to use. Cordless models are good buys as long as you have a heavier model to use for bigger jobs. Look for stainless steel beaters and a three-speed motor—

especially one that allows you to boost it to the top speed easily while working at a lower speed. A wall bracket for storage is a good feature, too. Trust name brands to use motors that will not burn out and switches that will not break.

IMMERSION BLENDER

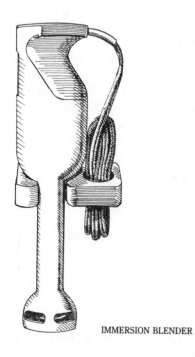

IMMERSION BLENDER

ALSO KNOWN AS: Hand blender

DESCRIPTION: Long, slender, plastic-covered electric tool, about a foot long, thick at the grip/control end, with a trumpetlike business end that contains a small propeller blade. Controls are usually limited to two speeds, but with immediate start/stop action. Supplied with a stand or wall bracket for storage. May come with a small workbowl or beaker.

USE: Convenient and rapid blending or pureeing of soft or liquid foods such as vegetable soups, dips, egg whites, mayonnaise, milk shakes, or bar drinks in the container in which they are originally cooked, mixed, or finally consumed in order to avoid cleaning an interim mixing bowl.

USE TIPS: Just stick the blender into the food you want to mix and push the button—but keep it below the surface to be sure that you won't spin the food out into the kitchen. Do not keep "on" for more than short bursts.

BUYING TIPS: Great way to avoid having to wash additional mixing dishes (you still have to wash the blender, though, but that is easy: Just hold it under running water). Allows for more control than a conventional countertop *blender* (see page 70).

MILKSHAKE/
MALT MAKER

MILKSHAKE/MALT MAKER

DESCRIPTION: Tall, chrome-plated stand with egg-shaped electric motor at the top, from which descends an agitating spindle with a small, wavy disc on the end. Supplied with a stainless steel 12-ounce cup.

USE: Rapid mixing and aerating of milk-based drinks.

USE TIPS: Can be used to make healthier combinations than tradition would dictate, like vegetable shakes.

BUYING TIPS: Intended as a gift item that resembles those machines at soda counters. Shakes can be easily made with a *blender* (see page 70).

MIXING BOWL

ALSO KNOWN AS: Sphere-shaped bowl, bowl, beating bowl

DESCRIPTION: All-purpose bowl available in sizes ranging from tiny up to 8 quarts for common usage (13-quart bowls are found, too). The sloping sides can extend all the way around, forming half a sphere, or the bowl may have a flat center bottom, or have a pouring lip, or have straight, vertical sides (and may be called a *U bowl* in this case). Some have lips that serve as grips or handles, and rubber nonskid bases. All are available in a variety of materials, including stainless steel, plastic, and glazed earthenware. Most do not have handles, but some have *hang rings*, two small loops hanging from the rim, that allow a bowl to be hung on a rack.

USE: Mixing both liquid and dry ingredients. Shallow bowls, as much as 14 inches in diameter, are excellent for serving pasta and salads, as well as for mixing large recipes.

USE TIPS: Check to see if your bowls are conventional oven- or microwave ovenproof. Vitrified stoneware (high-fired at 2,300° F) resists chipping, cracking, and holds yeast bread batter at room temperature as it rises. Put your thumb through the rings to hold the bowl.

BUYING TIPS: Usually sold in nesting sets of three or four. Look for metal bowls that can be hung from a ring on the edge of the bowl if you have a pegboard wall. Though *unlined copper bowls* (see opposite) must be used only for egg whites, the choice of material and color of bowls is largely a function of personal taste. Be sure to get something that you like, for you will be using these often. Using beautiful bowls adds to the pleasure of cooking.

MIXING BOWL RING

DESCRIPTION: Thick, tacky rubber ring about 6 inches in diameter.

USE: Placed on countertop underneath mixing bowls to prevent bowl from slipping or scratching countertop.

BUYING TIPS: Unique item that can be very helpful to some but that others will never need.

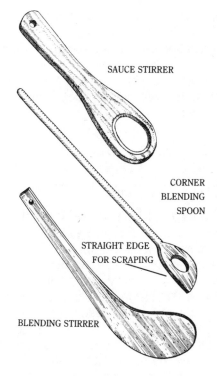

SAUCE STIRRER

CORNER
BLENDING
SPOON

STRAIGHT EDGE
FOR SCRAPING

BLENDING STIRRER

SAUCE STIRRER

ALSO KNOWN AS: Blending spoon, pierced stirrer

DESCRIPTION: A large wooden or plastic spoon with a large oval hole instead of the usual cup of the spoon. Usually oval but also made as a *corner blending spoon,* with an offset, straight-edged, one-point design. A flat model with an exaggerated offset point and a large hole may be called a *whipping spoon.* A plain, flat paddle without a hole is called a *blending stirrer* or just plain *stirrer,* and may have an offset end like a hockey stick.

USE: Stirring sauces, especially in delicate nonstick cookware. The opening creates more turbulence than a solid spoon does. Straight edges allow for scraping the sides of a pan or pot.

USE TIPS: Particularly good for stirring stews and other preparations with meat cubes or small pieces of chicken. The flat stirrer has the advantage over a cupped spoon in that it can be cleaned off by dragging it across the lip of a pan.

BUYING TIPS: Wood is the preferred material here because it won't melt if left standing in hot foods. Some *spatulas* (see page 138) can be used as stirrers.

UNLINED COPPER BOWL

UNLINED COPPER BOWL

ALSO KNOWN AS: Egg-white beating bowl, whipping bowl, copper egg-white beating bowl, copper egg bowl

DESCRIPTION: Large, deep, semispherical cooper bowl usually with one hanging brass ring on the narrow rim. Available in diameters ranging from 9 to 14 inches (a 10½-inch-diameter bowl may have a 4½ quart capacity). Also available as a *liner bowl* (see opposite) for electric mixers.

USE: Beating egg whites.

USE TIPS: Hang on to the bowl by hooking a thumb into the ring. Clean the bowl thoroughly with soapy warm water before cleaning with commercial copper cleaner (or 2 tablespoons of lemon juice or vinegar and a teaspoon of salt). Make sure the bowl is completely dry before using. Use a large *balloon whisk* (see page 78) with a contour that matches the shape of the bowl. Can also be used to cook zabaglione instead of using the specialized *zabaglione pan* (see page 174).

BUYING TIPS: This is something to get only if you use a lot of beaten egg whites in your recipes. You can beat egg whites in any kind of bowl, but a chemical reaction between the copper and the albumen in the egg whites causes them to "mount" better, to the extent of seven times their original volume. A bowl about a foot in diameter is most common. Heavyweight copper resists dents better than lightweight copper.

WHISK

ALSO KNOWN AS: Beater whisk, hand whisk, whip

DESCRIPTION: Large hand utensil made of high tensile strength stainless steel wire formed in a variety of shapes and sizes, from 6 to 12 inches long (some professional models are longer). Handles are thick stainless or chrome-plated steel tube or wire, wood, or nylon. Miniature models are still 7 inches long, but only about an inch wide at the whisk end. Whisks are also available in wood, made from two crossed hoops, as well as plastic, either in a balloon shape or a cone of stiff, straight strands. Many different designs have been developed to meet cooks' preferences and needs for various types of foods. The top brands are available in various wire thicknesses. Some cooks, especially professionals, may tend to call these *whips*, not *whisks* (perhaps because *whip* is the literal translation of the French term for whisk, *fouet*), but manufacturers tend to call the flexible, coiled models *whips* and all the others *whisks*. All can be referred to as whisks, though.

TYPES: *Balloon whisk* (Also Known As *egg whisk*): Light-bulb shaped group of about five to ten wire strands woven to form not only the bulb but gathered together in the handle to give it strength. Some are almost spherical, much wider than the *sauce whisk* (below), in order to incorporate more air.

Flat whisk (Also Known As *roux whisk* or *skillet whisk*): Has only half a dozen slightly bent wire loops. Good for reaching thick sauces in the corners of a saucepan, or for deglazing a skillet and many other cooking tasks. Very versatile item.

Sauce whisk (Also Known As *French whisk, French whip, pastry whisk,* or *pear-shaped whisk*): Standard, elongated pear shape, 10 to 14 inches long, with a thick handle and a narrow bulb shape tapering toward the handle, like a slender balloon whisk (see above). Most common model. A version made of thinner wires that resemble

PLASTIC WHISK

BALLOON WHISK

FLAT WHISK

SAUCE WHISK

piano wire may be called a *piano style whisk, piano wire whisk,* or *fine whisk*. Thinner wires help create a whipping action. A *mayonnaise whip* is an extra-long model.

Presto whisk (Also Known As *churn beater, dressing beater,* or *beater whip*): One wire that spirals out to a wide bottom, or a small ball. Very flexible on end of shaft so it can be whipped around.

Whip (Also Known As *coiled whip*): Single flat loop of thick wire around which is spiraled a thinner wire that looks almost like a spring. More common in Europe than in the United States. Handy with thin batters, eggs, and all sauces or gravies. Most versatile of all whisk types. Handy, important, and inexpensive.

Rod and ring: Unusual whisk design with about a dozen stainless steel rods with rings on the ends; the other ends are gathered into a plastic handle.

USE: Balloon whisks are used for whipping cream, light batters, and eggs, and other whisks are used for mixing and delumping light sauces, gravies and salad dressings. Balloon whisks are especially used for egg whites. The flat whisk is used to reach lumps on the bottom of a saucepan. Wooden and plastic whisks are for use on delicate porcelain or nonstick surfaces. The smallest are for things like individual cups of hot chocolate; the largest for a bowl of egg whites (the curve of the whisk should match the curve of the bowl).

USE TIPS: Prior to beating egg whites, make sure the whisk is completely dry and scrupulously clean. Any trace of water or grease will keep the eggs from mounting, or whipping up.

BUYING TIPS: Try the handle of a whisk before buying to see if it feels comfortable in your hand. Some people prefer thicker handles that offer a more solid grip, others prefer a thinner one. Get a selection of sizes for more efficient whisking. Wires should be solidly anchored, the best may have a ring holding wires together at the tip.

Mashing and Pressing Utensils

About Mashing and Pressing Utensils

A number of items are specially designed to help you make smooth portions of food, or to extract juices either in any vessel or in the utensil itself. Make sure to note how easy it is to clean a given tool of any residue.

BLENDING AND MASHING FORK

BLENDING AND MASHING FORK

ALSO KNOWN AS: Blending fork

DESCRIPTION: Short but wide, thick, cast-aluminum fork with four large prongs.

USE: Mashing and blending potatoes or pastry dough.

BUYING TIPS: Very handy for mashing small amounts of food. Takes up very little space in a drawer.

CITRUS JUICER

CITRUS JUICER

ALSO KNOWN AS: Juice extractor, lemon juicer, orange juicer, juicer

DESCRIPTION: Whether simple hand pressure, mechanical advantage or electric power is used, the basic idea is the same: a conical ridged device that fits inside a cut half of a citrus fruit. Unfortunately most manufacturers use these names interchangeably and indiscriminately for all types.

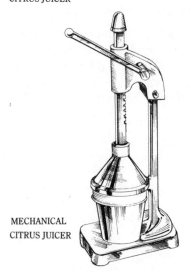

MECHANICAL CITRUS JUICER

TYPES: *Citrus juicer:* Classic, simple, commonly found item made of glass or ceramic more often than plastic or aluminum, this has the familiar fluted cone (the *reamer,* see below) in the middle of a wide, shallow cup. Usually has a coffee cup–type handle and a spout; may come with a cup, bowl, or jar that fits underneath a perforated base. Also available with a hand crank that causes the reamer head to rotate. Reamer heads come in two sizes: small for oranges, lemons, and limes, and large for grapefruits.

Electric citrus juicer: This is a short, thick cylinder of a machine, with a clear plastic top that when removed, exposes a fluted cone in the center of a metal dish. The cone spins when the machine is turned on. A spout comes out of the side, usually over an indentation for glasses.

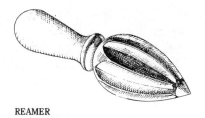

REAMER

Juice press: Two levers, hinged together at one end, with a small cap and crenulated cone at the hinge end. The levers are squeezed together to extract the juice from the halved fruit.

Mechanical citrus juicer (Also Known As *freestanding citrus juicer*): Sturdy cast-aluminum machine, about 8 inches high, with a domed top that is raised and lowered by revolving a 6-inch-long arm on one side. Inside the dome, attached to the base, is a ridged, flattish cone, at the outside of which are holes. A small glass fits nicely right underneath the funnel spout. The arm raises and lowers the dome with about 1½ turns; it can produce hundreds of pounds of pressure due to a rack-and-pinion gear system.

Reamer (Also Known As *citrus reamer, hand-held citrus juicer*): Small, fluted, pointed, cylindrical piece of wood or plastic, half of which is handle, which is twisted into a fruit half, while holding it over a bowl or glass to extract juice.

USE: Juicing citrus fruits by compressing the insides against the rind.

USE TIPS: The reamer is particularly easy to use for extracting the juice from a grapefruit.

BUYING TIPS: The mechanical model is very quick, but like the hand model, takes some energy on the part of the user. Strainer bases are helpful for separating the seeds from the juice. The electric model should have easy to use controls, and should separate the pulp and seeds from the juice.

CITRUS SQUEEZER

ALSO KNOWN AS: Lemon squeezer, lemon/lime squeezer

DESCRIPTION: Scissorlike device, but instead of cutting blades, both sides have flat surfaces that squeeze together. Available in plastic and stainless or gold-plated steel. A smaller citrus squeezer, usually called a *lime squeezer*, is shaped just like a *garlic press* (see page 82): two small bowls hinged together on one end, each with a long handle. One acts as a plunger when the handles are squeezed together. A larger version of this is called a *juice press,* and has the *juicer's* (see previous entry) distinctive crenulated cone on one side.

A smaller item, the *lemon slice squeezer,* is shaped like a

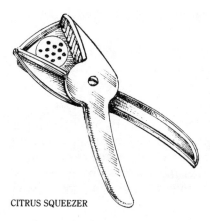

CITRUS SQUEEZER

wedge and has a ridge that separates the fruit from the rind for complete juicing. Yet another version is shaped like a miniature *gravy boat* (see page 381) with a small hinged lever than can be pressed down into it. Some are made with a charming, decorative bird design stamped into the sides. All versions are available in plastic or stainless steel.

USE: Squeezing lemons or limes one wedge at a time, when you wish to avoid wetting your hands.

USE TIPS: Particularly handy when you need to control the amount of juice you squeeze out very carefully.

BUYING TIPS: A small *potato ricer* (see page 90) can double as a fruit or even a vegetable juicer.

DUCK PRESS

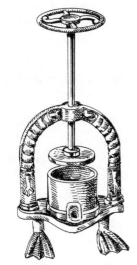

DUCK PRESS

DESCRIPTION: Heavy, solidly constructed machine about 1½ feet high, with a wheel on top that turns a screw which in turn lowers a piston slowly into a round cup filled with duck meat. Usually made of polished brass but also in plated steel (silver as well as nickel). On some models, the feet which support the press are shaped like a duck's. Presses can weigh from 25 to 50 pounds.

USE: Compressing a cooked duck carcass and innards. The fluid which drains out of the press is used to poach the duck breast. This is essentially done only for one duck recipe, *canneton rouennais à la presse,* or pressed duck.

USE TIPS: Intended to be used with dramatic flair at the dining table.

BUYING TIPS: An extraordinary gift item which is likely to be used very, very rarely.

GARLIC PRESS

DESCRIPTION: Two hand-sized levers, hinged at a point, that have a small round or rectangular hopper on one and a small plunger on the other. The hopper bottom is perforated and the plunger fits snugly into the hopper as the levers are squeezed closed. Most are made of cast-aluminum or other metal alloys, though recently some made of plastic have been found and there are some heavy ones made of stainless steel.

SELF-CLEANING
GARLIC PRESS

TYPES: *Garlic press/cherry pitter:* Has an extra small plunger just behind the main one, which serves as a cherry pitter. It goes through a hole in a small bowl on the other lever.

Press and store garlic press: Plastic tube which encloses the garlic clove for storage—you only press out what you need, usually by means of a large screw device rather than a lever, and store the device in the refrigerator, covered.

Self-cleaning garlic press: Has features for removing the leftover garlic from the perforations, such as a handle with a section of points on the back that folds the opposite way from normal use and pushes the leftover garlic out of the holes. Some are sold with a separate piece with lots of little points that can be pushed into the press holes to eject the leftover garlic.

USE: Pressing garlic cloves. Pressed garlic is more easily mixed into other foods for cooking than small pieces of chopped garlic.

USE TIPS: Peel the garlic clove before pressing, unless your model is specifically designed for handling the skin as well (it would have larger holes).

BUYING TIPS: Check that the press has tight hinges and that the plunger fits neatly into the hopper. A loose press wastes much garlic around the sides of the plunger. With some practice a large sharp knife and a decent chopping board can do the job faster and with less clean-up time. Just smash the clove down and dice for a few seconds.

GUACAMOLE MASHER

ALSO KNOWN AS: Mini masher

DESCRIPTION: Small masher, made of thick stainless steel wire formed into a flat zigzag shape that arches back into a short handle. Overall height is 7½ inches; about 2½ inches wide. Small version of the *potato masher* (see page 90).

USE: Reducing ripe avocado meat to the consistency necessary for guacamole.

USE TIPS: Don't mash too much or it may get watery.

BUYING TIPS: A fork suffices easily.

HAMBURGER PRESS

HAMBURGER PRESS

ALSO KNOWN AS: Patty press, burger press

DESCRIPTION: Two round, polished cast-aluminum disks, hinged together at one side. Capacity is either ⅕ or ¼ pound of chopped meat. ¼- and ½-pound models are also available in the form of a two-piece plastic item, a cylinder mold, which may be high enough to store eight ¼-pound patties, and a plunger. Some plastic molds have spiral ridges in them that form indentations on the patty, exposing more surface area to heat.

USE: Molding perfectly round hamburger patties of uniform weight. Often used for patties that are then individually wrapped and frozen.

USE TIPS: Cover the meat with waxed paper on top and bottom before pressing to ensure easy removal and storage. This item will help avoid crumbly hamburgers, but they come out rather small, dry, firm, and dense.

BUYING TIPS: Important where cost control counts, like in a restaurant, and not recommended for serious home use. Hamburgers should be formed by hand, handled as gently and as little as possible so that they will be light, juicy, and flavorful, not dry and dense.

JUICE EXTRACTOR

ALSO KNOWN AS: Vegetable juicer

DESCRIPTION: Solid, heavy electric appliance about a foot high and wide, and half as deep, with a spout on one side and an open feed tube on the top. Most models have a separate scrap container built in. They either produce continuously, dispensing into any containers you may have, or have their own built-in pitcher, typically with a 24- to 32-ounce capacity.

USE: High-speed extraction of juice from vegetables and fruits (carrots, apples, oranges, tomatoes, etc.) via centrifugal force. Machine spits out the pulp, seeds and skin into the scrap container and the juice pours out of the spout.

USE TIPS: Wash food prior to juicing; no need to peel most except for bananas.

BUYING TIPS: Look for quiet operation, a continuous feed chute, a nonslip base, and a good brand reputation for reliability.

LEMON SPOUT

LEMON SPOUT

ALSO KNOWN AS: Screw juicer, lemon juicer, juice extractor, citrus spigot

DESCRIPTION: Small hollow cone with spiral threads on the outside. Made of either plastic (in many colors) or cast-aluminum alloy. Some models have hinged caps and a base for vertical storage of the fruit in the refrigerator. Also available mounted on a jar top; the jar collects the juice without the seeds. Another version comes with a little cap and a storage jar for a lemon with the spout still in it, and a base for it to sit on.

USE: Inserted into lemons or limes to extract their juice when only a small quantity is needed. May be left in during storage in the refrigerator.

USE TIPS: If you are juicing a large number of lemons, a *citrus juicer* (see page 80) is considerably faster.

BUYING TIPS: Handy gadget.

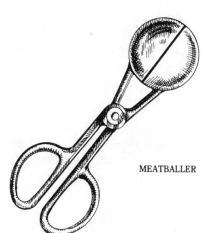

MEATBALLER

MEATBALLER

DESCRIPTION: Scissor-shaped instrument with large half-spheres instead of cutting blades that form a hollow sphere when closed. Standard ones form balls about 2 inches in diameter; a *Swedish* or *cocktail meatballer* makes smaller ones, about half that size.

USE: For shaping chopped meat into perfectly even meatballs.

BUYING TIPS: Helpful when you must make many meatballs, but hand-rolling should suffice for most cooks.

MEAT GRINDER

ALSO KNOWN AS: Grinder, grinder and chopper

DESCRIPTION: Either a hand-operated or electric machine with a gear mechanism that forces solid foods through a perforated plate. Some come with interchangeable heads for making pasta, slicing potatoes, mixing dough, and crushing ice as well.

TYPES: *Electric:* Similar to the hand-cranked version below, but with a large opening for meat, usually in the form of a flat dish, and often supplied with a plunger for forcing meat down the tube. Variable speed controls are normal.

Hand-operated: Zinc or chrome-plated cast-iron machine that clamps onto the side of a countertop, or a plastic machine with a suction-cup base that sticks to a countertop. A large hand crank is on one side, and a long, round protrusion on the other, with a perforated disk on the end that screws on and off. The whole machine disassembles for cleaning. A funnel-shaped opening for receiving the meat is on top. Inside the protrusion are a worm gear and cutting blades that force the food against and through the perforated disk. Accessories include extra disks and a sausage-making attachment, or *sausage-stuffing horn.*

USE: Grinding meat for sausage, fillings, and pâtés. Some grinders can also be used for crackers (for stuffing) and other foods, such as vegetables, cheese, nuts, or dried fruits, which it chops more than it grinds.

USE TIPS: Clean these tools extra carefully, for any meat left on them will certainly spoil.

BUYING TIPS: This is really a tool for a specialist like a caterer. Most cooks might do better by using a *food processor* (see page 73) or with an *electric mixer* (see page 71) that has a meat grinder attachment. Most people buy ground meat these days.

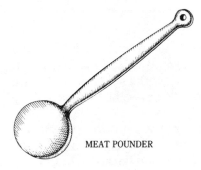

MEAT POUNDER

MEAT POUNDER

ALSO KNOWN AS: Pounder, meat flattener, meat bat, meat mallet

DESCRIPTION: Solid, heavy stainless steel disk or square blade with a vertical, angled, or horizontal handle. One version of the square model is thicker in the middle and tapers to sharp edges. The 2-pound, 3-inch-diameter disk with a vertical handle in its center may be called a *meat pounder* while the model with handles off to the side may be called a *meat flattener,* a *scallopine,* or a *chicken and veal pounder.*

USE: Used to flatten meats such as veal to form scaloppine, or for flattening boneless chicken breasts.

USE TIPS: Stretch scaloppine and thin them out as you work. Placing the meat between two pieces of wax paper helps to keep the meat from sticking to the pounder or the counter. Pound evenly and not too hard. Use an arching, gently sweeping motion.

BUYING TIPS: More popular with cooks who make a lot of veal scaloppine than a *meat tenderizer* (see next entry), probably because it offers more control.

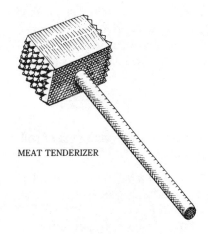

MEAT TENDERIZER

MEAT TENDERIZER

ALSO KNOWN AS: Meat hammer

DESCRIPTION: Commonly found as a block-headed mallet made of hardwood, plastic, aluminum, or stainless steel. The head has a pattern of pyramid points about ¼ inch deep, usually on both sides and sometimes on four sides—each side being a different size point. Some wooden models have one metal end. Another version has three rows of fifty or more small vertical blades set into a pump handle.

USE: Used on tough cuts, such as flank steak, to tenderize them by breaking up the fibers in the tissue.

USE TIPS: Be sure to pound lightly or you might open up a large hole through the meat.

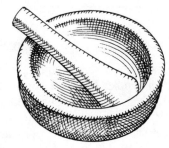

MORTAR AND PESTLE

MORTAR AND PESTLE

DESCRIPTION: A small, club-shaped stick (*pestle*) paired with a small, deep, slope-edged bowl (*mortar*). Made of marble, wood, stoneware, pottery, or porcelain; the mortars may have a matte or glossy finish, and the gloss may only cover the outside and top inside rim.

Sometimes the pestle is made of wood no matter what the mortar is made of, but usually they are of the same material. One design for a pestle departs from the traditional—a mushroom shape that conforms to the mortar shape. A special two-toned design, called a *suribachi,* has sharp ridges in attractive wedge-shaped patterns; the pestle is always of wood and is called a *surikogi* or *Japanese mortar.*

USE: Grinding nuts, seeds, beans, tofu (suribachi), spices, or herbs to a fine powder or paste. Usually this makes for a much stronger aroma than achieved with industrial grinding. The food is placed in the mortar and ground with the pestle, using a quick, circular motion.

USE TIPS: Good for making a base for special sauces such as aioli or pesto. Marble models can be quite handsome and are considered by some people to be purely decorative.

BUYING TIPS: Smaller models are more popular, but in fact the *food processor* (see page 73) largely replaces the need for a mortar and pestle. Sometimes sold in sets of three different sizes. Get a beautiful mortar and pestle and keep it on the counter for all to admire.

PASTA MACHINE

DESCRIPTION: Hand-operated or electric machine with sets of rollers or a feeder bowl with extruder heads.

TYPES: *Extruder:* Electric or hand-cranked machine. The electric version of an extruder type is either a free-standing machine or an attachment for a *food processor* (see page 73) with an extruder cylinder onto which you can screw at least four different flat, circular heads with holes for forming different types including spaghetti, flat noodles, macaroni, and lasagna. The free-standing model is a foot-high plastic-covered metal box, about 8 inches deep and wide, with a motor inside and a feeder bowl on top. As many as nine different pasta discs are included, as well as three for cookies, pretzels, even bagels. It can produce 1½ pounds of fresh pasta in ten minutes because it automates the mixing, kneading, and shaping processes, and even blows warm air to aid in drying the pasta.

The *hand-cranked* version looks like a *meat grinder* (see page 86)—a large plastic funnel with a suction-cup base that clamps down onto a counter. A hand crank and an extruder cylinder, onto which you can screw at least four different flat, circular heads with holes for forming different types of pasta, is in the narrow midsection. Another version is a metal device made of several components including two arms that jut out of each side of the top, with a large hand crank on one side. It clamps to the kitchen counter, and has sets of rollers similar to the electric machine in various removable heads which fit on the top. One side rolls out flat pieces up to 9 inches wide (depending on the model) and the other side cuts them. Cutting heads may include 1mm-wide angel hair, 2mm spaghetti, and 50mm curly lasagna. Specialized attachments are available for making nonstrip type pasta, such as ravioli.

These are small machines, about 5 inches high, 5 to 7½ inches wide, and 7 or 8 inches deep, made of chrome and nickel-plated steel. An electric motor, a *machine motorizer,* is available that can replace the hand crank. A *cavatelli and gnocchi maker,* a small, simple hand-cranked disk with two rollers, is also available.

Roller: The electric model is a C-shaped, heavy but small, plastic-covered machine that has a motor in the base and a gap at the top that holds three different attachments: a smooth roller for kneading the dough into sheets and two notched or gear sets for cutting the smooth, large pieces into noodles of various widths.

USE: Cutting pasta dough into fresh pasta shapes, and in the case of the roller type, kneading the dough into plain sheets prior to cutting.

USE TIPS: Relatively easy to use. The problem is making dough of the right consistency.

BUYING TIPS: Look for models that can be adjusted to produce sheets of different widths and thicknesses, and with some texture. Mirror-smooth rollers produce a smooth finish that is less appetizing to some, and it doesn't hold sauce well. Pasta machines were once very popular, but since there is now such a good selection of fresh pastas sold in gourmet stores, they have become less popular.

HAND-CRANKED
PASTA MACHINE

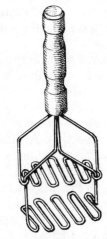

SPRING-ACTION MASHER

POTATO MASHER

ALSO KNOWN AS: Vegetable masher, masher, wire potato masher

DESCRIPTION: Two popular designs: One is a flat circle of steel with an open mesh at the end of two long, sturdy prongs; the other is thick wire formed into a flat zigzag shape that arches back into a long handle. A *spring-action masher* has two mashing heads, one over the other—the upper one comes down next to the lower one with each stroke. A *bean masher* is a 25- or 31-inch-long stainless steel professional model. All are chrome-plated, stainless steel, or aluminum with plastic handles. A stiff, all-plastic model, with vertical slats about an inch high, is also available, as is an old design, My Mother's Potato Masher, which is plain steel and L-shaped, with a wooden handle—the steel is slotted, so there is much more solid area for mashing the potato than with the wire or grid designs. And then there is the rather basic wooden club, round with a flat or mushroom-shaped end, also known as a *champignon*.

USE: Mashing cooked potatoes or other cooked vegetables such as refried beans.

USE TIPS: Also useful for preparing the vegetables in chunky-style soups.

BUYING TIPS: The spring-action masher is especially useful for making refried beans.

POTATO RICER

ALSO KNOWN AS: Ricer and fruit press

DESCRIPTION: Stainless steel or aluminum device with two lever-type handles that converge on a small basket, permeated with holes, attached to one of them. The top lever pushes a disk down onto a boiled potato or other soft food in the basket, mashing it down and through and out the small holes. Some models come with two interchangeable disks with different sized holes that fit in the bottom. Available in 1 cup or ½ cup ("mini") capacities. When the basket is covered by an outer shell with a pouring spout, it serves as a *fruit and vegetable juicer* (see page 84).

USE: Making lump-free mashed potatoes, as well as applesauce, baby food, and the like.

USE TIPS: Be sure potatoes are fully cooked. If they are too firm, they will not pass through the ricer. Remove seeds from fruit prior to use.

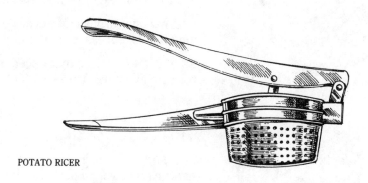

POTATO RICER

TOMATO PRESS

ALSO KNOWN AS: Tomato strainer

DESCRIPTION: Hand-cranked machine that attaches with a suction cup or a clamp to a countertop. A large hopper is on top, and a chute comes out of one side. Just under a foot high; made of stainless steel and plastic.

USE: Separating juice and pulp from the skin and seeds of tomatoes, cooked apples, pumpkins, and other such fruits and vegetables.

USE TIPS: Cook your tomatoes quickly after running them through this machine. Note whether your model can only take quartered tomatoes or if it can take whole ones, which is very rare. Ideal for baby food, applesauce, tomato sauce, and the like.

BUYING TIPS: Make sure you get one that is easily cleaned. Most can come apart for this purpose.

TORTILLA PRESS

TORTILLA PRESS

DESCRIPTION: Two cast-aluminum disks, hinged on one side, 6½ inches in diameter. A long handle locks the top one down.

USE: Making tortillas (Mexican corn or wheat pancakes) by pressing a ball of tortilla dough until it is flat and thin.

BUYING TIPS: Only experienced, adept Mexican chefs can make tortillas by hand. A press is necessary for everyone else.

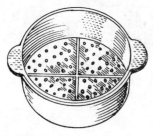

TUNA SQUEEZER

TUNA SQUEEZER

DESCRIPTION: Small plastic cup with straight sides, the size of a flat tuna can, with a perforated bottom and two ear-type handles.

USE: Squeezing the water out of canned tuna.

USE TIPS: Do this in or over the sink.

CHAPTER 3

Measuring Equipment

About Measuring Equipment

If it is important to you, get items with both American and metric markings—most have both. However, dual and triple markings can be very confusing and lead to a greatly increased chance of making a mistake in measuring. Buy measures with metric markings only if you plan to make a lot of foreign recipes, many of which specify quantities by weight, not by volume.

Dry and Liquid Measures

About Dry and Liquid Measures

It is pointless to buy a poor-quality measuring device that may be inaccurate. Get a good one. Test scales by weighing a package of food that is clearly labeled as to weight or capacity.

The greatest accuracy is required for baking, because that depends on specific chemical reactions. Take advantage of the latest in high-tech gadgetry if you are a serious baker. Measuring for much stovetop cooking can be done more by feel. Of course, too much "feel" and there is not much recipe. For example, one noted chef used to consternate fans when she would give a recipe with a notation like, "Fill yellow bowl . . . then cook until done." So much for accurate measurements.

BOWL SCALE

BOWL SCALE

ALSO KNOWN AS: Portion control scale

DESCRIPTION: Flat, round scale, which comes with either a deep bowl on top, usually the same width as the scale, or a flat surface that can be used under any plate or bowl. The weight readout can be reset to zero while food is in the bowl in order to make successive readings simpler as different ingredients are added to the same bowl. Usually gives both metric and American measures. Small models measure only up to 1 pound while large ones measure as much as 6½ or even 11 pounds (5 kilograms).

USE: Measuring various foods as components of the same recipe that are placed together in the bowl.

KITCHEN SCALE

ALSO KNOWN AS: Spring scale

DESCRIPTION: Available in a wide range of sizes and shapes with maximum capacities from 1 pound to 10 pounds. Almost all have a bowl or pan of some sort on top to hold the food being weighed. Readouts may be electronic (digital) or analog (dial face) and either metric (grams) or American (ounces) or a combination of the two. Usually the pan, often made of plastic, can be inverted and placed over the scale or the scale face when it is not in use. A smaller model may be called a *diet scale*. Another type is a *beam-balance scale,* a low, flat, larger scale with two horizontal beams in front on which small weights slide from side to side, just like the scales used for measuring your weight in a doctor's office. One beam measures pounds, the other ounces (or kilos and grams).

USE: Weighing nonliquid foods, either for recipe measurement or for individual portions in order to determine calorie intake (for dieters).

USE TIPS: When recipes call for ingredients by the ounce, as is often the case with meat ingredients, a small scale is very useful. Also helpful for portion control when feeding large groups from large cuts of meat or fish. If you don't have a good eye or hand for estimated weight, this eliminates the guesswork.

BUYING TIPS: Ranges up to 2 pounds are most common and useful. Beam-balance scales are only for the most serious cooks who use a lot of large foods, which fit better on its large tray. The self-contained models whose bowls fit over them travel and store well.

MEASURING CUP

DESCRIPTION: Either one large cup or a *measuring set* of four or five variously sized nesting cups, usually attached at their pan-handle ends key-ring style, with their capacities clearly marked on the edges or handles. Large ones start at about 1½ cups and go on to 2- and 4-cup capacities, and are often made of heat-resistant Pyrex glass with red markings, but are available in plastic and aluminum as well. The smaller ones are made in only plastic, stainless steel, and aluminum. Sets usually are made of cups which measure ⅛, ¼, ⅓, ½, and 1 cup. Sometimes a set of nesting cups is called *Mary Ann cups*. An *adjustable measuring cup* is made of two cylinders. One slides inside the other, adjusting to the amount you desire at the top. In this case, you set the cup for the quantity of liquid or solid food you want prior to putting the material in it. Finally, at least one manufacturer has cemented two plastic 8-ounce/250ml measuring cups together at their bottoms so that you can dedicate one to wet ingredients and the other to dry ingredients—a *wet and dry measuring cup*.

USE: For the measure of dry and liquid ingredients.

USE TIPS: The smaller cups, which are often marked with only their full capacity, are good for dry ingredients, but not liquids—use the larger clear glass or plastic cups and read at eye level for exact liquid measurement. All dry measurements should be leveled with the flat side of a knife blade, but without tamping down. Note whether your recipe tells you to measure flour sifted or unsifted. To prevent sticking when measuring viscous ingredients such as honey or syrup in a glass measuring cup, spray with vegetable oil spray or rinse it first with water and do not dry it, then measure the ingredient. After use, the liquid will pour out easily and the cup will be easier to wash.

BUYING TIPS: Do not buy lightweight metal cups: if they become dented, the measure will be inaccurate. May be sold as part of a set of *measuring spoons* (see next entry) and cups ranging from ⅛ teaspoon to 1 cup. Some plastic models have magnets on them for convenient storage but risk melting if left near a hot stovetop. Be sure to have several sets to speed your cooking by allowing you to measure different ingredients simultaneously.

MEASURING SPOONS

MEASURING SPOONS

DESCRIPTION: One or a set of four or five small spoons banded together at the end of their handles, key-ring style, with their capacities clearly marked on their handles. One make is available that has magnets in the handles instead of a ring. Typical range of size is ¼ teaspoon to 1 tablespoon in the small set and ¼ cup to 1 cup in the larger set. Some include a tiny one labeled "just a pinch." Made of plastic in a variety of colors, or aluminum or stainless steel. A variation on this simple design is the *adjustable measuring spoon,* a long, narrow plastic or metal trough with a short handle and a sliding bar that effectively shortens or lengthens the size of the open area. Measurements are marked along the edges and are for dry ingredients only. Finally, some sets include one spoon with a palette-shaped flat end used to scoop food out of the spoons after measuring.

USE: For the measure of dry and liquid ingredients.

USE TIPS: Plastic spoons may melt and aluminum ones may corrode in your dishwasher.

BUYING TIPS: An essential tool for any kitchen. May be sold as part of a set of *measuring cups* and spoons ranging from ⅛ teaspoon to 1 cup. Those with magnets are convenient to store. Good stainless spoons are dishwasher-safe.

RECIPE ADJUSTER

DESCRIPTION: Flat plastic sheets and wheels with various markings and windows. All rotate on a rivet point in the middle to make a crude computer. Most markings concern numbers of portions and measurements of ingredients.

USE: Calculating how to adjust quantities for more or fewer servings than indicated in the original recipe.

USE TIPS: Keep in mind that baking requires very accurate measurements, as many ingredients actually react with each other.

Specialized Measuring Equipment

About Specialized Measuring Equipment

Though timers can help any cook, the other items in this section are for only those who have specialized needs or a personal preference for gadgets to assist them in estimating. Test timers for accuracy with a watch.

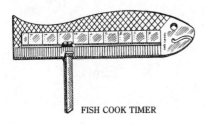

FISH COOK TIMER

FISH COOK TIMER

DESCRIPTION: A 6-inch-long measuring guide with a sliding measuring stick, with cooking times on a chart related to the thickness of fish being measured. Made from aluminum or plastic, and often shaped like the profile of a fish.

USE: Determining accurate cooking times for fish. As the sliding part is moved to measure the thickness of the fish, the time necessary for proper cooking is indicated on the scale.

BUYING TIPS: Direct observation and testing are probably more accurate, and in any case this kind of information is found in most recipes.

SACCHARIMETER

ALSO KNOWN AS: Pèse-sirop (Fr.), syrup-density meter, densometer, densimeter, hydrometer, Baumé hydrometer, water measure

DESCRIPTION: A long glass tube that looks like a thermometer with one end thicker and heavier than the other. Instead of temperature markings, it has a Baumé scale running from 0 to 40. Often used with a tall, narrow, stainless steel pitcher for holding the syrup, called a *syrup holder, syrup density-meter test tube,* or *eprouvette* (Fr.).

USE: Measuring the density or water content of sugar syrup for various dessert recipes such as ice cream or sherbert, or in the jelly-making process.

USE TIPS: Density affects freezing characteristics. Add syrup or water to your mixture as necessary.

BUYING TIPS: Easier to use with a syrup holder pitcher. Relatively inexpensive item.

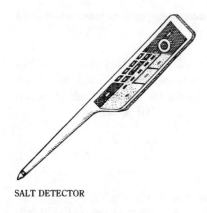

SALT DETECTOR

SALT DETECTOR

DESCRIPTION: Plastic-encased, 7½ inch, steel-tipped electronic probe with an on/off button. Looks like a modern thermometer, with a scale on the side indicating sodium content. A *salometer* is a glass tube similar to the *saccharimeter* (see previous entry).

USE: Measuring sodium content in cooked foods and beverages. Hold power button on for a few seconds with the steel-tipped end inserted into the food until readout indicator lights up. A salometer is used to measure the salt content of pickling brine.

USE TIPS: Not recommended for use at fancy dinner parties.

BUYING TIPS: Very helpful for those on low sodium diets. Unfortunately, this is a very expensive item.

SHORTENING DISPENSER

DESCRIPTION: Plastic, disk-shaped pump that attaches to the top of a 48-ounce can of vegetable shortening. The handle serves also as a dial that is set to a desired volume of shortening to be dispensed.

USE: Dispenses predetermined amounts of shortening through a small spout.

BUYING TIPS: Saves cleaning additional measuring utensils.

SPAGHETTI MEASURING STICK

SPAGHETTI MEASURING STICK

ALSO KNOWN AS: Spaghetti measure, spaghetti portioner, pasta portioner

DESCRIPTION: Flat plastic or wooden round or paddle, about 8 inches long and 2 inches wide, with three to six holes progressing from small to large. Holes are unlabeled on many, or else next to each hole is the number of servings that a bunch of pasta that diameter will make. Labels may read, "one adult, two adults, one child," etc. Also, some *spaghetti forks* (see page 133) may include a measuring hole in the handle.

USE: Eliminating the guesswork when determining how much spaghetti to cook. Take a handful of spaghetti and place some of it into one of the appropriate holes, eliminating the excess.

USE TIPS: Obviously, this is an average. It doesn't take into account very small and very big appetites or those influenced by the sauce (tomato sauce, that is). Use only with uncooked spaghetti.

BUYING TIPS: Inexpensive item easily replaced by a little experience.

TIMER

DESCRIPTION: Any of four basic types; all contain a timing mechanism and an on/off procedure.

TYPES: *Digital timer*: Compact and high-tech electronic device (battery powered) which displays time in a liquid-crystal display (LCD) for periods up to twelve hours. Some of the better models have several different modes, such as countdown or countup, and may keep track of up to three different times simultaneously, with three different alarms. Usually controlled by pushing a variety of buttons. One model comes with a lanyard and can be hung from your neck as you move around the house.

Egg timer: Solid plastic egg shape with a red color and three doneness markings (soft, medium, hard). The "egg" is placed in the water with the real eggs and changes color as they cook; the edge of the colored area indicates the doneness on the scale. Though any timer can be and often is called an egg timer, this one is specifically designed for timing boiled eggs due to its unique design.

Hourglass timer (Also Known As *3-minute egg timer, telephone timer,* or *egg timer*): Small glass tube, filled with fine sand, inside a wooden frame, usually no more than a few inches high. The tube is enlarged at either end and very, very narrow at the middle. It is turned on its end to work. The sand takes three minutes to pour out of the top part and into the bottom.

Wind-up timer (Also Known As *kitchen alarm timer, spring-type timer*): The most common and traditional design for a timer. Usually a metal or plastic box with a dial that goes up to one hour or sometimes two, divided by minutes, marked in five- or ten-minute increments. Dial is often at an angle and has a knob in the center, or a top half, that is twisted to the desired time; the timer then winds down from that time to zero. It has a loud automatic bell that rings for a few seconds at the end. Designs range from practical and simple white geometric to shaped and

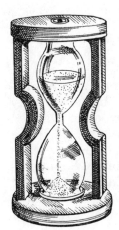

HOURGLASS TIMER

WIND-UP TIMER

colored like a pear, green pepper, tomato, orange, onion (either purple or yellow), or a chef with toque. A *clip timer* can be clipped onto an apron or belt; a *magnetic timer* can stick to a metal appliance door. And now there is a wall mounted, 8-inch-diameter version with a face that can be read from across the backyard.

USE: Timing items to be baked, broiled, boiled, simmered, etc., a certain amount of time.

USE TIPS: Can be used to time noncooking items too, such as phone calls. Digital model can also be used as an alarm clock. Keep plastic timers away from hot stovetops.

BUYING TIPS: Plastic egg-shaped timer is the only one to give satisfactory results when cooking eggs, regardless of the altitude or number of eggs in the water. The fancier digital models can be quite expensive, but also much more versatile. They can handle multiple items, and some even double as a clock. The wind-up timers have a tendency to be very inaccurate, especially with short amounts of time.

Thermometers

About Thermometers

Mercury is the most accurate medium for a thermometer, as metal coils may wear out and batteries may weaken. But calibrations on metal or wooden plaques attached to glass mercury tubes may be a bit off if the plaque has moved slightly. Etched glass mercury thermometers are the most accurate and reliable. Some professional thermometers are quite specialized, and not included here (for dough, or milk). Always store thermometers carefully—don't let them bounce around in drawers.

CANDY/DEEP-FRY THERMOMETER

ALSO KNOWN AS: Candy and jelly thermometer, candy/jelly/deep-fry thermometer, fat/candy thermometer, deep-fry/confectionery thermometer, sugar thermometer, fat thermometer, deep-frying thermometer

DESCRIPTION: Usually a large glass thermometer that looks like a thick standard medical thermometer but measures temperatures from 50°F or 100°F to about 400°F (25°C to 200°C). Also available as a T-shaped metal thermometer, with a horizontal dial on top. All models are large, from 8 to 12 inches long. Celsius measure is usually marked as well. Equipped with a clip, hook, or handle for hanging inside a vat of something very hot and sticky. Also available in a microwave-safe version.

USE: Measuring the extremely high temperature of candy (sugar syrup) or deep-frying fat as it is cooking, and when making preserves and jellies to establish the temperature at which they will "set."

USE TIPS: A must-have item if you make candy since the temperature rises very quickly and a few degrees is the difference between perfect and perfectly burned with such recipes. Be extra careful when working with high-temperature liquids such as these.

BUYING TIPS: Best to look for one that will have cool handle of wood or plastic, though the plastic should not extend to a place that would touch the pot while in use. Look for clear, easily read numbers. Handy if you are inexperienced at deep-frying.

CHOCOLATE THERMOMETER

DESCRIPTION: A thick, long, glass mercury-filled thermometer that measures from about 50°F to 140°F. Markings are large and clear.

USE: Accurate measurement of melted chocolate temperature for use in candy and pastry recipes, usually as part of a delicate process called tempering that involves rapid heating and cooling.

USE TIPS: Handle and store this large, glass object with extreme care, as it is extremely fragile.

BUYING TIPS: For the professional and serious amateur pastry chef.

GRILL THERMOMETER

DESCRIPTION: Lightweight metal dial thermometer geared to high temperatures from about 100°F to 600°F. Usually made of stainless steel, sometimes with a magnetic back so that it sticks conveniently to the hood at grill level, or else just directly to the grill.

USE: Measuring the cooking temperature at the grill surface for barbecuing but also of particularly hot or big ovens.

USE TIPS: Keep clean—don't let smoke and food residue build up. Adjust the height of your rack for appropriate temperature.

BUYING TIPS: Not an essential item.

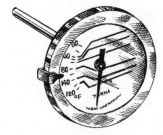

MEAT AND POULTRY THERMOMETER

MEAT AND POULTRY THERMOMETER

ALSO KNOWN AS: Meat thermometer, roast meat thermometer

DESCRIPTION: Any of several designs which include a probe and a gauge of some sort. Internal temperatures for cooking common foods are usually marked, such as "Lamb, medium," or "Beef, rare." May also be called a *roast-yeast thermometer* and include the appropriate markings for yeast.

TYPES: *Stainless steel insert:* Stainless steel spike, about 5 inches long, with a plastic or glass-faced dial 1¼ to 1¾ inches in diameter, on one end. The spike is a temperature probe and the dial has a needle and temperature markings up to about 220°F and the equivalent in Celsius. Some models start at 0°F and others at 100°F. Spikes on older models are about ¼ inch thick, while newer and specialized models are very thin. May be dishwasher-safe.

    Glass insert: Glass probe, about 5 inches long, filled with nontoxic liquid. Extremely accurate. Sometimes has a metal safety shield on the end, with a metal plaque behind about a third of the glass on which temperature and doneness markings are etched or painted. Supplied with a skewer for puncturing the meat prior to insertion.

    Microwave thermometer: Similar to the glass insert model, but made of only plastic and glass; a metal skewer is used to puncture a hole for the probe in the meat prior to insertion.

    Instant-read thermometer (Also Known As *instant thermometer* or *rapid-response thermometer*): Long, thin probe with a dial at one end. Good for use with microwave ovens or rotisseries, where the thermometer cannot be left in the meat. A similar electronic probe model can be used on barbecued meat (or meat cooked anywhere)—one touch of a button gives a reading as to doneness. A 1-inch-wide dial reads from 0°F to 220°F on most models. The top-of-the-line models are digital, reading from 68°F to 220°F to 160°F or − 40°F to 120°F, and have an updating feature adjustable from 1 to 15 seconds. Battery powered, LED or LCD readout. Not intended to be left in the food as it cooks. Carrying case provided.

Barbecue meat thermometer: Stainless steel insert style (see above) designed to be used over open flame or other intense sources of heat; the gauge part is protected inside a stainless steel cylinder.

USE: Inserted into the meat at the start of cooking time, or in the case of specially designed models, when checking to see if done. When the proper meat temperature is attained, as read on the thermometer, the meat is done. Yeast temperature is very important—an error of a few degrees can kill it, and if it's not hot enough, then nothing will happen.

USE TIPS: Check your cookbooks or use common sense to place the probe properly. Your reading will be way off if it is touching a bone or dangling inside a carcass. Also, the idea of doneness may vary from manufacturer to chef. Finally, remember that roasts continue to cook a bit after removal from the oven.

BUYING TIPS: Look for one with a clear, readable face—the digital models are best in this respect, and the instant reading feature is very convenient. Also, be sure to get one with both Fahrenheit and Celsius degrees in case you are following a European recipe with metric measurements. An important tool to have, especially if you ever cook pork, which must be well done. In general, a reassuring way to avoid embarrassment and delay resulting from serving an underdone roast.

MEAT BUTTON

MEAT BUTTON

ALSO KNOWN AS: Steak button

DESCRIPTION: T-shaped miniature thermometer that inserts directly into the meat, leaving a small, round face visible. The needle reaches points marked "rare," "medium," or "well-done" instead of degrees as on a regular thermometer. A simpler version, a *roast beef timer,* is a plastic, naillike device that pops up when the correct temperature is reached. Made also in a pork and a lamb version.

USE: Measuring the doneness of meat. You remove the meat from the oven when it reaches the doneness desired.

USE TIPS: Do not use over open flame unless specifically designed for that purpose. Wash carefully.

BUYING TIPS: A regular meat thermometer is more accurate. The plastic pop-up style is a disposable item.

OVEN THERMOMETER

OVEN THERMOMETER

DESCRIPTION: Small, rectangular, squarish, or round dial-type (spring-style) or glass, mercury-filled tube thermometer, about 3 inches in diameter or 5 inches long, made of stainless steel and glass. Generally has a small foot and a top hook so it can hang from an oven rack. Available with both Fahrenheit and Celsius measure going from 100°F to about 650°F. A *folding oven thermometer* is a more accurate, long model made of stainless steel with a glass mercury-filled tube and a base stand.

USE: Measuring the temperature of an oven, not only to second-guess the thermostat, but to see if the temperature varies in different areas of the oven as it usually does.

USE TIPS: Move to various positions within the oven to test for even temperature distribution.

BUYING TIPS: Look for clear, easily readable numbers. The folding model is more accurate but is intended mainly for professionals. A good and inexpensive item to have, as most ovens can be off by as much as 10°F (and sometimes more) from the dialed setting of the thermostat. Mercury tube style lasts longer than the spring-style.

POULTRY BUTTON

DESCRIPTION: A T-shaped mini-thermometer measuring about 2 inches in length, with a round face with a needle and/or a small flag. A simpler version, a *poultry timer,* is a disposable, plastic, naillike device with a core that pops up when the desired temperature is reached.

USE: Automatically signals that poultry is cooked enough.

USE TIPS: The needle end of the thermometer is inserted into the center of the poultry so that the face of the thermometer can be seen clearly. Wash carefully. Do not use over open flame unless it is specifically designed for that purpose.

BUYING TIPS: The pop-up version is not reusable.

REFRIGERATOR-FREEZER THERMOMETER

DESCRIPTION: Stainless steel, dial-type thermometer which looks almost identical to the *oven thermometer* (see opposite). The dial, about 3 inches in diameter, is marked for both Fahrenheit and Celsius from about $-20°F$ to $80°F$. Designed to both hang from a rack or sit on a shelf.

USE: Measuring the temperature in the refrigerator or freezer accurately.

USE TIPS: Will register vast differences if the appliance is crammed full of food or if the door is opened frequently.

BUYING TIPS: As with all thermometers, this one should have a clear, readable face. Some models are available with a fog- and frost-free face.

Separating, Grating, and Milling Tools

About Separating, Grating, and Milling Tools

Any serious cooking involves more than just mixing or cutting, and at one point foods need to be transformed in a more complex way. That is where these tools come in. Although you can chop anything quite finely with a knife, grating and grinding tools generally can do this better and faster. And many of these are quite specialized, useful for certain foods or dishes only.

This is one area where you may have to buy an item because of one particular recipe that you are determined to make.

Separating Tools

About Separating Tools

Almost every item in this section is a traditional kitchen workhorse. Happily, they are relatively inexpensive and widely distributed.

CHEESE FUNNEL

ALSO KNOWN AS: Yogurt cheese funnel, yogurt strainer, soft cheese maker

DESCRIPTION: Large, shallow funnel made of stiff, plastic micronized mesh (with microscopic openings). Yogurt is poured into the funnel and left to sit over a large glass overnight in the refrigerator. Made in 1- and 2-cup capacities.

USE: Separating the whey from the yogurt, creating a low-fat cream cheese.

USE TIPS: Superb for cheesecake. Substitutes for mayonnaise or sour cream in some recipes, too.

BUYING TIPS: Good item for those people trying to cut back on cholesterol.

CHEESECLOTH

ALSO KNOWN AS: Bouillon cloth

DESCRIPTION: Very loosely woven white cotton cloth sold in small bolts or rolls of about two square yards. Usually lint-free.

USE: Straining soups or stocks, jelly, or clarifying butter. Wrapped around delicate fish and certain other foods to retain their shape and moisture during the cooking process. Also used for making *bouquet garni bags* (see page 107). Originally used to hold large pieces of cheese together and to maintain moisture. Often used for poaching fish.

USE TIPS: Lay cheesecloth in a strainer or colander. Use two or more layers when clarifying a consommé.

BUYING TIPS: Good to have around for its multiple uses.

COLANDER

ALSO KNOWN AS: Spaghetti strainer

DESCRIPTION: Large stainless or enameled steel, plastic, aluminum, tinned copper, porcelain, or earthenware bowl with a pattern of small holes and two small grip handles, plus a round base or feet. Similar to a *strainer* (see page 113), which is a lighter item made of wire mesh, with a long handle and no feet. Some patterns are plain, with evenly spaced slots or holes, and others have repetitive stars. Capacities are typically 3 or 5 quarts, though sizes actually range from 1½ to 13 quarts. A variety of types are made.

COLANDER

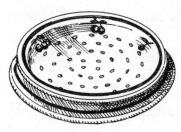

CHERRY DRAINER AND PLATE

TYPES: *Berry colander* (Also Known As *fruit colander and tray*): Flat copper or stainless steel bowl supplied with a close-fitting tray that sits underneath to catch water.

Colander/bowl: Hybrid model that is a wire mesh bowl with no feet.

Fruit drainer (Also Known As *berry bowl, grape drainer,* or *cherry drainer*): A specialized, fancy porcelain model—a perforated flat bowl that comes with a plate to catch water as it drips off freshly washed fruit. Some bowls have more holes than others. Intended for use on the tabletop.

Scoop colander: Hybrid model which has the colander's solid, perforated bowl, but the strainer's handle and lack of feet. Bowl usually measures about 7 by 9 inches but can be smaller.

USE: Draining water from cooked pasta or vegetables or rinsing food. Stands on its own in a sink or hangs from the lip of a pot. A heavier-duty item than a strainer. Fruit drainers or colanders that come with matching plates or trays allow you to serve the fruit without waiting for it to drain completely.

USE TIPS: At least one restaurant placed these over light bulbs for a food-related interior decoration solution. If you try this, be aware of the star patterns as well as plain or random patterns and handles that might interfere with the smooth interpretation of your grand design plan.

BUYING TIPS: Look for solid feet that won't loosen with use over a long period of time—a round base is best. These things should last forever. An essential tool.

EGG SEPARATOR

ALSO KNOWN AS: Egg yolk separator

EGG SEPARATOR

DESCRIPTION: Small, open, dish-shaped device a few inches in diameter, usually made of stamped aluminum or plastic as well as glazed ceramic. The center is just large enough to hold an egg yolk, and it is surrounded by an open slot. There is a tongue on the side which is just large enough to grip with your thumb and forefinger. One plastic model actually hangs on the inside edge of a cup. Other models are rectangular, with winged handles that sit on both edges of a glass or cup.

USE: Separating egg yolks from egg whites one egg at a time.

USE TIPS: Crack the egg very carefully into the separator. It is very important that the separator be very clean. Even a trace of grease in egg whites will keep them from forming stiff peaks when beaten. You can use a broken shell to remove traces of yolk in the white.

BUYING TIPS: Usually very inexpensive. Most cooks can separate eggs by carefully breaking the shell, leaving the yolk in one half, thus avoiding having to wash another utensil.

FAT-OFF LADLE

FAT-OFF LADLE

DESCRIPTION: Large stainless steel *ladle* (see page 129) with two levels. The center part is a small, deep, cut shape, which is surrounded by a flat rim with slots on one side. This is in turn surrounded by a short vertical edge.

USE: Skimming fat off the top of stews, stocks, or soups.

USE TIPS: Have another bowl ready into which you can pour the skimmed-off fat.

BUYING TIPS: Good idea for those who make soup or stock often.

FISH BONE TWEEZER

DESCRIPTION: Large, wide tweezers made from one piece of flat stainless steel, the tips of which are plain.

USE: Removing fish bones from fish prior to cooking and serving.

USE TIPS: Make sure you get every bone. It only takes one to cause an accident.

BUYING TIPS: Pliers are better for removing some large bones from raw fish.

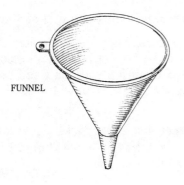

FUNNEL

FUNNEL

DESCRIPTION: Basic cone shape with a small opening at the point, usually at the end of a short neck. Made of plastic, stainless steel, or aluminum, usually with a small lip and hole for hanging. Some brands are available with interchangeable tips that may contain a small screen. Also available is a *folding funnel*, which flattens for easy storage, and an enormous bowllike *canning funnel*, which has a collar that fits into jars.

USE: Pouring liquids from one vessel into another one, such as from a pot into a bottle with a narrow neck.

USE TIPS: Screened funnels are ideal for cleaning used cooking oil.

BUYING TIPS: Usually sold in sets of various sizes. Look for canning funnels with a vented design for fast flow. Good to have several on hand.

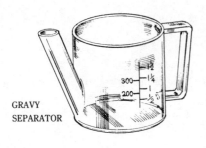

GRAVY SEPARATOR

GRAVY SEPARATOR

ALSO KNOWN AS: Gravy skimmer, fat separator

DESCRIPTION: Plastic or glass mug with large spout extending from bottom of mug (a regular pitcher's spout extends from the top). Markings on side show cups, ranging from 1½ to 4. Particularly large ones are made for use with soups. Another version is a large ladle that has a trap door on the bottom that is opened by a trigger in the handle; you scoop up the gravy or soup and wait for the fat to come to the top, then pull the trigger; a cup model with a toggle on the bottom that you pull to open is also available.

USE: Separates fats and oils from gravies, sauces, and soups. The fat rises to the surface while the gravy itself pours from the opening near the bottom. The ladle or cup with a hole in the bottom is dependent on your eye—you close the opening when the gravy is all poured out, just as the fat reaches the opening.

USE TIPS: Just fill the mug with liquid requiring separation and let sit a moment. Oils rise to top so you can pour out fat-free sauce from the bottom of the mug. Clear plastic lets you see when all is separated.

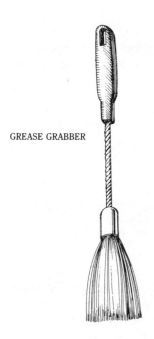

GREASE GRABBER

BUYING TIPS: The cup version can also be used as an egg separator, butter clarifier, strainer, or a syrup dispenser. Handy item.

GREASE GRABBER

DESCRIPTION: Long brush with plastic handle and twisted wire shaft, with round set of long white, fine, soft, polyester bristles.

USE: Soaking up fat from gravies and soups.

USE TIPS: Rinse well in hot soapy water.

JELLY STRAINER

DESCRIPTION: Simple wire rack about 6 inches in diameter and a foot high, made of a ring suspended by three legs. The bottoms of the legs are splayed out and hooked so that they can hook over the edge of a pot or bowl as well as sit on a countertop. A cheesecloth bag called a *jelly bag*, made especially for this, hangs from the ring.

USE: Straining jellies, juices, and stocks.

USE TIPS: Make sure you have several replacement bags on hand.

BUYING TIPS: Handy item for those who strain a lot.

PAN DRAINER

ALSO KNOWN AS: Pan edge drain(er), pot drainer, pan drain

DESCRIPTION: Odd-shaped flat plastic or metal tool with one large flat edge and one curved edge and a short handle. The curved part has holes and a small lip. Rarely more than a foot long. Also available shaped like a kidney and without the handle.

USE: Draining any small pot or pan by holding it against the pot or pan as you pour out the liquid and block the food. Also performs as a scraper, turner, and fish lifter, depending on strength and design.

USE TIPS: Don't expect it to hold extra-heavy and large quantities of food that come sliding down the inside of a big pot. Practice to learn its limits and yours. This takes up less space than a colander, so it is very useful to have in a tiny kitchen.

BUYING TIPS: For small quantities only—works only with pots and pans you can hold with one hand. Experiment until you find the one or two that serve you best.

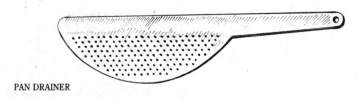

PAN DRAINER

SALAD SHREDDER

DESCRIPTION: A smaller version of the *food mill* (see page 119) but without a hopper. Available in many different models from various manufacturers, it consists primarily of the horizontal crank, a triangular stand, and a set of different cutting disks or cones. Made of tinned or stainless steel, cast aluminum, or a mixture of steel and plastic.

USE: Shredding vegetables for cooking.

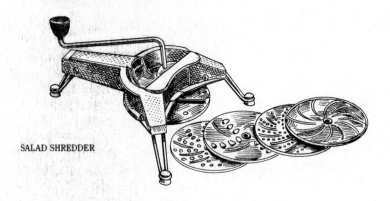

SALAD SHREDDER

SKIMMER

ALSO KNOWN AS: Drainer, scum strainer, skimmer ladle

DESCRIPTION: Generally a long-handled, stainless steel or cast-aluminum spoonlike utensil with a large, round, flat disk on the end where the cup would be on a spoon or ladle. Also available in a large, square or round version from 8 to 10 inches wide. This

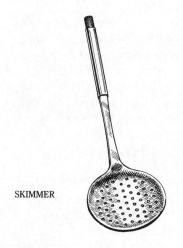

SKIMMER

disk is slightly concave and may be a stainless steel mesh (fine, open, or wide open) or just perforated. Made also as an oriental or wok version, usually in woven brass with a fairly open mesh and a bamboo handle, 5 to 7 inches in diameter. A *Mongolian skimmer* is a small brass wire basket on a lightweight, twisted wire handle, used for fishing food out of Mongolian hot pots (Chinese fondue)—it may be considered a piece of tableware. A *tempura skimmer* is almost a *strainer* (see next entry), with its fine, bowl-shaped mesh.

USE: Removing scum from broths, stocks, or preserves as they cook, or removing the food or herbs from same. Some models, such as the oriental ones, are used exclusively for removing food from hot deep-frying oil.

BUYING TIPS: Though a slotted spoon substitutes nicely, some cooks prefer the extra-wide, pot-sized model that removes everything at once.

STRAINER

ALSO KNOWN AS: Sieve

DESCRIPTION: A wire mesh basket with a long handle off the rim, available in a variety of designs. Strainers do not have feet, but a similar item, a *colander* (see page 107), does.

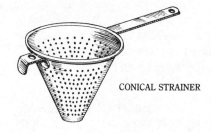

CONICAL STRAINER

TYPES: *Conical strainer* (Also Known As *chinois, china cap, bouillon* or *conical bouillon strainer, passe-sauces* [Fr.]): Cone-shaped aluminum or tin-plated or stainless steel strainer, usually with a fine wire mesh, about 7 inches long and wide, and with a long handle off the rim. There is often a small tab and a lip that allow you to rest the strainer in a pot. A solid and slightly larger version called a *perforated sieve* (also called a *chinois*) is made of finely perforated metal and supplied with a conical wooden *pestle,* a hand-sized, cone-shaped tool for forcing the food through the perforations to puree it. May be supplied with a stand, and sometimes referred to as a *rotary food press.*

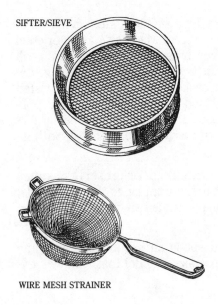

SIFTER/SIEVE

WIRE MESH STRAINER

Sieve (Also Known As *sifter/sieve, drum sieve, tamis* [Fr.]): Round, shallow, flat-bottomed wooden or stainless steel bowl with a fine-mesh bottom grid of wire or nylon, and straight sides. 7½ or 8½ inches in diameter (professional sizes up to 16 inches) and about 2 inches high. One version is a *tammycloth,* a worsted cloth strainer used for sauces. Sometimes the mesh is expressed in terms of the number of holes per square inch, such as "14 mesh," which is a medium mesh. Screens were traditionally made of horsehair.

Wire mesh strainer: Bowl-shaped mesh made of stainless or tinned steel, aluminum, or nylon, ranging from extra fine to coarse, with a long handle. Available in a range of sizes from 2½ to 7 inches in diameter. Handles and frames are made in stainless steel, wood, or plastic. All have a small hook or hooks opposite the handle for support from the rim of a pot. Generally a lighter-duty tool than a *colander*. A *strainer/colander* has the handle and hooks of a strainer and the feet of a colander. A *pasta strainer* is a wider-mesh, heavier-duty model. A hand crank and blade that pushes food around and through the strainer can be added, turning a strainer into a *food mill* (see page 119).

USE: A strainer is used for draining pasta, stocks, or vegetables after cooking or cleaning, and can also be used to sift flour or strain tea leaves out of a teapot, depending on size of the mesh. The loops are for resting on the rim of a pot or sink (they form a triangular support along with the handles) and also for hanging the strainer on a tool rack. A sieve is most frequently used for sifting dry ingredients, but can be used interchangeably with a strainer.

USE TIPS: The more open, coarse mesh strainer can also be used as a colander. Generally, a strainer is used for lighter foods (because you have to hold it in one hand) and a colander used for heavier foods (because it sits in a sink).

BUYING TIPS: This item, or a set of graduated sizes and meshes of this item, is one of the essentials in a well-equipped kitchen. Look for a solidly made one with loops on the edge opposite the handle. All stainless steel is best.

Graters

About Graters

Although electric appliances that can do many of the jobs of graters are common, in many cases a hand grater will give the best results. These are always good items to have. Many innovative designs are available.

FISH SCALER/GRATER

FISH SCALER/GRATER

ALSO KNOWN AS: Fish scaler

DESCRIPTION: Flat aluminum oval a little over 4 inches long, with numerous holes punched in it, each of which has rough cutting edges. A loop handle is on the back. Other types include a small oval frame with a jagged, saw edge (often with a pointed blade parallel to it for convenience), a short rod with many sharp ridges or rings, mounted at the base of a cast-aluminum hopper that collects the scales as they fly off, or a slightly offset metal shaft with a heart-shaped scraper blade.

USE: Grating the scales from fish.

USE TIPS: Work in an area that you can easily clean with lots of water—fish scales tend to make a mess.

BUYING TIPS: Not necessary for most store-bought fish, this is an item for fishing enthusiasts.

GRATER

DESCRIPTION: Any one of a number of designs, all of which incorporate a metal sheet, either flat or curved, with holes or slots that each have a sharp cutting edge, like a rasp. Usually made of stainless steel, but also available in tinned or chrome-plated steel, aluminum, plastic, and porcelain. Some manufacturers consider the sheets with the finest-sized cutting holes *graters,* the medium ones *shredders,* and the largest ones *slicers,* but these are not consistently used terms. A *safety grater* is slightly different, being a large, rectangular, very open stainless steel wire mesh with a short handle.

BOX GRATER

LEMON/ORANGE GRATER

GINGER GRATER

TYPES: *Box grater* (Also Known As *4-sided grater* or *grater and shredder*): Slightly tapered, 4-sided pyramid (6-sided models are found, too) with an open bottom and a handle on top. In the most common model, each of the four vertical sides has different sizes of cutting holes; the smallest create crumbs, the medium-sided holes create longer pieces, or shred food, and the large ones create small slices. One model, a *measuring grater,* is made with a sliding plastic bottom and clear plastic side with measurements etched in; another version comes with three different cutting sheets that each fit on a plastic box that catches the grated food, and another version of this combines all three types of cutting holes in one round plastic sheet that fits over a bowl. A modified and common version is an *all-purpose* or *combination grater,* which is one flat sheet with three different types of cutting holes: small, for crumbs (or grating), large, for long pieces (or shredding), and a slot (for slicing).

Lemon/orange grater: Small, round, plastic item made with a perforated top with sharp cutting points and a fitted bottom that catches the small gratings, called zest, and the flavorful oils. A small, flat, metal mini-shredder with a very fine cutting surface may be called a *lemon grater,* and may be slightly convex. Note that a lemon grater can be used on all citrus fruit skins, of course.

Mini shredder (Also Known As *cheese grater, hand grater,* or *mini-grater*): One flat or curved metal piece with a small handle on one end and one size of cutting holes. Handle may be a large loop or a straight grip. Some models have a self-cleaning feature in the form of a flap the same size as the shredding surface that lifts up after use, bringing all the leftover food with it. Sometimes a smaller curved model is referred to as a *lemon shredder.*

Nutmeg grater: Usually long, tapered, and convex to the point of being a half cylinder or even a cone, with a fine rasp surface. May have a container inside for storing whole nutmegs. Also used as a *cinnamon grater,* for grating other hard spices, or for grating chocolate. Another design consists of a flat rasp area in a curved plastic casting that provides a good grip.

Ginger grater: Either a small, flat, ceramic plate with small, sharply pointed teeth for grating ginger root, daikon radishes, or citrus fruit rind, or a round stainless sheet with a rasp surface inserted in a plastic bowl to catch the

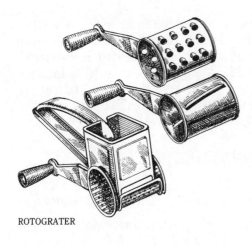

ROTOGRATER

grated ginger. The ceramic plate may be decoratively shaped and can double as a spoon or sponge rest.

Rotograter (Also Known As *drum grater, rotary grater with three cylinders,* or *salad maker*): Device with a large grip and a hopper, with a large hole on the side into which various small, cylindrical grater drums can fit. A crank handle is attached either to each drum or to the device itself. Food to be grated is inserted into the hopper. Interchangeable drums come with different-sized cutting holes, similar to the flat graters. Some are sold in sets of three, called *triple rotograters.* A model that does not accept interchangeable drums is called a *single rotograter* or a *grater mill.* Made as both a hand-held model about 7 inches long and a countertop model, which has a lever-activated suction cup on the bottom to hold it in place. An elegant version of this is used only for Parmesan cheese, and intended only for table use—sometimes called a *table grater* or a *cheese grater.* The fancier designs have only a small knob to turn, and a collar holds the cheese snug inside; a small stand may be incorporated. All are made in left-handed versions as well. Also available in a similarly designed, battery-powered model.

USE: Grating food, usually firm cheese, vegetables, spices, nuts, chocolate, or fruit peel. When you rub the food against the cutting points, the food is cut into small pieces which fall through the holes or accumulate around the cutting points in the case of the smallest holes. The size of the holes determines the width and depth of the pieces; the texture of the food determines the overall size of the cut piece. For example, one hole might cut short strips of carrots but only hunks of cheese. The smallest openings or points merely crumble the food or create a mush of softer foods. Safety graters are good for very coarse cuts of the softer foods and will not cut your fingers.

USE TIPS: Watch your fingers and knuckles to prevent cutting them, especially as the piece of food gets small. Especially when using the larger cutting blade sizes, turn the food piece often to get a more efficient cut, otherwise you'll just get deep furrows in the food where the blades can't cut anymore. Be sure to take out rotograter drums and clean thoroughly with soap and water before storing. Grate only the outside rind, not the bitter white, of citrus fruits.

BUYING TIPS: Stainless steel is preferable to tinned steel for this tool. Some models of all types are often included in sets sold either as *slicing sets* or *salad makers*. A similar item is the *electric slicer-shredder* (see page 36). Many ingenious gadgets incorporate several different types of graters, choppers, and cutters such as a *mandoline* (see page 40) in a design that may include a serving and storage bowl as well.

LEMON ZESTER

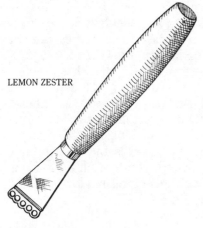

LEMON ZESTER

ALSO KNOWN AS: Citrus zester, zester, citrus-peel shredder

DESCRIPTION: Short-handled tool with a short, wide, stainless steel blade that has five small sharp-edged holes at the end. Available in a combined model with a *lemon stripper* (see page 345), called a *canelle knife, zester/stripper,* or a *zest and strip,* with a hole in the middle and a raised cutting edge on one side. Certain designs of *graters* (see previous entry) qualify as zesters, such as a round plastic *lemon/orange grater.*

USE: Grating off very thin strips of lemon, lime, or orange skin for use in recipes that require a delicate addition of flavor. Gentle removal of only the outer layer avoids the bitter taste of the pith.

USE TIPS: May cause some citrus oil to drip, so be sure to catch it for use along with the zest.

BUYING TIPS: Do not confuse with a *lemon stripper* (see page 345), with which this is often combined.

SPAETZLE MAKER

SPAETZLE MAKER

DESCRIPTION: A very specialized machine, this flat, rectangular, stainless steel and plastic shredder has a box that slides up and down over the cutting surface. The box holds the batter, small pieces of which are shredded off through the bottom. Also made in a rotary model that resembles a *food mill* (see next entry). Spaetzle, a Germanic noodle dish, are sometimes called dumplings.

USE: Making spaetzle by dropping small bits of batter into boiling water.

BUYING TIPS: A *sieve* (see page 113) or *colander* (see page 107) with large holes substitute nicely for this specialized item.

Mills

About Mills

Mills generally combine a crank or motor and a blade of some sort, and yield a finer product than graters. They are also used on the smaller, harder foods. Many are made with fine materials and workmanship.

FOOD MILL

FOOD MILL

ALSO KNOWN AS: Roto-mill

DESCRIPTION: Large, open, conical, plastic, stainless or tinned steel (or tinned steel combined with plastic), mechanical *sieve* with a large handle on the side and a horizontal hand crank on top. The narrow bottom contains a perforated plate or interchangeable plates and a paddle-shaped blade that pushes against it. The blade is moved by cranking the handle on top. Capacity is commonly between 2 and 3½ quarts. The bottom may have arms that extend out to fit over a bowl.

USE: Pureeing food, or mushing soft, usually cooked foods, like vegetables and fruits, against the plate in order to separate the meat from the skin and seeds. A grating effect may be achieved with some hard foods such as cheese with the appropriate plate.

USE TIPS: Less likely to turn delicate vegetables into mush than a *food processor* (see page 73).

BUYING TIPS: Very useful to have in any kitchen.

GRAIN MILL

DESCRIPTION: A box-shaped stainless steel and plastic electric machine, about 8 or 10 inches on a side, weighing about 8 pounds, with a high-speed grinding mechanism inside and a bin which reverses to act as a cover. A smaller, cast-iron, hand-cranked version called a *grain grinder* is also available. It has a high, narrow funnel and clamps to a countertop.

USE: Grinding any dry grain into flour, such as rice, wheat, barley, corn, or oats, generally for use in bread baking.

USE TIPS: Freshly ground grains should be kept in the freezer to keep them from going stale.

BUYING TIPS: The better machines maintain a low temperature in the gear chamber. The flavor of bread baked with freshly ground flour is definitely different from that of bread baked with store-bought flour. Really only of interest to extremely serious bread-makers.

HERB GRINDER

DESCRIPTION: Small version of a *pepper mill* (see opposite), this plastic cylinder has a clear top so you can see which herb or spice is inside. Works by twisting the top against the bottom.

USE: Grinding whole spices and herbs such as orange peel, cloves, and specially prepared, flavored peppercorns.

USE TIPS: Fresh-ground herbs and spices provide more flavor and aroma than the preground kind.

BUYING TIPS: Many herbs can be crushed in your hand just as easily.

NUT MILL

DESCRIPTION: Small hand-cranked mill, usually made of enameled cast iron with a horizontal tinned steel grater drum and a small hopper. A small plunger is used to push the nuts down against the drum. Most models clamp onto the side of a table or counter. A *nut chopper* is a very small, lightweight mill that merely breaks up nuts into small pieces. Typically made of a glass jar with a plastic funnel and crank mechanism that sits on top.

USE: Fine grinding of shelled raw or toasted nuts for baked or pastry items.

USE TIPS: This yields a more even, finer result than food processors and other alternative grinders, which also release the nut oils.

BUYING TIPS: Easy and simple to use, and essential for fine grinding.

NUTMEG MILL

NUTMEG MILL

ALSO KNOWN AS: Nutmeg grinder

DESCRIPTION: Small mill, usually of wood, a few inches high with a horizontal hand crank. A spring-loaded device holds a whole nutmeg down as it is cranked against a steel cutting blade at the bottom. Capacity may be only a few whole nutmegs.

USE: Grating nutmeg in order to obtain full aroma and flavor.

BUYING TIPS: Simpler and more efficient than a *nutmeg grater* (see page 116).

PEPPER MILL

DESCRIPTION: Cylinder, from a few inches to a few feet in length (though commonly no more than 18 inches long) and about 1½ inches in diameter, with either a small hand crank on the top or else two sections that twist in opposite directions. A steel shaft runs inside from the top to the bottom grinding mechanism, and the hollow inside is filled with peppercorns. The cylinder can be made of clear acrylic plastic, wood, stainless steel, brass, porcelain, pewter, or even rare metals. The most traditional material is dark walnut. It may be decorative or functional in design. One model even has a built-in light. Also available in a plastic, electric version, and a one-handed version that has a trigger which is squeezed to grind and release pepper. Some electric models can also grind nutmeg and other spices.

USE: Fresh grinding of pepper from peppercorns. Intended to be used directly over the plate in order to capture the maximum aroma.

USE TIPS: This item has become synonymous with fine and would-be-fine restaurants, but unfortunately, some overemphasize the need for fresh-ground pepper, and lots of it, on every dish. Never put salt in a pepper mill or it may corrode the grinding mechanism.

BUYING TIPS: Most kitchens need only one, but if you use different colored peppercorns, several mills are useful and can be color coded. Be sure to get a good-quality model that is adjustable as to coarseness (and that holds this setting) and is easily filled, with a superhardened or stainless steel grinding mechanism. The grinding mechanism is the heart of the machine. Good gift item, and a good item for all cooks to have.

Cooking Items

Holding, Turning, and Cooking Hand Utensils

About Holding, Turning, and Cooking Hand Utensils

One-piece construction of large spoons, forks, and ladles, usually found in better stainless steel models but also in plastic and wood, means less chance of breakage or bending and no places for food debris to hide or bacteria to grow. Most come with a hole in the handle for hanging up, but some have a bent end that forms a hook, convenient for hanging from any rack. Many are sold in sets.

Note that many manufacturers give a name to an item that suggests a specific use, such as *pancake turner* or *corn tong,* but that quite often those items can be used for any general handling job. In fact, in some cases the same items are placed in different packages with different names. Be sure to examine a use-specific product carefully before buying it in order to see if it is substantially different from the general-use model.

There is a wide range of sizes, weights, and designs of small utensils, so feel free to have plenty on hand. You'll find that using the right tool for the job makes cooking much easier.

ABOUT WOODEN HAND UTENSILS

One of the most common materials used for spoons and other hand utensils is plain old wood. Indeed, almost every utensil is made out of wood by some enterprising manufacturer.

Some chefs swear by wooden spoons and the like, and

keep trusty, worn ones in their kitchen for years. In order to help them last, do not soak them or put them in the dishwasher, as this will dry out the natural oils and allow them to absorb detergent. Clean and dry them quickly after use. Keep in mind that wood does absorb some flavors, so you may want to keep the ones that stir garlic separate from the ones used on, say, batters. Do not use wooden utensils on raw fish, poultry, or meat— they can harbor harmful bacteria.

Wooden utensils should be made of hard, smooth wood, though don't feel obliged to get only the fancy, exotic stuff like olivewood, hornbeam, or cherry. The top-quality woods are identifiable by their hard, silky smooth surface and visible dark grain. Maple, birch, or beech is fine (most utensils made of these woods come from Europe), even though they are light-colored with little grain visible. Avoid any wood which is soft enough to be dented by your fingernail, has a rough surface, or that has an odor. Soft pine is commonly used in the least expensive tools, but the price difference is only slight. Wood should be properly dried before being packaged or shaped, and low-quality wood utensils are often packaged while still moist, creating an odor.

Good-quality wooden utensils should last for generations. They do not scratch delicate nonstick surfaces, and they don't melt if they touch the edge of a hot pan, though the handle can get burned if left leaning over the edge for some time.

ABOUT PLASTIC HAND UTENSILS

There is plastic, and then there is plastic. We say this because there is stuff that is oven-safe to 500°F, though it may be labeled as safe only to 400°F as a margin of safety for the manufacturer. The latest material can be bent or used at high heat without damage, and won't damage your most delicate pans. Some have design features not found on their metal counterparts, such as a jagged inside edge on a fork for better holding power, or a texture for easier handling. They don't break and are easy to clean. These are labeled as high-temperature–resistant plastic, actually an engineering resin developed for industrial use, which is hard and smooth and can be used in both conventional and microwave ovens.

Some softer plastics, like nylon, are porous and absorb food colors and odors. Look for stain and grease-resistant plastic that will not do this. Most should be heat resistant, safe for nonstick surfaces, and dishwasher and microwave safe. Materials that usually meet these criteria include the harder, smoother plastics. Check the labels for detailed information, including a rare "FDA Approved" note.

Nylon is soft, will not scratch delicate nonstick surfaces, and is relatively inexpensive. But it has a low melting point—it will melt or distort if left touching a hot pan, and it tends to absorb colors and odors. It outsells all other plastics because it is the best known of the plastics, it is more pliable, and it is inexpensive.

Melamine is more heat-resistant than nylon, though it is more brittle and not microwave-safe. It can scratch delicate nonstick surfaces, and is more expensive than nylon.

Forks, Spoons, Ladles, and Tongs

About Forks, Spoons, Ladles, and Tongs

Keep all your most frequently used utensils in a large utensil holder or pitcher on your countertop so that they are always at hand.

COOKING CHOPSTICKS

DESCRIPTION: Extra long and thick bamboo sticks, slightly tapered at one end and generally with a small string loop at the blunt end. Typically 14 inches long.

USE: Manipulating food while cooking in a *wok* (see page 155).

USE TIPS: Particularly well-suited to stirring long, stringy food such as noodles or bean sprouts. Being made of wood, they do not conduct heat, an appreciable attribute for those of us who insist on tasting directly from the cooking pot.

BUYING TIPS: Their extra length makes these safer to use in a hot wok but too large to use at the table. Inexpensive and handy.

GRANNY FORK

KITCHEN SPOON

GRANNY FORK

ALSO KNOWN AS: Cook's fork, cooking fork

DESCRIPTION: Three-pronged fork about 6 inches long, with stainless steel tines that curve slightly outward. Usually has a wooden handle.

USE: General utility fork for turning and holding small food items. Can also be used as a large table fork.

BUYING TIPS: Can become a personal favorite in the kitchen.

KITCHEN SPOON

ALSO KNOWN AS: Basting spoon, cook's spoon, cooking spoon, deep spoon, mixing spoon, chef's spoon, basting and serving spoon

DESCRIPTION: Large, solid spoon, usually oval but also round and sometimes with a squared-off tip. Available in nylon, aluminum, stainless steel, and wood, and in a range of sizes averaging from 9 inches to as much as 18 inches long (the longer sizes usually have very thick handles). Although terms vary in their usage and accuracy, *kitchen spoon* often refers to a larger spoon and *mixing spoon* refers to a flatter model. Stainless steel *basting spoons* generally have the largest capacity. Wooden models are made in slightly varying shapes such as oval, round, square- or blunt-ended, and one with a straight edge and an offset point, called a *corner blending spoon,* for more efficient scraping of pots, and can be found made in common soft pine as well as better woods such as boxwood, olive, beech, cherry, and hard maple. Some of the fancier models have extra thick, comfortably designed handles. One has a *rack jack* configuration on the end—a hook and a V-slot for pulling or pushing oven racks in and out. A *chocolate spoon* is a long, shallow, varnished version usually with a decorative handle. A *stew spoon* is short, thick, and flat.

USE: Mixing liquid recipes as they cook, basting roasting meat as it cooks, and removing food from cooking utensils. Nylon is recommended for nonstick cookware, and wood for tin-lined copper, enameled cast-iron, and other delicate surfaces.

USE TIPS: Most cooks have a favorite spoon that is in constant use. However, some wooden spoons absorb strong flavors such as garlic, and you should not use a tool that smells of one strong flavor to cook delicately flavored ingredients. Do not put wooden spoons in a dishwasher. Never use a wooden spoon on raw poultry, fish, or meat—it can harbor bacteria.

BUYING TIPS: Look for a hook or hole in the handle so you can hang your spoon when not in use. Buy a range of sizes for simplicity in use, as spoons are used for cooking almost everything. Beechwood is usually the best material for wooden spoons. Straight-edge, blunt-tipped models are most useful and efficient.

LADLE

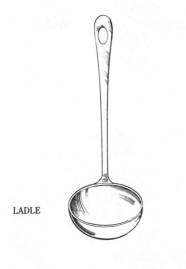

LADLE

SAUCE LADLE

ALSO KNOWN AS: Cook's ladle, soup ladle

DESCRIPTION: Long-handled utensil with large, hemispherical, cuplike end at a right angle to the handle. Usually about a foot long, though some special models have much longer handles, and a miniature size is commonly found. Available in various capacities ranging from 1 to 16 ounces. Made of nylon, plastic, cast aluminum, wood, and tinned as well as stainless steel. Nylon models come in various colors such as white, slate, and mauve; acrylic is available clear, for serving punch. One comes with its own stand for countertop use. Various specialized designs are sold, as noted here.

TYPES: *Chinese ladle:* Wide and shallow, designed for wok cooking.
    Pierced ladle: Holes in the bottom for drainage.
    Sauce ladle (Also Known As *sprinkling spoon, pouring ladle,* or *gravy ladle*): Spouts on one or both ends, or just a smaller ladle, about a 1½-ounce capacity. A small model is called a *sauce spoon.*
    Soup ladle: Quintessential model, deep cup, at least a 3-ounce and as much as a 16-ounce capacity.

USE: Removing or serving large quantities of liquid, such as soups, from the cooking pot. The pierced model is used to remove large quantities of food from cooking liquid. Smaller models are helpful for degreasing sauces.

USE TIPS: Certain batters are best used with a ladle, such as crepes, which are often made with 2 ounces of batter.

BUYING TIPS: Make sure the handle has a hook or hole for hanging. You may find that a really large-capacity ladle is of more use than you would expect if you serve soups often. Get ladles of particular capacities for your recipes, such as a small one for cooking crepes or a large one for serving soup. Usually it is helpful to have a small range of sizes at hand.

POT FORK

POT FORK

ALSO KNOWN AS: Utility fork, cook's fork, chef's fork, meat fork, fork

DESCRIPTION: Generally a relatively wide, two-pronged fork made of nylon, aluminum, or stainless steel, about a foot long, with a wooden or plastic handle. Nylon models are available in assorted colors. The tines are usually slightly curved. Wooden forks with three or four tines are also available. Extremely long forks (22½ inches) are called *broiler forks,* and the longest are *barbecue forks* (see page 275).

USE: Removing large pieces of food, such as a whole chicken, from a cooking vessel, such as a pot (hence the name). Also used for steadying food held on a turner or being handled in any other way.

USE TIPS: Sometimes used to hold meat while carving, but a carving fork with straight tines is better suited to this purpose.

BUYING TIPS: One per kitchen usually suffices.

POTATO FORK

ALSO KNOWN AS: Potato peeling fork, piercing fork, blanching fork

DESCRIPTION: Small, wooden- or plastic-handled fork with three short offset tines in an equilateral triangular pattern—not flat, as with a regular fork.

USE: Holding hot or cold potatoes (or other foods) for peeling or eating, as well as piercing them prior to baking in order to vent steam. Also used for removing pickles or olives from a jar, and called then a *pickle fork.*

BUYING TIPS: Any fork can be used for these things, but this one does them better, with its sharp points and insulated wooden handle. Often sold with a curved *paring knife* (see page 18) in a potato-peeling set.

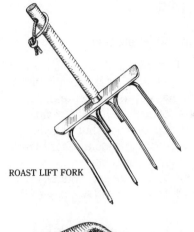

ROAST LIFT FORK

BEAR CLAWS

ROAST LIFT FORK

ALSO KNOWN AS: Meat lifting fork, oven fork

DESCRIPTION: Extraordinarily large forks with wire tines about 4 inches long. From 5 to 6 inches wide overall. Some are just two tines formed from one wire, with a simple wire handle, while others have four tines and wooden handles with a flat plate at the base that keeps the roast from sliding onto the handle. Sold by the pair. May be called a *meat lifter,* which is actually the term for an extra-wide *turner* (see page 140), or *roast and poultry lifter,* (see page 140), which is the term for a chainlike device. A similar but unusual item is a pair of thick plastic *claw*-shaped tools.

USE: Lifting large, heavy roasts or poultry out of roasting pans or off of barbecue grills. Used two at a time. Claws are used also for shredding cooked meat and serving pasta.

USE TIPS: Always use two forks at once or the roast might fall, being too heavy to handle with one fork. Can also be used to hold the roast for carving.

BUYING TIPS: Inexpensive, handy item.

SALAD FINGERS

ALSO KNOWN AS: Salad and pasta servers

DESCRIPTION: Short, thick beechwood dowel with four thinner, longer dowels embedded in the side. 4 inches wide by 6½ inches long. Sold in pairs.

USE: Mixing, blending, and serving salad, pasta, popcorn, stuffing, or other light foods.

BUYING TIPS: Very handy, easy to use item.

SCOOP

SCOOP

ALSO KNOWN AS: All-purpose scoop, canister scoop

DESCRIPTION: Comes in a variety of shapes and sizes, but most often it is one unit made of plastic or light cast metal, with a handle attached to an open rectangular cup or spoon end that is narrow at the open end and widens toward the handle. Capacity may be marked, usually around a cup or two, but this is not intended to be used for accurate measuring; graduated sizes may be denominated from 0 to 4 and then by dimensions in inches. Large ones are up to 7 inches long by 2⅜ inches wide. A *food scoop* is just another name for an *ice-cream scoop* (see page 266) intended for use with any food.

USE: Lifting small, loose material such as flour or rice from one large container into another, often smaller, container or cooking utensil.

USE TIPS: Good to keep one in each canister (flour, sugar, rice, cereal, etc.) so you don't have to hunt one up each time you need that ingredient.

BUYING TIPS: Different sizes make it possible to get one that fits each canister or food type, so measure your canisters before buying scoops to make sure they'll close tightly with the scoop stored inside. Smaller ones are commonly sold in sets of three or four.

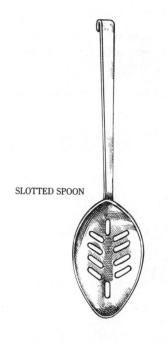

SLOTTED SPOON

SLOTTED SPOON

ALSO KNOWN AS: Cook's spoon, strainer spoon, pierced spoon, skimming spoon, draining spoon, perforated spoon

DESCRIPTION: Large, long-handled spoon between 9 and 15 inches long, with slots or holes in the cup part, generally made of nylon or aluminum but also available in stainless steel and wood. Nylon spoons are available in assorted colors.

USE: Removing foods from cooking liquid, or straining a pot of food by holding it at the lip of the pot as you pour out the liquid. Nylon spoons are best for nonstick cookware.

BUYING TIPS: Look for spoons with a hook or a hole in the handle for hanging on your tool rack, and for a comfortable grip. Important, handy item.

SPAGHETTI FORK

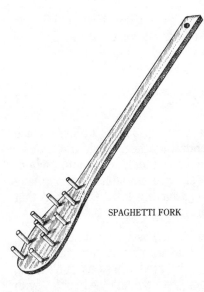

SPAGHETTI FORK

ALSO KNOWN AS: Spaghetti rake, spaghetti claw, pasta fork, pasta lift, pasta and egg lift, pasta server

DESCRIPTION: Long-handled, slotted, spoonlike utensil with crenulated or spiked edge, made of nylon, wood, or stainless steel. Plastic models are available in various colors. Some apply the name *spaghetti rake* only to the wooden model, which looks more like a leaf rake, being flat with tines at a right angle.

USE: Handling or serving spaghetti or other pasta, and in the case of the cupped version, lifting eggs out of boiling water (see page 136 for the *egg lift*).

USE TIPS: Wet spaghetti may slip off this—be careful.

BUYING TIPS: Some people find the *spaghetti tongs* (see page 135) easier to use and more versatile.

SPURDLE

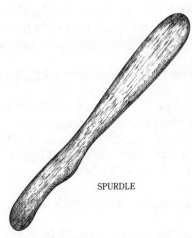

SPURDLE

DESCRIPTION: Flat, long, wooden tool about a foot long with rounded ends and a smooth surface that tapers to a thin edge all around. The edges are curved a bit in and out. American folk-art item; not mass-produced.

USE: Stirring, scraping, tasting, and turning food. Flat shape allows for easy removal of food from it after use.

USE TIPS: Wash and dry after use to keep from cracking.

BUYING TIPS: Hard to find—not widely distributed. Often found at craft fairs or in gift shops.

TASTING SPOON

TASTING SPOON

DESCRIPTION: Small, shallow, porcelain spoon with a longish handle. Also made of wood with two cupped ends, one larger than the other. The handle is hollowed out so that the hot liquid cools down as it flows from the large spoon end to the small one.

USE: Tasting food as it is cooking. Porcelain is a neutral material which does not absorb heat or affect the taste of foods in any way.

USE TIPS: Porcelain is delicate. Handle with care.

BUYING TIPS: A *Chinese soup spoon* (see page 358) substitutes nicely, but has a short handle. Wood is a poor choice of material for this tool as it can absorb flavors.

TONGS

DESCRIPTION: Long, V-shaped or giant scissorlike utensil, which when squeezed brings the two ends together. Made of chrome-plated steel (wire or band), stainless steel, aluminum, wood, bamboo, nylon, and plastic. Steel wire versions usually have vinyl-coated handles. *Locking tongs* have a little steel loop that locks larger tongs closed for storage.

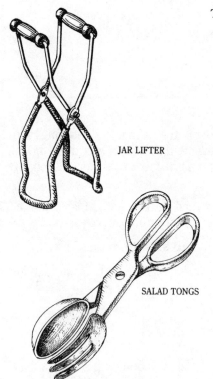

JAR LIFTER

SALAD TONGS

TYPES: *Ice tongs* (Also Known As *kitchen tongs*): Stamped out of sheets of stainless steel, these are the plainest models, in the professional version. Decorative versions of all kinds can be found, too. Either one-piece, V-shaped, with slightly curved gripping ends that have large jagged teeth, called *pan tongs,* or two-piece construction, *spring-action tongs,* with a small spring in the joint. Gripping ends may have a 3-inch-long scalloped rather than jagged-tooth pattern.

Jar lifter (Also Known As *canning jar lifter*): Parallel sets of wire forming extra-wide scissorlike tongs, the ends of which are plastic-coated and curved for holding onto hot, wet jars such as used in canning preserves.

Microwave tongs: Plastic tongs, usually of a sort of flat design with large, solid gripping ends. Plastic can be left in the microwave, though it is unclear just why you would want to do this.

Bread tongs: Similar to *utility tongs,* with larger, cupped, round tips.

Salad tongs (Also Known As *salad servers, salad scissors,* or *spoon and fork tongs*): Wide, plastic, scissorlike tongs, with a fork and a spoon for gripping ends. Usually relatively short.

Snail tongs (Also Known As *escargot tongs*): Hand-sized tool, usually made from one stainless steel wire with a coil at one end to spring-load the business end, which consists of two small, shallow, roughly oval bowls. Their form is perfect for holding snail shells firmly so you can extract the meat.

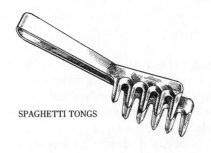

SPAGHETTI TONGS

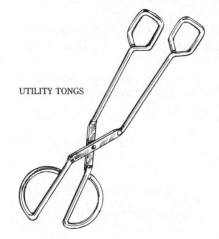

UTILITY TONGS

Spaghetti tongs: Relatively short metal tongs made from one piece of stamped stainless steel, bent in a V shape, with large tines on the business ends that face to the side.

Steamer tongs: Large, rectangular, wire and plastic tool, spring-hinged at one end. Being a few inches wide allows it to grip underneath bamboo steamers used in woks, as well as jars used in home canning.

Toaster tongs: Small hardwood or bamboo tongs with a squared off, solid jointed end and two parallel, straight legs with no gripping ends. A small magnet is glued to the back for convenient storage on the toaster. Made of wood so as to resist the heat of toaster elements and also to prevent electrical shock in case it touches a heater element that is on—metal tongs would cause a short. 10-inch-long *bacon tongs* and *Chinese tongs* are the same thing, without a magnet.

Utility tongs (Also Known As *serving tongs, corn tongs, cook's tongs,* or *scissor tongs*): Standard design for large scissorlike tongs with large finger grips and inch-square, slightly curved loops on the gripping end. Typically 10 or 12 inches long. Also available in an offset version, called *angle tongs.* Because of the curved gripping ends these are equally suitable for ears of corn and for baby bottles. Usually made of chrome-plated or stainless steel wire.

USE: Picking things up that would be too difficult to pick up with any other implement or even your hand because the item is too hot, cold, slippery, or messy. Useful for turning food on the grill and serving ice or salad as well as handling raw or breaded fish or poultry.

USE TIPS: Using tongs instead of a fork or hands avoids piercing juicy meats and saves washing your hands, too.

BUYING TIPS: It is good to have a range of sizes and types in every household. Pan and spring-action tongs are the most useful. Great gift item.

Lifters, Turners, and Spatulas

About Lifters, Turners, and Spatulas

Most people confuse the terms *turner* and *spatula*. Turners usually have a handle at an angle, while spatulas are usually entirely flat (more detailed differences are found in the text, below). Look for solidly made models that are securely riveted or molded. If you use a lot of delicate nonstick cookware, you will need plastic or wooden utensils. For most cooking, turners and spatulas can be used interchangeably. The choice is largely one of personal preference (there are trends from one country to the next, it seems); so is the choice between flexible or stiff.

Every cook needs a few good, favorite turners and spatulas. Be sure to get a small selection of these generally inexpensive items.

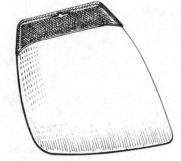

CAKE AND PIZZA LIFTER

CAKE AND PIZZA LIFTER

ALSO KNOWN AS: Universal lifter, giant spatula, tart and pizza lifter

DESCRIPTION: Almost foot-square sheet of stainless steel or plastic with slightly curved edges. Plastic version is slotted. Metal version has plastic handle along one side.

USE: Lifting and moving cakes, pizzas, tarts, and other large, light, flat items.

BUYING TIPS: Very handy item.

EGG LIFT

EGG LIFT

DESCRIPTION: Long, plastic, spoon-shaped fork, with tines rising perpendicularly to the bowl. The bottom of the bowl has a hole in it for drainage.

USE: Lifting hard-boiled eggs out of hot water. Also may be used as a *spaghetti fork* (see page 133), and indeed, some manufacturers combine these two items into one.

BUYING TIPS: Consider this a spaghetti fork with a large hole in the center and get one item instead of two.

FISH LIFT

FISH LIFT

ALSO KNOWN AS: Pan spatula, cook and strain spatula

DESCRIPTION: Large, perforated, flat, stainless steel blade about 6 inches long, with one straight edge with a ¼-inch-high ridge and one curved edge that comes to a point. The handle rises at a slight angle. Another version is an extra-wide, slightly concave turner called an *asparagus and fish cradle*.

USE: Lifting fish from poachers or pans, or any large food from cooking liquid, including hamburgers.

USE TIPS: Curved edge allows for easy scraping of any food from a skillet, including heavy meat; perforations allow it to be used to drain cooking liquid from a pan or pot as a *pan drainer* (see page 111).

BUYING TIPS: Versatile tool.

MEAT LIFTER

ALSO KNOWN AS: Wide turner

DESCRIPTION: Extra-wide-bladed *turner* (see page 140), usually made of heavy gauge stainless steel with a short handle covered by plastic. Blade is about 5 inches wide and usually has a few drain holes and two grooves in the blade for strength.

USE: Lifting meat or poultry out of cooking dishes.

USE TIPS: A fork should still be used to steady the meat on the lifter, or it may slip off.

BUYING TIPS: Handy item to have.

POT AND PAN SCRAPER

ALSO KNOWN AS: Scraper, bowl and surface scraper

DESCRIPTION: Stiff nylon in various shapes, including a square, about 2 by 2 inches, with rounded corners and feathered edges, and no handle. Some are curved like an artist's palette, to fit all sizes of bowls, and others have one curved side and one straight side.

USE: Scraping and scooping food from pots and pans as well as cutting boards.

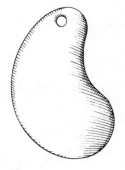

POT AND PAN SCRAPER

USE TIPS: The lack of handle gives you better control and concentrated scraping action.

BUYING TIPS: Inexpensive handy item. Try several different shapes. May replace or supplement a *spatula, dough scraper, spreader, or flat chopper* (see index for these entries).

RICE PADDLE

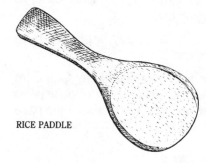

RICE PADDLE

ALSO KNOWN AS: Rice-serving spatula, bamboo spatula, rice-serving paddle

DESCRIPTION: Wide, flat, short bamboo spoon with only a slightly shallow depression for a bowl. Bamboo is the traditional material for both Chinese and Japanese manufacturers. Rounded edge is ideal for scooping rice.

USE: Serving rice from the cooking pot.

USE TIPS: Dip paddle in cold water before each scoop to prevent rice from sticking to it.

BUYING TIPS: Very functional design. Bamboo doesn't warp, shred, or suffer in the dishwasher as wood does. Inexpensive item.

SPATULA

FLEXIBLE, SLOTTED FISH SPATULA

ALSO KNOWN AS: Turner (incorrect), cook's palette knife

DESCRIPTION: A thin, flat, and flexible blade made of rubber, plastic, wood, bamboo, or stainless steel, of various shapes and sizes. Many are particularly designed for use with nonstick cookware. A *turner* (see page 140) is usually wider and stiffer, though the two terms are often confused.

TYPES: *Bamboo spatula:* 15-inch-long, flat, bamboo paddle with a very slightly cupped, shallow, spoonlike tip and a long flat handle. A *wok spatula* is an entirely different item, made of metal (see page 156).

Cookie spatula: Small stainless steel blade about 2½ inches wide and 7 inches long, with a long angled handle. Correct term is *cookie turner* (see page 141). Small size makes it easy to reach between cookies on a sheet, and the edge is thin for scraping up sticky ones.

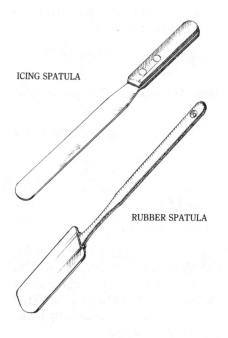

ICING SPATULA

RUBBER SPATULA

WOODEN SPATULA

Flexible, slotted fish spatula: Long, slotted stainless steel blade with sturdy wooden handle. Blade is wider and slightly curved upward at tip.

Icing spatula: Long, narrow, flexible stainless steel blade (see page 260 for more details).

Rubber spatula (Also Known As *bowl scraper, plate and bowl scraper, pot and pan scraper, cooking spatula,* or *spatula*): Squarish, tapered flat, rubber or nylon blade attached to a long narrow plastic or wooden handle, or else a one-piece design of nylon. One corner is usually squared off while the others are rounded. Common blade size is about 2 by 3 inches, though some are larger and slightly cupped (one brand calls its large, deeply cupped model a *Spoonula™*); handles range up to about a foot long. *Mini-* and *jar spatula* models have inch-wide blades, the latter having a long handle. May be sold in sets of three: narrow, long and narrow, and wide. Some plastic models with stainless steel wire handles are heat-resistant to 450°F. Especially tiny ones are called *bottle and jar spatulas.*

Wooden spatula: Any of three basic designs, such as a thick, short flattened spoon with a blunt tip; a wide, slightly curved model with a thin, straight tip; and moderately wide, flat model with a sharply beveled, angled tip.

USE: Scraping, applying, or smoothing soft food material, such as applying icing to cakes or scraping food from the insides of pots, pans, woks (the bamboo model), and bowls. Also folding (slowly mixing) batters. The cookie spatula is good for scraping cookies from a sheet or for lifting and turning crepes and tortillas on a griddle.

USE TIPS: Do not use plastic spatulas on hot cooking utensils unless you are certain that they are heat-resistant. Wooden spatulas make excellent stirrers as well. Straight-sided models are best for removing food from straight-sided food processor workbowls.

BUYING TIPS: Sometimes sold in sets of various sizes. Don't buy a set unless you need extra spatulas for baking. In that case, sets are helpful for the various sizes of bowls and wet and dry ingredients.

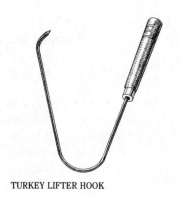

TURKEY LIFTER HOOK

TURKEY LIFTER HOOK

DESCRIPTION: Long, thick, pointed wire rod bent in half to form a V shape. Long, narrow wooden handle on one end.

USE: Lifting turkeys from roasting pans onto carving boards or platters.

USE TIPS: Remember that the bird may rotate on the hook—hold it steady with a large fork.

BUYING TIPS: Not as efficient as other tools, such as noted in the next entry.

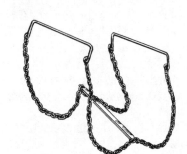

TURKEY LIFTER/ROAST LIFTER

TURKEY LIFTER/ROAST LIFTER

ALSO KNOWN AS: Poultry lifter, turkey and roast lifter

DESCRIPTION: Beltlike tool, about 1½ feet long and 4 inches wide, made of an aluminum sheet with aluminum wire handles at both ends. A lighter version is made of two small chains separated at the middle by a small aluminum bar, and attached to a handle at either end. And yet another version is made of woven poly mesh with large handles, almost 3 feet long altogether.

USE: Lifting large turkeys or roasts out of cooking vessels without piercing the skin and releasing the juices (as you would if you used a fork).

BUYING TIPS: A very good way to lift huge turkeys.

TURNER

TURNER

ALSO KNOWN AS: Spatula (incorrect), server, flipper, utility turner

DESCRIPTION: Long-handled, wide and flat-bladed hand tool, about a foot long, with handle at a slight angle ("offset") to the blade. Blade may be of various sizes from short to long and narrow to wide, which may be solid or have a pattern of holes or slots, and designed to be used for a variety of foods and purposes. Turners are often confused with the term *spatulas* (see page 138), for a tool that is flat and narrow, often like a knife, and used for working with soft foods. Made of nylon, aluminum, wood, or stainless steel, either as one piece (nylon only) or assembled via riveting or welding. May have a wooden or plastic grip. Nylon models come in assorted colors. Blades can be square, rectangular, half oval, or vaguely triangular. Manufacturers use the terms *pancake turner* or *hamburger turner* quite often to describe items that are very different, rendering these terms useless. They further confuse things by incorrectly labeling many *turners* as *spatulas*.

TYPES: *6-in-1 spatula:* Slotted, with a sharp edge for lifting, a spiked edge for tenderizing meats, a serrated cutting edge, and a hole that works as a bottle opener.

Cookie turner: 2 inches wide (the width of a brownie) with a very sharp front edge (or side edges) for scooping up cookies.

Crepe turner (Also Known As *Normandy style pancake turner*): 13- or 15-inch-long, 2-inch-wide, flat wooden bat with tapered edges. May be same as an *icing spatula* (see page 260). A *Breton style pancake* or *crepe turner* is much wider.

Hamburger turner: Squarish, about the size of a larger hamburger patty, with a very short handle. May be of very heavy construction.

Lasagna spatula: Large, rectangular, wide turner about the size of a serving of lasagna.

Lefse turning stick: 24-inch-long, flat, narrow, wooden stick used for turning the large, thin, Scandinavian pancake, *lefse*.

Pancake turner (Also Known As *jumbo turner*): About the size and shape of a pancake, with a long handle. Do not confuse with the flat, wooden crepe turners described above.

Slicing turner (Also Known As *slicing spatula* or *griddle scraper*): Thick and stiff blade, which is almost always solid, with beveled edges, either on the front or sides (at least the left-hand side), or both. May be quite sharp but usually not. Left-handed models, with a cutting edge on the right-hand side, are also available.

Slotted turner (Also Known As *pierced turner*): Thin and flexible or thick and rigid turner with a slotted or perforated blade. A long, slotted, flexible turner is excellent for use with fish filets. Wooden versions are often slightly curved and may have slots or holes, and have an angled front edge.

Triple turner (Also Known As *spread turner* or *spreading turner*): Three long, narrow, slotted blades on a hinge: Moving a lever on the handle causes them to fan out in order to flip something large, like an omelet.

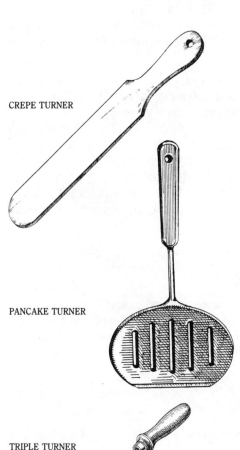

CREPE TURNER

PANCAKE TURNER

TRIPLE TURNER

USE: Serving or flipping all kinds of food when sautéing, or taking cookies off of baking sheets. Nylon turners are ideal for delicate nonstick cookware.

USE TIPS: Avoid using too narrow or short a blade on a soft piece of food that might fall apart when lifted if not entirely supported, such as a fish filet (a specialized tool called a *fish lift* [see page 137] is made for this). Some tools with wooden handles are not intended to be dishwasher-safe. Don't attempt to lift something heavy with a very long-handled turner—it is too hard to balance and you may drop the food. Do not leave plastic items in hot pans or near burners.

BUYING TIPS: Look for handles with hooks or holes in the end for hanging on tool racks. Wooden handles should be securely riveted. Check rivets attaching *tang* (see page 4) to blade for solidity. One-piece items never fall apart. Good, thick turners have sharp, beveled edges on the sides for easy lifting. Be sure to have a variety of lengths and widths in your collection, but do not feel compelled to buy a specialized model for any particular food unless you make that food all the time. See Chapter 9 for barbecue turners and other tools especially designed for barbecue use.

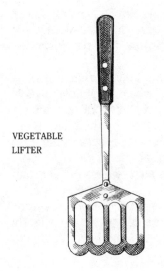

VEGETABLE LIFTER

VEGETABLE LIFTER

DESCRIPTION: Extra wide, slotted, or perforated *turner* (see previous entry), made of heavy-duty stainless steel with a short handle, often of plastic or rosewood. Some brands call their slightly concave, extra-wide version an *asparagus cradle* or *asparagus and fish cradle*.

USE: Lifting cooked vegetables or other delicate foods, such as fish, from a cooking vessel.

USE TIPS: Hold vegetables in place with a fork or they might slip off.

BUYING TIPS: Sometimes an extra-wide, round *turner* (see previous entry) can serve the same purpose.

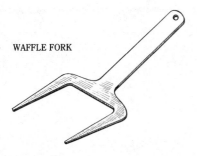

WAFFLE FORK

WAFFLE FORK

DESCRIPTION: Extra-wide, plastic, two-pronged fork.

USE: Lifting two Belgian waffles at a time from a *waffle iron* (see page 143).

USE TIPS: Be careful not to touch the hot iron with the plastic.

BUYING TIPS: Less likely to harm nonstick finish than a metal fork.

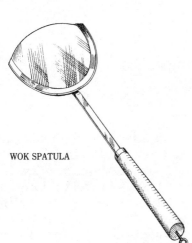

WOK SPATULA

WOK SPATULA

ALSO KNOWN AS: Wok shovel, Chinese turner, stir-fry spatula

DESCRIPTION: Flat shovel with short curved sides and a very long handle. The front edge is slightly curved to conform to the curve of a wok. Normally made out of black steel although also available in heat-resistant plastic as well as stainless steel. The handle is usually two-thirds metal ending in wood.

USE: Turning and removing stir-fried foods from a wok.

USE TIPS: Be careful not to leave the spatula in the wok with the handle hanging over the edge—it might get too hot to handle or even burn. Dry black steel carefully to prevent rust.

BUYING TIPS: Nothing else works as well when stir-frying in a wok. This is a necessary item for wok cooking and useful in other pans as well. Often included in wok sets.

Stovetop Cooking Equipment

About Stovetop Cooking Equipment

The choice of cookware is largely personal and budgetary, two considerations that are often, alas, in conflict. Many cooks feel comfortable only with what their mother used, or their cooking school teacher, or favorite TV chef, or something that looks brand-new at all times, or could be considered a work of art. Others need something that they can serve from and store food in. Most are limited by low budgets or, thankfully, we hope, by what they receive as gifts. But they should get the best they can afford.

Some cooks consider the cookware part of any recipe, and indeed that is often true. Although good cooks can use almost anything to prepare a meal, they will be restricted with inappropriate utensils. Even on a limited budget one can find decent cookware. You might just have to buy less of it if money is a consideration (indeed, most people do not need full sets), but in stovetop cooking, size and shape are not essential considerations as they are in baking, where the recipe for a cake will specify the dimensions of the cake pan to use.

Get at least *some* good equipment—it is a pleasure to use, and in any case, some good will come of using equipment that cooks particularly well. A comfortable handle and good balance are important advantages. Though you can ruin a dish in the finest cookware, to be sure, it always pays to hedge your bets. The manufacturers are falling over themselves in the competition to make the "perfect" cookware. And good cookware lasts practically forever.

In order to help you sort out similar claims, an explanation of the most common terms and points of comparison between types of cookware follows. Divided into two sections, the first covers the basic materials used either in the body or on the surface of utensils, and the second section covers the way these materials are used in various designs and types of construction.

About Pot and Pan Materials

There are two holy grails of cookware manufacture.

One is a base material that conducts heat well, heats up evenly and quickly, looks great, cleans easily, is lightweight, doesn't dent, rust, or react with any foods, needs little maintenance, and doesn't cost much.

The other is perfect nonstick surface that doesn't chip, crack, or peel, resists high heat, doesn't cost much, and that can be put on a good heat-conducting base.

No one material meets all these criteria. Some meet more than others, and some combinations meet almost all, but the problem ultimately is a personal criteria: budget, style of cooking, and aesthetics.

BASE MATERIALS, COATINGS, AND FINISHES

Cookware is made from six basic materials: Copper, aluminum, glass, stainless steel, cast iron, or plain steel, all of which are used both plain and with some kind of coating or finish.

Copper may be the ultimate cookware material and is generally considered the benchmark against which all others are measured. This is primarily because it conducts heat so well, is greatly sensitive to temperature changes, and is beautiful when polished, but it is extraordinarily expensive, heavy, and still very delicate. Hammered copper is a little stronger, and prettier, than plain. Copper reacts with certain foods in a toxic manner, so it is lined with tin (most common), nickel, or stainless steel (some copper utensils are lined with the best conductor of all, silver, but most of us can't even begin to consider purchasing those). The best tin-lining is done by hand and leaves thick brush strokes visible. Copper is difficult to keep clean; it tarnishes quickly, so it must be kept polished. Tin-lined pans must not be used at high heat and must be relined often if used in a regular manner, due to wear. They must not be scoured, nor should metal utensils be used in them. The heaviest, professional pans have iron handles, while the domestic variety has brass handles. Only the most serious, traditional, and richest chefs can handle a whole set of copper pots and pans.

Aluminum (actually aluminum alloy) is inexpensive, a quick and even heat conductor (almost as good as copper), and easy to maintain. Thick aluminum alloy is very dent-resistant and popular in commercial kitchens due to this, plus its relative lightness and low cost. Thicker is better both in terms of heat conduction and durability. The surface of some heavyweight aluminum utensils are hammered for extra strength. But plain, soft aluminum reacts badly with certain minerals and foods, turning the pan black. To solve this problem, some high-quality aluminum cookware is electronically altered, or *anodized,* so that the surface is sealed and becomes dark and so much harder—up to 800 times harder—that it is scratch-and-stick-resistant. Aluminum is the most common material for nonstick coated cookware. Once thick aluminum is coated or anodized, it is one of the best all-around solutions.

Glass is used for some pans, even frying pans, but it is not a good conductor of heat, though it does transfer it quickly to the food directly over the flame (it works best with dishes that are stirred constantly or have lots of liquid). It is generally good-looking and can be used in the microwave oven or freezer. Still, glass lacks most of the characteristics one looks for in cookware. Glass lids should be heavy-duty, break-resistant, heat-tempered glass with a stainless steel band around the edge to prevent chipping. One advantage to glass lids is that you can see food cooking and perhaps prevent boilovers or burning once liquids have been absorbed.

Stainless steel is strong, inert, and easy to clean, but has a major drawback: It does not conduct heat well. However, when combined with copper or aluminum cores or layers, it is terrific. The elemental makeup of stainless steel is often noted on a label. 18/10 is typical, meaning that the steel contains 18 percent chromium and 10 percent nickel. Lower quality stainless steel has lower figures.

Cast iron is famous for its excellent heat transmission, even heating, and long retention of heat, and certainly is the most durable of materials—it never warps or dents. Most cooks have a favorite cast-iron pan. It is common and relatively inexpensive, and after years of use or "seasoning" develops its own "nonstick" surface. (Seasoning involves coating the utensil with peanut or similar oil and heating it to the smoking point; it can only be wiped clean—not washed—afterward or it will need to be reseasoned.) But plain cast-iron utensils do not cook liquids well, they retain the flavors of some foods that have been cooked in them, and they react badly with others. The most common alternative is to make it with a porcelain enamel coating. **Enameled cast iron** is easier to maintain and nonreactive, but a little delicate—it can chip easily or crack if overheated while empty. It is very popular in certain designs such as skillets as it can be used equally well in the oven or on the stovetop (though it does not brown foods very well and may have some hot spots) and is generally offered in bright colors good-looking enough to use for serving at the table. Unfortunately, cast-iron utensils are too heavy for some cooks. Most are European-made.

Plain steel (Also Known As *mild steel, carbon steel, black steel, rolled steel,* or *untreated steel*) is thin and strong and an excellent heat conductor, especially for utensils used over high flames, like woks and crepe pans. It is inexpensive, but the surface easily rusts and food sticks to it easily. Most cooks treat steel by seasoning it (see above) but it is more commonly available with an enamel coating.

Enameled steel (Also Known As *porcelain enamel*) is popular in two extremes of the budget line. Expensive pans with a bright, thick coating are popular with those who put looks at the top of their priority list. Relatively inexpensive thin-coated pots are workhorses in many households and found in every store (and culture). They are light and conduct heat well. The enameled steel surface also has a slight nonstick ability, does not react to foods or absorb odors or flavors, and is easy to clean. Brightly colored enameled cookware is a good combination of beauty and function, mainly by being designed to be placed on the table for serving. The best enameled steel cookware is made with thick steel, has three coats of enamel, and has a stainless steel rim to prevent chipping.

NONSTICK SURFACE MATERIALS

While the base materials incorporate mostly familiar names like copper and steel, the nonstick surface materials or finishes used are largely high-tech and trademarked brand names. They are chemical- and heat-resistant and permit cooking with reduced amounts of fat. Some food might stick to these coatings, but they are very easy to clean. The best ones can brown food as well as a plain metal pan and are so tough that metal utensils can be carefully used in them, but most require the use of wooden or plastic turners, spatulas, spoons, forks, and other utensils to prevent scratching. The use of high heat or plunging a hot pan into cold water is discouraged by the manufacturers, but that goes for almost all cookware. Most have to be seasoned before use (see directions), and some should be preheated before food is put in them. Almost all nonstick-coated cookware is aluminum, although cast iron, stainless steel, plain carbon steel, and glass versions are found as well, though usually just on individual models and not on whole sets.

Teflon® is the best known nonstick coating, a fluorocarbon resin invented by Du Pont in 1938. It is often applied in thin layers to cookware and bakeware that does not need a lot of durability. Recently Teflon has been incorporated into more advanced and durable nonstick coatings called Teflon 2®, SilverStone®, and SilverStone SUPRA®, and is used on all cookware, bakeware, and small electrical appliances as well as in a host of industrial applications. There are two- and three-coat systems. These coatings represent the good, better, and best in terms of quality (effectiveness and durability). Other brands that are similar include T-Fal®, Super T+, Amourcoat, Xylan, and Greblon. All use the same base but have different formulations, application processes, and licensing requirements.

Cookware manufacturers are licensed to apply these coatings and state which one they are using on the packaging. The overall quality of the utensil varies somewhat with the manufacturer. They vary in their thickness (the number of layers), the method of application, and the thickness of the cookware it is used on. In general, thicker is better.

Teflon® coatings do not begin to deteriorate until the temperature of the cookware reaches about 500°F and only decompose significantly at about 660°F—long after anything cooking in them has turned into acrid smoke (a fried egg is cooked at about 374°F). If a coated utensil is burned to this temperature while empty, the fumes may cause temporary and apparently harmless flulike symptoms, especially if there is poor ventilation. Pet birds, especially small ones with a high respiration rate, are likely to suffer more dramatic consequences, however. Particles of destroyed Teflon® coatings are harmless to eat, as they are nontoxic and inert. This kind of surface does wear out over time, depending on the type of usage to which it is subjected. For all practical purposes it is not repairable.

Some of the best new nonstick aluminum pans are anodized (electronically altered) prior to receiving their coatings, in order to create a harder surface and to actually incorporate the coating into the pan. Furthermore, some top-quality products have nonstick surfaces with microscopic cavities, stainless steel mesh, or small grooves in order to retain the coating more effectively and to brown foods better. This fused style is often guaranteed for long periods—up to twenty years.

Ceramic is an uncommon alternative to this fluorocarbon coating, which is fired in at 36,000°F. It is literally diamond-hard, so you can use metal utensils on it without fear of damage. It is essentially a permanent coating. The most common brand puts this on moderately priced cast-aluminum pans and pots which are ovenproof to 500°F. This type of surface comes with a lifetime guarantee.

About Stovetop Cookware Construction

If only shopping for cookware were as simple as picking out your preferred base material and cooking surface. Far from it. Most cookware materials are found in combination with others, and with handle or lid styles which further distinguish them from one another. While this is confusing, it also allows you to choose the cookware which truly suits your cooking style and sense of aesthetics—or your budget.

MATERIAL COMBINATIONS

Much cookware is made of one basic material, but most of the better cookware is made of combinations that manage to benefit from the good qualities of each material while minimizing the shortcomings. For example, an easy-to-maintain but poor heat-conducting material is combined with a hard-to-maintain but excellent heat-conducting material in such a way that you get cookware which is easy to maintain and also conducts heat well. Most combination cookware is damaged by use over very high heat or if left on a burner while empty, though the thicker the material, the less likely it is to warp.

Unfortunately, the best combination is usually too expensive for most cooks, so manufacturers try other combinations emphasizing price over performance. Every cook should be able to find cookware with the attributes desired if they search these out.

Here are some typical material combinations. See the

prior section on materials (pages 145-47) for characteristics of each material.

Clad: Also called *cladded,* this usually refers to a moderately priced item which has a top and sides of a durable, easily cleaned and cooked-in material such as stainless steel and an outside bottom of another which has better heat conduction. Some of the least expensive, popular lines have only a thin layer of the good heat conductor (such as copper) because it is very expensive, and because it is so thin you do not benefit all that much from its conductivity. It does look good, though. The better clad cookware has a thick, high-conductivity bottom section, usually of aluminum, that goes partway up the sides.

Sandwich: Some of the finer cookware being made these days incorporates a visible flat layer of copper or aluminum in a thick, disklike bottom. If the aluminum is about ¼ inch thick or the copper is about ⅛ inch thick, it will provide excellent heat conduction; the thicker the sandwich, the less likely it is to warp. Innovative, primarily European cookware designed for use without any fat or water added usually features an extra-thick sandwich bottom and insulated sides (they also have special, airtight lids to trap moisture).

Lined: The most common use of lining is in the finest, expensive copper cookware, as noted on page 145. Traditionally it is a thin layer of tin, but silver and (rarely) nickel are also used, albeit more expensively. Tin melts at 450°F and wears out with use, and silver is too expensive, so more modern versions are lined with a layer of durable stainless steel.

HANDLE AND LID CONSTRUCTION

Cookware of any material needs handles. Some pans have insulated handles, even if made of metal, which are a great convenience. Unless you leave them over another burner, you won't burn your hand when you touch them. Look for plastic handles that are ovenproof (at least to 350°F or 400°F) if you think you will want to put the utensil in the oven as part of the stovetop cooking process. Plastic handles are generally not meant to be placed under the broiler. Metal handles are presumably oven- and broilerproof, but check the labels to be sure.

Old, fine copper cookware may have lids with long pan handles. Most handles are riveted, but those which are also screwed on have the added benefit of being replaceable if need be. On the other hand, they may need to be tightened from time to time. Make sure the rivets are solid and large. Avoid spot-welded handles. Handles with holes or rings in the end can be hung up for storage. Some of the better lines are designed with aesthetics in mind, if that matters to you. The arched angle and good length contribute to the coolness, balance, and ease of handling. Large pans should have a second, helper handle on the side opposite the main handle.

As for general design, look for flared rims which allow for dripless pouring and lids that fit tightly. Choose a set of utensils which shares some lids so you don't have to get a lid for each item. Lids that are tight-fitting and designed to cause moisture to drip back into the utensil are superior to plain, loose-fitting lids.

About the Terms for Pots and Pans

Although many specific types of pots and pans are described in detail here, manufacturers often conjure up fancy names that confuse the uses and designs. Many general-use utensils share the functions of specialized pots and pans. Your best bet when shopping is to look closely at your cooking needs, storage space, and the design of the item rather than to go by its name. Also, note whether lids are included. Often one lid will fit several items in a set, which saves on storage space but is a problem if you use all of the items at once.

Some people even confuse "pots" with "pans." The only thing that is sure is that pots have two small loop handles, while pans have one long one. Of course, there is an exception (the *paella pan,* page 169), but only one—officially, anyway.

The bottom line is to call it whatever you want, but use the right utensil for the job. The terms presented here are correct, but not what you might hear in a kitchen or store. That's where the AKAs come in handy. AKAs are not necessarily even close to being correct, common, or acceptable—but you will find them used from time to time by some manufacturers, stores, catalogs, or cooks. Don't accept any one name as gospel, but look at the dimensions and your need instead.

A French regulatory agency long ago set the only

standards that manufacturers should follow. The French system follows the relationship of diameter to height in order to determine what kind of pan or pot it is.

The French rule is, in ascending order of size (all of these items are described in detail later in this chapter):

A *skillet* is a shallow fry pan with sloping sides.

An *omelet pan* is a shallower fry pan.

A *sauté pan* is 3⅔ or almost 4 times as wide as it is high, and has a long pan handle.

A *braising pan* is 2⅔ times as wide as it is high, but is made in larger capacities than the *sauté pan* and so has two loop handles instead of a pan handle.

A *saucepan* is only twice as wide as it is high, with one long pan handle, though it is also made in a 25 to 50 percent higher version called a *high-sided saucepan.*

A *casserole dish,* more often called a *Dutch oven* or *saucepot,* is also twice as wide as it is high, but is made in larger capacities, and so has two loop handles to carry the additional weight. It is generally made so it can go into the oven as well as on top of the stove.

A *deep saucepot* is 1½ times as wide as it is high.

A *stockpot* is as wide as it is high, even though it always looks tall and narrow. This gives it twice the capacity of a *saucepot* with the same diameter.

Standard Fry and Sauté Pans

About Standard Fry and Sauté Pans

Though you can fry or sauté in any kind of pan, these different designs allow you to cook with different styles or make different sauces. Even though they are considered standard, it is not unusual to have some or all of them in a well-equipped kitchen. Look for handles that are designed to stay cool. Keep the number of people you usually cook for in mind and select pans of an appropriate size. And as usual, thicker is better.

RONDEAU

ALSO KNOWN AS: Braising pan (incorrect), brazier, braisière, sauteuse (incorrect), sautoir, saucier (incorrect), low casserole, casserole

DESCRIPTION: Pot version of the *sauté pan* (see next entry) in larger proportions, this is a large, flat, round, medium deep pot with two loop handles—often called a *double-handled sauteuse (plat à sauter à anses)*. Ranges in size from 8 to 16 inches (usually one foot) in diameter but no more than 4½ inches high and up to 18½-quart capacity. By definition, it's about 3⅔ or 4 times as wide as it is high. Generally offered by the better manufacturers only, in a fairly heavy construction overall and usually with a reinforced bottom.

USE: Browning, braising, and poaching in relatively large quantities or of large pieces of meat, both on the stovetop and in the oven.

BUYING TIPS: This is not a widely distributed item, but is very popular with professionals and generally offered by the more serious distributors.

SAUTE PAN WITH LID

SAUTE PAN

ALSO KNOWN AS: Sauteuse (Fr.), deep frying pan, open fry pan, poêle à frire (Fr.) (incorrect), straight-sided saucepan, plat à sauter (à queue) (Fr.), sautoir (Fr.)

DESCRIPTION: A straight-sided, relatively deep and heavy frying pan that ranges from 8 to 14 inches in diameter, and made in the usual range of materials for pans: aluminum, treated aluminum (anodized or nonstick surfaced), lined stainless steel–aluminum, plain stainless steel, tin-lined copper, enameled steel, or cast iron. Sides are 2½ to 4½ inches high and capacity is about 2½ or 3 quarts but can be found in up to 7-quart capacities. Not more than four times as wide as it is high. Should be of thick construction; heaviest models may have a small loop *helper handle* opposite the main handle. Lid may or may not be supplied but may be shared with other items in a set. Though no two sources agree, a deeper version is more often supplied with a lid and is often called a *sautoir* or *plat à sauter* in French.

Americans sometimes call this a *skillet* (see next entry), which is similar but has lower, curved sides. Not too different from the smaller, heavy *low saucepan,* which has about an 8-inch diameter and a 1½-quart capacity, and is generally 3 inches deep.

USE: Frying (sautéing) food in fat, liquid, and/or sauces (hence the high sides). Also for stir-frying, browning vegetables, quick stewing, and poaching.

USE TIPS: Because this is a pan, food in it can be stirred by shaking it while holding the long pan handle.

BUYING TIPS: Larger models need a second small "helper" handle opposite the main handle or else they will be too hard to lift. Be sure to get the heaviest and largest model possible, and the best quality you can afford. Popular with serious cooks.

SKILLET

SKILLET

ALSO KNOWN AS: Frying pan, fry pan, frypan, chef pan, poêle (Fr.)

DESCRIPTION: Very common item available in a wide range of materials, sizes, designs, and quality. Round, with sides that are usually slightly curved or angled out, and somewhat low (Americans sometimes call a skillet a *sauté pan* [see previous entry], which is similar but actually has higher, straight sides). Typically made of cast iron (plain black or enameled), anodized and non-stick coated aluminum, stainless steel, cast aluminum, or tin-lined copper, and at least one company makes a glass one, coated with a nonstick surface. Ranges in size from 5 to over 12 inches in diameter, and one manufacturer makes a "jumbo" 20-inch model. Cast-iron skillets are available in 5-inch and 9-inch square designs for cooking efficiency. *Fish fry pans* are oval or rectangular.

The largest models may have a small loop *helper handle* opposite the main handle, and in that case may be called a *Dutch skillet*. A cast-iron model with ridges across its bottom designed for use in the broiler is the *ribbed skillet* or *grill pan* (see page 187). Also available in a self-standing electric version, usually square. And one manufacturer offers a pressure-cooker version, called a *pressure fry pan*, with a special, reinforced lid that locks on for combination pressure cooking and sautéing.

USE: Basic frying of almost all foods over heat with a small quantity of fat.

USE TIPS: Be sure to follow the use and cleaning tips that pertain to the particular material your pan is made of. Choose a pan size that fits the amount of food you usually cook.

BUYING TIPS: A solid, thick bottom prevents scorching, but otherwise it is the feel of the pan—its overall weight and handle—that is most important. Look for a thick pan that transmits heat evenly, no matter what material it is. A variety of sizes is helpful, like small, medium, and large—6 or 8, 10, and 12 inches. Nonstick models are extremely practical, but get only a good-quality one. Metal handles should be designed not to transmit heat. Skillets with metal handles can be placed in the oven or broiler for finishing off certain recipes. Brand names are a good indication of quality. It is not a bad idea to have some shallow, lightweight aluminum skillets along with some heavy cast-iron ones for use over high heat. Restaurants buy lighter-weight models by the case—they don't last long when used constantly at high heat.

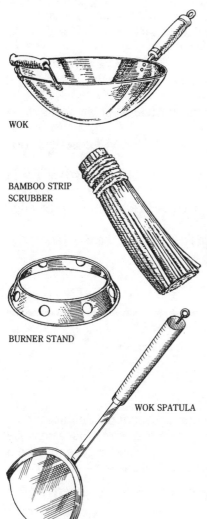

WOK

BAMBOO STRIP SCRUBBER

BURNER STAND

WOK SPATULA

WOK

ALSO KNOWN AS: Chinese wok

DESCRIPTION: Large, wide, bowl-shaped pan. The average diameter for home use is about 12 to 14 inches, with a depth of about 3½ inches. Diameters up to several feet (yes, feet!) are available for professionals or large families. Most have two small wooden or wire U-shaped loop handles on the sides, but some have one straight plastic or wooden handle sticking out to the side. Only a small section of the bottom may be flat. Some manufacturers make a slightly Westernized version with steep sides and more of a flat surface, combining aspects of the wok with a large sauté pan, and may call this a *stir-fry pan;* others call all woks by this name. May be plain or nonstick-coated carbon steel, enameled steel, anodized aluminum, or stainless steel, both plain and copper-clad—and even cast iron (made with a flat bottom). Traditional carbon steel woks are slightly thicker on the very bottom and quite heavy. Also available in a self-standing electric version (see page 289).

USE: Fast, hot stovetop cooking—oriental "stir-fry" style in particular. Woks are well-suited to stir-frying and deep frying but also are suitable for use with the cover on for braising and steaming.

USE TIPS: Plain steel woks absolutely must be well-seasoned (see page 146), as must some nonstick types. Do not scrub clean after seasoning. Woks can replace most other pans due to their unique shape. When cooking in a rough-textured, hand-hammered wok, you can push food up the sides and let it sit to remove it from the hot bottom temporarily.

BUYING TIPS: Most any cook can benefit from having a wok for cooking whole meals quickly. Woks are often supplied with many accessories that may be sold as part of a wok set, but all are available separately too. The basic ones are noted here.

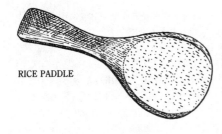

RICE PADDLE

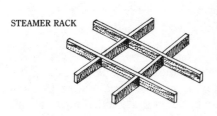

STEAMER RACK

TEMPURA RACK

Bamboo strip scrubber: Short cylindrical brush made of either fine or thick strips of bamboo, for cleaning food particles out of a wok.

Burner stand (Also Known As *wok ring, burner ring,* or *fire ring*): Light metal, slightly cone-shaped ring made from a band about 2 inches wide, containing large holes, with an opening about 7 inches in diameter it fits around your burner and supports the wok over the flame at just the right height. Common, essential item.

Wok spatula (Also Known As *cooking and serving spatula*): Flat blade at an angle to a long handle. Blade is sort of triangular. Flat outside edge is rounded to fit shape of wok and other edges have a slight lip (see page 143).

Cooking and serving chopsticks: 14-inch-long, heavy-duty chopsticks, often with a small string loop at the back end (see page 127).

Cover: Dome-shaped, aluminum, for use when steaming or to keep spatter down to a minimum.

Rice paddle: Short, wide, flat bamboo spoon for serving rice (see page 138).

Steamer rack: Circular wire rack or bamboo cross that fits in bottom of wok to suspend *bamboo steamers* (see page 166).

Tempura rack: Half circular wire rack that hooks over the edge for draining fried foods.

Wok ladle: Shallow, round ladle with long handle (see page 129).

Specialized Fry and Sauté Pans

CREPE PAN

DESCRIPTION: Shallow plain steel or aluminum pan, no more than 8 inches and as small as 5 inches in diameter. Sides may be slightly curved or angled. A pan 4 or 5 inches across may be a *blini pan,* for making the Russian buckwheat version.

USE: Making crepes (thin French pancakes) or other, similar pancakes.

USE TIPS: Wipe with oil after making each crepe and keep the pan hot. The smaller models are for dessert crepes, the larger models for entree crepes. Keep steel pans well seasoned for best results.

BUYING TIPS: It is much easier to get good results with a high-quality, well-seasoned crepe pan than with a regular skillet. Plain steel or thick anodized aluminum and nonstick pans are good choices here. Do not confuse this with the fancy, flat *crepes suzette pan* (see below).

DANISH EBELSKIVER PAN

DANISH EBELSKIVER PAN

ALSO KNOWN AS: Danish Ableskiver pan, Aebelskiever pan, Ebleskiver pan, munk pan

DESCRIPTION: Large, flat, round or hexagonal cast-iron pan with seven moderately deep, cuplike depressions. These can be 1, 1¼, 2, or 2¼ inches in diameter.

USE: Making a Danish apple dumpling dish called ebelskiver.

BUYING TIPS: A very rarefied need. Serves as a decorative or a gift item for most people.

CREPES SUZETTE PAN

FLAMBE PAN

DESCRIPTION: 11- to 13-inch diameter round or oval shallow frying pan, usually made only in the finer materials such as polished copper or stainless steel exteriors. Long brass handles are typical. A *crepes suzette pan* is a specialized type, with extremely short, vertical sides.

USE: Dramatic, tableside flambéing of dessert dishes. Those with short, vertical sides are used for flambéing precooked crepes suzette, which do not need much depth. The low sides make it easier for the alcohol in the spirits to catch fire when the pan is moved to the side and the flame curls over the edge.

USE TIPS: Be careful—some flames can be enormous under the right conditions. Follow recipes or expert advice closely.

BUYING TIPS: You can flambé anything in any pan, but these are designed both for use with high heat and for dramatic, beautiful presentation at tableside.

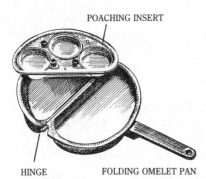

POACHING INSERT

HINGE   FOLDING OMELET PAN

FOLDING OMELET PAN

DESCRIPTION: Round or oval pan, about an inch deep, which folds in half. Usually made of a light metal, such as aluminum, and usually coated with a nonstick finish. May be sold with a three-egg poaching insert (see page 167 regarding *egg poachers*). Available in plastic for use in microwave ovens.

USE: Cooking an omelet with a filling. Cook the eggs until they are done and the filling warmed, and then fold the pan over, making a pocket for the filling.

USE TIPS: May also be used to cook two separate dishes simultaneously in one pan.

BUYING TIPS: Most cooks use a regular *omelet pan* (see next entry) and fold the omelet in half with a spatula. It's easy with a little practice.

OMELET PAN

OMELET PAN

ALSO KNOWN AS: Omelette pan

DESCRIPTION: 8- to 10-inch-diameter frying pan with gently sloping, curved sides, made out of cast aluminum, plain steel, cast iron, anodized or nonstick aluminum, or tinned copper. Usually the handle is quite long and angled. Some manufacturers put concentric ridges in the bottom for even distribution of oil or melted butter.

USE: Cooking omelets.

USE TIPS: Though omelets can be and are often made in any other kind of frying pan, this one is the easiest to use both for its shape, which enables you to fold the omelet in half or slide it onto a plate, and for its heat conduction, which helps cook the omelet evenly and quickly. Plain steel or aluminum pans should not be washed, but just wiped out with paper towels. Sticky food may be gently "scoured" away with a little salt. Reseason (see page 146) from time to time as necessary.

BUYING TIPS: An excellent gift item. Three-egg omelets are best cooked in an 8- or 9-inch pan with a 6-inch-wide flat bottom. Nonstick pans are easier for beginners to use, and in many cases are preferred by the top pros as well.

PLETT PAN

ALSO KNOWN AS: Swedish plett pan, platte pan

DESCRIPTION: Flat, cast-iron pan with seven 2½- or 3-inch-diameter shallow, straight-sided depressions. There is a pouring spout on the side.

USE: Making evenly sized Swedish pancakes, or plättar. Also good for making blini, Russian pancakes.

USE TIPS: Commonly served as a dessert item, with lingonberry preserves.

BUYING TIPS: Uncommon, usually decorative item.

Standard Saucepans and Pots

About Standard Saucepans and Pots

Good saucepans are a pleasure to use and low-quality pans problematic; they may easily dent, they may have hot spots, and in general be a false economy. Good ones last for generations. Get heavy, thick ones.

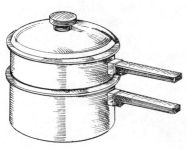

DOUBLE BOILER

DOUBLE BOILER

ALSO KNOWN AS: Bain-marie (Fr., incorrect)

DESCRIPTION: Set of two saucepans that nest one inside of the other. The lid should fit either one. Made of glass as well as all the usual metals, though the traditional design is a thin copper bottom with a thick porcelain insert, and available in a wide range of sizes. Inserts designed to fit a saucepan are available for this purpose as well. Actually, there is no item called a bain-marie, which is a cooking technique, though there is a pan designed for this purpose (see page 165).

USE: Gentle heating of delicate foods, such as butter, chocolate, milk, egg custards, and making emulsified sauces such as hollandaise and béarnaise. Water is boiled in the bottom unit and that steam heats the top unit.

USE TIPS: A bain-marie, or water bath, is made by placing a bowl or cooking vessel in a larger bowl of warm water to cook or poach delicate foods like custards or mousses or to keep food warm. A double boiler is heated by steam, not by immersion in the water. The diffused heat prevents sauces from breaking.

BUYING TIPS: Look for a set in which both saucepans can be used separately in conventional manner. If you don't need this item much, make your own by stacking two saucepans that are about the same diameter, nest a metal mixing bowl over a saucepan with boiling water, or just get a double boiler top, or insert.

DUTCH OVEN

DUTCH OVEN

ALSO KNOWN AS: Casserole (incorrect), roaster (incorrect), French oven, braising pan, brazier (incorrect), covered oven, cocotte (Fr.)

DESCRIPTION: Large, deep, heavy, uncoated or enameled cast-iron pot, usually oval but also round, with two loop handles and a tight-fitting lid. Sometimes referred to simply as an *oven,* such as a *round oven* or an *oval oven.* A common size is 8 quarts, but ovens are made from 2 to 13 quarts in the round shape and 3½ to 9½ quarts in ovals. May be supplied with a flat, perforated metal disk called a *meat rack* that sits in the bottom. Porcelain enameled cast-iron ovens are available in a wide range of bright colors. A variation made for use in campfires, with short legs, is called a *camp oven* in the East and a *legged Dutch oven* in the West. A 5-quart model with a large bail handle may be called a *jambalaya pot* in the New Orleans area. A similar, self-basting model called a *doufeu* has a concave top in which one puts cold water.

The term *Dutch oven* derives from its popularity with the Pennsylvania Dutch, who set them in the coals of an open hearth and piled more hot coals on the (then) concave top. A Dutch oven is generally larger than a casserole dish. Many manufacturers call a *saucepot* (see page 162) a Dutch oven, but this is incorrect.

USE: Slow cooking of dishes with liquid, such as beef stew, pot roast, or braised beef. The cast iron transmits heat from all sides, causing hot air to circulate within the vessel, hence the name *oven.* Generally used on top of the stove at a slow simmer but also in the oven. The meat rack suspends large pieces of meat over the bottom so that the fat drains away. The self-basting model's lid causes condensation to drip back onto the food as it cooks.

USE TIPS: Do not cook with wine in a plain cast-iron Dutch oven, as it will defeat the seasoning (see page 158) and the food will acquire an odd taste. To prevent rusting, dry it carefully and store in a dry place. Do not scour enameled ovens with steel wool, and they will last virtually forever without damage.

BUYING TIPS: Enameled Dutch ovens, popular in Europe, are easier to use and maintain than plain cast-iron models. They are easy to clean and look good enough to serve from directly at the table. Make sure that the handles are heatproof and can go into the oven.

FLARE-SIDED SAUCE PAN

FLARE-SIDED SAUCEPAN

ALSO KNOWN AS: Fait-tout (Fr.), flared saucepan, splayed sauté pan, Windsor saucepan, French-styled saucepan, French sauce pan, conical sauté pan, sauteuse évasée (Fr.), slanted sauteuse

DESCRIPTION: Large, thick, heavy pan, 1½- to 2½-quart capacity, that is somewhat cone-shaped. The bottom is smaller than the top and the whole pan is more than several inches high. Normally not supplied with a cover. Made in the usual variety of materials. Same ratio of width to height as a sauté pan.

USE: Boiling down (reducing) liquids in order to make sauces.

USE TIPS: You can reduce a cooking liquid in any kind of pan or pot, but this one makes it faster by concentrating the heat under a larger surface due to the conical shape. The slanted sides make for easier stirring, too.

BUYING TIPS: Tin-lined copper is the best material for this pan, because the diffusion of heat is essential to proper reduction of a sauce without burning. This is an excellent choice for your one "good" pan.

SAUCEPAN

SAUCEPAN

ALSO KNOWN AS: Sauce pan, pot (incorrect), casserole

DESCRIPTION: Deep, straight-sided pan made from one of the usual variety of materials: copper, anodized aluminum, stainless steel, glass, ceramic, enameled steel, or enameled cast iron. May have a pouring spout. Capacity ranges from 1 pint to 5 quarts or so. A saucepan is twice as wide as it is high, except for a *high-sided saucepan*, which is 25 to 50 percent higher. Usually sold with a snug-fitting lid. The hybrid low saucepan is noted in the *sauté pan* entry (see page 153). A small saucepan with one or two pouring spouts, about 3 inches in diameter, is often called a *butter warmer*. A larger saucepan with pouring spouts may be called a *milkpan*. Ironically, some manufacturers offer the saucepan with two loop handles instead of the one long pan handle.

USE: Cooking or reheating any food that has liquid in it. The lid is essential when cooking some items that depend on the retention of moisture.

USE TIPS: Always cook with a little liquid or fat. A low saucepan is extremely versatile for cooking dishes in which meat and vegetables might be combined—a cross between a sauté pan and a regular saucepan. The butter warmer is often just a decorative addition to a set of pans but can also be used to flame alcohol. Select the size appropriate to the quantity of food you are cooking—too large a pan causes too much evaporation.

BUYING TIPS: One of the most common pans in the kitchen. Look for a model that feels comfortable to hold. A hole in the handle end for hanging is a plus. Decide if you want one with a pouring spout or not. Better brands have rims that are designed to facilitate pouring. Highly polished pans need more upkeep than others, so bear the maintenance of the material in mind when you buy. It is good to have a selection of sizes for more efficient cooking. A good saucepan will become a favorite tool.

SAUCEPOT

SAUCEPOT

ALSO KNOWN AS: Pot, oven, casserole, deep casserole, low marmite, marmite base (Fr.), marmite (Fr./Canadian), low stockpot, Dutch oven (incorrect), saucier, bassine à blanchir (Fr.), bassine à ragoût (Fr.), braisière (Fr.), stew pot, brazier, cocotte (Fr. Canadian), marmite à ragoût (Fr. Canadian), fait-tout (Fr.), everything pot. (Note that many of these names depend on the size of the pot and vary tremendously from culture to culture and brand to brand.)

DESCRIPTION: Large, wide, deep, two-handled pot, holding from 4 to 14 quarts of liquid; 7 or 8 quarts is typical. Made of the standard materials, such as enameled iron, enameled steel, plain and anodized aluminum, stainless steel, or copper. Sold with a lid. The flat, deep lid of one brand is made of the same material as the pot and because it has two loop handles on the side rather than a knob on top, it can be used as frying pan as well as a lid. Decorative styles suitable for tabletop serving are available. It's lower and wider than its deeper cousin, the *stockpot* (see next entry), with which it is often confused. It's lighter in weight than a *Dutch oven* (see page 160). Plastic versions, looking like plain storage containers, are available for use in microwave ovens, as are plastic basket inserts for steaming vegetables or pasta.

TYPES: *Casserole:* Common name for lower version.

Pasta pot (Also Known As *deep saucepot, spaghetti cooker, pasta cooker, vegetable steamer, covered steamer, blancher,* or *steamer pot set):* Higher version only 1½ times as wide as it is high. A larger saucepot (or any other deep pot, such as a *stockpot* [see next entry] in the 8 quart range may be sold with a shallow perforated metal basket insert about 2¾ to 6 inches deep, called a *steaming basket, vegetable basket,* or *steaming insert* for steaming vegetables. Some deep pots include a very deep perforated basket for making pasta, sometimes made of fine aluminum or stainless steel mesh, called a *spaghetti* or *pasta basket* or *pasta insert.* Some people call this a *blanching pot* and *blanching basket* or *insert.* One *steamer* model actually sits on, not in, the pot with the water, which has a spigot for draining. Others have two stackable, perforated-bottom steamer sections that stack on top of a solid one.

USE: Stovetop cooking, especially for simmering liquid recipes like soup, beans, stews, and cooking pasta, and, with the appropriate inserts, steaming large quantities of vegetables or shellfish. Inserts allow for quick removal and draining of vegetables and pasta.

USE TIPS: In heavier models the food does not need to be stirred as frequently because the heat is more evenly diffused. When steaming vegetables, boil the water gently and make it sure it does not boil away or touch the vegetables.

BUYING TIPS: 4 to 8 quarts is the most common and useful capacity range, with the 8-quart size lending itself well to steaming or boiling large quantities of vegetables or pasta. Look for comfortable handles on both the lid as well as on the sides. Thick, heavy models cook the most evenly (hence the name *saucier*—even cooking is necessary for slow-cooking sauces). Some pots are sold with a low, perforated platform called a *trivet steamer* that sits in the bottom and allows for steaming large items, such as puddings. Everyone needs a good, big pot.

STOCKPOT

STOCKPOT

ALSO KNOWN AS: Spaghetti pot, marmite (Fr.), boiling pot, marmite haute (Fr.), marmite traiteur (Fr.), stock pot, fait-tout (Fr.)

DESCRIPTION: The largest pot in the kitchen, this is traditionally very high and narrow in order to present the smallest open surface to avoid the reduction of liquid (it is actually only as high as it is wide). Capacities begin at about 4 quarts and go as high as 22 quarts, for restaurant use; 6 to 10 quarts is useful around the home. The French terms noted above generally indicate a larger, professional model. Made of the usual materials, such as anodized or plain aluminum stainless or enameled steel, or copper. Always supplied with a tight-fitting lid. Essentially a deeper version of the *saucepot*, with which it is often confused. The French term, *marmite*, also refers to a rarely found pottery cooking vessel.

USE: Cooking large quantities of liquid, such as soups or stocks, cooking pasta, or for bulky vegetables such as corn and artichokes, or for steaming or boiling lobsters.

USE TIPS: Handy for cooking large quantities of food on a crowded stovetop because it has twice the capacity of a *saucepot* (see page 162) with the same width.

BUYING TIPS: 8- or 12-quart-capacity models are the most commonly used in the home kitchen, but it you are really serious about making stocks, get a bigger one. Some manufacturers offer a variety of sizes of stockpots and large saucepots, and instead of merely listing the sizes, they give them different names—*bean pot, chili pot, fiesta pot, tamale pot, menudo pot, pasta cooker, corn pot,* and so on. Many stockpots are sold with the inserts described in the *saucepot* entry (page 162), making them somewhat interchangeable with that more common and useful item.

Specialized Saucepans and Pots

About Specialized Saucepans and Pots

Certain recipes call for specialized cookware, whether for cooking, presentation, or both. Other specialized cookware simply does a better job of cooking certain dishes, but can easily be done without.

RACK INSERT

ASPARAGUS STEAMER

ASPARAGUS STEAMER

ALSO KNOWN AS: Asparagus cooker, vertical steamer, tall steamer

DESCRIPTION: Tall, deep, narrow pot with tall rack insert. 3-quart capacity is normal. Commonly available in stainless steel and anodized or plain aluminum. Supplied with lid.

USE: Steaming asparagus vertically. Because the thick stems are in the bottom (full of boiling water) they cook more rapidly than the tender tips, which are steamed. Can also be used for a few ears of corn.

USE TIPS: Some chefs swear that this is the only way asparagus can be evenly and perfectly cooked.

BUYING TIPS: Buy the handsomest pot you can afford—some even have decorative brass handles. A steamer is the perfect complement to a lifelong devotion to asparagus, if that is your thing. Good gift item for asparagus lovers.

BAIN-MARIE PAN

DESCRIPTION: Tall, narrow pan. Do not confuse with the two-part *double boiler* (see page 159).

USE: Sits in a large container of hot water (a water bath, or, in French, a *bain-marie*) to poach or keep delicate foods warm. Commonly used for custards or mousses.

USE TIPS: Smaller pans can be floated inside this, and heated with warm water, as well.

BUYING TIPS: Rarely needed by the average cook. You can put any pan into a larger container to keep it warm.

BAMBOO STEAMER

BAMBOO STEAMER

ALSO KNOWN AS: Stacked bamboo steamer

DESCRIPTION: 8- or 10½-inch-round, woven bamboo basket set, usually consisting of 2 bottoms and a top. The bottom is about a 2-inch-high bamboo band with a rack inside made of bamboo slats about a half-inch apart. The top fits over bottom very tightly. Generally sold with a crisscross bamboo or circular wire *steamer rack* (see page 156).

USE: Steaming vegetables, dumplings, fish, and the like in a wok. The steamer is suspended over boiling water on top of a steam rack for cooking, and may be brought to the table for serving.

USE TIPS: Keeps food warm for up to half an hour after cooking.

BUYING TIPS: Not only is this traditional, but it is the best way to steam food in a wok. Buy several to increase your capacity.

CANNER STEAMER

CANNER STEAMER

ALSO KNOWN AS: Steamer canner, jar steamer

DESCRIPTION: Shallow but wide aluminum pot with perforated shelf that sits on top lip and a very high cover. Up to seven quart-sized jars can sit on the shelf. The lower part is filled with water.

USE: Steaming jars as part of the canning process.

USE TIPS: Certain foods require a pressure cooker for this purpose, depending on their acid level. Be sure to check the instructions very carefully.

BUYING TIPS: Proper equipment is a must for canning.

CHESTNUT ROASTING PAN

CHESTNUT ROASTING PAN

ALSO KNOWN AS: Chestnut pan

DESCRIPTION: Large, shallow, black steel pan that looks like a regular *skillet* (see page 154) but has large holes perforated throughout the bottom. Long handle.

USE: Roasting chestnuts over a gas or wood flame.

USE TIPS: Think holiday-related thoughts while roasting chestnuts.

BUYING TIPS: Good gift item.

COUSCOUSIERE

COUSCOUSIERE

DESCRIPTION: Large, bulbous two-part aluminum pot with cover and small loop handles. The upper part is totally perforated on the bottom and somewhat perforated on the top. Typical capacity of the lower pot is 8½ quarts. The whole thing should be about a foot high.

USE: Cooking couscous (semolina or cracked wheat) in the upper pot with steam from vegetables and meats being cooked in the lower pot. This is a traditional North African one-dish recipe. May also be used to cook rice.

USE TIPS: Condensed steam should not drip back onto the couscous, which is meant to be served dry and fluffy.

BUYING TIPS: This is the best way to cook this wonderful dish, but not a commonly needed item.

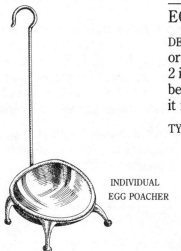

INDIVIDUAL
EGG POACHER

EGG POACHER

DESCRIPTION: Round or triangularly shaped nonstick coated metal or plastic dish with three or six shallow indentations, each about 2 inches across. Fits on top of a shallow pan that may or may not be sold with the dish as a set (it can be used in any size pan, as it is the depth of the water that poaches).

TYPES: *Egg poaching pan:* The smallest aluminum saucepan found, only 4 inches in diameter and 1¾ inches deep, sold with a cover and poacher insert to hold one egg.
  Individual egg poacher: Shallow, spoonlike cup on inch-high feet, with one 6-inch-high wire handle jutting straight up, or with a hook on the end of the handle that allows it to hang from the side of a deep pan. Also made as a *double poacher,* with two cups joined back to back. The bottom of the bowl is perforated for drainage.

USE: Poaching eggs; that is, cooking them in a shallow pan of gently boiling water. Each indentation holds one raw egg. Plastic models are for use with microwave ovens. Either version will produce a neat egg "package" without trailing wisps of egg white. Can also be used to gently warm such things as baby food.

USE TIPS: Even with models that have a nonstick finish, put a dab of butter, margarine, or nonstick spray in the poacher to keep eggs from sticking.

BUYING TIPS: If you like poached eggs, try one of these.

REMOVABLE RACK

FISH POACHER

FISH POACHER

ALSO KNOWN AS: Poissonier (Fr.), double-handled fish poacher, fish kettle

DESCRIPTION: Long, narrow, deep metal pan with small loop handles at each end and a removable rack at the bottom. Common size is about 2 feet long by 4½ to 7 inches wide and about 5 inches deep, though an 18-inch-long model that is a little narrower and shallower is also found. Available in stainless and nonstick steel, plain and anodized aluminum, and copper. Supplied with a lid. A *French style steamer and poacher* is the name sometimes given to a rectangular utensil (8¼ x 12 x 5 inches deep) with an insert that is adjustable for either steaming (high) or poaching (low). A French *turbot poacher,* also known as a *turbot kettle* or *turbotière,* is an enormous elongated diamond shape, 25 inches wide.

USE: Poaching whole fish as well as boiling or steaming vegetables such as asparagus.

USE TIPS: Rack is used for easy removal of fish without danger of it breaking up. The longer models fit over two burners. Use low heat only—this is usually made of thin metal and high heat will damage it. *Poaching* is cooking in water that is almost hot enough to boil, but not quite—there is only an occasional bubble that rises gently to the surface. The water should barely simmer.

BUYING TIPS: Be sure that the rack is included with your poacher. Measure your stovetop and your cabinet—as well as your favorite fish—before purchasing. This is a big item.

FROZEN FOOD COOKER

DESCRIPTION: Small, rectangular, stainless steel pan with lid.

USE: Exactly the right size for cooking a typical box of frozen vegetables. Small size retains most moisture.

USE TIPS: Cook slowly and check the label of your food to see if water should be added.

BUYING TIPS: Any pot or pan will do as long as it is not too big.

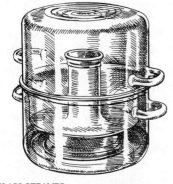

GLASS STEAMER

GLASS STEAMER

DESCRIPTION: Two large pots made of borosilicate glass (a shock-and-heat-resistant glass that can be used on a gas burner), one of which fits upside down over the other. The lower one holds a footed insert bowl with a tube in the center; food to be steamed, such as cut vegetables, is distributed around the tube and water is placed in the very bottom of the pot. The lower pot holds 1½ quarts and the upper one 2 quarts. Microwave and dishwasher safe.

USE: Steaming small amounts of food, especially vegetables, as you watch. Place directly on table for serving.

USE TIPS: Both halves double as regular *casseroles* (see page 192).

BUYING TIPS: Great for dramatic cooking, but not entirely practical.

PAELLA PAN

PAELLA PAN

ALSO KNOWN AS: Buffet server

DESCRIPTION: Large, shallow pan with two loop handles and short, angled sides. About 13 to 17 inches in diameter. Made of enameled steel, plain steel, stainless steel, aluminum, clay, or copper.

USE: Cooking any stovetop recipe but primarily for the Spanish or Portuguese seafood and rice dish known as paella.

USE TIPS: Paella normally is made with a base of saffron rice with a stew of lobster, shrimp, clams, mussels, chicken, chorizo (hot sausage), tomatoes, onions, and peppers.

BUYING TIPS: Because paella is usually served directly from the cooking vessel, try to get a decorative model. Measure your stovetop and oven to see if it can handle such a big dish before you invest.

POLENTA POT

ALSO KNOWN AS: Paiolo (Ital.)

DESCRIPTION: Flat-bottomed, conical, deep, unlined copper pan. May be hammered copper, with a helper handle opposite the long pan handle. Available in capacities ranging from 1½ to 12 quarts, with 4- or 7-quart capacities being most common.

USE: Making the Italian yellow cornmeal dish, polenta.

USE TIPS: Clean thoroughly before and after use, and do not use for acidic or salty foods—they will react with the unlined copper.

BUYING TIPS: Polenta can easily be made in any large pot but this one allows you to get a nice crust on it.

HAND CRANK

MOVIE-THEATER-TYPE
POPCORN POPPER

POPCORN POPPER

DESCRIPTION: Container into which oil and popcorn are poured according to directions. The 4-quart "movie theater" type is a round bucket that has a manual stirring device designed to make all kernels pop. Other versions include a deep pan with a screen top and 24-inch-long handles that snap together (one comes from the top, one from the bottom) and a rectangular metal pan about a foot long with a sliding top that has large perforations in it. A long, insulated handle extends from the end.

Microwave version is merely a footed, clear plastic bowl with a vented top. Electric versions are heated by a hot plate in the bottom, though hot-air models are also common.

USE: Making popcorn.

USE TIPS: Use good-quality popping corn. Butter can be melted in a special cup in the top of some models.

BUYING TIPS: Hot-air models are useful in places where you are unlikely to have oil on hand, such as in an office.

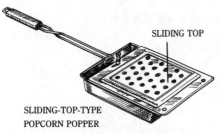

SLIDING TOP

SLIDING-TOP-TYPE
POPCORN POPPER

PORTUGUESE CATAPLANA

DESCRIPTION: Squat sphere of hammered copper, usually made in a decorative manner, with two hinged halves. Side handle loops are clips that hold the two halves together tightly for cooking.

USE: Steaming and serving seafood and vegetables.

USE TIPS: For added drama, do not open until you are right at the table. The steam will rush out, making a great display.

BUYING TIPS: Excellent gift item.

PRESSURE CANNER

ALSO KNOWN AS: Canner

DESCRIPTION: 12- to 22-quart-capacity, polished, heavyweight aluminum pot with *pressure cooker* features (see next entry) and a canning rack that holds any number of mason jars, depending on their size. Typical capacity is seven 1-quart jars, ten pint jars (17-quart-model), or twenty-four half-pint jars. Sold with a jar rack.

USE: Cooking food in sealed jars, usually mason jars, for preserving as part of the canning process.

USE TIPS: Pressure canning is the only method recommended by the U.S.D.A. for low-acid foods. Follow directions closely and carefully.

BUYING TIPS: Doubles as a large capacity *pressure cooker* (see next entry).

PRESSURE COOKER

PRESSURE COOKER

DESCRIPTION: Large, thick, aluminum or stainless steel pot with very solid lid that fastens down. Common size is 7½ quarts; available from 4- to 10-quart capacities. May come with a jar rack for canning (see previous entry).

USE: Cooking all kinds of food with water and under pressure in order to cook faster. Ideal for stews and soups with long cooking times, such as bean soups. Can also be used normally for slow cooking with a regular lid.

USE TIPS: Cooking times can be three to ten times faster with a pressure cooker than with ordinary methods.

BUYING TIPS: Look for an extra clamp across the lid as a safety device. The latest models have been redesigned with safety in mind.

STEAMER/JUICER

STEAMER/JUICER

DESCRIPTION: Large, 8-quart-capacity stainless steel pot with a perforated basket insert and a panlike base a few inches high. There is a spigot with a plastic hose at the bottom of the pot. The pot has a wide tube in the center.

USE: Steaming fruit to release the juice. Water is boiled in the bottom pan, juice collected in the middle pot, and fruit held in the basket.

BUYING TIPS: Not as popular as pressure or mechanical juicers and extractors. Several seconds in a microwave can produce similar results with some fruit.

STOVETOP POTATO BAKER

STOVETOP POTATO BAKER

ALSO KNOWN AS: Potato baker, warmer/crisper, warming oven, old-fashioned potato baker

DESCRIPTION: Stainless steel or aluminum inverted panlike utensil with a very deep cover. The pan's "bottom" is actually its top surface, and is fairly thick. It has holes around the outside edge. The top fits tightly over it. Holds four to six potatoes.

USE: Baking potatoes without the benefit of an oven. This baker sits on a gas flame. A shallower version is more likely to be used for warming bread and rolls.

USE TIPS: Useful if an oven is not available. Can be used to warm rolls, too.

BUYING TIPS: Good camping item.

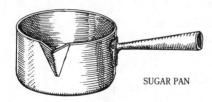

SUGAR PAN

SUGAR PAN

ALSO KNOWN AS: Sugar pot, caramel pan, sugar melting pot, sugar boiler, sugar melter

DESCRIPTION: Unlined copper pan, often with a large pouring spout, from 3-cup to 2½-quart capacity, with a flat bottom and a large, hollow handle. A *jam pot, confiture pan, maslin,* or *preserving pan* is a similar, extremely large, flat, angle-sided version, commonly with a 12-quart capacity and two loop handles, one on either side.

USE: Exclusively for melting sugar for syrups, candy, or caramel recipes. The larger version, the jam pot, is for making fruit jams or jellies without loss of taste or color.

USE TIPS: Do not stir the sugar as it melts into liquid caramel, or add water to the dry sugar—it will turn to steam and can cause a severe scald. Even the handle gets very hot at these temperatures—be careful. Only use for caramelizing sugar or making jam.

BUYING TIPS: Look for a hollow copper handle. Unlined copper is used to achieve the high temperatures that are necessary for turning the sugar into caramel, as a tin lining would melt at this point. A very rare item, indeed.

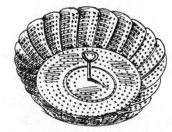

VEGETABLE STEAMER

VEGETABLE STEAMER

ALSO KNOWN AS: Steamer, folding vegetable steamer, health steamer

DESCRIPTION: Stainless steel or plastic bowllike device with sides made of sections that fan out like the blades of a fan when the steamer is lifted but collapse to the diameter of a pot when the steamer is placed inside. Most have a removable center post and pull ring. One has different-sized posts attached to the opposite sides of the base. Another has handles on the sides, eliminating the center post and creating more room for vegetables.

USE: Steaming average quantities of vegetables, fish, and shellfish in pots usually up to about 10 inches in diameter (each model opens up about 4 inches larger than its closed diameter). The plastic version is for use with microwave ovens.

USE TIPS: Steaming is best for making crisp, tender vegetables that are not waterlogged. The water level should be below the vegetables, not touching them, but be sure not to let it boil away. Use one with high feet or the double model if you need to use lots of water. Make sure your pot has a tight lid to retain all the steam.

BUYING TIPS: Look for a pull ring on the center post for easy lifting, and a removable post so that you can steam large vegetables. Some plastic models are made of a special material which resists heat, allowing the plastic to be used not only in the microwave but also on the regular stovetop.

ZABAGLIONE POT

ZABAGLIONE PAN

ALSO KNOWN AS: Zabaglione pot, zabaglione bowl

DESCRIPTION: Unlined copper pan with a spherical bottom. 1½- to 2½-quart capacity.

USE: Making the egg dessert zabaglione—wine custard.

USE TIPS: The rounded bottom allows for continuous whisking while cooking evenly. Don't forget and try to set it down on the counter. The height is necessary to accommodate the greatly increased size of the dish after beating and the addition of wine.

BUYING TIPS: Talk about specialized—this tool is for one dish only, and a rare one at that. Buy the 6-cup capacity. Larger ones are for restaurant use.

Deep-frying Utensils

About Deep-frying Utensils

Deep-fried foods can be delicious but it does entail cooking with a large amount of hot oil or fat, so you want to be sure that your pot is very stable and has short handles that are less likely to be hit by mistake. The second most important aspect of success here is maintaining the right temperature, for which a special thermometer is required (see page 100). Make sure all your accessories are of good quality.

CHICKEN FRYER

CHICKEN FRYER

ALSO KNOWN AS: Deep covered skillet

DESCRIPTION: This large, deep frying pan is often made of cast iron, either plain or enameled, and comes with a snug-fitting dome-shaped cover, often made of glass. Most measure about 9 or 10 inches across but can be found as wide as 12 inches. Should have a small loop handle opposite the main handle.

USE: Frying and braising chicken or other meats.

USE TIPS: The lid is essential to keep the fat from splattering out over the stove and to retain the steam. Chefs have a never-ending controversy about whether the chicken is better cooked with the lid on for more tender chicken or off, for crispier skin. Most chefs use a combination. Keep the fat at 375°F—if it gets too hot, it may catch fire. Leave the fat to cool when done and then pour into a can for disposal when it solidifies.

BUYING TIPS: Some are available with a basket for easy removal of chicken.

DEEP-FAT FRYER

DESCRIPTION: Foot-wide and 4-inch-deep pot with two handles, usually sold with a wire mesh basket that fits inside and also perches on top, and a tight-fitting cover. Most are made of aluminum, some of enameled or plain steel. 5-quart capacity is normal. Also available in an electric version (see page 287).

USE: Deep-frying foods ranging from doughnuts to potatoes and chicken. The basket is made to perch on top of the pot for draining.

USE TIPS: Always deep-fry with great caution—boiling oil can spatter and burn skin easily. Keep the fat temperature at 375°F and don't let it get higher—it may catch fire. For best results, fry food twice—a preliminary cooking and then after allowing the food to dry and cool, a final one to the point that it is crisp and brown.

FRY BASKET

ALSO KNOWN AS: French fry basket

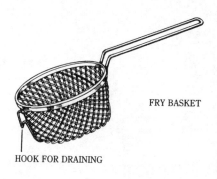

FRY BASKET

HOOK FOR DRAINING

DESCRIPTION: Open mesh, wire basket, about 8 inches in diameter, with handle extending horizontally from open edge of basket. May have a hook on lip across from handle or on base.

USE: Deep-frying foods ranging from doughnuts to potatoes to chicken. Provides for easy plunging and removal from hot oil in a large, deep cooking vessel such as a *deep-fat fryer* (see previous entry).

USE TIPS: The basket should be used in a fryer with sufficient depth for the oil or shortening to rise 2 to 3 inches above the food. Never allow a wet basket to be plunged into hot oil—it will cause splattering.

BUYING TIPS: Sold as an accessory with deep-fat fryers (see previous entry) or separately.

POTATO BIRD NEST MAKER

ALSO KNOWN AS: Potato-nest basket, bird's nest fryer

DESCRIPTION: Large chrome-plated or stainless steel mesh spoon-like contraption that actually is two large spoons that fit one inside the other, in order to press raw potatoes or dough into a nest-shaped mold, about 3 or 4 inches in diameter. A larger, wider mesh version is used for molding tortillas, thin Mexican corn or wheat pancakes, into baskets, called a *tortilla basket fryer* or *tortilla basket maker*. (Non-Spanish speakers may call these *taco baskets*.) Also available in a nonstick coated wire version.

USE: Making bird's nests by deep-frying shredded or grated potatoes which are compressed tightly between the two baskets to form a bowl shape. These "nests" are then used to serve miniature vegetables or chicken salad and the like. Tortilla baskets can be made with either the potato or the tortilla model.

USE TIPS: Practice to get the consistency of the potatoes right for best results.

BUYING TIPS: Not a common home kitchen item.

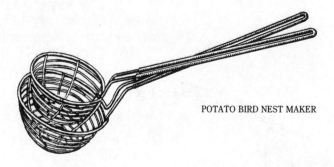

POTATO BIRD NEST MAKER

SPATTER GUARD

ALSO KNOWN AS: Splatter shield, splatter screen

DESCRIPTION: Very fine mesh, round screen, about a foot in diameter, with wire rim and plastic handle. Available in various sizes. Also available is a *microwave splatter shield* with all-plastic construction. (The correct term is really spatter, but splatter—a combination of splash and spatter—is acceptable.) A *splatter shield* for regular stovetop cooking is a folding wall made of three 8-inch square pieces of aluminum hinged together so it can fit around a burner.

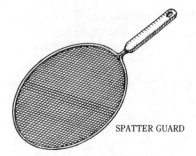

SPATTER GUARD

USE: For covering or shielding frying pans while cooking foods that spatter, such as bacon, in order to protect your kitchen and yourself.

USE TIPS: Can be used to protect the cook when adding liquids to a hot fry pan—just pour them right through the guard. Some spatter will still get through, but not much. Also helpful for draining vegetables.

BUYING TIPS: Very handy and inexpensive item.

TACO FRYER

TACO FRYER

ALSO KNOWN AS: Taco tongs

DESCRIPTION: Large, scissorlike wire tongs that have V-shaped, semicircular business ends about 4 inches in length—the size of a taco. One end fits inside the other, forming a taco shell from a flat tortilla. Made of either chrome-plated or nonstick-coated steel wire.

USE: Holding soft, thin, Mexican pancakes, called tortillas, in a soft V-shape as they are deep-fried to a crisp in order to make them into tacos.

BUYING TIPS: Preformed taco shells are commonly available and much easier to use. This is for strict purists.

Stovetop Cooking Accessories

About Stovetop Cooking Accessories

Included here is a wide variety of generally inexpensive items that can help make a special dish easier to cook, protect your cookware, make cleanup easier, and in general be a convenience to you when cooking on the stovetop. However, most cooks will have no call for many of these, so choose according to your needs.

ARTICHOKE COOKER

ARTICHOKE COOKER

ALSO KNOWN AS: Artichoke steam rack

DESCRIPTION: Stainless-steel stand made of horizontal loops of wire. An artichoke fits neatly in and on it.

USE: Holding an artichoke vertically and off the bottom of a pot for steaming.

USE TIPS: Use only enough water to touch the base, or stem, of the artichoke. Steam until leaves are easily removed.

BUYING TIPS: Any regular vegetable steamer or basket does the same job well.

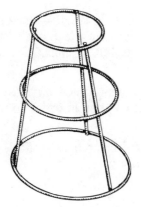

ASPARAGUS STEAM RACK

ASPARAGUS STEAM RACK

ALSO KNOWN AS: Pastry bag holder, asparagus cooker/holder

DESCRIPTION: Tall, cone-shaped rack made of three horizontal rings supported by three vertical rods. All made of chrome-plated steel.

USE: Holding asparagus stalks upright for cooking in any large pot or for holding full pastry bags (see page 263) facing down between uses.

USE TIPS: Let thick stalks sit in boiling water while the delicate tips are steamed.

BUYING TIPS: An inexpensive alternative to the *asparagus steamer* (see page 165). Ideal way to cook asparagus and a good gift for the asparagus lover.

BACON PRESS

BACON PRESS

DESCRIPTION: Heavy, cast-iron sheet either rectangular, about 5 × 7 inches, or circular, 9 inches in diameter, often with a picture of a pig etched into one side and a horizontal handle on the other.

USE: Pressing bacon or burgers down to cook flat and evenly on a griddle or in a frying pan. Increases overall crispness.

BUYING TIPS: Most cooks prefer to let bacon cook without a press.

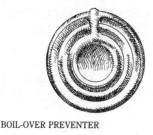

BOIL-OVER PREVENTER

BOIL OVER PREVENTER

ALSO KNOWN AS: Boilmaster, boil alert, boil control, pot watcher

DESCRIPTION: Stainless-steel or heat-resistant glass disk, about 3 inches in diameter, with indentations and ridges.

USE: Place in the bottom of a pot prior to filling with liquid. Rattles against the bottom of a pot when the liquid begins to boil, alerting the cook to help avoid letting the liquid boil over. Prevents milk from boiling over by helping the air bubbles release themselves.

USE TIPS: Can double as a spoon rest on the stovetop.

BUYING TIPS: If you are cooking with distractions like small children or a busy phone, this may avert a disaster or two. Otherwise, just keep stirring for the same results.

BOUQUET GARNI BAG

DESCRIPTION: Small cheesecloth bag with drawstring, usually sold in packages of ten. Another version is the aluminum *spice infuser,* a small screw-top perforated cylinder.

USE: Holds a small quantity of herbs and spices for flavoring soups, stews, or stocks via infusion—traditionally thyme, parsley, bay leaf, and peppercorns. Removed after cooking. Can also be used as your own giant, custom tea bag.

USE TIPS: These herbs and spices can be placed directly in the cooking broth, but then they can be difficult to remove.

BUYING TIPS: Normally sold filled and ready to use as a food item, this is offered for those cooks who want to do everything themselves. A *tea ball* (see page 313) can do the same job as this but the bag has more room.

BURNER COVER

DESCRIPTION: 8- to 10-inch round or square, lightweight piece of enameled, chrome-plated, nonstick-coated, or stainless steel, hammered-finished copper, or painted aluminum, with a small angled edge. Some have stainless steel rims. Fits over gas or electric burners when not in use. Available in different colors.

A cast-iron version fits tightly over electric coil burners and stays on during use.

USE: Keeping electric or gas burners covered when not in use. They protect burners from spills and splatter, are easy to clean, and provide additional workspace. However, it seems that the main reason for using these is one of aesthetics. The cast-iron burner cover enhances an electric coil burner to create a more evenly heating element that allows you to use a lower setting more effectively.

USE TIPS: Good to have when children are in the kitchen. May also be used as *trivets* (see page 393).

BUYING TIPS: Sold in sets of two or four.

BURNER DRIP PAN

ALSO KNOWN AS: Burner liner, range pan, burner bib, reflector bowl, reflector pan

DESCRIPTION: Cupped metal disk, either chrome-plated, nonstick steel, or aluminum foil, 6 or 8 inches in diameter, or square, about 6 or 8 inches on a side, with large hole in center. Designed to fit particular brands and styles of stoves. Bright, triple chrome-plated *electric range reflector pans* fit any range with hinged elements.

USE: Fits into the well of a gas or electric burner stovetop to catch drips from pots and pans, or to reflect heat upward.

USE TIPS: These are easier to remove and clean than cleaning the wells themselves.

BUYING TIPS: Take your old one along to the store to be sure you are getting the right size.

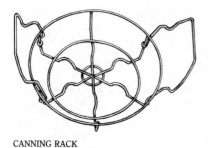

CANNING RACK

CANNING RACK

DESCRIPTION: Two concentric wire rings, the smaller one forming the bottom and the larger one forming the top, with several other wires radiating out from the center, and two large wire loop handles with notches. Sort of a basket made from a minimum of wires. Seven 1-quart canning jars fit snugly in it.

USE: Removing canning jars from a pot (see *canner,* page 171) full of boiling water. Loop handles rest on edge of pot for more convenient individual removal of each jar.

BUYING TIPS: Handy if you do much canning.

DOUBLE BOILER MAKER

DOUBLE BOILER MAKER

ALSO KNOWN AS: Bain-marie (incorrect)

DESCRIPTION: Cast-metal ring, about 4 inches in diameter, made of a band about ¾ inch wide. There are three dips in the ring that form feet.

USE: Supports a smaller pot within a larger pot of boiling water for gentle heating, either substituting for a specially designed pot set called a *double boiler* (see page 159), in which the upper pot sits *above* the boiling water, and is heated by steam, or creates a *bain-marie,* in which the upper pot sits *in* the boiling water, which is filled about ¾ of the way up the pot sides.

USE TIPS: Note that a pot may be unsteady on this—be careful when stirring.

BUYING TIPS: Very handy, inexpensive, and small substitute for a useful but rarely needed item.

EGG CODDLER

EGG CODDLER

DESCRIPTION: Small canisterlike china dish, with a metal top.

USE: Making and serving coddled eggs. A shelled egg is placed inside the dish along with butter, salt, and pepper, and the dish itself is heated in gently boiling water (a *bain-marie*).

USE TIPS: Don't rush it—this can take as much as twenty minutes.

BUYING TIPS: A rarely used, one-dish item.

EGG/PANCAKE RING

ALSO KNOWN AS: Egg ring, pancake ring, egg fry ring, egg and pancake ring, egg corral

DESCRIPTION: Stainless-steel or nonstick-coated metal band formed into a circle, square, or the shape of any number of animals, including Mickey Mouse, with handle attached at a 90-degree angle.

USE: Frying perfectly round eggs or pancakes, or in the case of the animals, an amusing and familiar shape. Also keeps eggs or pancakes from running together.

EGG/PANCAKE RING

EGG/PANCAKE RING

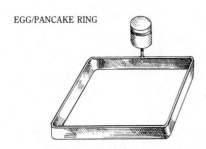

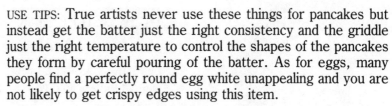

USE TIPS: True artists never use these things for pancakes but instead get the batter just the right consistency and the griddle just the right temperature to control the shapes of the pancakes they form by careful pouring of the batter. As for eggs, many people find a perfectly round egg white unappealing and you are not likely to get crispy edges using this item.

BUYING TIPS: This is actually a little difficult to use—the batter or egg often runs underneath it. Not a recommended item.

GLASS COOKWARE PROTECTOR

GLASS COOKWARE PROTECTOR

ALSO KNOWN AS: Stove ring, heat diffuser, burner shield

DESCRIPTION: Zig-zag or clover-shaped wire, about 4 inches across.

USE: Sits on a burner being used to heat glass cookware so that the cookware does not touch the electric burner or the iron pot supports of a gas burner.

USE TIPS: Particularly helpful on electric coil burners.

BUYING TIPS: Good, inexpensive insurance that reduces cracking of glass coffee pots.

LID WAND

DESCRIPTION: Pencil-size plastic stick with a magnet on one end.

USE: Retrieving canning lids from the bottom of a pot of boiling water.

USE TIPS: Wear an *oven mitt* (see page 432) when working around boiling water.

BUYING TIPS: Only for the serious canner.

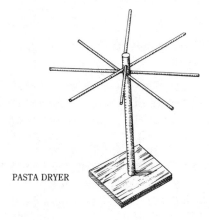

PASTA DRYER

PASTA DRYER

ALSO KNOWN AS: Pasta dryer rack, pasta rack

DESCRIPTION: Wooden dowel about a foot high with a square base and eight small dowels jutting out at a right angle from the top in a radial pattern. Another version, consisting of a long block with many dowels jutting out from one side, mounts under a cabinet or on the wall. Others, several feet in length, resemble laundry racks.

USE: Air-drying freshly made strips of pasta.

BUYING TIPS: Slightly dried pasta holds up better in the cooking water.

POT LID HOLDER

POT LID HOLDER

DESCRIPTION: Plastic stand, about 8 inches high, with a notch for holding pot lid and a drip-catching basin/spoon rest in the small, circular base.

USE: Provides a convenient place to stick a hot, wet pot lid while working with its pot.

BUYING TIPS: Good space-saving device, if you don't like putting pot lids on the stovetop.

SHELLFISH STEAMER BAG

DESCRIPTION: Small white pouch made of an open cotton mesh. A large bag, about 1 by 2 feet, can hold about a dozen large clams.

USE: Steaming shellfish. The bag keeps the shellfish (clams, mussels, oysters, crabs, etc.) together in a large pot, making for easier retrieval when cooked.

USE TIPS: Place individual servings in each bag for convenience.

BUYING TIPS: Good idea if you start servings at different times.

SIMMER RING

SIMMER RING

ALSO KNOWN AS: Heat diffuser, flame tamer, flame diffuser, simmering pad, radiant heat plate

DESCRIPTION: Any of four designs that fit over a gas burner flame. One is a large, flat, double-layered steel disk, about 7 inches in diameter, with a wooden handle. The metal is perforated with small holes. Another is a thin disk made of woven asbestos or ceramic fiber, with a slightly larger diameter, and a similar one is a fine steel mesh ring. Finally, there is a stamped, chrome-plated steel or cast-iron, raised platform that fits over the burner and raises the cooking vessel up an inch or so. Adjustable models are found that are made of enameled steel and that can raise utensils up as much as 3 inches.

USE: Placed over low heat to keep liquids at a very low simmer by diffusing a gas flame. Also serves to protect glass and ceramic cookware from too much direct heat.

BUYING TIPS: Handy for those cooktops with large, professional burners which tend to be too hot on even low settings.

STERILIZING RACK

DESCRIPTION: Two small, cast-aluminum racks with twelve slots each, attached by four legs. The lower rack is smaller than the upper one. A long wire handle ending in a wooden knob is on one end.

USE: Sterilizing canning lids thoroughly and conveniently. The wooden knob remains cooler than the metal, making retrieval from boiling water easy.

TACO RACK

TACO RACK

ALSO KNOWN AS: Taco fill rack

DESCRIPTION: Long, stainless-steel wire rack, shaped like three rows of waves, which holds six taco shells.

USE: Holding taco shells for filling or serving.

BUYING TIPS: Helpful if you are making more than one at a time, in advance.

UNIVERSAL LID

ALSO KNOWN AS: Sauce pan and fry pan lid, replacement lid

DESCRIPTION: Aluminum disk with a slight conical form and small circular ridges, measuring from 8 to 11½ inches in diameter, with a handle in the center.

USE: Replacing lost pot or pan lids or reducing the need to store matching lids.

BUYING TIPS: It is better to get one that fits exactly or you may run into problems on the stovetop when things really get cooking. Always replace bent or buckled lids.

Grills, Griddles, Irons, and Toasters

About Grills, Griddles, Irons, and Toasters

Despite all the specialized pots and pans available, some food is cooked by exposing it directly to the heat source. Many people seek this kind of cooking because it is fat-free or at least cooked with a minimum of fat. And in the case of irons, the food is shaped by the pan it is cooked in.

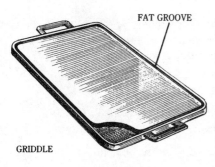

FAT GROOVE

GRIDDLE

GRIDDLE

DESCRIPTION: Large, square, round, or rectangular thick metal sheet with only a slight lip along the edges for a side, often smooth on top and ridged on the bottom, with a handle. Ridged griddles are usually considered *grills* (see page 186). Some have a deep groove around the outside edge to drain fat into a corner depression. Old-fashioned ones are made of cast iron and are smooth; more modern ones have a nonstick finish and are made of lightweight metals such as cast aluminum. Also available in a self-standing electric version, with a thermostatic control.

TYPES: *Breakfast griddle:* A square griddle with a pan handle.
Fajita kit: Small, 10-inch-round or oval griddle (or sometimes very shallow skillet) sold with fitted wooden trays for tableside serving of this Mexican dish.
Tortilla griddle (Also Known As *comal* [Sp.]): 9-inch-diameter flat, round piece of thick steel with a wooden handle at a slight angle.

USE: Frying simple food like hot dogs, hamburgers, or pancakes in quantity. Also useful for browning sandwich breads and whenever a wide, hot surface is needed, and there is no liquid involved. Lack of sides makes it easier to slip a turner under the food. Thickness prevents warping.

USE TIPS: Meats are cooked on the ridged side in order to drain away fat, and everything else is cooked on the smooth side (meat can be cooked there, too). A griddle does not hold fat like a frying pan does, draining it off the sides into channels; in fact, one manufacturer calls its model a *dry fry griddle*.

BUYING TIPS: While a griddle may not be used daily, it always comes in handy sometime.

SANDWICH GRILLING IRON

SANDWICH GRILLING IRON

ALSO KNOWN AS: Croque monsieur, sandwich cooker, sandwich grill

DESCRIPTION: Two cast-aluminum molds that hold sandwich-sized bread, hinged together. Each half has a long handle that is locked onto the other in the closed position. Also available in an electric model, usually with a nonstick coating on the inside, and in a plastic microwave version.

USE: Browning cheese/ham/egg sandwiches over a burner. The French café snacks, *croque-monsieur* and *croque-madame* (battered grilled cheese and ham and egg), are made this way. The microwave version can also be used to brown hamburgers and potatoes.

USE TIPS: Experiment to get your timing down. Avoid putting too much batter on your sandwiches.

BUYING TIPS: Decent gift for the very young and not-so-rich setting up a first household.

STOVETOP GRILL

DESCRIPTION: Three different designs are available. All are metal and fit over gas burners.

TYPES: *Open mesh:* Round, 10-inch-diameter, plain black iron or nonstick-coated steel grill made from expanded, open

RIDGED, ONE-PIECE STOVETOP GRILL

STOVETOP GRILL—
TWO-PART WITH DRIP PAN

mesh and a 1-inch-high outside band. Two short wooden handles extend from the sides.

Ridged, one-piece (Also Known As *skillet grill, grill pan,* or *ribbed skillet* [see page 154]): Very similar to the *griddle* (see page 185), this is a round, square, or squarish, cast-iron item with very low sides, a spout for pouring off grease, and a big handle on one side. Ridges run lengthwise and may or may not be continuous. May have a special finish to prevent sticking or rusting. Available in a single-burner, fry pan style, or as a rectangle that covers two burners.

Two-part, with drip pan: Cast-iron or -aluminum, nonstick-coated surface with shallow grooves and open slots around edges, either about a foot round or rectangular, designed to cover one or two burners. The fat runs off through the grooves and drops through the slots into a porcelain, enamel-coated, steel drip pan underneath. The drip pan has an open center for the gas or electric burner. Drip pans are usually filled with a small amount of water to prevent flare-ups and reduce smoke. Dishwasher safe. May be sold with domed cover and grill-lifting gadget.

USE: Grilling foods over the stovetop as an alternative to frying in a frying pan with grease, or as an alternative to grilling outdoors.

USE TIPS: Use over moderately high heat for maximum benefit. Only high temperatures will sear beef properly. Do not cook anything that drips fat on the open mesh grill. It is best to cook only vegetables on this type.

BUYING TIPS: Good choice for those on low-fat diets who seek to avoid pan frying in fat wherever possible. The two-part model is also offered with a companion, portable, one-burner gas stove for tabletop cooking.

STOVETOP TOASTER

DESCRIPTION: Bright tin or stainless-steel contraption of various designs intended to sit over a gas-burner flame or a campfire.

TYPES: *Flat toaster:* 9½-inch square, double-level grid, with a wire loop handle. Ideal for campfire use.

Folding toaster: 9-inch-diameter, perforated disk with four wire frames the size of bread slices that fold up to a point. Slices rest on each frame and are toasted on the side facing the burner only.

PYRAMID STOVETOP TOASTER

Pyramid toaster: 6½-inch square base with 5-inch-high pyramid of slotted sheets in the middle. Two wire frames hold two slices of bread for toasting on the side facing the pyramid.

USE: Toasting bread slices one side at a time over an open flame, either gas or wood fire.

USE TIPS: Some models might work over an electric burner, but this is not recommended. Allow to cool before removing.

BUYING TIPS: Inexpensive alternative to an *electric toaster* (see page 293). However, these do require vigilance and dexterity. Old-fashioned and quaint.

WAFFLE IRON

DESCRIPTION: Cast-aluminum mold of two halves with long handles that lock together in the closed position. The mold has a distinctive crenelated pattern of small square holes. Usually configured to make either two or four waffles at a time, either wedge-shaped (round exterior) or square (rectangular exterior), and some models can make unique shapes like hearts. Most models are nonstick coated. More commonly found in a free-standing electric version (see page 294). Standard models are shallow; Belgian models are deeper. May be sold with a cast-iron ring that goes directly onto the flames and diffuses the heat for the iron, which fits inside the ring.

USE: Making waffles from batter.

USE TIPS: This is for making waffles only. These can become a specialty of your house when served with a variety of toppings—everything from chicken in a cheese or white sauce to fresh fruit and ice cream.

CHAPTER 7

Ovenware and Utensils

About Ovenware

For the purposes of this book, ovenware covers items that are used for baking and roasting all foods except pastries, breads, and desserts, which are covered in chapter 8. There is some overlap between the two categories, though, so be sure to check both chapters for any item (such as molds) that you can't find right away or that you think has an incomplete entry.

Some of the terms are interpreted particularly loosely by the manufacturers, distributors, and stores, causing some minor confusion. The aim of this book is to straighten that kind of thing out, but we are still left with items like casseroles and Dutch ovens that defy consensus.

About Ovenware Materials

The choice of materials for baking items is much less critical than for the stovetop items covered in chapter 6 or the bread and dessert baking items covered in chapter 8. Results are affected much more by the evenness of the heat in the oven, the time baked, and the food itself. Nonetheless, there is a choice to be made from the wide variety of materials available.

Enameled cast iron has become one of the most popular materials, and with reason. It is easy to clean, transmits heat extraordinarily well, and is available in good-looking colors. The edges of the enamel can chip, however, if they are hit by a falling lid.

Enameled steel is another popular material, especially for roasting pans. It is very inexpensive, lightweight, lasts for generations, and is traditional. Typically dark blue with white specks.

Stainless steel is probably the most common material for use in the oven. It is inert, scrubbable, strong, easily made in any common shape, and not too expensive. It is virtually indestructible.

Aluminum foil utensils are usually disposable but are often heavy-duty and can be reused.

Earthenware is the oldest and most traditional of oven utensil materials, and is usually heavy, glazed, and inexpensive. Typically pale creamy yellow. It absorbs heat slowly (it should never be placed in an already hot oven—start cold or it may break) and is used for slow-baking items. Do not use earthenware or other unvitrified, slightly porous ceramics for cooking, storage, or marinating with acidic liquids such as lemon juice or vinegar. Although some are now labeled as lead-free, lead seepage may occur on older, hand-crafted or highly decorated ceramics. Earthenware is somewhat fragile.

Stoneware is semivitrified, usually fully glazed, and impervious to liquids. Fired at a higher temperature than earthenware, it is more costly and less delicate. Good for slow baking.

Terra cotta is usually unglazed or partially unglazed and is sometimes intended for oven use (do not use if you are not sure). The reddish, unglazed surface absorbs heat very well and also absorbs oils from foods that season it. It also absorbs water, so do not wash with a detergent. Relatively inexpensive.

Porcelain is vitrified (glasslike) and totally nonporous, and very durable except when subjected to rapid temperature changes. It is generally decorative enough for serving use and can be fairly expensive.

Heat-resistant glass and **Pyroceram,** a glasslike ceramic, are made and treated especially for oven use. Many can go directly from the freezer or refrigerator to the oven, and some flameproof glass types are specially designed to be used on the stovetop burner as well. Be sure to check your labels before trying.

Conventional Baking Dishes

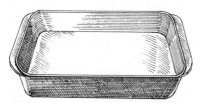

BAKER

BAKER

ALSO KNOWN AS: Baking dish

DESCRIPTION: Large, shallow (2-inch deep), oval or rectangular dish with almost vertical sides, made of a variety of materials but most often stoneware, glass, porcelain, or earthenware, but also copper or enameled steel as well as foil. Usually made without lids or handles but possibly a lip. Capacity ranges from 1 pint to 4 quarts, and dimensions 10 to 16 inches long by 7½ to 15 inches wide. A smaller version is a *shallow baker* with fluted sides, usually made of porcelain. One type of terra-cotta baker is glazed to be nonstick and scratchproof and is made with a handle.

USE: Baking large main courses or desserts such as lasagna or pudding. Metal ones can be used for roasts as well and are similar to *roasting pans* (see page 194). The shallow version is for multipurpose baking.

USE TIPS: Terra-cotta versions, one of which is called a *baker pan*, retain their heat and keep the baked goods warm at the table.

BUYING TIPS: Every kitchen needs one or even several good bakers.

BROILER PAN

BROILER PAN

ALSO KNOWN AS: Broil pan, broiler tray

DESCRIPTION: Either of two types. One is a large, shallow rectangular metal pan with corrugated bottom. Usually made of aluminum, foil, or lightweight stamped metal with a nonstick or baked enamel finish. Also made in plastic for use in microwave ovens. Available in many sizes, but on average, about a foot long, by 9 inches wide, and 1 or 2 inches deep. The other, sometimes called a *low fat broiler pan*, is a two-part pan, with a base that is a deep, plain pan much like a *roasting pan* (see page 194) and an insert, which fits on the top edge, that has shallow ridges separated by open slots.

USE: Broiling foods. The corrugated bottom forms ridges which allow the fat to flow away from the food; the slots in the two-part kind allow the fat to drain into the base.

USE TIPS: The bottom half of the two-part kind can be used for baking all kinds of foods.

BUYING TIPS: Disposable foil is popular here, as cleanup can be messy.

CASEROLE

ALSO KNOWN AS: Casserole dish

DESCRIPTION: Round, oval, or square dish with loose-fitting lid of clear, heat-resistant, tempered glass or the same material as the dish. A casserole has small handles or lips and a cover, a certain heft or weightiness, a few inches of depth, and is generally smaller than its heavier cousin, the *Dutch oven* (see page 160). Made of special, sturdy, tempered glass-ceramic that looks like porcelain, high-fired porcelain, enameled cast iron, or pottery. Sizes range from 1½ to 7 quarts, with 2½ to 5 quarts being the most popular sizes. A casserole is usually designed for oven use, though most glass-ceramic or cast-iron ones can be used on the stovetop as well, primarily for starting or finishing off a dish.

USE: Baking food, especially recipes that combine several different types of food and liquid that are served as one-course meals.

USE TIPS: Nonmetallic models can be used in microwave ovens, and some glass and porcelain models can go from the freezer directly to the oven or broiler and dishwasher without risk of cracking, so that they can be used for storage as well as cooking with a maximum of convenience.

BUYING TIPS: Often sold in sets. Buy only what you need or you may have a storage problem. Look for a material that can go from the refrigerator or freezer directly into a hot oven or microwave, and you can save both time and storage dishes.

CLAY BAKER

ALSO KNOWN AS: Clay chicken pot, clay cooker, terra-cotta baker, Roman pot, clay cook pot

CLAY BAKER

DESCRIPTION: Two-part oval casserole made of unglazed terracotta, often with a decorative relief on outside. Available in a range of shapes and sizes, but commonly large enough to hold a whole chicken along with a little broth and some root vegetables. Based on an ancient Etruscan utensil. Most are microwave safe. Small models can accommodate a 2- to 6-pound chicken, while the large size can take up to a 14-pound turkey.

USE: Baking chicken or roast meats along with vegetables with a steam effect. Meat self-bastes and moisture is retained.

USE TIPS: Soak in cold water first for at least fifteen minutes before placing in a cold oven and cooking at high heat. The water will "steam" the meat. Clean clay pots carefully, using baking soda instead of soap or detergent because they are unglazed and they absorb water. Not intended for dishwasher cleaning. Decorative style makes it suitable for serving directly on the table.

BUYING TIPS: Many people think this is the best way to cook chicken.

EARTHENWARE CLOCHE

ALSO KNOWN AS: Instant brick oven

DESCRIPTION: Round, 11½-inch-wide, shallow earthenware dish with short, angled sides, and a huge domed cover of the same material—it is just about as high as it is wide.

USE: Baking bread with a thin, crisp crust by trapping steam.

USE TIPS: Handle with care. Never expose to extreme temperature changes. Wipe dry—not intended to be immersed in water.

GRATIN DISH

GRATIN DISH

ALSO KNOWN AS: Boat, au gratin dish, au gratin server

DESCRIPTION: Shallow, oval or round dish ranging in size from small individual serving size (7 to 10 inches long) to platter size (7 to 10 inches across and 13 to 16 inches long), made of a range of materials including porcelain (most common for individual-size dishes), tin-lined copper, earthenware, glass, stainless steel, ceramic, and enameled cast iron. Sides are usually short and slightly angled. Handles are either small metal loops or else extensions of the clay material, usually like a fish tail at the oval ends. There are always two on a gratin dish.

USE: Cooking and serving baked or broiled dishes, most often with browned cheese on top ("au gratin").

USE TIPS: The copper version can also be used over a burner.

BUYING TIPS: Excellent for freezing single servings that can be reheated without changing dishes. Inexpensive, handy item.

LIFT-OUT RACK

ROASTING PAN

ROASTING PAN

ALSO KNOWN AS: Roaster, bake-roast pan, bake and roast pan

DESCRIPTION: Large, deep, rectangular or oval pan made of aluminum (plain or anodized), enameled or stainless steel, tinned copper, plain or enameled cast iron, glass, ceramic, or heavy-duty aluminum foil. Made in a very wide range of sizes, including 7½ or 10½ inches wide and about 10 or 14½ inches long and 2 to 4 inches deep. Traditional enameled steel pans are dark blue with white specks. Loop handles are on either end, sometimes slightly offset in certain models; some may be bail-type loop handles that hang down when not in use. May come with a cover or lid, which may be vented; a *double roaster* has a lid that is the same as the bottom, giving you two open roasters or one covered roaster. A *French-style roaster* is just a large, rectangular, covered roasting pan, although it may be a deeper model. The deepest is called a *brazier,* about 6 inches deep and over a foot and a half long and a foot wide. A *lasagna pan* is the same basic item, at least 10½ inches by 12½ inches by 1¾ inches deep, but usually larger and deeper. Also available with a lift-out rack as well, which allows drainage and use as a large steamer (a rack with vertical partitions allows for steaming different types of vegetables separately).

USE: Holding large cuts of meat, such as beef, pork, or chicken, for roasting, or for cooking custards in a hot water bath, or for large recipes of Italian dishes such as lasagna or eggplant parmagiana. Thicker ones are also used for making gravies on the burner. Lift-out rack allows for poaching or steaming.

USE TIPS: Measure your oven before trying to fit a large roasting pan (loaded with a 20-pound bird or not) inside. Allow room for air to circulate freely around the roasting pan, too. Choose an extra-deep (3 inches or more) pan for anything with a sauce, like lasagna or moussaka. Support pans with heavy loads with a metal tray or *cookie sheet* (see page 224).

BUYING TIPS: This is an extremely useful item that may be used forever, so get a good, strong one you like. Look for models with comfortable handles—the offset ones fit better in smaller ovens, and bail-type loop handles that hang down when not in use save space and look better on the table. Lasagna pans should be heavy to prevent scorching and about 3 inches deep to prevent overflow. Decorative models suitable for serving from are easily found. Foil pans may be sold in pairs, but don't buy in pairs unless you really think you need the second pan. Also, foil pans vary in design, especially in the use of beaded rims or deep ribs for strength. Try out a variety before you choose one for an especially heavy item, such as a Thanksgiving turkey—holidays are not the time to see your bird plop unceremoniously onto the kitchen floor.

Specialized Baking Dishes

About Specialized Baking Dishes

Though the average cook is interested in having items that are versatile, some equipment, especially baking dishes, is intended for one type of food or recipe only. Having a few of these items is convenient in some cases, allowing for slow cooking that you could not do with conventional cookware. At the very least, they are fun to try.

BAKING SHELL

BAKING SHELL

ALSO KNOWN AS: Bake shell, canape shell, shell baker

DESCRIPTION: Scallop-shaped cup made of porcelain, stainless steel, or natural shell and measuring 2½ to 6 inches across. Usually only available in white or natural shell color. Also available as an oval-shaped conch shell.

USE: Baking coquilles St. Jacques and other seafood dishes au gratin, such as scampi or deviled crab. The food is served directly from the baking shell.

USE TIPS: Those made of natural shell are especially delicate—be cautious when washing.

BUYING TIPS: Usually sold in sets of four or eight, depending on the size. Rarely used these days.

CEDAR BAKING PLANK

ALSO KNOWN AS: Chinook cedar baking plank

DESCRIPTION: 10½-inch-wide, 17-inch-long, 1½-inch-thick plank of cedar wood with an oval depression cut out of one side. Made of Western Red cedar, which is high in oil content.

USE: Baking and serving fish fillets, such as salmon. Cedar oil adds some flavor, reduces "fishy" taste, and keeps fish moist as it cooks.

USE TIPS: Do not wash in dishwasher.

BUYING TIPS: Good gift item.

CLAY CAZUELA

DESCRIPTION: Shallow, large, round earthenware baking dish glazed only on the inside. Generally made with straight, short sides.

USE: Baking Spanish dishes, especially stews and paella. Absorbs and holds heat particularly well.

USE TIPS: Dry thoroughly before storing. Use over low flames only if it is well seasoned and protected by a *heat diffuser* (see page 184). Place in cold, not preheated oven.

BUYING TIPS: Traditional, attractive material.

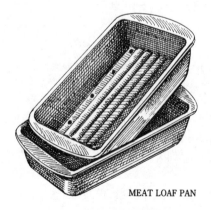

MEAT LOAF PAN

MEAT LOAF PAN

ALSO KNOWN AS: Loaf pan

DESCRIPTION: Two-part set, made of a 2- to 3-inch deep rectangular pan, about 4 inches across and about 8 to 10 inches long, usually made of sheet metal with a baked enamel finish (often with a hammered texture), tin-plated or nonstick steel, or aluminum. Comes with an insert whose perforated bottom allows the fat to drain from the loaf as it cooks. The insert, called a *meat loaf drain,* is also sold separately. A 6-cup capacity is common.

USE: Baking meat loaves.

USE TIPS: Coat with oil first.

BUYING TIPS: You can use any *loaf pan* (see page 228) for meat loaf, but the double pan allows excess fat to drain out.

OEUF EN GELEE MOLD

ALSO KNOWN AS: Oval aspic mold, oval dariole

DESCRIPTION: Shallow ovals a few inches long, with no covers. Usually made of porcelain, but also of aluminum or tinned steel.

USE: Making and serving individual eggs poached or baked in aspic. Doubles as an individual mousse dish.

BUYING TIPS: Tin is easier to unmold.

OVEN PANCAKE PAN

OVEN PANCAKE PAN

DESCRIPTION: Shallow, 11-inch-diameter, round, bowl-shaped, nonstick coated steel pan with two loop handles.

USE: Baking thick German or Dutch apple pancakes.

USE TIPS: This design helps create the sugar glaze that is essential to the recipe.

BUYING TIPS: Many cooks claim this is essential to the recipe.

POMMES ANNA PAN

ALSO KNOWN AS: Pommes Anna dish

DESCRIPTION: Small, round, two-handled copper casserole with snug-fitting lid that matches the base.

USE: Baking the potato dish Pommes Anna, named after Anna Deslions, a high-society French lady of the Second Empire. The potatoes are flipped as a unit to continue cooking.

BUYING TIPS: Rarely used pan but a delicious (and simple) recipe.

PIZZA PAN

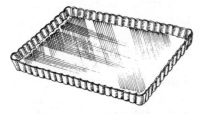

SICILIAN OR DEEP-DISH PIZZA PAN

ALSO KNOWN AS: Pizza pie pan, pizza tray

DESCRIPTION: Flat, round pan, 12 to 17 inches in diameter with an angled edge about ¼ to ½ inch high. A *Sicilian* or *deep dish pizza pan* is a little deeper (about 1½ inches), rectangular as well as circular. Both are available with a removable bottom. Often made of tinned steel or aluminum foil. Another version is a specially designed flat, round, aluminum or steel pan usually 12¾ inches in diameter with a perforated bottom; still another is an insulated model with an air pocket inside. Deep dish pans are often sold with a lever-operated *pan gripper* for holding deep dish pizza pan while cutting and serving.

USE: Baking pizzas in the traditional, eight-slice size, or in the case of the perforated model and rack, baking pizzas with crisp, even crust.

USE TIPS: Perforations or a rack allow for hot air to contact the bottom of the dough.

BUYING TIPS: Some chefs prefer to place their pizzas directly on the oven floor or to use a stoneware *pizza brick* (see page 210), but if you have only a metal oven rack and limited resources, then you need a pan. Look for a removable bottom in the deep dish model for easier serving.

PAN GRIPPER

TERRINE AND PATE MOLDS

ALSO KNOWN AS: Loaf pans

DESCRIPTION: Sheet metal, enameled cast iron, porcelain, or earthenware loaf pan, rectangular, oval, or triangular in shape. The sides may be fluted and the cover may be sculpted with a relief representing rabbits, ducks, or other animals. Capacities range from 1 pint to 2 quarts (from ½ to a little over a foot long) depending on the type. *Terrine* denotes both the utensil and the food.

TYPES: *Enameled cast iron pâté terrine:* Always supplied with a cover that may or may not be vented, this is the most popular model because the terrine is easily served from and stored in the same container in which it is baked.

Galantine mold: Usually made of white porcelain and not supplied with a cover; intended to be used for presentation and service.

Pâté en croûte mold: Tinned steel mold in which the sides and the bottom are separate pieces that can be easily removed from the baked loaf through a series of locking pins or clips that are inserted or removed as needed. The rectangular size is popular and often measures 10 by 3 by 3 inches. May have an embossed herringbone pattern. Oval and fluted shapes are also popular; 9-inch diameter is the norm.

White porcelain or earthenware pâté terrine: The basic item, very similar to an ovenproof casserole, supplied with a lid. Some with small handles on either end, most with no handles.

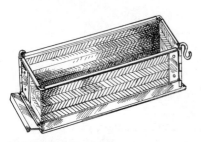

GALANTINE MOLD

PATE EN CROUTE MOLD

USE: Cooking small meat loaves known in French as terrines, galantines, or pâtés.

USE TIPS: To unmold, dip a knife in cold water and run it around the edge. Wet the serving plate slightly so you can move the loaf to the exact center. Also used for cooking small portions of any kind of casserole dish. Make a cover of aluminum foil if need be.

BUYING TIPS: Some of the larger terrines can also be used as *casseroles* (see page 192). Look for one that you feel can be used this way and you will be better off than if you buy a "one-dish" item that you use only rarely.

TORTILLA STEAMER

DESCRIPTION: Low, terra-cotta pot with cover and unglazed interior, 8¼ inches wide and 2⅜ inches deep. Thick, unglazed bottom soaks up water prior to use.

USE: Keeps tortillas warm throughout a meal after the pot has been soaked in water, filled with tortillas, and baked in oven or microwave.

USE TIPS: Dishwasher safe only if labeled so.

BUYING TIPS: Next best thing to fresh-cooked tortillas.

Entree Molds

About Entree Molds

Purists will complain that included here are items not necessarily used in the oven. They are correct. Some aspics and fish mousses are merely blended and refrigerated, but it is impossible to classify these items anywhere else.

ASPIC MOLD

ASPIC MOLD

ALSO KNOWN AS: Gelatin mold, fancy mold, dessert mold

DESCRIPTION: Lightweight metal mold, typically a half-cylinder, either round (with a tube in the center, or "tubed") with fluted edges and ribs, or curved in the shape of a fish, rabbit, turkey, owl, cat, or other decorative item such as a Christmas tree.

Capacities range from 1 to 9 cups, and sizes vary accordingly. Commonly made of aluminum but also of tinned steel or copper, glass, pottery, or even plastic.

USE: Giving shape to solidified aspic, gelatin, or mousse. These dishes are usually made by cooling or freezing, not baking. Metal aspic molds may be too thin for baking. Most make a good decorative wall-hanging.

USE TIPS: Dip the mold in cold water before filling to enable the molded food to slip out easily after it has set. You may need to run it under hot water briefly to unmold it anyway.

BUYING TIPS: Soft-edged patterns are hard to see in a finished item; look for sharp-edged designs. Good to have, even if only for decoration.

FISH MOLD

FISH MOLD

ALSO KNOWN AS: Aspic mold

DESCRIPTION: Lightweight, bright, tin-plated steel or copper mold in the shape of a fish, with a hanging hook that acts as stand. Usually a few inches deep and about 10 inches long, with a 2½-cup capacity, but many are available with capacities of up to 4½ cups, and one is made with a 9-cup capacity. 1-cup models are sold in sets of six or attached to a frame holding six. A similar item, a *lobster mold,* is in the shape of a lobster.

USE: Preparing fish pâté or other fish recipes which call for molding fish mixtures.

USE TIPS: Oil the mold lightly before filling so the fish will slip out easily after baking.

BUYING TIPS: Decorative wall hanging as well as a utensil.

Microwave Oven Cookware

About Microwave Oven Cookware

Although the extraordinarily useful microwave oven is a welcome addition to most kitchens, one constraint that immediately presents itself is that traditional metal utensils cannot be used in them. Even glass or porcelain dishes with metal trim present problems because the

metal reflects the microwaves and in some cases may cause electrical problems. Furthermore, not all non-metalic items are suitable—some may break and others may melt in contact with hot, fatty, or sugary foods.

Be sure to check the manufacturer's directions for use and care prior to putting anything not specifically designed for microwave use into such an oven. Most oven-proof glass, ceramic, glass-ceramic, and pottery dishes are fine, and many heavy platsic items work well. Always look for something that is "microwave transparent," that is, something that does not heat up when bombarded with microwaves. A few microwave-safe materials have been developed just for use in microwave ovens. In the meantime, gathered here are items designed expressly for this use, followed by a section on items that are microwave versions of conventional items.

BROWNING GRILL

DESCRIPTION: Foot-long oval dish made of special, nonstick composite material that is conducive to browning.

USE: Browning foods that normally would not brown in conventional microwave cookware.

BUYING TIPS: Not necessary if your oven has a convection feature.

MICROWAVE BACON RACK

ALSO KNOWN AS: Oinker oven

MICROWAVE BACON RACK

DESCRIPTION: 1½-quart, glazed crockery pitcher with rack that fits on top. Rack holds twelve strips of bacon draped over the rungs of the rack.

USE: Microwaving bacon without use of paper towels to absorb the fat. Fat drips into pitcher for disposal or storage.

USE TIPS: Pitcher can be used for any other purpose you wish.

BUYING TIPS: Some people say microwave-cooked bacon is the best-tasting.

MICROWAVE COOKING BAG

DESCRIPTION: Biodegradable, recyclable, specially treated, heavy paper bag that is heatproof to 400°F. Similar in feel to parchment and wax paper. About a foot long and ½ foot wide.

USE: Holding food for cooking in microwave (and conventional ovens) without a cooking dish—even microwave popcorn. Also for storing food in refrigerator.

USE TIPS: Due to the use of a specialized material, no venting is necessary. You may want to seal it with a *bag lock* (see page 411).

BUYING TIPS: Usually sold in sets of eight.

MICROWAVE CRISPING/BROWNING WRAP

DESCRIPTION: Paper sold in roll form with a special foil coating that attracts microwave energy. Similar to coating used on much commercial frozen microwave food product packaging.

USE: Concentrates microwaves to increase browning and crisping of food.

USE TIPS: Leave a slight opening for venting.

LEFTOVER TRAY

MICROWAVABLE FOOD CONTAINERS

DESCRIPTION: Plastic containers of various shapes with tight-fitting covers, including small, medium, and large casseroles, roasters, leftover trays, bowls, and mugs. Designed to be stacked in the microwave oven. Some are sold with a slotted basket, or colander, for draining fat from meats or steaming vegetables. Also available is a plastic cone that inserts in the center of large quantities of food to help it cook more evenly.

USE: Cooking food in a microwave oven and whenever possible, storing it in the refrigerator or freezer without having to use another dish. Entire meals made of three dishes can be cooked simultaneously when stacked.

USE TIPS: Follow microwave cookbook directions very closely for stack cooking. Tight-fitting covers must be left partly open to vent steam.

BUYING TIPS: This can be a great convenience, but many different traditional materials are microwave- and refrigerator-safe and therefore are less costly than specialized alternatives.

MICROWAVE HAMBURGER COOKER

ALSO KNOWN AS: Drainer-cooker

DESCRIPTION: Clear plastic, 9½-inch-wide dish with perforated bottom.

USE: Precooking ground beef or other meat in order to drain off the fat. May also be used as a steamer.

MICROWAVE LID

ALSO KNOWN AS: Banquet cover

DESCRIPTION: Clear plastic dome with small hole in flat top, 11 inches in diameter and 3 inches high.

USE: Covering and stacking plates with food on them for microwave cooking or banquet-style serving.

BUYING TIPS: Avoids having to use plastic wrap or paper towels.

MICROWAVE METER

ALSO KNOWN AS: Leakage tester

DESCRIPTION: Plastic-covered gauge, in a spoon shape with a ball instead of a cupped spoon area, about 6 inches long, or a small, rectangular plastic-covered electronic device with a meter on one end. Generally has only a green and red scale, indicating "no leak" or "leak."

USE: Testing seams and seals of a microwave oven for radiation leakage.

USE TIPS: Have your oven serviced if meter indicates a leak.

BUYING TIPS: Leakage is not a common problem, but this inexpensive device does bring peace of mind.

MICROWAVE POPCORN BAG

ALSO KNOWN AS: Microwave bag popper

DESCRIPTION: Special paper bag that holds one large serving of popcorn kernels. Sold both with and without popcorn inside.

USE: Making popcorn in a microwave oven.

USE TIPS: Wet thoroughly before use. Can be reused up to three times, or according to label. Do not overfill with popcorn.

BUYING TIPS: No oil is used in these bags, but some people do not like the resulting taste. Very inexpensive.

MICROWAVE POPCORN POPPER

DESCRIPTION: Large plastic dish, 10 inches high and almost as wide, with domed, vented lid and cone-shaped bottom, sometimes with several V-shaped channels.

USE: Popping popcorn in a microwave oven.

USE TIPS: Works without oil, but butter can be added by placing pats in the vents in the lid so that it drips down onto the popcorn.

BUYING TIPS: Specially designed cone-shaped channels in bottom help to concentrate the microwave energy on each kernel so few are left unpopped; a flat or plain bowl would not be nearly as efficient.

MICROWAVE ROASTER

DESCRIPTION: Ceramic oval or round roasting pan with clear glass cover and a metal tray insert. The pan walls incorporate small amounts of strategically placed metal that do not cause harmful microwave deflections. Small model is intended for use in less powerful ovens only.

USE: Browning roast meats in a microwave oven. The metal rack drains juices and the metal-filled walls prevent juices from creating steam, which is what prevents meat from browning. It cooks in dry heat, as in a conventional oven.

USE TIPS: Experiment to make this work.

MICROWAVE TURNTABLE

DESCRIPTION: 9-inch-diameter, 1½-inch-high turntable which rotates on a manually-wound, spring-loaded mechanism that can run for up to about 30 minutes.

USE: Rotating food while it cooks in a microwave oven for even heat distribution.

BUYING TIPS: Some ovens have a food turntable built in, and others need none because the microwave source rotates itself.

MICROWAVE UTILITY BOARD

DESCRIPTION: Small plastic board, 8 by 11⅝ inches, with one flat side and one grooved side. White.

USE: Reheating foods. Grooves catch melted frostings, cheese, or grease. Flat side serves as tray and cutting board.

BUYING TIPS: Handy if you do not have microwave-safe dishes.

PLATE STACKER

PLATE STACKER

DESCRIPTION: Plastic ring made of a slotted band about 2 inches wide with a slight taper to it. Approximately 7 inches in diameter.

USE: Stacking plates with food for reheating in a microwave oven.

BUYING TIPS: Helpful, inexpensive item.

BACON RACK/BAKING SHEET

REVERSIBLE BACON RACK/BAKING SHEET

DESCRIPTION: 10-inch-square, 1-inch-thick, plastic, two-sided cooking utensil. Bacon rack side has ridges that suspend strips of bacon to drain away the fat; the baking sheet side is smooth and flat.

USE: Cooking bacon or baked goods in the microwave oven.

BUYING TIPS: Bacon can also be cooked on a special *microwave bacon rack* (see page 201). Very useful item.

Conventional Equipment Made in a Microwave Version

In addition to the specialized items noted above, many pieces of kitchenware are made in two versions—those that are suitable for conventional ovens and a modified version suitable for use in a microwave. Rather than duplicate the descriptions and uses written for the conventional models, those items are listed here by name only, in the order in which they appear in the book, with a cross-reference to the place where you fill find a full description. Of course, many nonmetallic cooking and serving items are suitable for use in a microwave oven without being specially modified, such as baking parchment or coffee mugs. Always check the label of any item prior to use in a microwave, or do a brief test following the oven's directions.

Mixing Bowl (see page 76)
Meat and Poultry Microwave Thermometer (see page 102)
Instant Read Thermometer (see page 102)
Candy Thermometer (see page 100)
Tongs (see page 134)
Egg Poacher (see page 167)
Fish Poacher (see page 168)
Folding Omelet Pan (see page 158)
Vegetable Steamer (see page 173)
Spatter Guard (see page 176)
Sandwich Grilling Iron (see page 186)
Broil Pan (see page 191)
Casserole (see page 192)
Clay Cooker (see page 192)
Vertical Poultry Roaster (see page 206)
Roasting Rack (see page 214)
Cake Molds (see page 219)
Cake Pans (see page 222)
Flan Pan (see page 229)
Muffin Pans (see page 230)
Portable Convection Oven (see page 448)
Potato Baker (see page 172)
Potato Ring (see page 211)
Rice Cooker (see page 291)
Drip Coffeemaker (see page 309)
Percolator Coffeepot (see page 309)

Ovenware Accessories

About Ovenware Accessories

A number of common items have been developed for use on baked or roasted foods that speed up cooking or cleaning, while others help attain more even or moist results. However, not all are equally useful, so be sure you make an informed purchase.

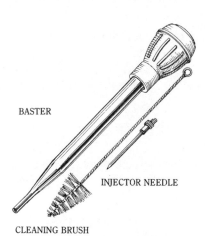

BASTER

INJECTOR NEEDLE

CLEANING BRUSH

BASTER

ALSO KNOWN AS: Bulb baster

DESCRIPTION: Long, hollow plastic, metal, or glass cylinder with narrow, open tip and squeezable rubber, lightbulb-shaped hollow top found in various colors. Some have graduated markings on the side, usually ¼ ounce up to 1 ounce. Some plastic models are made of heatproof nylon. A stainless steel *injection baster* has a long, narrow point, sometimes supplied with a needle that screws on to the tip, and may have a plunger-type handle. Smaller models that resemble syringes or guns are called *flavor injectors*.

USE: Basting roasts, that is, moving cooking juices that have accumulated in the cooking pan onto the item being cooked in order to keep it moist and flavorful. An injection baster is for internal basting—actually putting the juices inside the piece of meat.

USE TIPS: Don't squeeze the bulb of a fully loaded baster too hard or the juices will splash as they hit the roast. Remember, these are usually mostly hot fat, a very dangerous liquid to handle. When finished with use, use a *bottle brush* (see page 402) for a thorough cleaning.

BUYING TIPS: Plastic basters must be kept from touching hot metal surfaces, and may take on some of the flavor of the juices used in them. Stainless steel basters clean up more completely, but you can't see how much juice is inside. Glass has none of these problems, but is fragile.

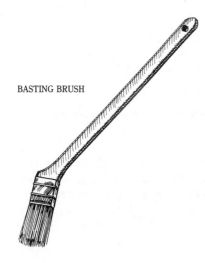

BASTING BRUSH

BASTING BRUSH

ALSO KNOWN AS: Pastry brush

DESCRIPTION: Large brush, often with bristles at an angle, with a flat wooden or plastic handle from ½ to a foot long, or else a loosely gathered round bunch of bristles on a shorter twisted wire handle. Round, artist-paintbrush-like models are known as *barbecue basting brushes*. Bristles are made of natural bristle (tampico) or fine nylon, usually 1 or 1½ inches long. Often sold for barbecue as part of a *basting set* (see page 275).

USE: Basting roasted or barbecued meat and fish, as it cooks, with butter or other fats and sauces to keep the food moist and to add flavor.

USE TIPS: Wash in hot soapy water and dry thoroughly before storing.

BUYING TIPS: Some sanitation experts prefer the round, loosely gathered and easily cleaned kind to the fine, paintbrushlike kind whose ferrule can harbor food. Get the longest-handled model you can find for use as a barbecue basting brush. Very handy item.

BROILER PAN RACK

DESCRIPTION: Two narrow loops of chrome-plated steel wire in an X-shape, curved upwards at the ends, usually available in two sizes.

USE: Supports foil *broiler pans* (see page 191) and provides handles for more controlled lifting of these light items when they are loaded with heavy food.

USE TIPS: Always be careful when working with heavy items in aluminum foil pans.

COLLAPSIBLE ROASTING BASKET

DESCRIPTION: Oval, chrome-plated steel wire basket made of a bottom rack and an upper rim, both of which are connected by a half-dozen small chains. A large bail (loop) handle is on either end. Bottom rack has small feet, keeping it slightly above the bottom of a roasting pan. Fits an 18-inch-long *roasting pan* (see page 194).

COLLAPSIBLE ROASTING BASKET

USE: Easy removal of large turkeys or roasts from roasting pans.

BUYING TIPS: There are several more common alternatives to this item, such as a variety of special lifters (see pages 131, 137 and 140).

LARDING NEEDLE

ALSO KNOWN AS: Larder, boeuf à la mode needle, lardoir

DESCRIPTION: Concave, stainless-steel, knifelike tool, about 10 inches long, with a wooden handle. The blade is less than ½ inch wide. A *larding knife* is a straight-bladed knife about 4 inches long. Another version has a small set of jaws on one end to hold fat.

USE: Inserting seasoned pork fat into roasts prior to cooking for internal basting.

USE TIPS: Go with the grain and insert every few inches or more.

BUYING TIPS: The needle is much more efficient than the knife. Not for practitioners of lean cuisine. Not a common item, now that fat reduction is called for in most recipes.

LARDING NEEDLE

OVEN LINER

ALSO KNOWN AS: Oven guard

DESCRIPTION: Large, shallow, rectangular, lightweight aluminum tray in a variety of sizes that fill an oven bottom.

USE: Catching drips of food that fall to the floor of the oven during cooking, especially when baking pies or making large roasts.

USE TIPS: Place underneath electric burner elements; do not block gas heat vents. Check manufacturer's directions. Can also be used as a cookie sheet.

BUYING TIPS: There are two good alternatives to this: cleaning your oven often or using a well-placed *cookie sheet* (see page 224) on the lowest rack.

OVEN RACK PUSH-PULLER

OVEN RACK PUSH-PULLER

ALSO KNOWN AS: Oven pusher puller, rack jack

DESCRIPTION: 12-inch-long, flat, inch-wide utensil with a V-shaped, forked end and a cut-in hook or notch a few inches back. Made of fine hardwood. Sometimes incorporated on the end of a wooden spoon.

USE: Pushing and pulling wire oven racks in and out of the oven.

BUYING TIPS: Inexpensive but unnecessary item. You can grab a rack with an *oven mitt* (see page 432) or *hot pad* (see page 433) more easily.

PIZZA BRICK

ALSO KNOWN AS: Pizza stone, baking stone, bread stone

DESCRIPTION: Flat, round or rectangular, ½-inch thin piece of stoneware with two loop handles or a chrome-plated steel rack for it to sit on. A typical rectangular size is 14 by 16 inches. At least the top surface is very smooth. Typically a foot or so in diameter. Another version is a set of 4- by 8-inch *baker's tiles,* sometimes called *fire clay tiles* or *hot bricks,* usually sold in a set of eight that fit into a 16-inch-square aluminum tray (may be sold together with tray).

USE: Baking crusty pizza or bread without metal pans.

USE TIPS: This works as it does because the hot stone conducts heat much as a brick oven floor does. Do not immerse in water— wipe clean only.

BUYING TIPS: Unglazed quarry tiles intended for use on floors can do an adequate job too. They are usually 6 inches square, so four will do nicely in an average oven. However, specialized stoneware does the best job.

PIZZA PEEL

ALSO KNOWN AS: Oven peel, baker's peel, bread peel

DESCRIPTION: Large, flat, wooden square with rounded, beveled tip and long handle. Typically 13 to 16 inches across. An *oven shovel* is a smaller version only 4 inches wide.

USE: Inserting and removing pizzas or other large baked goods from oven. Also provides a surface for preparation and serving, if need be.

USE TIPS: Sprinkle with flour to reduce the possibility of the pizza sticking to the peel.

BUYING TIPS: Helpful only if you bake on a *pizza screen* (see next entry) or a heavy *pizza brick* (see opposite), which is placed in the oven prior to the pizza itself.

PIZZA SCREEN

PIZZA SCREEN

ALSO KNOWN AS: Pizza rack, pizza crisper

DESCRIPTION: Expanded stainless-steel or aluminum grid, 12 to 16 inches in diameter.

USE: Slips under fresh or frozen pizza in pan or on oven floor to allow for air circulation underneath the dough. Prevents soggy crusts.

USE TIPS: Excellent help for cooking extra-well-done crisp pizzas without burning the bottom. Best used with a *pizza peel* (see opposite) for support.

BUYING TIPS: Even used by some professionals on stone oven bottoms. Very effective.

POTATO BAKING HOOK

POTATO BAKING HOOK

PLASTIC MICROWAVE POTATO BAKER

DESCRIPTION: Stainless steel band about ¼ inch wide and about 6 inches long, with a slight twist to it and a hook at one end, for holding one potato. A stainless- or chrome-plated steel wire *potato rack,* also known as a *potato baker,* has four upright tines (for holding up to four potatoes). For use in the microwave, there's a plastic model called a *microwave potato baker* with two U-shaped, pointed, plastic rods, bent into four vertical spikes on a base with a handle in the middle. There are simpler models for the microwave—an X-shaped base with points on each end or a circular model called a *potato ring* with four prongs spaced evenly apart.

USE: Inserted into raw potatoes in order to hang them from an oven rack for baking. Saves space on the oven rack for cooking vessels and promotes even roasting. A potato rack holds them vertically from below.

BUYING TIPS: Many cooks believe the metal also helps heat penetrate the potato to cook it faster and more evenly. This does not apply to the plastic, microwave versions. Not necessary for anyone who bakes small quantities of potatoes.

POTATO NAIL

ALSO KNOWN AS: Baking nail, baking spike

DESCRIPTION: Large aluminum nail that looks just like a regular steel ten-penny nail used in carpentry. Also available is a *potato bake rod,* a 6-inch-long form with a ring for pulling out at one end.

USE: Transmits heat to the center of a baking potato or other food.

BUYING TIPS: It is scientifically unproven but widely accepted that this helps food cook more evenly and quickly. Usually sold in sets of four or six.

POTATO SHELL

DESCRIPTION: Small, oval, aluminum foil pan, 4¼ by 2⅜ by ⅞ inches, sold in bulk quantities of twelve or twenty-four.

USE: Baking potatoes normally or baking dishes which call for the potato meat to be removed from the skin and then baked, such as deviled potatoes.

USE TIPS: You may still wish to line these with thin foil prior to use so that they can be easily unmolded.

POULTRY LACER AND LACING

DESCRIPTION: Thin metal rod, about 3 to 6 inches in length, with a finger loop at one end and a sharpened tip at the other. Lacing is called *butcher's twine* or *kitchen twine,* a specially made strong linen string. Sets of smaller rods and lacing, called *poultry lacers,* are sold for chickens, and larger rods in sets, intended for turkeys, are sold as *turkey lacers.* Do not confuse with a similar item, a *trussing needle* (see page 215).

USE: Lacers are anchors for poultry lacing. An even number of lacers are placed on either side of the opening of a bulging, overstuffed bird, and the lacing is crisscrossed, through the lacers, to

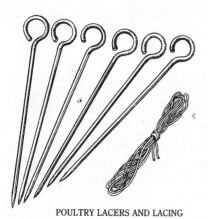

POULTRY LACERS AND LACING

hold the wings and legs close to ensure even cooking, and to seal the stuffing inside. Also used on stuffed roasts, chops, and fish.

USE TIPS: Lacers double as small *skewers* (see page 283) and *cake testers* (see page 246).

BUYING TIPS: Usually sold in sets of six rods.

POULTRY STUFFING BAG

DESCRIPTION: Cotton bag with drawstring, about 6 inches across the top when flat.

USE: Holds stuffing together inside a bird in case you don't like to put it in or scoop it out of poultry after cooking. Fill bag and place inside poultry.

USE TIPS: Machine washable.

BUYING TIPS: It is not so hard to remove stuffing from a roast bird that you need this, but it does speed things up.

ROAST FEET

ALSO KNOWN AS: Rackless roast rack

DESCRIPTION: Small aluminum or steel arches, about an inch wide, 2 or 3 inches long, and an inch high, with a spike or two sticking straight up from the center.

USE: Stuck into the bottom of a roast to suspend it over the roasting pan enough to allow heat to circulate underneath it. Makes for more even cooking and eliminates sticking to bottom of pan.

USE TIPS: Place in a manner that creates a stable base; insert with roast bottom-side up. Can also be used to support large melons in buffet display.

BUYING TIPS: Inexpensive item that does the job, replacing *roasting rack* (see next entry).

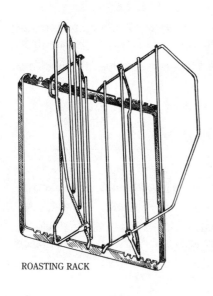

ROASTING RACK

ROASTING RACK

ALSO KNOWN AS: Roast rack

DESCRIPTION: Stainless, chrome-plated, or nonstick-coated steel wire platform that fits in a *roasting pan* (see page 194). Some are flat, others are V-shaped, some are adjustable to either configuration, and some are semicylindrical baskets. Usually designed as a folding model. Also made of plastic for use in microwave ovens, though some manufacturers use a heat-resistant plastic that can be used in conventional ovens as well.

USE: Holding meat above a pan for better hot air circulation.

USE TIPS: Prevents the bottom from stewing in its own juices and acquiring a tough texture.

BUYING TIPS: Folding models take up less space in storage. Very important item to have.

ROULADEN RING

DESCRIPTION: Small, metal ring, about ½ inch wide, adjustable from 1¾ to 2¼ inches in diameter. Spring tension in the metal holds an end hook in the hole you choose to fit the food.

USE: Holding stuffed foods together for cooking. Typical recipes include veal, birds, chicken Kiev, or fish and vegetable timbales, as well as dessert dishes made of rolled cakes.

USE TIPS: Remove prior to serving.

BUYING TIPS: Easier than string and better than toothpicks.

TOASTER OVEN TRAY

DESCRIPTION: Aluminum foil tray, average size 8 by 4¾ by ¾ inches.

USE: Holding items to be placed in *toaster oven* (see page 293), such as open-faced sandwiches or other items with a tendency to drip, such as is common with melted cheese toppings.

TRUSSING NEEDLE

ALSO KNOWN AS: Lacing needle, butcher's needle

DESCRIPTION: Stainless steel needle, ranging from 4 to 10 inches long, with a wide point. Sort of a major league sewing needle.

USE: Stitching or trussing poultry and boneless roasts together for cooking. Threaded with *butcher's twine,* a specially made linen string, and then inserted through the roast or poultry.

USE TIPS: Slightly more secure than just holding string wrapped around a roast with *poultry lacers* (see page 212). Keep needle stuck in ball of twine so you don't lose it in your gadget drawer.

BUYING TIPS: Not expensive and not hard to use. Makes for moister roast birds.

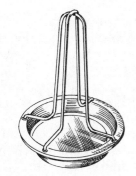

VERTICAL POULTRY ROASTER

VERTICAL POULTRY ROASTER

ALSO KNOWN AS: Upright chicken roaster, vertical roaster

DESCRIPTION: Stainless, chrome-plated, or nonstick-coated steel wire configured to form a trumpet-shaped cone. Base wires may flare out with spikes for potatoes. Many fold flat; about 7 inches tall. Some models come with a shallow 5½-inch-wide gravy pan, usually nonstick-coated, for collecting juices at the base. There are 6-inch-high models called *game hen roasters.* May be sold with racks for both poultry and potatoes, called a *roasting set.*

USE: Inserted into a chicken or duck up to 8 pounds in size to hold it vertically for baking; fats drain down into tray and heat surrounds bird evenly.

USE TIPS: Provides for more even cooking and, it is claimed, cooks a bit quicker than a conventional roasting position allows. Not for use with stuffed birds. Bake potatoes at same time if spikes are provided. Make gravy with the juices collected in the gravy pan. Can also be used on a barbecue grill (see page 269). It is possible to carve the bird still on the rack, if you wish.

BUYING TIPS: Also available in plastic for microwave oven use, but a *plastic roasting rack* (see opposite) will do.

Baking, Pastry, and Dessert Equipment

About Bakeware Terms

The term "baking" is subject to interpretation. This chapter concerns itself with bread and pastry items that are baked. You'll find equipment for baking meats and fish in chapter 7.

Bakeware is a loose term for baking utensils, including bread pans and cake molds. Many of the terms are interchangeable. You can bake a flan on a cookie sheet and freeze ice cream in a mold that can also be used for baking a cake. Plastic molds called *dessert molds* can be used for parfaits as well as pudding, butter, jelly, mousses, aspics, and some entree dishes too. It is important to look beyond the name and examine the description of any item to see if it may have multiple uses.

The difference between the terms *pan* and *mold* is really quite blurred because you can mold cold desserts or even entrees in molds that are also used for baking cakes. Molds generally can be of quite a bit lighter construction and are measured by capacity, while pans are measured by dimensions. In many cases they are used interchangeably. In this chapter pans and molds are organized according to their primary use. The shallowest are often called *plaques* or *sheets;* a *tin* is in between. Shop by function, not by name, to be on the safe side.

About Bakeware Materials

There are many options in bakeware material. Some models come with clear plastic covers for storage or transportation. If you alter your baking to suit the material, you can get good results in any of these—there is no one "best" material. However, most bakers swear by their favorite material and probably feel unable to use any other.

Shiny metal pans and molds may produce a light brown crust because they tend to deflect heat away from the cake. Darker metal may produce a more attractive nicely browned crust because it absorbs heat and promotes fast, even baking and browning. You may have to lower your oven temperatures if you use dark metal pans as recipes are often geared to shiny pans. Of course all baking results depend on many variables, such as the particular oven and the way the ingredients are handled.

The wide variety of choices available most definitely has to do with personal preferences, as some materials possess characteristics totally opposite from others. People have strong opinions about what works, often thinking that nothing else does besides what they are accustomed to. These opinions are not often based on fact but rather on cooking style, habit, or expectations. Most manufacturers make a variety of materials for this reason.

The following are the most popular materials, in addition to stoneware and porcelain, which are discussed in detail in the introduction to chapter 7 (page 190).

Tinned steel, often just called "tin," must be handled carefully to avoid scratching. Though less expensive than aluminum, it is less popular because it may rust if scratched. It is an excellent heat conductor, however—it transfers heat particularly slowly and evenly—which does not interact with food and is nontoxic. It can be soaked, but not scoured, and it darkens with age.

Aluminum is one of the most versatile materials. Many experts prefer it uncoated and medium to heavy in weight for the best, most even baking results. The coated (nonstick) kind seems to get too hot and dries out or over-browns the baked goods, as does thin aluminum. Aluminum is lightweight, doesn't rust, and is very durable. Anodized aluminum is smoother and may be easier to clean, but not necessarily any better for baking. Some manufacturers claim gold anodized bakeware bakes quicker, but faster is not always better, though it may be better for crusts. Both can be soaked and scoured. Aluminum foil is meant to be disposable but can be reused if you are careful.

Black or blued steel is ordinary, thin steel that is chemical- or heat-treated until it turns a very dark blue-black. This makes it slightly rust-resistant but it still rusts wherever it is scratched and must be dried thoroughly after washing. The darker steel bakes quickly and evenly and helps produce a thicker crust, which you want for items such as French bread. Avoid using salty or acidic foods on this surface as they will damage it. This is not a problem if the steel is coated with a *baked enamel* finish.

Glass is avoided by many because it gets too hot and bakes too fast, causing the outside of a baked good to be done before the center and doesn't make a crusty crust. It does, however, look better than most of the other materials and is often selected so it can be used on the dinner table. It is also better than aluminum or non-stainless steel for storage due to its inertness.

Stainless steel is a good-looking, strong, and solid material that you can soak and scour and even polish with commercial cleansers so that it always looks brand-new. It never reacts to foods. On the other hand, it is a poor heat conductor and relatively expensive.

Nonstick (silicone) coated steel or aluminum pans and molds are generally delicate and must be handled carefully to avoid scratches. Even this kind of pan needs a little greasing before it gets filled with batter (vegetable oil spray is the way to go). Its main advantage is that it cleans easily without scouring and the surface does not interact with foods. However, if the thin coating gets a scratch the coating can peel off over time. Many experts find that it heats up too fast and dries out the food, but you can adapt cooking times and temperatures to compensate for this.

Insulated bakeware is a recent innovation that is made from two sheets of aluminum or steel separated by a layer of air and is found in a variety of types of bakeware. This construction protects the bottoms of cookies and cakes from the direct, intense heat coming from below and ostensibly results in even browning, something particularly good for sugar cookies and shortbread, but not necessarily for other items such as aerated cakes like angel food. The heat might not reach inside fast enough, and would cause sinking. Foods generally take longer to bake because of the insulation, as much as 10 to 15 minutes for some cakes. Test first to see if you must modify your cooking time.

Bakeware

About Bakeware

As noted above, there is much innovation and variety in this area, and most items are quite specialized. Buy only according to your needs. Experiment to find what works best for your repertoire and in your oven, and follow recipes closely for best results.

BISCUIT PAN

ALSO KNOWN AS: Roll pan, jelly-roll pan (incorrect)

DESCRIPTION: Rectangular, shallow-edged, tinned steel or aluminum, or aluminum foil pan, 11 by 7 by 1 inches or slightly smaller.

USE: Cooking biscuits, rolls, or other light foods, like cookies.

USE TIPS: Height of lip makes it difficult to get a turner under biscuits or cookies.

BUYING TIPS: Very useful item. Good substitute for *jelly-roll pan* (see page 225).

BRIOCHE PAN

BRIOCHE PAN

ALSO KNOWN AS: Brioche mold

DESCRIPTION: Usually made of tinned steel, cone-shaped, with exaggerated fluted sides and a small base. Diameters range from 3½ to almost 10 inches, or from 2 to 7½ cups capacity.

USE: Baking the French bread item brioche.

BUYING TIPS: Look for seamless model. This is a very specialized mold, more often used by professionals than by home cooks.

CAKE MOLD

ALSO KNOWN AS: Cake pan, dessert mold form

DESCRIPTION: Lightweight aluminum (cast, plain, or nonstick), foil, blued or black steel, nonstick-coated steel, baked enamel steel, stainless or tinned steel pans available in various shapes. They are also made in plastic for use in microwave ovens or for gelatin or ice cream molding. Molds are measured in terms of capacity, and they tend to be deeper and come in more decorative shapes than regular cake pans, but many cooks and manufacturers use the terms interchangeably. In fact, many of the items in each group serve the same purpose.

TYPES: *Bundt® pan* (Also Known As *fluted tube pan, crownburst mold*): 4-inch-deep, 8½- or 9-inch diameter, semispherical tubed mold with a wide, deeply fluted pattern of six sections. Typically a 12-cup capacity. Also available in minisize, either as an individual 6-cup Baby Bundt® pan or a six-piece, 1 cup each, muffin tin–type Bundt-lette® pan. Available in thick cast or thin stamped, nonstick-coated aluminum. Good for all dense pound cakes. Also available is a special plate and locking handle that, along with the inverted mold, form a *tote set* for carrying the finished cake.

Cake cup: Small, individual-size mold, about 3 inches in diameter by 2 inches in height. Handy item.

Charlotte mold: Heavy tinned steel pan with high, straight but slightly angled sides, usually with two grip handles. Available from 2 to 6 quarts in capacity (a 2½-quart size is common and measures 7 inches in diameter).

Decorative mold (Also Known As *jelly mold* or *fancy mold*): Found in a wide variety of designs, including crowns, hearts, stars, scallop shells, flowers, melons, Christmas trees, clowns, owls, cats, rabbits, turkeys, rosettes, fruits, and yule logs. Average size is 6 to 12 inches in length or diameter and 1 to 3 inches deep, with capacity also noted in cups (2½ to 6). Miniature versions are available. A 6-inch-deep version of the star mold is called a *starburst mold,* and is often used for gelatin dishes.

Fluted cake or *aspic mold* (Also Known As *fluted tube pan*): About 3 inches deep and 8½ to 10 inches in diameter (or long, in oval shapes), 6- to 12-cup capacity, as well as minisize. Slightly angular, fluted sides with a scalloped top.

Kugelhopf pan (Also Known As *turban mold, crown mold, Kugelhopf mold,* or *Gugelhupf, Gugel-* or *Kugelhof pan*): Similar to the Bundt® pan (above) but deeper, with a slightly more convoluted design and a narrow tube, this is a round, fluted mold available from 1½ to 3 quarts in capacity; most popular models have about a 9½ inch diameter. The fluted design is slightly angular or spiraled with an enlarged bottom to suggest the weave of a Turk-

BUNDT® PAN

DECORATIVE MOLD

KUGELHOPF PAN

ish turban. Used for making heavier, yeast-raised cakes with dried and candied fruit. Made out of the usual range of light metals.

Panettone pan: 4 inches high, 7½-inch-diameter pan with removable sides, like a *springform pan* (see page 232). Named for the Italian fruit bread that requires this mold. Usually made of tinned steel. A similar item, a *Panettoni mold,* is 6 inches high, with a 7½-cup capacity and deeply fluted sides.

Petit four molds: Wide variety of shapes in a miniature version, usually measured in millimeters. For example, common round and square shapes are 35 to 40 mm (1⅝ inches) on a side. Also made as minibrioches, diamonds, plain or fluted ovals (barquettes), fluted rounds, rectangles, and triangles.

Ring mold (Also Known As *rice ring*): large, deep, circular mold in tinned steel, aluminum, or glass, with a large hole in the center. Popular models hold from 5 to 12 cups and are available from 2 to 12 inches in diameter. Besides cakes and breads, a ring mold is used for making rice rings as well as aspic and gelatin preparations. A *Trois Frères mold* is a scalloped ring; a flattened version without the tube is known as a *Viennese swirl pan.* Most cooks should have one or two sizes.

Ring cake mold (Also Known As *Kransekake forms*): Set of as many as fifteen flat, ridged molds of progressively smaller sizes, each with a hole in the middle. Used to made Scandinavian cake of the same name, a multitiered, festive dish.

Savarin mold: Wide, shallow, circular mold, about 9 inches in diameter, with a small hole in the center, like a shallower, narrower version of the ring mold (above). 4 to 6 cups is the average capacity, but also made in an individual serving size 3 or 4 inches in diameter (¼- to 1-cup capacity). Usually made of seamless tinned steel with a reinforcing bead around the rim; popular for making the rum-soaked cake called a *savarin.* Also available in a fluted style.

TROIS FRERES RING MOLD

USE: Baking cakes and making other desserts with these distinctive shapes or names. All cake molds but especially decorative molds may also be used for aspics, gelatin, mousses, and ice cream if they are seamless and can contain a liquid, but extra thin *aspic molds* (see page 199) are not suitable for baking cakes.

USE TIPS: Smaller cakes can be unmolded as soon as they are baked but wait ten to twenty minutes for larger cakes to settle. Run a spatula around the edge of the mold to loosen the cake, pressing outward so as to avoid touching the cake more than necessary. Invert it onto a wire cake cooling rack and then immediately turn it right side up to prevent the surface from cracking. Most of these require thorough greasing if they are not nonstick coated.

BUYING TIPS: An ovenproof tumbler can be set, open-end up, in the middle of a cake pan (see next entry) to substitute for a ring mold, if need be. Professionals use a conical *heating core* for this purpose, converting any plain pan to a tubed pan.

CAKE PAN

ALSO KNOWN AS: Cake mold (see above), cake tin

DESCRIPTION: Lightweight or heavyweight aluminum, tin, aluminum foil, black or blued steel, nonstick coated steel, baked enamel steel, stainless or tinned steel pan available in various shapes. Also made in plastic for baking in microwave ovens. Pans, which are measured in terms of dimensions, tend to be shallower and have plainer shapes than molds, but many cooks and manufacturers use the terms interchangeably. Some round and square pans are sold with tight-fitting plastic covers for transport and storage of the finished cake. Ordinary cake pans are .015 inch thick, while heavy-duty pans are .060 to .065 inches thick.

CHECKERBOARD CAKE PAN

TYPES: *Checkerboard cake pan:* Sold in a four-piece set consisting of three 9-inch diameter pans and a plastic divider with two concentric circular bands suspended from a brace. The bands are the same depth as the pan and form a total of three concentric circles of cake batter, alternating light and dark colors. The divider is removed prior to baking (raw batter is thick and does not mix easily). Pans can be used for plain layer cakes without the divider.

German loaf cake pan: About the size of a long, narrow loaf of bread, made in a wide range of light to heavy metal, and with a strong beaded rim. As much as 12 inches long by about 4 inches wide and 3 inches high.

Round pan (Also Known As *layer cake pan*): With or without a removable bottom, 8- or 9-inch diameter, 1- to 3-inch-high straight sides. Consumer models are made of plain, nonstick, or anodized aluminum, stainless or black steel; professional models are made of the same as well as tinned steel. Some are sold in sets of progressive sizes for making tiered wedding cakes *(separator plates* and *pillars* are also available for making these elaborate constructions). One 9½-inch-diameter, 1-inch-deep pan comes with a *cutter* attached to a rivet in the center. The cutter, a narrow strip of steel flush with the bottom and the side, is bent over the top edge, and releases the cake from the pan as it is drawn around.

Square cake pan (Also Known As *brownie pan*): 8 or 9 inches square, with straight or very slightly sloped sides. Available in plain, nonstick, or anodized aluminum, as well as tinned steel or even glass, and foil. Better models have perfectly square corners and welded sides for durability. Most have a lip for convenient handling. Rectangular cake pans are similar, of course, but one model, sometimes called an *educated cake pan,* comes with twelve hollow aluminum 2-inch cubes that can be arranged to take up space in order to create letter- or number-shaped cakes. Most useful and versatile item.

Tube Pan (Also Known As *Angel food cake pan*): 4-, 5- or even 6-inch-deep by about 9-inch-wide, round, tubed mold, usually with small feet on the open end or an extra-long tube that raises the pan off a counter to allow air circulation while cooling. Most have a removable bottom. Usually made of lightweight aluminum or tinned or nonstick steel, though professional models are heavier. Most common capacity is about 9 cups, or about 10 inches in diameter. Also available in heart, daisy, and square shapes as well as individually sized ("mini") molds sold in plaques of six. Another version, a *high tube pan,* is a plain model with no bottom, which is 6¾ inches high but only about 7 inches wide, with a 12-cup capacity, and no feet. Common, popular item.

ANGEL FOOD CAKE PAN

USE: Baking cakes and other desserts with these common or distinctive shapes or names.

USE TIPS: Use a pan that is as high as the cake will be when it reaches full height during baking (almost all cakes settle back a little), and that is no more than twice the volume of the batter. Too large a pan will yield a dry cake and cause it to cook too slowly; too small and you may have a mess in your oven. As with all baking, follow directions closely. Straight-sided pans make cakes that are easier to frost.

BUYING TIPS: Check the fit of removable bases or sides. Non-stick-coated steel or baked-enamel steel may be worth the extra cost. Heavier-weight pans are less likely to warp or dent, and distribute heat more evenly. Look for seamless corners for durability and smoothness, and good-sized lips for easy lifting. Good pans will last forever.

CAKE STRIP

DESCRIPTION: 1½-inch-wide by 30-inch-long strip of absorbent, heat-resistant, metallic cloth.

USE: Keeps pan edges from heating so fast that the edges of the cake cook faster than the center. Helps create moist, level cakes.

USE TIPS: Moistened and wrapped around side of cake pan prior to baking.

BUYING TIPS: Some pros swear by these.

CANAPE BREAD MOLD

ALSO KNOWN AS: Bread and cake mold

DESCRIPTION: Long, tinned steel canister with cap, in either of three shapes: heart, flower, and star. About 11 inches long and 3 to 4 inches wide. Dough is actually baked in this mold.

USE: Molding loaves of bread into these distinctive shapes as bases for canapés.

USE TIPS: Follow directions carefully as you must put only the right amount of dough into the mold.

COOKIE SHEET

COOKIE SHEET

ALSO KNOWN AS: Baking sheet, cookie and baking sheet

DESCRIPTION: Rectangular or square, flat metal item with one edge turned up about half an inch; some models have two or even three edges turned up. Materials range in weight from very light to very heavy, including insulated aluminum (with an airspace inside), plain, anodized (silver or gold), or nonstick coated aluminum, aluminum foil, and stainless or tinned blued steel. Size should be as big as you and your oven can handle, but 12 by 14 inches square (or by 9 inches wide) is typical. A *cookie pan* or *cookie/jelly roll pan* has a low edge all the way around, usually ⅝ to ¾ inch high). The edge gives the thin tinned steel some strength.

USE: Baking cookies—put the dough directly onto the sheet, or place *baking parchment* (see page 249) on first to prevent sticking. May also be used to support other pans or to make any other baked items, such as bread, placed directly on the sheet.

USE TIPS: Make sure that there is a gap of at least 2 inches between the edges of the sheet and the oven walls to insure proper baking. Lightweight sheets may cause burning. Put one plain sheet atop another to create your own version of an insulated model.

BUYING TIPS: Models with two or three edges turned up are less likely to warp. Buy two; one can be filled while the other is in the oven. Any of the new nonstick, insulated models is worth a try. Important item for all cooks.

CORNBREAD PAN

CORNBREAD PAN

ALSO KNOWN AS: Cornstick pan, ear of corn pan

DESCRIPTION: Heavy, cast-iron tray, either shaped like a frying pan with eight wedge-shaped compartments (*corn bread skillet*), or a rectangular tray ¾ inch deep, 6½ or 8 by 10 or 11 inches with five to seven deep, corncob-shaped depressions (*corncob pan*) or twenty-two plain shallow troughs (*breadstick pan*). The smaller tray may have one or two handles.

USE: Baking cornmeal muffins or cornbread in wedge or breadstick shapes. Small sections allow for browning on three sides, as opposed to just the top and bottom of pieces cut from a loaf.

USE TIPS: Experiment with batters and oven temperatures to find the best way to get cornbread browned on both the bottom and the top.

BUYING TIPS: Avoid any other material than cast iron. Handled models are easier to use and help you avoid damaging the bread with your oven mitts.

CUSTARD CUP

CUSTARD CUP

DESCRIPTION: Looking like a small drinking cup, this is often made of porcelain but is also found in heatproof glass or glazed earthenware. Typical capacity is 4 or 5 ounces.

USE: Baking or serving individual desserts such as custard or pudding.

BUYING TIPS: Sold as a piece of tableware as well as bakeware. Very handy, versatile item.

ECLAIR PLAQUE

ALSO KNOWN AS: Ladyfinger plaque, eclair and finger sheet

DESCRIPTION: Tinned steel sheet with a dozen oblong-shaped shallow depressions about 3 inches long. A similar item is *langue du chat plaque,* with ten small depressions, narrower in the middle.

USE: Baking pastry for eclairs and ladyfingers or similar items.

ENGLISH MUFFIN RING

DESCRIPTION: 4-inch-diameter tinned steel rings, about an inch high. Usually sold in sets of four.

USE: Baking English muffins or crumpets on a baking sheet. The dough is poured inside the ring which forms a mold.

BUYING TIPS: Similar to *egg rings* (see page 181) but lacking a handle.

FLAN RING

FLAN RING

ALSO KNOWN AS: Tart ring, cake ring

DESCRIPTION: Inch-wide metal band, usually tinned steel, which may or may not have a reinforcing beaded rim. May be square, rectangular (up to 14 inches long), or round (8 to 12 inches in diameter). Also available as an *expanding deep flan ring,* a 3- or 4-inch-wide strip of stainless steel bound into a coil that slides from 7 to 14 inches in diameter. A *Marguerite flan ring* has a 12-inch diameter and a large scalloped, instead of a plain, edge. A larger, deeper version of a ring is a *frame,* often called a *mousse frame,* or *entremet ring.* They are available in a wide variety of basic geometric and decorative shapes.

USE: Baking various simple pastries, such as a pastry shell or thin sponge cake, directly on a *cookie sheet* (see page 224). May be used to make basic tart and quiche shells. Frames are used to assemble mousse cakes or layered sponge cakes with fillings.

USE TIPS: Use on a cookie sheet without a rim so that the baked, filled flan can be slid easily onto a serving dish.

BUYING TIPS: Get a sturdy one so it won't bend or fall apart easily.

FRENCH BREAD LOAF PAN

FRENCH BREAD LOAF PAN

ALSO KNOWN AS: Baguette pan, bread mold, French bread tray

DESCRIPTION: Two 2¾-inch-wide half cylinders, about 1½ feet long, stamped from one piece of metal, usually aluminum or black or tinned steel. Available in heavy weight, and in half size (usually with four molds, each 8½ inches long). May be either smooth and open-ended or slightly ribbed and close-ended. More popular in the perforated versions than the plain. A model that has places for six loaves is called a *baguette frame*. An *Italian bread pan* is shorter and wider, typically 15 inches long by 4 inches wide.

USE: Baking two loaves of French or Italian bread simultaneously in the traditional, long shape.

USE TIPS: Some chefs discourage the use of molds for bread, feeling that they trap moisture. They prefer to place the bread directly on the oven floor, if the oven is designed for that, or a slab of stone.

BUYING TIPS: Look for the models that have a slotted center strip, which allows air to circulate in the oven. Good for a bread-baker to have.

HALF-SHEET BAKING PAN

HALF-SHEET BAKING PAN

ALSO KNOWN AS: Baking pan

DESCRIPTION: Flat, heavy aluminum pan with short, angled edges and a rolled rim. The ends have a slight overhang that serves as a handle. At 13 by 18 inches, it is half the size of a commercial sheet baking pan—hence the name. Also available in perforated, tinned steel. A very similar item is the *jelly-roll pan*, which at a maximum of 12 x 18 inches is just a bit smaller (it is often only ¾ inch high, too, less than the half-sheet model), and has no handles on the ends.

USE: Baking sheet cakes or any other baked item. This size fits into a regular consumer oven; the full-size model fits only large commercial ovens. The low sides of the jelly-roll pan make it suitable for use as a *cookie sheet* (see page 224) too.

USE TIPS: Jelly-roll pans substitute easily for half-sheet baking pans (or cookie sheets) if you take into account their low sides.

BUYING TIPS: Very useful—get two. Handy for browning chicken in the oven.

LOAF PAN

ALSO KNOWN AS: Bread pan

DESCRIPTION: Rectangular pan, usually measuring about 8 to 10 inches long by 4½ to 5 inches wide by 2½ to 3 inches high and holding about 6 cups at the maximum. Available in a variety of materials, such as tinned or black steel, plain or nonstick aluminum, blued steel, cast iron, terra-cotta, or glass. Large and miniature sizes are found, as an in-between size, for small loaves or fruitcake, only about 6 inches long. Some specialized types are available as follows:

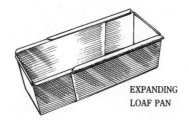

EXPANDING LOAF PAN

LOAF PLAQUE

TYPES: *Expanding loaf pan:* Two-piece pan. One half slides into and out of the other, expanding the pan from 8¾ to 15¼ inches long.

Folding loaf pan: 10 or 11 inches long, with one end that snaps up and can be pulled open so you can slide the loaf out.

Loaf plaque: Rack or *banded frame* holding four or eight miniature loaf pans, each 4 or 5 inches long and about 2½ inches wide, sometimes called a *miniloaf* model.

Pullman pan (Also Known As *Pullman loaf pan*): Has a sliding cover and is usually over a foot long. For baking *pain de mie,* or Pullman bread.

Ribbed loaf pan: Curved version with a ribbed pattern. Another version of this for use with cakes is the *Rehruecken cake form.*

USE: Bake anything that is traditionally loaf-shaped: bread, meat loaf, pound cake, fruit cake, etc.

USE TIPS: Make sure the pan size is appropriate for the recipe you choose. Miniature sizes tend to tip easily if they are not enclosed in a frame. Some materials are not good for all recipes; check to see if a pan you use for bread is suitable for meat loaf before trying it. Some pans intended for use with bread only may not have leakproof seams. Anodized aluminum, darkened sheet metal, or glass pans tend to give crustier breads.

BUYING TIPS: The perforated pans allow moisture to escape and make for a slightly crispier item. Very useful item. You may want to use a *meat loaf pan* (see page 196) if you bake that often.

MADELEINE PLAQUE

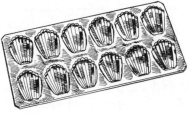

MADELEINE PLAQUE

ALSO KNOWN AS: Madelaine mold, Madelaine pan, Madelaine plaque (incorrect), Madeleine biscuit sheet

DESCRIPTION: Flat, rectangular, aluminum or tinned steel tray with multiple shallow depressions. Traditionally, these are of a shell design, and there are eight to twenty-four of them, each about 3 inches long and about 2 inches wide. Another model, known as a *Madeleinette plaque,* has as many as forty depressions only half that length. An alternative shape is provided by a *sea shell plaque.*

USE: Baking sponge-cake cookies known as Madeleines (named after a nineteenth-century French pastry chef, Madeleine Paumier).

BUYING TIPS: Very specialized item with nice decorative pattern, even if you don't use it.

MARYANN PAN

MARYANN PAN

ALSO KNOWN AS: Sponge tart pan, indented fruit tart mold, continental flan, flan tin, flan pan, shortcake pan, flan/shortcake pan, continental, Obsttortenform

DESCRIPTION: Shallow, 8- to 12½-inch-diameter textured pan with a gutter around the fluted edge. Also available individually sized at 3 to 4¾ inches with about a 4-ounce capacity (may be called a *shortcake pan* in this case). The effect is that the bottom appears to be raised. Made of tinned or nonstick steel or aluminum foil, as well as plastic for use in microwave ovens. Also available in long rectangular shape.

USE: Baking thin sponge cake or pastry shell bases for fruit tarts and other filled desserts. The cake is turned upside down so that the "gutter" in the mold forms a ridge of cake that holds the cream or fruit filling in. Note that flans of this nature are called flans in England and France, but the Spanish flan is a custard baked in a soufflé dish.

USE TIPS: Be careful when unmolding, as a thin sponge cake is very fragile.

BUYING TIPS: Heavier and nonstick types may be easier to unmold.

MUFFIN PAN

MUFFIN PAN

ALSO KNOWN AS: Muffin tin, cupcake pan, muffin tray

DESCRIPTION: Rectangular metal tray with 6 or 12, 1⅜-inch-deep cups molded in place, each 2¾ inches in diameter (2 inches at the bottom); usual capacity is 3 to 4 ounces (all dimensions vary slightly from one manufacturer to another). Aluminum or tinned steel are the most common materials, but also made in stainless steel, nonstick aluminum, aluminum foil, and cast iron, both plain and nonstick. Made in plastic for microwave ovens.

TYPES: *Drop biscuit pan:* Has eight shallow but straight-sided depressions. Usually made of cast iron.

English muffin pan: Large, shallow depressions.

Fancy bun pan: Cups in the shape of teddy bears, the alphabet, stars, Christmas trees, hearts, and a host of other designs. The more decorative kind of pan is fairly shallow and may be called a *cookie mold* or a *muffin plaque* (often made of cast iron with a nonstick coating). The cast-iron types have some of the more whimsical shapes, such as fruit, roosters, and daisies.

Giant muffin pan (Also Known As *Texas-size muffin pan*): 2-inch-deep, 3½- to 4-inch-wide cups (at the top), starting at 10-ounce capacity, each. Made two, four, and six to a pan.

Jam tart plaque: 2½-inch-wide, ¼-inch-deep, slope-sided indentations. A similar item is the *jelly tart plaque,* which has nine very shallow, round depressions.

Miniature muffin pan (Also Known As *gem pan* or *Pixie bun pan*): Holds from twelve to twenty-four 1½-inch-diameter muffins.

Miniature tea cake pan: 1¼ inches wide at the base of each cup, and only ¾ inch deep. Twelve to a pan.

Yorkshire pudding pan: Very wide and shallow, sloped-sided, 4-inch-wide (at the top) by ½-inch-deep depressions, four to a pan.

USE: Baking muffins or cupcakes.

USE TIPS: If you don't use paper *baking cups* (see page 244), spray with a vegetable-oil spray prior to use. If you don't use every cup in a pan, fill the empty ones with water so you don't scorch the surface. Use heavyweight pans for slower-cooking, dense muffins. Fill two-thirds full. Allow lots of air around; place them side by side.

BUYING TIPS: Very useful item—get a set of small, medium, and large sizes. The nonstick versions are very handy here. Look for sturdy models.

PIE PAN

PIE PAN

ALSO KNOWN AS: Pie plate

DESCRIPTION: Classic, round, sloped-sided pan, 1½ inches deep, made of a variety of materials, such as black or tinned steel, nonstick or plain aluminum, Pyroceram, glass, aluminum foil, and even terra-cotta or stoneware. Popular sizes are 8 to 10 inches in diameter (9 inches is standard but models are available up to 12 inches) and about an inch or more deep. A deeper, oval version with a wider rim, called a *deep oval pie dish,* is only slightly wider than a regular pie pan, at about 9 to 11 inches in diameter, and is made of earthenware or ceramic. A perforated pie pan, usually made of heavyweight tinned steel, has small holes that allow moisture to escape and heat to enter. Also available in mini-size, and for fruit pies, with a wide drip-catching lip around the edge.

USE: Baking traditional American pies. Deep oval pie dishes are used for British deep-dish meat or fruit pies that have a sharp crust top. Bright tinned steel will get darker with use, which is desirable.

USE TIPS: Try to avoid cutting into nonstick metal pans or the surface may be damaged. Lightweight metal pans can also be flown, inverted, with a flick of the wrist. If this sounds suspiciously like a Frisbee®, that is no surprise. The pans of Mrs. Frisbee's pies in New Haven, Connecticut, provided the inspiration for today's popular plastic toy.

BUYING TIPS: Experiment to find the material that works best for you. Some cooks find that nonstick pie pans are generally unnecessary because of the high amount of fat in their pie dough. Standard kitchen equipment. It is often convenient to make two pies at once, especially with canned pie fillings, so get two pans.

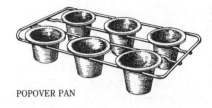

POPOVER PAN

POPOVER PAN

ALSO KNOWN AS: Popover tin

DESCRIPTION: A variation on the *muffin pan* (see page 230) is the *popover pan* which has deeper cups set into plain or enameled cast iron as the traditional material. Some models can be found set in a wire frame instead, in tinned or black, nonstick steel. One model, with 2-inch-deep and 3½-inch-diameter cups, has an extra-wide collar for a puffed crown shape.

USE: Baking popovers.

USE TIPS: Preheat 15 minutes at 400°F.

BUYING TIPS: Not sticking is of primary importance with this recipe, so be sure to either grease your pan well or get the nonstick kind.

SHORTBREAD MOLD

SHORTBREAD MOLD

DESCRIPTION: 8-inch-wide round or square stoneware plate with eight decorative sections molded in.

USE: Baking Scottish shortbread.

USE TIPS: Normally dishwasher and microwave safe, but be sure to check nonetheless.

BUYING TIPS: Very specialized.

REMOVABLE TUBED AND
SCALLOPED BOTTOM
REMOVABLE QUILTED BOTTOM

REMOVABLE
SCALLOPED BOTTOM
SPRINGFORM PAN

SPRINGFORM PAN

ALSO KNOWN AS: Springform mold

DESCRIPTION: Two-part cake pan available in heavy tin, stainless steel, and nonstick metal, as well as plastic for use in microwave ovens. Flat or fluted, and tubed or untubed, 5 to 12 inches in diameter, with a removable side 2½ or 3 inches high. The side has a tongue and latch, such as found on a suitcase. The bottom part of the pan is just an insert, usually with a small quilted, scalloped, or corrugated pattern; it is also available perforated and in any case springform pans are commonly sold with a set of three different bottoms. A heart insert is also made. Standard size is about 9 or 9½ inches diameter, with a capacity of about 12 cups.

USE: Baking cakes of all kinds, especially those that would be difficult to remove from a solid pan or mold. Removable side allows you to use these with soft, sticky cakes like cheesecake as well as traditional batter cakes.

USE TIPS: Check to see that the bottom and sides are securely attached before pouring batter inside.

BUYING TIPS: Also available in three-piece sets of increasing sizes. If you like cakes, buy good ones as they will get lots of use. Some cooks prefer standard pans with removable bottoms that can be used to support the cake when moving it.

TARTELETTE MOLD

DESCRIPTION: Small (2- to 4-inch-wide), cone-shaped, oval (barquette) or round, fluted or plain-sided, lightweight mold in a wide variety of designs. Generally made of tinned steel or aluminum foil. Most often has a solid bottom, but also available with a removable one.

USE: Baking small pastry items, such as individual serving-size tarts or quiches.

USE TIPS: Those with wider bases are less likely to tip over when placed on a baking sheet and transferred in and out of the oven.

BUYING TIPS: Buy sets of twelve or twenty-four molds

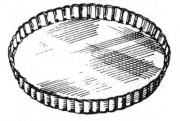

TART PAN

TART PAN

ALSO KNOWN AS: Fluted tart/quiche pan, quiche dish, fluted quiche mold

DESCRIPTION: Shallow, round pan with slightly angled, fluted sides and either a solid or removable bottom (a disk that sits on top of a bottom rim). These are usually 8 to 13 inches in diameter, and 1 inch high. Also available in a square or long, narrow, rectangular shape (may be called a *French tart pan*) 4½ by 14 inches, 8 by 12 inches, or 9 by 9 inches. Almost always made of heavy tinned or black steel, but also available in porcelain, aluminum foil, or blued steel.

USE: Baking tarts or quiches with delicate crusts, whether filled or empty. The removable bottom makes the removal from the pan less risky.

USE TIPS: Models with removable bottoms can be used for either a filled or empty crust shell, and should be used if you intend to serve the tart by removing it from the baking dish, such as for firmly set custard tarts or quiches. Use a solid dish, such as a porcelain one, if you intend to serve from a baking dish itself, such as for fruit tarts.

BUYING TIPS: Porcelain models can be well decorated and make good gifts.

Cutters, Guns, and Stamps

About Cutters, Guns, and Stamps

A number of very useful and usually inexpensive items have been developed to cut or shape raw dough before it is baked into biscuits, buns, cookies, or pastries. Many are recipe-specific.

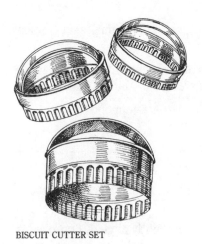

BISCUIT CUTTER SET

BISCUIT CUTTER

DESCRIPTION: Open cylinder about an inch high and from a couple to several inches in diameter, made of metal or plastic, often with a loop handle across the top. Metal models are available with crimped edges. Usually sold in sets of three, from a little over an inch in diameter to about 3 inches in diameter.

USE: For easy, traditional shaping and cutting of biscuits. Simply press cutter into rolled-out dough and lift.

USE TIPS: Dip in flour before each use to prevent the dough from sticking to the cutter.

BUYING TIPS: Common, inexpensive item, though a small drinking glass can suffice.

CAT COOKIE CUTTER

COOKIE CUTTER

DESCRIPTION: Plastic or metal (stainless or tin-plated steel) circular designs, open at top and bottom and about 1 inch deep, or closed and about ¼ inch deep, available in myriad sizes and shapes: boats, cartoon characters, cars, flowers, dinosaurs, farm and zoo animals, Christmas trees, numbers, letters, greetings, geometrics, stars, clouds, hearts, and so on. *Gingerbread cookie*

DINOSAUR COOKIE CUTTER

cutters are shaped to make little people. They range in size from 2 to 8 inches. Some models have rolled top edges while others have beaded edges, and some have loop handles on top, but all have sharp bottom cutting edges.

A particularly complex model is the *four-way cookie cutter*, used for linzer tarts, doughnuts, vol-au-vent, etc., with four edges—scalloped, smooth, scalloped with hole, and smooth with hold. Other similar items are *canapé cutters* (with one solid side) and *garnishing cutters*, both for cutting thin layers of vegetables, meat, cheese, and aspic.

USE: Cutting and shaping of cookie dough or other soft foods.

USE TIPS: Dip in flour to avoid sticking. Experiment by cutting thin slices of vegetables or bread for a festive effect.

BUYING TIPS: Look for stainless or tinned steel or plastic thick enough to hold a shape, but with very sharp edges. May be sold in sets or singly. Some sets are grouped with other pastry items necessary to make certain holiday dishes, such as gingerbread houses or Christmas trees, or else are sold in theme sets, such as animals, Valentine's Day, and so on.

COOKIE GUN

ALSO KNOWN AS: Cookie press

COOKIE GUN

NOZZLES   PLATES

DESCRIPTION: Long aluminum or plastic cylinder, with either a large trigger and ratchet mechanism or a screw device on the back end, and a tip that holds various plates or nozzles. Ten to twenty-four of these tips are sold with the gun with various patterns of holes or slots.

Some models come with cone-shaped nozzles for applying icing to cakes, making it function like an *icing syringe* (see page 261). This may be called an *icing set* or a *cake decorator*.

USE: Squeezing soft cookie dough out in various decorative patterns for making large quantities of butter cookies, or when used with icing nozzles, for decorating cakes with icing in various patterns and textures.

USE TIPS: Clean thoroughly after use.

BUYING TIPS: Almost a professional item; in any case, only for the dedicated butter cookie maker. An *icing syringe* (see page 261) is dedicated to making decorations only. Look for a model that can do both cookies and icing.

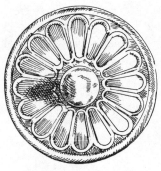

COOKIE STAMP

COOKIE STAMP

DESCRIPTION: Wood, glass, or ceramic disk or square, usually no more than a few inches across, with a small handle on top and a reverse (mold image) decorative design on the bottom. Another, smaller glass version merely presses a design into cookies before cooking. Typical designs include flowers and geometrics.

USE: Making cookies one at a time by pressing down on a small wad of dough. Maintains even thickness.

USE TIPS: Dip in flour or water between pressings to keep dough from sticking. Small, shallow patterns are hard to see.

BUYING TIPS: You can also use any kitchen utensil, such as a meat tenderizer.

COOKIE STENCIL

DESCRIPTION: Long, flat aluminum sheet that looks like a plain *turner* (see page 140) with a leaf or other design cut out of the blade, and a slightly offset handle. Available in a range of sizes and shapes, such as double leaves.

USE: Forming thin cookies in particular shapes, such as for wafer leaf cookies. The dough mixture is forced through the stencil onto the cookie sheet.

BUYING TIPS: Inexpensive item that is easy to use for thin cookies.

CROISSANT CUTTER

CROISSANT CUTTER

ALSO KNOWN AS: Rolling croissant cutter

DESCRIPTION: Stainless steel cutter blades in the shape of a small rolling pin, with wooden handles. The blades are slightly twisted, like lawn mower blades, with round blades for wheels. Available in regular or triple version; regular comes in four sizes that cut triangles from 4 by 8 inches to 4½ by 6 inches to 6¾ by 8 inches; the triple version cuts three triangles 5½ by 6¾ inches. A similar item is a 4-inch-wide *lattice dough roller,* which cuts pie dough into a crisscross pattern.

USE: Cutting triangles in quantity by rolling over long sheets of croissant dough.

BUYING TIPS: Only for the most serious bakers.

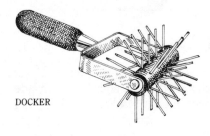

DOCKER

DOCKER

ALSO KNOWN AS: Roller docker, pastry prickers

DESCRIPTION: Thick roller about 6 inches wide with many long plastic or steel spikes protruding from it; axle mounted on a short handle.

USE: Poking holes in puff pastry prior to baking.

BUYING TIPS: A real convenience to use when baking large quantities of pastry; otherwise a fork will do the job.

DOUGHNUT CUTTER

DOUGHNUT CUTTER

ALSO KNOWN AS: Donut cutter

DESCRIPTION: Two concentric circles of polished aluminum or stainless steel, joined by a handle that spans the overall 3- or 4-inch diameter. About an inch high. On some models the inside cutter is removable. Also made in a *crinkled* (crenulated) version.

USE: Cutting doughnut dough for cooking. The inside cutter can be used alone as a *biscuit cutter* (see page 234) or a *cookie cutter* (see page 234).

USE TIPS: Dust with flour to prevent sticking.

DOUGHNUT MAKER

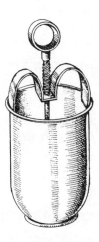

DOUGHNUT MAKER

ALSO KNOWN AS: Donut maker

DESCRIPTION: Large, stainless-steel or aluminum cylinder with a plunger handle on top and a slit around the bottom. Made to hold raw doughnut batter.

USE: When plunger is pushed down, a perfectly formed piece of raw doughnut batter is forced out and into hot fat for cooking.

USE TIPS: Be careful not to get splashed with hot fat. Can be used to dispense thick pancake batter as well.

DROP COOKIE MAKER

DROP COOKIE MAKER

ALSO KNOWN AS: Cookie dropper, ejector spoon

DESCRIPTION: Hand-sized, stainless-steel, tonglike tool with one horizontal blade that goes though a slot in a vertical blade. Made from one piece of steel and bent into a U-shape with spring tension. The blades are a little over an inch wide. A similar item is the *cookie drop scoop,* a small stainless-steel *ice-cream scoop* (see page 266). A similar item is the *ejector fork,* for stiffer food.

USE: Neatly depositing dollops of cookie dough onto a baking sheet without worrying about its stickiness. The squeeze motion pushes the dough off the blade.

USE TIPS: Also useful with peanut butter, baby food, pet food, honey, jam, and jelly.

PASTRY CUTTER SET

PASTRY CUTTER

DESCRIPTION: Wide tinned steel band formed into a large circle, plain or fluted, or an oval, star, or heart shape, with one rolled edge and one sharp, cutting edge. Sold in sets of six to sixteen nesting sizes, depending on the shape (circular shapes can be sold in a set of sixteen concentric circles). Typically 1⅝ inches high and ¾ to 4¾ inches in diameter. The oval shape is longer—up to 6 inches.

USE: Circular cutters are for cutting any size of pastry dough into portions with either plain or fluted edges for use in decorations, vol-au-vent cases, or large cookies, one at a time.

USE TIPS: The circular, one-at-a-time design wastes dough (which can be recirculated of course) and is much slower than the *rolling cookie cutter* (see next entry) if you are using this for cookies.

BUYING TIPS: These are sold in large sets; buy a biscuit cutter (see page 234) if you need only one or several.

ROLLING COOKIE CUTTER

ALSO KNOWN AS: Cookie pin, roll along cookie cutter, pastry cutter

DESCRIPTION: 2½- to 5½-inch-wide, stainless-steel or cast-aluminum roller or drum, axle mounted on a short wooden handle. Depending on the design, the rollers have sharp edges that pro-

ROLLING COOKIE CUTTER

RAW COOKIE DOUGH

duce one to ten patterns repetitively (as long as there is dough and it is rolled). Patterns range from simple jagged-edged rectangles to complex bird and animal designs, all placed next to one another so there is no waste. Also available is a set of eighteen interchangeable plastic cutters that can fit on a drum that holds six of them at a time.

USE: Cutting infinite numbers of cookies, jigsaw-puzzle style, from long pieces of rolled-out cookie dough.

BUYING TIPS: Wastes less dough than individual cookie cutters, and faster to operate as well.

Dessert Molds

About Dessert Molds

With the exception of the versatile ramekin and the soufflé dish, these are one-recipe items. However, most are popular recipes and the items are not so expensive as to preclude their addition to most kitchens.

BABA MOLD

ALSO KNOWN AS: Baba au rhum mold

DESCRIPTION: Small metal mold, either round or oval, about the shape of a drinking cup, sometimes with a rolled lip, available with a capacity from about 1 to 7 ounces. A lighter-weight but similar mold is a *timbale*. A shallower oval mold is more accurately called a *dariole* though for some, it is the name of any baba mold. Found in tinned or stainless steel as well as aluminum. Sometimes this name is used for a small ring mold that is really a *savarin mold* (see page 221).

USE: Making the rum-soaked pastry, baba au rhum, or individual mousses, crème caramel, ice cream, and other individual servings of desserts or appetizers.

CANNOLI FORMS

CANNOLI FORM

ALSO KNOWN AS: Cannoli tube

DESCRIPTION: Tin-plated steel tube about an inch in diameter and 6 inches long.

USE: Cannoli dough is rolled and cooked around this simple form.

USE TIPS: Do not remove tubes from fresh-cooked cannoli until thoroughly cooled down.

BUYING TIPS: Sold in sets of four.

CHOCOLATE MOLD

CHOCOLATE MOLD

ALSO KNOWN AS: Candy mold, plaque

DESCRIPTION: Flat, rectangular item, commonly made of plastic but also in tin-plated steel, with a shallow ridge and over a dozen indentations of various shapes, such as flowers, fruits, or nuts. Two-part stainless-steel molds are also available, as are collections of tiny, individual molds approximately 2 inches long or wide.

USE: Making chocolate candies. Plaques are used for solid pieces while the two-part model can be used for hollow or filled pieces.

USE TIPS: Experiment to get the right mixture of chocolate and timing for refrigeration. Chocolate should pop out like ice cubes out of a tray.

BUYING TIPS: Dutch-made molds are usually top quality.

CREAM HORN MOLD

ALSO KNOWN AS: Pastry horn, cornucopia mold

DESCRIPTION: Ice cream cone-shaped tinned steel mold.

USE: Dough is pressed around this form for deep-frying to make a cone for holding ice or whipped cream. A more exaggerated cone shape is called a *lady lock form*.

USE TIPS: Avoid handling after removal from hot fat until thoroughly cooled down.

BUYING TIPS: Sold in sets of six.

CUP MAKER

CUP MAKER

DESCRIPTION: Small wooden block with a bowl carved out of its middle, and a mushroom-shaped plunger that fits the bowl's lines.

USE: Making cups out of freshly made thin waffles, such as for cup-shaped ice cream "cones."

USE TIPS: Fill cups with fruit or other desserts.

GINGERBREAD HOUSE MOLD

GINGERBREAD HOUSE MOLD

DESCRIPTION: Heavy, thick, cast-iron plaque, 8 inches wide by 13 inches long, with indentations on either side that form the components of a gingerbread house: side, front, chimney, roof, etc. Each side forms a different style of house.

USE: Molding the components of a gingerbread house.

BUYING TIPS: Some cooks prefer to use plain, flat pieces of gingerbread that are then decorated with icing for the distinctive details.

ICE CREAM MOLD

DESCRIPTION: Available in as wide a range of shapes and designs as there are creative chefs to use them; the most popular are squarish, for cakes, and figurines, for holiday theme servings, such as Christmas (Santa Claus is the most popular). May be made of pewter, plastic, stainless or tinned steel. Smaller ones are usually three-dimensional, with two similarly shaped halves that fasten together. They may or may not be supplied with a cover for the bottom (actually the top as it is being frozen). Cake-style molds usually have relief on the top only. A *bombe mold* is a 1½-liter capacity, plain or truncated cone, with a top. A larger cone, 10 to 20 inches high and 3-liter capacity, can be used to make extra-large, elaborate French desserts such as an enormous *bombe* or as a *croquembouche mold* or support. A *log mold* is a long, narrow mold rounded on the top (for making Yule log, or *bûche de Noël*).

USE: Molding ice cream.

USE TIPS: Mix several flavors for dramatic effect.

BUYING TIPS: Molded ice cream is always a festive dish.

PARFAIT MOLD

PARFAIT MOLD

DESCRIPTION: Heavy aluminum, 3½- to 5½-ounce, rounded, cone-shaped mold with tight-fitting lid.

USE: Molding ice cream for the dessert dish *parfaits*.

USE TIPS: Run under warm water very briefly to unmold.

POT DE CREME CUP

POT DE CREME CUP

DESCRIPTION: Small porcelain cup with lid. Some have lion heads on side of cup; most have small loop handles. Decorative style.

USE: Cooking and serving custardlike desserts (*crème* in French), or mousses.

BUYING TIPS: Usually sold in sets of six.

PUDDING MOLD

PUDDING MOLD

ALSO KNOWN AS: Pudding bowl, steamed pudding mold, steam pudding tin, pudding basin

DESCRIPTION: A deep container, made either of tinned steel formed into an appealing design with fluted and sculpted or plain sides and a scalloped top (*mold*), or a deep, glazed earthenware bowl with a pronounced rim (*basin*). Some molds have a tube in the middle and a lid or cover that clamps onto the base. A tubed model with vertical, fluted sides is called a *crown pudding mold*. 1- to 2-quart capacity, and 5½ inches deep. One of the more intricate designs in a *cathedral mold,* with multiple arches on six sides.

USE: Making Christmas plum pudding and other traditional British steamed puddings, though both types can be used as a mold for any other kind of dish, too.

USE TIPS: The deep, heavy earthenware basin doubles nicely as a basic kitchen mixing bowl.

BUYING TIPS: The 1½-quart bowl is the most useful size.

RAMEKIN

RAMEKIN

ALSO KNOWN AS: Individual casserole dish.

DESCRIPTION: Small, deep, straight-sided porcelain dish, typically 3-ounce capacity (3¾-inch diameter). A wide and shallow ramekin, either round or oval, is known as a *crème brûlée ramekin* or *custard cup* (see page 226), used for desserts. Usually finished with a high-quality, glossy glaze and decorative exterior—traditionally fluted.

USE: Baking and serving individual servings of dessert or entrée soufflés and mousses.

BUYING TIPS: Very useful, versatile item that makes a nice gift, too. Get good-looking ones.

SOUFFLE DISH

ALSO KNOWN AS: Soufflé mold, casserole dish

DESCRIPTION: Almost invariably made of white porcelain, this clean-looking dish is smooth on the inside but has a fluted pattern on the outside, similar to the smaller *ramekin* (above). It is usually found in the 1½-quart size, but is available in other sizes as well.

USE: Baking and serving soufflés and casseroles.

USE TIPS: Because it is good-looking, this is a useful serving dish, too, even if the item served was not baked in it. Excellent for reheating leftovers, too, and can be used in the microwave.

BUYING TIPS: Very handy item to have, even if you never make a soufflé.

Baking and Pastry Accessories

About Baking and Pastry Accessories

Even if your attempts at baking are only annual, you will find many of these items essential to success, if only for an improvement in preparation and cleanup tasks. Some may seem too small or simple to make a difference, but appearance has much to do with the success of a dessert, and many accessories help with some important details along this line. Happily, most of these things are inexpensive and readily available, and quality is not a major issue.

BAKE CUPS

BAKE CUPS

ALSO KNOWN AS: Baking cups, bake paper, bake cups, cupcake pan liners

DESCRIPTION: Muffin-shaped paper or light foil cups, pleated and available in a wide range of sizes and shapes and colors, in Christmas patterns, floral patterns, Disney characters, and so on. Sizes include giant, regular (about 2½ inches across), or mini. The mini-sizes are also known as *candy cups,* and the smallest are called *petit fours cups.* Also available in the oblong shape of eclairs, as much as 4½ inches long.

USE: Insert one into each *muffin pan* or *cupcake pan* (see page 230) cup and fill with batter. Batter will bake in the cup and you can either serve them that way, or peel the cups off. Either way, you avoid having to clean baked-on crust from the pan.

USE TIPS: These make using muffin tins much, much easier. They reduce the washing time dramatically, permit the cupcakes or muffins to slip out of the tin easily and neatly, and reduce burning on the bottoms of the cakes. However, they may make the cakes a bit smaller than they would be if cooked directly in the pan.

BUYING TIPS: Sold in packages of large quantities, such as twenty-four, forty-four, or eighty-eight cups. Often found in display stands for bake paper of all sizes and shapes. Not always necessary in nonstick-coated pans.

BAKE-IN PIE LIFTER

BAKE-IN PIE LIFTER

ALSO KNOWN AS: First out pie spatula, bake-in pie spatula, lift & serve spatula, pizza slice lifter, pizza lift

DESCRIPTION: Triangular sheet of stainless steel bent to fit the angled side of a pie pan. About the size of an average wedge-shaped serving of pie, but with a large overhang for a handle. Looks almost like a section of a pie pan. A squared-off, rectangular version is called a *bake-in brownie lift* or *brownie spatula*.

USE: Placed under the crust when building the pie and baked along with it. When the pie is cut and ready to be served, this lifts the first piece out without any mess. It can be slid under the other pieces very easily.

USE TIPS: Prevents awkward breaking of crust when inserting a *pie server* (see page 373) to remove the first piece.

BUYING TIPS: Helpful item. As an alternative, make your first slice slightly larger than your pie server.

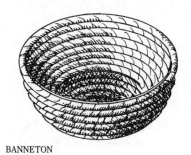

BANNETON

BANNETON

ALSO KNOWN AS: Dough basket

DESCRIPTION: Basket made from a spiral of thick, round reeds, typically about 8 to 10 inches in diameter and 3 inches high; also made in an oval shape.

USE: Gives shape and surface pattern to rising dense, heavy bread dough.

USE TIPS: Do not place in oven. Dust with flour to prevent sticking.

BUYING TIPS: Reeds increase ventilation for improved yeast rising, if that is a problem for you. Also a decorative item.

CAKE BASE

ALSO KNOWN AS: Cake circle, cardboard round

DESCRIPTION: Heavy white cardboard circle, 6½ to 12 inches in diameter, or square, from 11 by 15½ up to 14 by 19 inches. Rectangular model may have scalloped edge. Also available with decorative foil surface.

USE: Supporting cake for serving.

USE TIPS: Do not bake on cardboard.

BUYING TIPS: Removable bottoms of cake pans work just as well at home; these are best for cakes served elsewhere.

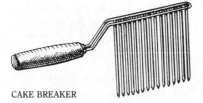

CAKE BREAKER

CAKE BREAKER

ALSO KNOWN AS: Angel food cake cutter

DESCRIPTION: A large, rectangular comblike tool with a small handle, made of long, chrome-plated steel wire teeth.

USE: Cutting and serving large, soft cakes, such as angel food cakes.

BUYING TIPS: Useful if you bake a lot of angel food cake, as a regular knife tends to squish the cake down.

CAKE TESTER

DESCRIPTION: Long metal needle with plastic or wood handle at one end.

USE: For testing the doneness of cakes. Inserted into the center and removed, it if comes out clean, the cake is fully cooked.

BUYING TIPS: A toothpick or a *bamboo skewer* (see page 283) is just as effective.

CAKE TESTER

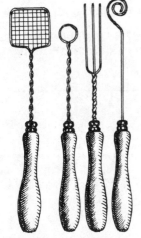

CHOCOLATE DIPPING FORK SET

CHOCOLATE DIPPING FORK

ALSO KNOWN AS: Dipping pin, candy dipping tool

DESCRIPTION: Long, stainless-steel wire tool bent into various shapes, with a wooden handle. Sold in sets of ten different shapes, including a variety of small loops, a square grid, a curlique, and a range of very long-tined forks.

USE: Dipping nuts, fruit, or other fillings for chocolate pieces in the process of candy making. The design of each fork varies according to the shape of the item dipped and leaves a distinctive mark on top of the piece.

BUYING TIPS: Superior to any nonspecialized item by design. The chocolate can drip away properly, and there is no need to pierce fruit or hold nuts in several spots.

COOLING RACK

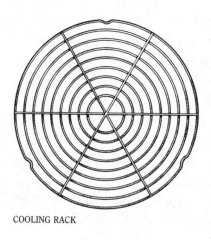

COOLING RACK

ALSO KNOWN AS: Wire rack, cake cooling rack, baker's cooling rack, cake cooler

DESCRIPTION: Flat, round or square rack of thin wires spaced about half an inch apart, with feet that suspend it from about ½ to an inch off the countertop. Usually made of chrome-plated steel, but also made of tinned, nonstick, and stainless steel. Average sizes are from about 10 to 13 inches across. One model has legs a few inches long instead of little feet, and can stack one upon the other up to three high.

USE: Cooling cakes or cookies, or any item just out of the oven. The air circulates underneath and prevents sogginess. Stacking racks save space.

BUYING TIPS: Be sure to get three if you bake a lot of layer cakes—you'll need to cool all layers simultaneously. Avoid racks with large gaps between the wires. Essential item.

CREAM WHIPPER

DESCRIPTION: Foot-high, aluminum, reinforced bottle with non-corrodible lining and three protrusions on top: one is a large nipple onto which a N_2O cartridge is screwed for charging, one is a button, and one is the nozzle by which whipped cream is dispensed. All are removable for cleaning or storage. Supplied with a cleaning brush and cartridges. One-pint capacity.

USE: Making and dispensing whipped cream as a topping for any dessert. Also works with nondairy toppings, mousses, mayonnaise, and various sauces.

USE TIPS: Mix the cream and sugar with different flavorings as an experiment. Do not shake. Clean carefully and thoroughly. Make sure you have plenty of cartridges on hand. One pint of cream yields up to 4 pints of whipped cream. Stores for up to two weeks. Uses different chargers than its cousin, the *seltzer bottle* (see page 326).

BUYING TIPS: Very popular item.

DOUGH BOWL

DOUGH BOWL

ALSO KNOWN AS: Colonial dough bowl

DESCRIPTION: Oblong, deep wooden bowl, about a foot and a half long, made of porous tupelo gum wood.

USE: Provides a handy place for vigorous kneading, and speeds rising by retaining heat generated.

USE TIPS: Insulating properties of the wood retain baked bread's warmth for serving.

BUYING TIPS: Good gift for the serious breadbaker.

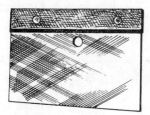

DOUGH SCRAPER

DOUGH SCRAPER

ALSO KNOWN AS: Scraper, pastry scraper, pastry/dough scraper, bench scraper, corne (Fr.), chopper dough divider, baker's helper, bench knife

DESCRIPTION: Stainless-steel or plastic, square or slightly off-square, thin blade, with a wood or plastic handle usually attached to the full length of the top side. The squarish stainless-steel model with a wooden handle may be called a *scraper/cutter*. Also available as a one-piece, heavy stainless-steel unit, with a handle formed from a rolled edge.

USE: Lifting and turning soft dough, or scraping dough or pastry off of countertops after kneading. Angle the scraper against the counter and push the scraps of flour and dough off into a bowl or your hand. Also used for chopping soft foods.

USE TIPS: Definitely speeds cleanup. Also good for carrying chopped ingredients from the board to the saucepan.

BUYING TIPS: Very handy item, especially if you bake bread. Similar items are the *flat chopper* (see page 33) or the *pot and pan scraper* (see page 137).

OVEN SPLATTER GUARD

ALSO KNOWN AS: Oven guard

DESCRIPTION: Extra-wide, shallow pie pan with a large hole in its center. Made of tinned steel.

USE: Placed under a pie to catch drips of filling.

BUYING TIPS: A similar function can be performed by the larger, general use *oven guard* listed on page 209.

PARCHMENT PAPER

ALSO KNOWN AS: Baking parchment, parchment liner, cooking parchment

DESCRIPTION: Literally, paper made of parchment, usually sold in rolls or folded sheets from 20 to 40 feet long, with a cutting edge to tear off appropriate size. Also sold in precut 8- to 10-inch-diameter circles that may be called *baking circles* and 12- by 16-inch *baking sheets*. Parchment triangles are used for making disposable *pastry bags* (see page 263). Treated so it will not burn in the oven, some models designed for cake pans, called *nonstick pan liners*, have silicone added for additional nonstick performance.

USE: Lining baking pans and molds so that the food will not stick to the cooking utensil. Very commonly used when baking cookies, candy, or meringues, as well as for making cones to apply icing or chocolate piping. The precut circles are used for lining the bottoms of cake pans of the same size. Sheets are also used to make envelopes for baking seafood dishes *en papillote,* and are popular for microwave use for covering dishes or lining the oven.

USE TIPS: Lining cake pans for yellow or white cakes is not essential, but it certainly is helpful with sticky chocolate cakes.

BUYING TIPS: Very useful material.

PASTRY BLENDER

PASTRY BLENDER

ALSO KNOWN AS: Dough blender

DESCRIPTION: U-shaped wires or thin blades of metal, about 4 inches wide at the opening, with a plastic or wooden handle grip. About 4 inches deep and an inch or so wide. Made of aluminum or chrome-plated steel. Some manufacturers call the wire model a *pastry blender* and the solid metal blade model a *dough blender*.

USE: Kneading dough by cutting and folding, and mixing shortening, or fat, into pastry dough, particularly for pie crusts.

USE TIPS: Also handy for making tuna or egg salad.

BUYING TIPS: Be sure to choose a sturdily made model. Wires may bend. This job can be done with your hands, but that would heat up the dough and butter. Good for mixing messy foods.

PASTRY BOARD

ALSO KNOWN AS: Marble pastry slab

DESCRIPTION: Usually just a very smooth, large, rectangular (16 by 22 inches), hard, wooden *cutting board* (see page 50) but one that is not used for cutting (some cooks use one side for cutting and one for pastry). Specialized models are made of the finest wood, rock maple, and may have markings scored in showing the standard sizes for tart and pie crusts. Also made of marble and in a 15- by 20-inch acrylic version with two lips, one facing up and one facing down.

USE: Providing a clean and smooth surface for rolling out pastry doughs of all kinds. The plastic model also serves as a drain board.

USE TIPS: Never chop on a wooden pastry board because you'll roughen the surface—use a cutting board. You can chill marble in the refrigerator before use.

BUYING TIPS: Marble keeps your pastry dough cooler than wood.

PASTRY BRUSH

FEATHER PASTRY BRUSH

DESCRIPTION: Looks just like a lightweight flat or round paint-brush. Typically 1 to 2 inches wide with 1½-inch-long bristles made of sterilized natural bristle or fine nylon. Handle of wood, metal, or plastic. Bristles are anchored to the handle with a metal or nylon collar or ferrule, which may slide back for cleaning purposes. Also made in some specialized designs.

TYPES: *Croissant brush:* Made of longer, unbleached bristles than the regular pastry brush, and is therefore softer.
English pastry brush: Round model.
Feather pastry brush: Made of six to eight sterilized goose feathers with a handle made from braided quills.

USE: For brushing butter, egg, or any liquid onto pastry dough or shaped pastries or desserts before, during, or just after cooking to create a glaze. Goose feathers are best for egg glazes. Also used to brush the same for sealing all kinds of dumplings.

USE TIPS: Dip brush in cold water and squeeze out excess before using for increased flexibility, otherwise it may be too stiff. Wash and rinse immediately after use, making sure to remove all food from the base of the bristles. Dry thoroughly and carefully.

BUYING TIPS: Try to find a model with a sliding ferrule, which permits thorough cleaning of the bristles. The best ones cause the bristles to fan out in a large V when pulled back on their wire handles. Wood handles may harbor some harmful microbes if not cleaned properly. Look for high-quality, well-anchored bristles. You don't want the bristles coming off on your pastries.

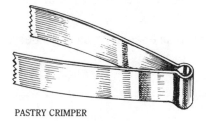

PASTRY CRIMPER

PASTRY CRIMPER

DESCRIPTION: Giant, half-foot-long tweezers, with corrugated edges on the ends. Made from one piece of chromed steel or plain brass. Ends are available in different patterns, such as S, U, and V. Also made in a miniature version for detail work. Not to be confused with a rolling cutter with a wavy blade, also called a *pastry crimper* (see page 43).

USE: Crimping the edges of open-face tart pastry shells, or crimping and sealing double-crust pies.

USE TIPS: May be difficult to use without practice.

PASTRY FRAME

DESCRIPTION: Pastry cloth stretched between two wooden slats by two wire rods. A scale of 18 inches is along the bottom, and two circles—8 and 9 inches—are in the center.

USE: Rolling dough out to precise sizes.

USE TIPS: Put plenty of flour on the cloth.

PIE AND CAKE DIVIDER

PIE AND CAKE DIVIDER

ALSO KNOWN AS: Cake slice maker, cake & pie divider

DESCRIPTION: Stainless or tinned steel or plastic ring with eight vertical blades forming a star. Each opening forms a wedge that is the size of a piece of cake. Another model is a knob with sawtooth arms protruding out. Professional models are available with seven to twenty slices.

USE: Cutting or just marking cakes into eight evenly sized pieces.

USE TIPS: Works best on solid, shallow cakes.

BUYING TIPS: Handy only if you have huge quantities of cakes to serve.

PIE BIRD

PIE BIRD

ALSO KNOWN AS: Pie vent, pie funnel

DESCRIPTION: Small porcelain sculpture of a blackbird with its mouth open and head tilted back. Plainer versions are inverted, footed funnels or small elephants.

USE: Placed in the center of fruit pies to aid ventilation as they bake.

BUYING TIPS: Make sure your bird is tall enough if you use a deep pie dish. Popular with children.

PIE CRUST MAKER

DESCRIPTION: 14-inch-diameter, zippered plastic bag. A ball of pie crust dough is placed inside it and rolled out by a rolling pin on the outside.

USE: Rolling out pie dough without it sticking to the rolling pin.

PIE CRUST MOLD

PIE CRUST MOLD

DESCRIPTION: Thin plastic rings, made of flat bands about an inch wide, available in bright colors. Inside diameters are 8, 9, and 10 inches. Usually sold in a set of all three. A knife or rolling cutter is drawn along the inside edge when placed on rolled-out dough.

USE: Cutting pie crust to the right size after it has been rolled out.

USE TIPS: This may be more convenient than measuring or cutting off an overhang from the pie tin, but it must be cleaned and stored. One alternative is to either get a rolling pin that has measurements on it or to measure and mark your pin (or your board) so that you can see how big your crust is.

BUYING TIPS: Fast and accurate.

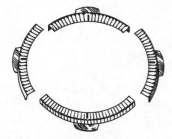

PIE CRUST SHIELD

PIE CRUST SHIELD

DESCRIPTION: Curved aluminum channel with an embossed corrugated pattern, sold in sets of four, with a small handle at the top of the curve. Each channel covers a quarter of a pie crust edge.

USE: Placed over pie crust edges to protect them from burning.

USE TIPS: This protects the crust, but it does not mold it.

BUYING TIPS: Experiment with your recipe before assuming you need these. Aluminum foil strips can do the same job as well.

PIE TOP CUTTER

PIE TOP CUTTER

ALSO KNOWN AS: Pie topper

DESCRIPTION: 10-inch-wide plastic disk with cut-out shapes of apples, hearts, tulips, birds, lattice design, etc. Cutting edges descend from the hole edges. Also available in a smaller, 5-inch size as either a *chicken pot pie topper* or an *apple/cherry deep dish topper*.

USE: Cutting decorative holes in the top crusts of pies prior to baking. Open areas let hot air out and prevent large bubbles from forming under the crust.

USE TIPS: Cut dough while on the cutting board, not on the pie.

BUYING TIPS: May be sold in a set with several pie topper patterns and other pie-baking accessories.

PIE WEIGHTS

ALSO KNOWN AS: Baking beans, baking weights

DESCRIPTION: Flat ceramic or aluminum beanlike pieces sold in bags of about 1 to 2½ pounds. Also available as a 6-foot-long stainless-steel beaded chain.

USE: Weighting down pie crusts that are being baked without a filling ("prebaked"). The weights not only hold down the crust to prevent bubbles but also conduct heat for even baking.

USE TIPS: Line dough with foil or oiled wax paper first.

BUYING TIPS: Dried beans or rice do the job just as well.

PIZELLE CONE ROLLER

PIZELLE CONE ROLLER

ALSO KNOWN AS: Kromkake roller or pin

DESCRIPTION: Wooden cone with short, round handle.

USE: Form that warm *pizelle* (Italian wafer cookies) and krumkakes (Scandinavian wafer cookies) are wrapped around to shape them into ice- or whipped-cream cones.

BUYING TIPS: Anything conical will do, or a wooden spoon for long cylinders.

PIZELLE IRON

PIZELLE IRON

ALSO KNOWN AS: Wafer grill

DESCRIPTION: Two small cast-aluminum disks, about 5 inches in diameter, with intricate embossed star patterns, hinged together, and with very long handles. Also available in an electric version that makes two or four at a time, with slightly different patterns, 5 to 7 inches in diameter. The Scandinavian version of this is called a *krumkake* (or *crumcake*) *iron,* sold usually with a base, or ring, that goes directly onto the flame. A *sugar cone iron* has a rounded triangular form with a shallow crisscross pattern, but is otherwise similar.

USE: Making *pizelle,* thin Italian wafer cookies, or other dessert waffles. These can be rolled to form ice-cream cones with a *pizelle cone roller* (see previous entry).

USE TIPS: The electric version is much easier to use.

ROLLING PIN

DESCRIPTION: Long, solid cylinder, often made of hardwood, usually with slim handles on either end but also made without handles. Handles are usually on an axle so that the pin can roll while you hold them. Typically 10 or 12 inches long and 2 or 2½ inches thick, though models 3 inches in diameter are used with lengths up to 18 inches. Available in brass, copper, nonstick material, plastic, marble, porcelain, and ceramic as well as hardwoods such as rock maple, beechwood, boxwood, or mahogany. There are even hollow models that you fill with ice in order to keep them cool (or hot water to soften a hard dough). Small pins are made as well, about 1 inch thick and 7½ to 10 inches long. Some *die cut rolling pins* are textured with grooves *(corrugated)* or checker *(knobbed)* patterns for adding texture to any kind of dough, especially flatbread or marzipan, and ridged pins can be used on puff pastry dough. (Marzipan is shaped with marzipan sculpting tools.)

TYPES: *Baker's rolling pin:* Large and heavy, usually 15 inches long by 3½ inches in diameter, and has a steel rod in it for extra weight. Handles on an axle.

Dough roller: 3½-inch-long, 1½-inch-diameter wooden roller, axle mounted, with a short wooden handle.

French rolling pin: Long, handleless, thin wooden cylinder, tapered from the center for rolling out circles. About 18 to 20 inches long; about 1⅝ inches in diameter at the thickest part.

Measuring pin: Regular handled rolling pin with small ruled measurements engraved or printed on it.

Pasta pin: Extra long and thin, about 26 inches long by 1½ inches in diameter, or only 20 inches long and 2 inches in diameter with no handles.

Pastry/pizza rolling pin (Also Known As *dough, pastry, & pizza roller*): Small handle with two axle-mounted pins at right angles on either end. One pin is about 2 inches long and slightly tapered, the other is about 4 inches long and straight.

Springerle rolling pin: 10-inch-long wooden pin with embossed patterns, five per row. Rolled over dough to create decorative German Christmas cookies. This just embosses a shallow design on the dough and does not cut the cookies as a *rolling cookie cutter* does (see page 238).

Straight rolling pin (Also Known As *tapered rolling pin, bakery rolling pin, French rolling pin*): Plain wooden cylinder about 1⅝ inches in diameter, no handles, about 18 to 20 inches long. May be tapered at the very ends.

USE: Stretching and rolling doughs as part of pastry recipes, such as cookies or biscuits, pie crusts, pasta, and similar preparations.

USE TIPS: Look for a heavy rolling pin that rolls easily for rolling bread and brioche doughs. The weight enables the dough to be rolled smoothly and easily. Many cooks prefer using tapered wooden rolling pins without handles. The additional length is useful for rolling a wide sheet of pastry with a minimum number of turns, and the less it is "handled," the lighter the pastry will be. Marble, being smooth and cold, is less likely to pick up the dough or flour or melt the fat; it even keeps the pastry cool. Marble rolling pins may be chilled in the freezer for pastry use on a hot day or in a very warm kitchen. All wooden pins should be

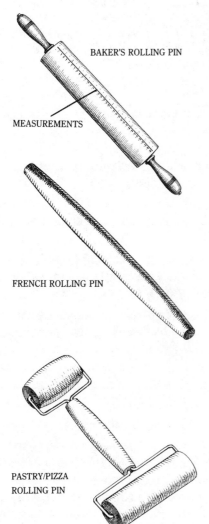

BAKER'S ROLLING PIN

MEASUREMENTS

FRENCH ROLLING PIN

PASTRY/PIZZA
ROLLING PIN

washed and dried thoroughly but never submerged in water or put in the dishwasher.

BUYING TIPS: Marble rolling pins, really about the best material for this kind of work, are often sold as a set with a marble or wooden cradle and a marble rolling slab or *pastry board* (see page 250) about 1 by 1½ feet. Pins with ball bearings roll extremely well but are expensive. Every cook needs one eventually.

ROLLING PIN COVER AND PASTRY CLOTH

ALSO KNOWN AS: Pin cover

DESCRIPTION: Canvas tube (cover) and flat rectangle (cloth). The cover stretches to fit most pins and the cloth is usually about 1½ by 2 feet wide.

USE: When thoroughly covered with flour, makes a smooth surface for rolling dough.

USE TIPS: To clean, brush rinse thoroughly and hang to dry completely. Washing often ruins the cloth, so be gentle. On the other hand, not washing well is bad for kitchen hygiene.

BUYING TIPS: Covers are often sold two to a package. Marble rollers and boards achieve the same effect—rolling neatly—more efficiently. Not a popular item with serious cooks.

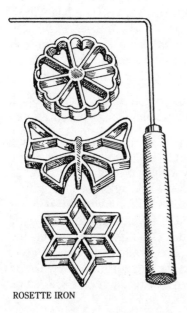

ROSETTE IRON

ROSETTE IRON

ALSO KNOWN AS: Rosette set, cookie waffle, cake maker

DESCRIPTION: L-shaped wire rod about a foot long overall, with wood or plastic handle sold with a variety of metal forms about 3 inches wide. Some models have two rods in one handle. The forms are usually snowflake (rosette), butterfly, and star shapes. Also sold with cuplike timbale forms as a *timbale iron* or more appropriately, a *rosette/timbale set.*

USE: Dipped into batter and then into hot, deep fat for cooking. Rosette irons make thin, pretzellike pieces, while the timbale irons make cups that can later be filled as an individual hors d'oeuvre or dessert.

USE TIPS: Practice to get the batter and cooking time right. Avoid splashing hot fat.

BUYING TIPS: Often sold as part of set (see above description).

SALAMANDER

SALAMANDER

ALSO KNOWN AS: Caramelizer

DESCRIPTION: Small, thick metal disk suspended at the end of a long metal rod with wooden handle. Also made in an electric version, a *carmelizing rod*, which is essentially a long heating element with a handle.

USE: After heating over a gas flame, passed over the tops of breadcrumbs or custard-type desserts to brown or caramelize them.

USE TIPS: Also used on meringues and some gratin dishes. Works best on sugar-based glazes.

BUYING TIPS: Rarely used item.

SHORTENING BRUSH

DESCRIPTION: Wide, plastic brush with stout handle. Bristles are cut at an angle. Dishwasher safe.

USE: Greasing baking pans and sheets with shortening prior to baking.

USE TIPS: Clean thoroughly to avoid spoilage.

BUYING TIPS: Convenience item for those who seek to avoid using basting or pastry brushes or cloths.

SIFTER

ALSO KNOWN AS: Flour sifter, shaking sifter, screen sifter

DESCRIPTION: Muglike container usually made of stainless steel or aluminum but also of plastic, with a squeezable trigger handle or a hand crank and one, two, or three wire mesh screens inside. Squeezing the handle causes an internal blade to rotate (either on a flat plane or in a sphere), or shifts the screens back and forth, aerating the flour passing through. Available in 1-, 2-, 3-, 5-, and 8-cup capacities. The larger models have three screens. There is also a battery-operated model (in the trigger style) with a detachable funnel.

USE: For sifting (aerating) flour. Flour tends to pack down quite densely, and the difference between sifted and unsifted flour can be as much as ¼ cup in a 2-cup measurement. Sifting also helps the flour mix with liquid.

USE TIPS: Generally use prior to measuring any large quantity of flour. For accurate measurements, note whether or not your recipe says to measure the flour after or before it has been sifted. Some chefs sift even "presifted" flour in order to keep their products extra light.

BUYING TIPS: Sifters with capacities of 2 cups or less are considered very small. A fine mesh *strainer* (see page 113) substitutes for very small quantities, but is messy. Sifters are slow to use, but electric ones work faster if you do a lot of baking.

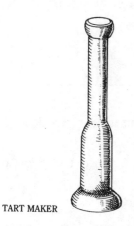

TART MAKER

TART MAKER

ALSO KNOWN AS: Pastry and tart tamper

DESCRIPTION: Small, 6-inch-long wooden club with two flat ends, one larger than the other. One is about an inch in diameter and the other about 2 inches.

USE: Tamping the dough for tart crusts down into the bottom of individual-size metal tart molds.

USE TIPS: Dust with flour before use to prevent sticking.

THICKNESS CONTROL RINGS

THICKNESS CONTROL RINGS

ALSO KNOWN AS: Adjustable thickness rings, thick and thin rings

DESCRIPTION: Flat, hard rubber or wooden rings of varying thicknesses, such as ¹⁄₁₆, ⅛, ¼, and ⅝ inch. Each thickness is a different color. These slide onto the ends of a smooth, hard maple, straight rolling pin. Usually sold as part of a set with the rolling pin, which may be called an *adjustable rolling pin*.

USE: Rolling out dough to a precise thickness.

USE TIPS: Typically ¹⁄₁₆ inch is for thin pie crusts or pasta; ⅛ inch for cookies or crackers; ¼ inch for puff pastry or Beef Wellington crust; and ⅜ inch for biscuits or thicker pizza.

BUYING TIPS: Recipes do not always specify dough thickness in all these tolerances, and you can learn to get a proper thickness through experience.

Cake Decorating Items

About Cake Decorating Items

Some cakes are decorated as a matter of course, and for this a good number of specialized items have been developed. It is very hard if not impossible to do much decorating without them. They are very widely distributed and usually not very expensive.

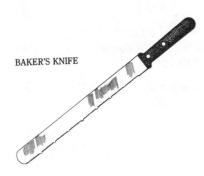

BAKER'S KNIFE

BAKER'S KNIFE

ALSO KNOWN AS: Cake knife, cake slicer

DESCRIPTION: 12- to 14-inch-long, narrow, flexible, stainless-steel knife. Round tip and serrated edge.

USE: Slicing thick cakes into thin layers.

USE TIPS: Work very carefully or you will have a lopsided cake. Use the pan edge as a guide.

BUYING TIPS: An ordinary *bread knife* (see page 10) suffices very well.

CAKE DIVIDING SET

DESCRIPTION: Large, flat plastic disk with lines radiating out from the center point marking 2-inch intervals on 6- to 18-inch-diameter cakes. Supplied with a plastic triangle marker with measurements on the side.

USE: Precise planning of cake decorations such as stringwork, garlands, and so on.

BUYING TIPS: Only for the absolutely serious cake decorator.

CAKE LIFTER AND DECORATOR

CAKE LIFTER AND DECORATOR

DESCRIPTION: Round, flat, plastic item about 9 inches in diameter, with a flat area extending out from one point to act as a handle. Perforated with geometric, decorative patterns—hearts are typical.

USE: Lifting and moving cakes while icing and layering them. The cutout design is for sprinkling powdered sugar on the top of the cake—it acts like a stencil.

BUYING TIPS: Very handy item.

FLOWER NAIL

FLOWER NAIL

ALSO KNOWN AS: Rose nail, rose pin, net nail

DESCRIPTION: Plastic or tinned steel nail or screw with a very wide top, ranging from an almost flat to a spherical, mushroom shape and from ½ to 3 inches in diameter.

USE: Provides a tiny turntable base for making flowers with icing for cake decoration. Nail is held in one hand and turned as icing is applied with the other.

USE TIPS: Attach a small piece of waxed paper to the top surface with a dollop of icing. Make flat flowers in a *flower former,* a long plastic trough, for a more natural look.

BUYING TIPS: Often sold along with icing tips. Screw threads provide more control and feel for your fingers.

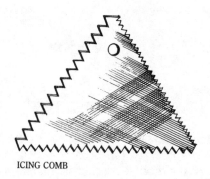

ICING COMB

ICING COMB

ALSO KNOWN AS: Decorating comb, cake comb, decorating triangle, comb scraper, serrated scraper

DESCRIPTION: Stainless-steel or plastic triangle with different sizes of jagged teeth on each edge. About 4 inches on a side. A long, narrow version of the same thing may be called an *icing ruler,* which looks like a jagged-edged foot-long ruler.

USE: Run around the frosting on the sides of cakes to give a professional ridged look.

USE TIPS: The measurements on an icing ruler help in the placement of decorations.

BUYING TIPS: Inexpensive, effective tool.

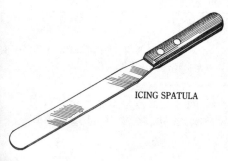

ICING SPATULA

ICING SPATULA

ALSO KNOWN AS: Spatula, pastry spatula

DESCRIPTION: Long, bladed hand utensil, about an inch or so wide, similar to a blunt-tipped knife, with a plastic or wooden handle. Usually flat, but also available as an *offset spatula* or a spatula with an *offset handle,* where the blade angles down from the handle a bit before angling back to be parallel to it. Blade is usually stainless steel or aluminum. Common length is usually about 8 to 12 inches, though some models are less than half a foot long and may be called *spreaders*.

USE: Applying and working with icing on cakes, or slicing sections and filling layer cakes. Also used for turning crepes or tortillas in pans or on griddles.

USE TIPS: Dip in warm water frequently to obtain a smooth surface and prevent the icing from sticking to the blade.

BUYING TIPS: Flexibility is a necessity here. Buy a short, 4-inch model if you have lots of detail work to do; otherwise a standard model is sufficient. There are many tools called spatulas, such as listed on page 138 in chapter 5.

ICING STENCIL

ICING STENCIL

ALSO KNOWN AS: Script pattern press, decorator pattern press

DESCRIPTION: Plastic disk or rectangle with various words or phrases and thematic decorations cut out. Commonly found items are: Happy Birthday, I Love You, Happy Anniversary, Congratulations, and so on. Decorations are simple shapes like hearts, flowers, cakes, and balloons. Another version is the *pattern press,* a ½-inch-wide plastic strip with these same words and shapes in raised patterns instead of cutouts.

USE: Stenciling these phrases or decorations on to cakes. Pattern press makes a guide for icing decorations.

USE TIPS: Practice on paper first.

BUYING TIPS: Inexpensive item that adds a professional touch.

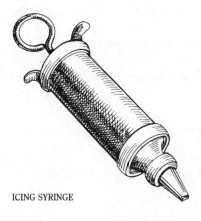

ICING SYRINGE

ICING SYRINGE

ALSO KNOWN AS: Cookie and decorating press (large model only), dessert decorator, cake decorator, creme syringe, decorating syringe

DESCRIPTION: Large syringe that looks like the hospital version, with two finger loops on one end, or an even bigger version that looks like a caulking gun, complete with trigger grip. Both come with many interchangeable *icing tips* (see next entry), usually made of plastic, which give shape or texture to the contents as it is squeezed out. The gun type also uses flat disks to provide even more variety, and some models may double as *cookie guns* (see page 235).

USE: Applying a wide variety of textures to extruded pastry icing. May also be used to fill pastries as well as deviled eggs and celery stalks, or to make decorations with mashed potatoes or mayonnaise.

USE TIPS: Some people prefer the simpler *pastry bag* (see opposite) for the same work because it offers more control.

BUYING TIPS: Often sold as part of a set, called a *decorating set* with all the tips and instructions.

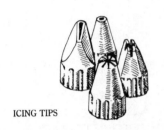

ICING TIPS

ICING TIP

ALSO KNOWN AS: Decorating tube, pastry tube, pastry tip, decorating tip, pastry and icing nozzle

DESCRIPTION: Small, plastic, tinned- or chromed-steel cone that fits into or screws onto a *pastry bag* (see opposite) and serves as a nozzle (the larger ones just rest inside the bag tip while the smaller ones screw onto it). Available in a range of sizes and shapes, most commonly including a plain small hole, star-shaped, X-shaped, a crescent, or a slit. Professional selections are much broader.

The plain, small hole is also called a *writing tip*. The X-shaped or scalloped slitted tip is also called a *leaf tip*. The asterisk-slit tip is also called a *star tip*. The crescent is also called a *lily of the valley tube*. And the long slit, usually slightly wider at one end, is also called a *petal tip* or *rose tube*. All are less than an inch across, some are just ¼ inch, and most no more than ¼ inch wide. Accessories sold include a metal and plastic cylinder *tip saver* for reshaping bent tips, *tip boxes*, and *tip covers* to save icing in the bag.

Tip sizes are noted by numbers and dimensions that vary by manufacturer. For example, one brand's No. 6 round tip is ½ inch in diameter; No. 9 is ¾ inch. Numbers and measurements of other shapes do not correspond, though. Sets range from a few to over fifty sizes and types.

USE: Shaping the flow of icing, dough, or other soft food as it is squeezed out of a pastry bag in a process known as piping.

USE TIPS: Clean thoroughly of all grease; try hot water and vinegar.

BUYING TIPS: Often sold as part of a cake decorating set with related equipment. Buy the set only if you are getting seriously involved with cake decoration. Look for smooth, welded seams. Do not rely on measurements or numbers of sizes—go by eye and by recipe. Often sold with miniature wire-shaft, nylon-bristle *icing tip cleaning brushes* for cleaning.

LAYER CUTTER

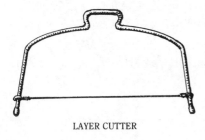

LAYER CUTTER

ALSO KNOWN AS: Wire cake slicer, cake leveler

DESCRIPTION: Fine steel wire about a foot long strung tightly between the ends of a U-shaped heavy wire frame. The distance of the wire from the ends is adjustable. A *cake saw* (Also Known As *confectioner's harp*), a saw blade set into a frame and adjusted by thumb screws, is available for the really serious baker.

USE: Slicing layers of cake into thin slices, and assuring that the slices are even.

USE TIPS: Drag the wire through the cake by keeping the ends of the frame on the counter in order to make an even cut.

BUYING TIPS: The same result can be achieved with a bit more effort by putting the cake back into a cakepan and drawing a *baker's knife* (see page 259) or any large knife, such as a *bread knife* (see page 10) or *slicer* (see page 19), across the rim. Put the cake on pieces of cardboard to bring it up the rim if need be.

PASTRY BAG

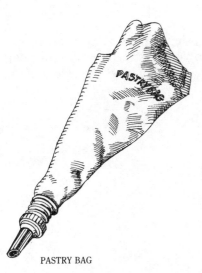

PASTRY BAG

ALSO KNOWN AS: Icing bag, decorating icing tube, pastry tube, cake decorator, decorating tube, decorating bag, forcing bag

DESCRIPTION: Tightly woven, cone-shaped cloth bag made of polyester, nylon, or plastic-lined cotton, as well as disposable paper. Almost always white, and available from 8 to 21 inches long. The small end is reinforced to hold metal or plastic *icing tips* (see opposite) of various shapes, which attach, in some cases, with the aid of a small cylindrical plastic piece called a *coupling* or *coupler,* which is also sold separately.

USE: Hand-squeezed cake and pastry decorating or assembly, known as piping. These are used for icings, buttercream decorations, eclair filling, and other pastry-related jobs as well as for forming doughs and even mashed potatoes into creative shapes.

The interchangeable tips have different shapes to give different patterns, such as plain (for writing) or star-shaped. Large ones are best for piping meringue, medium ones for piping whipped cream, and small ones for applying icing. Couplings allow you to change tips without having to change bags.

USE TIPS: Soak in hot water and vinegar to remove buttercream. Dry thoroughly after use (drape it over a bottle). Use paper or make your own from *parchment triangles* (see page 249) when using food coloring to avoid staining your pastry bag.

BUYING TIPS: Often sold in *decorating sets* or *icing bag sets,* which include at least five different tips. An *icing syringe* (see page 261) offers a solid alternative.

TOPPERS

ALSO KNOWN AS: Cake ornaments

DESCRIPTION: Little plastic figures such as clowns, cowboys, bears, numbers, trains, babies, various athletes, dumb-looking people, Mickey and Minnie Mouse, brides and grooms, Halloween characters, and the like. Most have small spikes protruding from their bases, while others have wide bases or stands with no spikes. More elaborate, romantic versions include porcelain and lace wedding cake ornaments in the shape of gazebos and wedding bells.

USE: Theme-decorating for the tops of cakes.

USE TIPS: Use sparingly.

BUYING TIPS: Professional sources have an amazingly vast array of figures to choose from. Wedding couples come in various combinations of white, black and silver, in regard to the colors of the tuxedo and gown.

TOPPER

Ice-cream Equipment

ICE-CREAM MACHINE

ALSO KNOWN AS: Ice-cream freezer, ice-cream/frozen yogurt maker

DESCRIPTION: There are three types of ice-cream machines, those cooled by ice, those cooled electronically, and those that are placed directly in the freezer. Basically, all of them have a stainless- or tinned-steel or aluminum container for the cream or sorbet mixture, and a paddle device for stirring as this mixture is cooled.

TYPES: *Countertop:* Self-contained stainless-steel and plastic unit with its own refrigeration system. The bowl holds from 1½ pints to 2 quarts and when closed, it is automatically stirred and frozen. Most recipes take about twenty-five minutes or less. Inexpensive versions are available which use ice cubes and salt instead of electric refrigeration. Some are sold with extra removable bowls and mixing blades so that you can make larger batches.

Freezer: The smallest type of ice-cream maker, this holds from a pint to a quart of ice cream and consists only of a stirring mechanism; the cold is provided by placing the entire device in your freezer and running the power cord out the door.

Old-fashioned wooden bucket: Made like a small barrel, the power models have an electric motor that sits directly on the top, while the hand-cranked models have a gear device on the top, connected to a large crank on the side. In both models, a paddle, known as a *dasher,* usually made of beechwood, hangs down from the center and fits into the cream. Both have a tinned-steel food container that holds 2 to 6 quarts, which is smaller than the tub so that it can be surrounded by ice. May be a foot and a half high overall. Most recipes take about forty minutes.

USE: Making ice cream, frozen yogurt, or sorbet (sherbet) at home. The ice is usually mixed with rock salt for better distribution of the cold, and to increase the coldness.

USE TIPS: Experiment with various recipes and cooling techniques—this is harder to get right than you might think. Mixing ice with rock salt actually maintains a lower temperature over a larger surface for a longer time.

BUYING TIPS: Hand cranking is fun if you've got an enormous supply of energetic youngsters to crank away; otherwise go for the power. Better models may have thermostats and timers for different temperatures at different points of preparation.

ICE-CREAM SCOOP

ALSO KNOWN AS: Food scoop

DESCRIPTION: Small, hand sized shovel in a variety of designs. Sizes range from one hundred scoops to six scoops per quart.

DIPPER

HALF-SPHERE ICE-CREAM SCOOP

TYPES: *Dipper* (Also Known As *roll dipper, scoop* or *digger*): Small, cast-aluminum or stainless-steel scoop with a deep, small, crescent-shaped bowl and a thick, round handle. Available in an anodized, nonstick version. Made of hollow plastic or metal filled with antifreeze type liquid or of plain nonstick plastic. No moving parts. Hollow models retain heat from your hand, which keeps the ice cream from sticking. Very popular design especially for those who do a lot of scooping. One plastic-covered model is self-heating—it actually has a battery-operated electric heater in the rim that aids in cutting through hard frozen desserts.

Half-sphere scoop (Also Known As *trigger scoop* or *disher*): The classic model. Full bowl with a small metal strip that moves from edge to edge when activated by a lever that you squeeze in or alongside the handle. Stainless-steel construction, usually with a plastic handle, and with metal or nylon gears. Also available in oval shape. The smallest model may also be sold as a *muffin scoop,* for scooping muffin or cookie batter. Typical ice-cream size is 2½ inches in diameter, or twelve scoops per quart, though the 1½-inch, twenty-four scoops per quart, is popular too. Only a model with two parallel handles that are squeezed tgether is suitable for use by both left-handed and right-handed users. Most have springs but at least one make is flexible plastic that has no springs to replace.

Plunger scoop: Deep plastic spoon with lever in handle that activates lever in bowl that pushes ice cream out. Another, 2½-ounce, professional, aluminum version has a spring-operated stainless-steel plunger that pushes the

SPADE

ice cream out very accurately. Suitable for use by both right- and left-handers.

Spade (Also Known As *transfer spade*): Slightly oblong, large, shallow spoon with blunt tip and large handle. Made of hollow cast aluminum, either plain or nonstick coated, filled with a self-defrosting fluid.

USE: For serving portions of ice cream, sorbet, or sherbet, from a bulk container. Also useful for serving other foods like mashed potatoes, rice, or cole slaw.

USE TIPS: Try to avoid dipping your scoop in hot water between scoops, as it can affect the texture of the ice cream. Just wet it with room-temperature water.

BUYING TIPS: You'll have to decide which is most effective for you. If the traditional ball shape is important, you'll probably like the sphere-shaped bowl with curved metal strip. If your ice cream is often very hard, or you are dealing with large quantities, the spade is most effective. If you often serve more than one spoonful, the dipper is a good choice. This seems to be the kind favored by ice-cream shops. 2½ to 3 ounces is a normal ice-cream-cone serving size, or about twelve servings per quart. Good item for any home.

Barbecue and Smoking Equipment

About Barbecue Equipment

Thanks to Henry Ford, who some say invented, but in any case popularized, charcoal briquettes and weekend barbecuing, 82% of American households now have barbecue grills (half use them year-round). As for the choice between gas-fired and charcoal, it is just a matter of personal choice between convenience, taste, and cost. There are devices to help charcoal users avoid using smelly charcoal lighter fluid now, solving one of the major drawbacks to charcoal. Gas-fired grills start faster, but you should still let the grill surface heat up thoroughly, and on some poorly designed or equipped models this takes quite a while.

Grills and Smokers

About Grills and Smokers

Because barbecuing is usually done outside over a source of very high heat, specialized tools have been developed to assist the cook and provide some safety and convenience. There is much ingenious competition in this area, so shop around for the items that please you and your budget.

GAS GRILL SMOKER

GAS GRILL SMOKER

ALSO KNOWN AS: Smoker

DESCRIPTION: Metal box, about 5 or 8 inches by 8 inches and a few inches high, which holds wood, and in some models, water. Cast-iron box holds wood chips only, and is covered. Cast-aluminum water smoker has a smaller box within that holds wood chips, and it is surrounded by 34 ounces of water in the larger box. Both boxes are designed to sit on the surface of a gas-fired grill with the food to be cooked alongside them.

USE: Smoking food on a gas-fired grill.

USE TIPS: Experiment to get the feel for the temperature needed for best results. Put the fire under the smoker box, not the food, if possible. It is the moist heat that does the job.

BUYING TIPS: Consult directions before buying to see which kind is suitable for your particular grill.

OUTDOOR GRILL

OUTDOOR GRILL

ALSO KNOWN AS: Barbecue, grill, barbecue grill

DESCRIPTION: Any of a number of designs that share these characteristics: a space that holds charcoal or artificial briquettes, a system of vents if it has a cover, a metal grilling surface, called a *grate, grid,* or *grill* that is suspended above the fuel space, and usually a cover. A sphere-shaped model with a tight-fitting cover and several vents is called a *kettle grill.* Smaller ones have stands and larger ones have long legs and wheels, with storage shelves and preparation spaces. May be fueled by wood, charcoal, electricity, or gas (with permanent cinders). Some gas grills can be attached to the house's natural-gas supply but all are intended for use with smaller, 5- or 20-pound refillable liquid propane tanks.

Grilling surface may be stainless, chrome- or nickel-plated steel wire, porcelain-enameled steel wire, or cast iron. Replacement grids are available. Exterior may be painted or enameled steel or aluminum. Designs range from spherical or kettle-shaped to small, rectangular shelves on wire legs. Some are designed to fold up and contain the coal ash for portability, while others are intended to be used in the same spot forever.

Sizes range from a portable 14-inch diameter or an indoor 12-by 13-inch model, to a family-sized 16 by 26 inches, or a giant 19-by 35-inch cooking surface. Standard family-sized kettle grills are either 18½ inches or 22½ inches in diameter (269 and 397 square inches, respectively). On gas grills, the heating capacity is measured in British Thermal Units, or BTUs. BTUs range from an enormous 46,000, to an average 32,000 or 36,000, to 12,000 for a portable model. Large models with a warming level as well as a cooking level have as much as 751 square inches of cooking surface. Electric grills tend to be smaller.

A *hibachi* is a small, oblong, round, or square Japanese grill that usually is made of cast iron and has a wooden base that permits its use on a table or floor. Some models have brackets allowing the grill height to be adjusted, and with models that have two grill surfaces you can cook on two levels at once.

Accessories for gas-operated grills include rubber *natural gas hoses, gas gauges and leak detectors, quick disconnect nipples,* and *reserve tank adapters,* as well as an extra, regular gas burner called a *side burner* (for keeping side dishes like baked beans warm). A *grid lifter* can be used on any kind of grill and consists of a slightly S-shaped piece of steel with a handle on one end and a small T on the other; a short bar crosses the middle. Chrome-plated steel wire racks are made for holding basting sauce or tools, usually made for each particular brand of grill. A large bucket-shaped *ash catcher* attaches under kettle-type grills. And then there is the *cordless clip-on BBQ light,* on a long, flexible gooseneck. Charcoal grills are also available with push-button gas starters. Other charcoal accessories include *hinged grates, charcoal rails* (to hold charcoal away from a drip pan for indirect cooking), and racks or tables for tools, condiments, or cutting.

USE: Cooking outdoors over coals or permanent cinders for barbecue flavor.

USE TIPS: Clean the grill with a good stiff wire brush often, and coat with oil to keep food from sticking so much. Special cleaning compounds are available, as is heat-resistant *grill paint.* Place a small metal drip pan directly underneath fatty meats to catch drippings and reduce smoke—the hot coals are placed around the outside edge for indirect cooking. Meat is placed directly over the coals for direct cooking.

BUYING TIPS: Look for a model that has a provision for holding the cover hooked on the side or tilted back when it is not in use. This is important because the cover gets very hot. Also look for a good venting system for more control of the fire and smoke if you use charcoal, and a device that catches ashes as they fall out of the vents. Some of the smaller ones are designed to be easily carried on picnics and feature designs that clamp the top down for this purpose. Note carefully that the grill surface area of some gas models is given in total square inches in order to take into account two cooking or warming levels. Look for accessories like side shelves and tool racks, push-button gas igniter, fuel gauge, thermometer, and dual burner controls. Check to see if larger grills have casters. Top-quality grills are made of thick metal and heavy castings, but are not necessarily the largest or most expensive. Even a small hibachi does a fine job.

PORTABLE BARBECUE PIT SMOKER

DESCRIPTION: Small enameled-steel drum, usually made from two almost equal halves, on legs. The domed cover has an insulated handle on top and the base has grip handles on either side. May be electric or wood/charcoal fired, or both. Typically about 2 or 3 feet high and about 1½ feet across. The base resembles a regular *outdoor grill* (see previous entry).

USE: Grilling (without the cover) and smoking meat, fish, or vegetables.

USE TIPS: It is hard to get the right blend of charcoal, wood chips, and water to create the perfect amount of smoke and heat. That is one reason why smoked foods are so expensive at the market. Experiment to get the right temperature and time down for each food.

BUYING TIPS: Some regular covered, outdoor grills can be used for smoking too, but a little less effectively.

RADIANTS

ALSO KNOWN AS: Permanent cinders, cinders

DESCRIPTION: The heat source in gas-fired or electric grills has two components: the gas flame or heating element, and the *radiant,* commonly known as *cinders.* There are several kinds, and they mimic, in a way, charcoal briquettes or wooden embers in traditional fires.

TYPES: *Ceramic diamonds:* Octagonal, angular, white ceramic pieces that resemble charcoal briquettes but that are attached to one another in an open grid formation. Material is nonporous, so all grease and fat is immediately vaporized when it touches the hot diamonds. Uniform size al-

CERAMIC DIAMONDS

RADIANT SMOKER PLATE

lows for excellent heat transmission and distribution. Not usable on electric grills. Very popular item.

Lava rocks: Genuine volcanic rock of odd shapes and sizes sold in packs of 3, 4, and 8 pounds intended for small, medium, and large gas or electric grills, respectively. Fats and juices are absorbed and burned off slowly.

Radiant smoker plate: Heavy cast-aluminum sheet consisting of a checkerboard pattern of recessed wells alternating with holes. The wells catch fats and juices and vaporize them immediately. Another version is a cast-iron grid, popular on electric outdoor grills.

USE: Radiating heat from gas or electric source and catching drips of fats and juices that are burned off to impart a smoky, barbecue flavor.

BUYING TIPS: Note whatever is recommended for your particular grill.

ROTISSERIE

DESCRIPTION: Attachment for large barbecue grill consisting of small electric motor (battery or household current operated), bracket, *spit rod* (long, square rod that goes through the food), and *spit forks* (to hold the food in place on the rod). Accessories include a number of specialized spit forks or baskets to hold food, such as a *tumble basket* (similar to a hamster cage), *4-prong spit forks* (for large cuts of meat), *flat basket* (for fish fillets or steaks), a *hot dog wheel* (with skewers for ten hot dogs), or a *shishkebob wheel* (actually two wheels that hold six skewers). A *counterbalance* that attaches to the spit for particularly large, uneven pieces of meat is available too. The spit rotates at a slow speed over a heat source.

USE: Quick and easy, self-basting roasting of food over the grill. Constant rotation guarantees even cooking and keeps any one part from burning.

USE TIPS: Although this is automatic, keep an eye on the fire for possible flare-ups when fat drips down onto the coals.

BUYING TIPS: Both standard and deluxe kits are offered, so shop around.

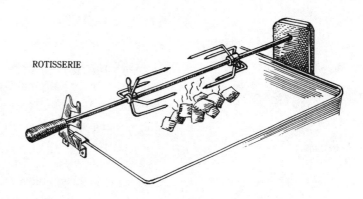

ROTISSERIE

TABLETOP GRILL

ALSO KNOWN AS: Indoor grill, smokeless grill

DESCRIPTION: Gas- (butane canister) or electric-fired grill, with either a chrome-plated or nonstick-coated wire grid or a solid metal, ridged top (or both), and thermostatic controls to set the level of heat. Base is ceramic or metal designed so that it is insulated from the heat and will avoid damage to the table. Most are designed to drain fats away from the heating elements and catch them in a cool drain pan in order to avoid smoke. A small range of sizes and shapes is available, such as 11-inch-diameter round, or 12-inch square, or 12 by 17 inches, and so on.

USE: Grilling food indoors. Popular for those who seek to cook with little or no fat.

USE TIPS: Though most new models claim to be virtually smoke-free, make sure you have adequate ventilation prior to starting. Do not wash heating elements; check directions to see what parts are dishwasher-safe. Does not cook with smoky taste.

BUYING TIPS: Look for models with easily detachable cord sets so you can move this around the table when serving. Look for low wattage, like 750 watts, for the electric models, and for one that disassembles easily for cleaning in the dishwasher.

TUSCAN GRILL

TUSCAN GRILL

ALSO KNOWN AS: Fireplace grill

DESCRIPTION: 18-inch-wide, 15-inch-high iron frame that holds a steel grate with long handles. Intended to fit in a fireplace. Vertical legs have notches for placing grate at different heights.

USE: Grilling over a wood fire, either in a fireplace or outdoors.

USE TIPS: Be sure to use over a small fire of glowing embers, like charcoal in barbecues, placed well back in the fireplace. Otherwise your food will burn and smoke up your house.

VERTICAL GRILL

DESCRIPTION: 11-inch-high and 16-inch-wide black metal frame consisting of two walls with notches along the upper edge and a shallow pan for a base. A 3-inch-wide basket holds charcoal briquettes in a vertical wall of heat. Steel wire *grill baskets* (see page 280) are placed on either side for cooking. Folds up for storage or transportation.

USE: Smokeless barbecuing. Because no fat drips onto the coals, they heat without creating smoke.

USE TIPS: Does not impart a smoky, barbecue flavor.

BUYING TIPS: Small, portable item not intended for cooking large meals. A little difficult to use.

Barbecue Accessories

MOP-STYLE BARBECUE
BASTING BRUSH

BRUSH-STYLE BARBECUE
BASTING BRUSH

BARBECUE BASTING BRUSH

DESCRIPTION: One of two styles, either a *brush* or a *mop*. Brushes usually have 15-inch-long handles made of flat or round wood or, more often, straight thick or twisted thin wire. Bristles may be plastic but more often are natural. A mop, also called a *Texas-style barbecue baster,* is just that: a ball of short, cotton cords a few inches long with a short wooden handle. Flat models may have angled heads for reaching underneath the meat. May be sold as a group of three, called a *basting set.*

USE: Basting meat with barbecue sauce as it grills.

USE TIPS: Clean well and carefully after each use to prevent bacterial growth.

BUYING TIPS: The longer-handled models are more comfortable to use over hot fires, but the shorter models of regular basters and brushes allow more control.

BARBECUE FORK

ALSO KNOWN AS: BBQ fork, toasting fork

DESCRIPTION: Extremely long (sometimes over 2 feet) fork with a large wooden or plastic handle. Usually only two prongs, rarely three or four. One model has an extension handle that slides the fork tip out to over 30 inches from the handle.

USE: Turning and moving food on a grill. Also handy for toasting marshmallows over any kind of fire.

USE TIPS: Don't pierce meat—you will release the juices and the food will taste dried out. Generally best to use a fork to hold food on a wide turner, or to move it around on the grill, not to pick it up.

BUYING TIPS: Usually sold as part of a set of barbecue tools. Important to have.

BARBECUE GRILL BRUSH

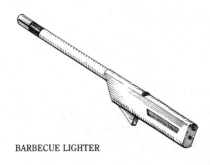

BARBECUE GRILL BRUSH

BARBECUE GRILL BRUSH

ALSO KNOWN AS: Barbecue grill cleaning brush, grid cleaning brush

DESCRIPTION: Wood-, wire-, or plastic-handled, brass-bristled brush with a 2½-inch flat, square head sometimes with a small metal blade protruding from the end. The blade has curved sides that fit over the wires in a grill for close and thorough cleaning. Another version is a double, forked, round steel bristle head on a short, 8-inch handle. One model is made of special wire bristles that do not damage porcelain, but most models do. Clean porcelain or other grills with a heavy-duty nylon *grill scrubber,* a tough, textured nylon sheet mounted on a fist-sized handle. An *oven rack cleaner* is a metal disk with four sets of prongs that is slid along the grill wires. The sets are for different diameter wires.

USE: Scrubbing and scraping charred food off of barbecue grills.

USE TIPS: Some people feel that the presence of charred food on grills adds to the flavor of the food being cooked.

BARBECUE LIGHTER

BARBECUE LIGHTER

ALSO KNOWN AS: Gas lighter, butane lighter, gas match lighter, gas match

DESCRIPTION: Butane lighter about the size of a very small flashlight. The grip area is relatively wide because it contains a large supply of refillable butane gas, and the forward part is more like a thick pen, with an open tip for flame. Most have a battery-operated piezoelectric trigger that sparks the flame.

USE: Safe and easy lighting of charcoal or gas fires in the barbecue grill, as well as pilot lights, candles in jars, and chafing dish candles. Particularly good for lighting birthday cake candles for older people—the flame lasts indefinitely.

USE TIPS: Think of this as an extra-large cigarette lighter, and treat with caution. It is also a miniature blowtorch when turned all the way up.

BUYING TIPS: Much safer and easier than using matches. An extremely efficient and helpful gadget.

BARBECUE
SAUCE POT

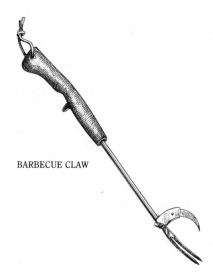

BARBECUE CLAW

BARBECUE SAUCE POT

ALSO KNOWN AS: BBQ sauce container and brush

DESCRIPTION: Small ceramic jar with a built-in brush for its top.

USE: Applying barbecue sauce to food as it cooks on the grill or *rotisserie* (see page 272).

USE TIPS: Aim carefully when replacing brush to avoid a mess.

BUYING TIPS: Especially helpful for homemade sauces.

BARBECUE TONGS

ALSO KNOWN AS: BBQ tongs, scissor tongs

DESCRIPTION: Extremely large (sometimes over 2 feet), V-shaped metal band, usually with forked ends and a hardwood handle. Some ends are inch-wide flat or angled pieces, and others are wire loops. One version, *turner/tongs,* has two different gripping ends opposite one another: a flat turner blade and a slightly curved, clawlike or forklike blade. An even wider version has two turners for gripping ends, called *burger tongs.* Handle section is squeezed to bring tips together. Some models are scisssorlike. And then there is a claw device, 19 inches long, with 4-inch fork prongs and a curved claw that can be forced down against them to pick up food via a squeeze of a trigger in the handle.

USE: Picking up food and coals from the grill.

USE TIPS: Don't pick up crumbly foods like fish and hamburgers with tongs because they might fall apart—use the *barbecue turner* (see next entry) instead. Tongs are best for solid things like vegetables or chops.

BUYING TIPS: Often sold in a set with a large *fork* (see page 275) and a large *barbecue turner* (see next entry), as *barbecue tools.* Your better sets also include a large *basting brush* (see page 272). Look for sturdy, wooden handles. Essential item.

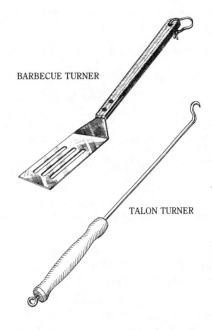

BARBECUE TURNER

TALON TURNER

BARBECUE TURNER

ALSO KNOWN AS: BBQ turner, grill spatula

DESCRIPTION: Very long (sometimes over 2 feet) tool with a small, flat, rectangular surface, often with slots in it, at a slight angle to the handle. Turner blade is usually about the size of a big hamburger, but double- and triple-width models are available. Wooden or plastic handle. One model has wide tines that are spaced far enough apart to fit into the gaps between the wires in the grill, allowing it to get under the food before touching it; another version has two sets of tines and works like giant, forked tongs. A *talon turner* is completely different, a 15-inch-long wire rod that ends in a curved point. The other end has a wooden handle. You must pierce the meat to turn it.

USE: Turning or flipping food on a grill.

USE TIPS: The shorter the handle, the more you must be careful when reaching across a hot grill.

BUYING TIPS: Look for one with a good-sized hole or lanyard for hanging between uses, and a sturdy wooden handle. Often incorrectly referred to as a *spatula*. Essential item.

BARBECUE WOK

ALSO KNOWN AS: Grill wok, BBQ stir fry

DESCRIPTION: 12- or 14-inch-diameter *wok* (see page 155) made of porcelain-enameled steel. The bottom is neither rounded nor flat as with normal woks, but has a small raised circular section with perforations; there is a channel around the circle which catches cooking oils. Available with either a long handle and a helper loop handle or, on the smaller model, two loop handles. Another version, also called a *grill basket,* is a square, slope-sided basket made of perforated, porcelain-enameled steel. Finally, there is now a porcelain-enameled steel *BBQ roaster,* which is a solid, slope-sided, 13-inch-square pan.

USE: Stir-fry cooking over a barbecue fire. The roaster is for roasting or smoking turkeys and the like.

USE TIPS: The flat-bottomed version does not retain sauces or juices like the round, stir-fry version does.

BUYING TIPS: Good way to add open-fire flavor to your stir-fry vegetables.

CHARCOAL CHIMNEY

CHARCOAL CHIMNEY

ALSO KNOWN AS: Charcoal starter, chimney starter

DESCRIPTION: Square or cylindrical sheet-steel device with grid in middle; charcoal is placed above the grid and newspaper or solid fuel fire starters underneath. The bottom half is vented. About a foot high and 8 inches across. Some models have a shielded and insulated handle. Holds 3 to 4 pounds of charcoal briquettes. The better models have a stainless mesh at the bottom to catch ashes.

USE: Rapid (15 minutes) and chemical-free lighting of charcoal. Place on the center of your charcoal rack and just touch a lighted match to the paper.

USE TIPS: Use plenty of paper, loosely crumpled up.

BUYING TIPS: This item is essential in some counties in California, where the use of lighter fluid to start charcoal fires has been banned. Some people make their own out of metal heating-duct piping from the hardware store.

COOKING SLAB

COOKING SLAB

ALSO KNOWN AS: Hot rock, hotstone

DESCRIPTION: 8-inch-square or 8 by 14½-inch, ¾-inch-thick marble slab, with or without grooves along the edges, with a stainless-steel wire frame that suspends it a few inches over the table. Comes with alcohol burners that fit underneath the slab when it is in the frame. Others come with reflector trays that sit in a hardwood serving base. Slab is heated to 450°F prior to use, and on the fancier models, kept hot by the alcohol burners. Others simply retain their heat long enough to cook at the table. This is derived from an ancient oriental cooking technique, though most cultures cooked on hot rocks at one point.

USE: Indoor, tabletop grilling with little fat.

USE TIPS: Experiment before trying this at a fancy dinner party.

BUYING TIPS: Good, fancy gift item.

FOOD UMBRELLA

FOOD UMBRELLA

ALSO KNOWN AS: Food tent

DESCRIPTION: 12- or 16-inch dome made of transparent, fine mesh nylon. Four metal wires covered by plastic hold umbrella upright. Collapses for storage. Available as a square from 13 to 24 inches on a side, and as a circular dome 30 inches in diameter.

USE: Covers food on outdoor tables, keeping flies and ants away.

USE TIPS: Not for use over flames. Not for protection from rain, either.

BUYING TIPS: Inexpensive item.

GRILL BASKET

ALSO KNOWN AS: Hamburger and meat grill, hamburger grill, steak basket, grilling basket

DESCRIPTION: Two-sided, square or rectangular steel wire basket, available in a wide variety of shapes, but a typical model measures about 9 by 12 inches or 1 by 2 feet with 2¼-inch-high sides. Wire may be plain stainless, nonstick, enamel- or chrome-plated steel. One side is hinged. The basket is held closed by sliding a wire loop over the long base handles. Handles come in a variety of materials or just plain wire. Some baskets are shaped to hold certain foods, such as ovals for fish up to 28 inches long (*fish basket* or *fish grilling basket*), rectangular ones with pockets for hamburgers (*burger basket*), or hot dogs (*hot dog basket*). One fish basket, a *triple fish grill,* holds three side by side (ideal for brook trout); another has folding legs that hold the basket at various heights over the coals. A *double shishkabasket* takes this to the extreme, with a deep, two-sectioned wire basket intended to be filled with vegetables that would otherwise be skewered.

USE: For grilling vegetables, meat, or fish over an open flame, or for small items that would otherwise fall through the more widely spaced wires on a barbecue grill, and for delicate items that might fall apart if turned by a narrow turner, or to avoid using *skewers* (see page 283). Allows you to turn a number of small items at the same time, making a much quicker job of it.

USE TIPS: Avoid using small pieces of food that may fall through the basket.

BUYING TIPS: Wooden handles are preferable to metal that can become quite hot. Handy item.

FISH GRILLING BASKET

GRILL COVER

ALSO KNOWN AS: All-weather cover

DESCRIPTION: Rugged PVC vinyl sheets tailored to fit over a particular type of outdoor grill (or lawn furniture). Heavy-duty, .6mm-thick (8-gauge), crack-resistant, fabric-lined material is typical of the better-quality items. Also available in a heat-resistant material that allows you to cover the grill while it is still warm.

USE: Protecting outdoor grill from sun, rain, wind, and snow.

USE TIPS: Don't put vinyl covers over a warm grill.

BUYING TIPS: Prior to purchase, measure your grill with all the attachments on. Look for models with elastic hems or Velcro® closures. Some stores include these with grills as part of a special promotion.

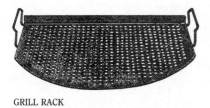

GRILL RACK

GRILL RACK

ALSO KNOWN AS: Grill screen, grill topper, barbecue grilling grid

DESCRIPTION: Fine stainless-steel mesh screen or grid with one upturned edge, about 10 inches square or 12 by 16 inches. Another version is flat, porcelain-enameled steel perforated with closely patterned holes, available with or without handles. Most brands offer round or rectangular screens with rounded edges to fit round, kettle-style barbecue grills.

USE: Keeps small items such as small vegetables or fish from falling through the wider grid of a normal barbecue grill.

USE TIPS: Upturned stop edge helps lifting with turner. Fine mesh screen can also be used as a *smoking rack* to hold wood chips over a gas grill.

BUYING TIPS: Enameled steel is virtually a nonstick surface, very easy to clean up, and smoother and easier to use than the stainless-steel expanded screen, but about three times as expensive. (Fine mesh stainless racks are priced in between the other two types). These racks are a new arrival on the market, but have become very popular due to the increased interest in grilling low-cholesterol foods such as fish and vegetables.

LIQUID PROPANE MONITOR GAUGE

ALSO KNOWN AS: Fuel gauge

DESCRIPTION: Large, colorful dial mounted on a heavy, weather-proof brass casting that screws into your propane tank.

USE: Indicates amount of propane left as well as any leaks.

USE TIPS: Follow directions for mounting. Very simple to use.

LIQUID PROPANE TANK CARRIER

ALSO KNOWN AS: Tank tote

DESCRIPTION: Plastic bucketlike item with a large, deep opening.

USE: Carrying or providing a steady base for a standard propane tank.

BUYING TIPS: Handy item if you have difficulty carrying tanks.

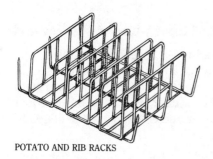

LIQUID PROPANE TANK CARRIER

POTATO AND RIB RACKS

POTATO, CORN, AND RIB RACKS

DESCRIPTION: Heavy nickel-plated or stainless-steel wire racks in various configurations and sizes.

TYPES: *Potato and rib rack:* Large enough to fill a small grill surface, this has vertical slots for ribs or chops and three spikes on either end for potatoes or corn cobs.

    Potato holder and *corn cob holder:* Two half cylinders that hold ears of corn or potatoes at an angle, or two U-shaped wires ending in four spikes that potatoes are set upon. About 6 inches wide and high.

    Rib rack (Also Known As *rib cradle*): Heavy-gauge, stainless-steel wire rack with nine slots for ribs, all at a slight angle, 18 by 11 inches, with handles.

    Warming rack: Small (6½ by 18½ inches) rack with feet that sit a few inches above the main grill surface.

USE: Holding food for roasting vertically and promoting self-basting and even roasting. Warming racks are used for toasting buns or keeping cooked food warm prior to serving.

USE TIPS: Spikes act like skewers, functioning as internal heating elements. May roast faster and more completely than normal cooking style.

BUYING TIPS: Increases grill capacity by as much as 50%.

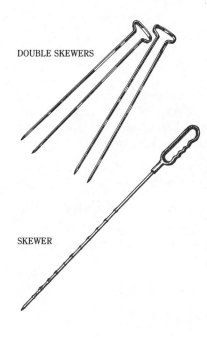

DOUBLE SKEWERS

SKEWER

SKEWERS

ALSO KNOWN AS: Kebab (or kabob) skewers, brochettes (Fr.), skews

DESCRIPTION: Long, thin, metal spikes with various decorative or functional designs on one end; the other end is always pointed. Most common are stainless steel with a ring on the end for easy removal, ranging from 10 to 18 inches long; they are usually flat or square, or may have a slight spiral. Others have decorative stamped brass plates, often with animal shapes. Small skewers made of bamboo, usually 6 inches but from 4 to 12 inches long and very thin, are readily available. Also made are *double skewers:* two pointed prongs that share a handle or are formed from one U-shaped wire. Certain models have a small block that slides down the skewers to push the cooked food off. Some skewers are made with wide, loop handles that provide more control when turning the skewers over. And a square metal frame, an adjustable *skewer rack* or *kabob rack,* is offered that holds up to six skewers over the grill. An *attelet* is a very fancy, decorative skewer used to garnish terrines.

USE: Holding small pieces of food together while making shish-kebab, either grilled in a barbecue or fried in a *wok* (see page 155). Double skewers are good for delicate foods that might not turn on a single skewer. The skewer rack allows for easier turning and carrying of all kebabs at once.

USE TIPS: Be careful not to burn off the ends of bamboo skewers completely when cooking over a hot charcoal fire. Simply hold a wide fork at base of skewer (near handle) and pull the skewer out to remove the food and, if done smoothly, the food will remain nicely aligned and in place on your plate or platter. Do not push the food off the skewer—it may resist for a moment and give way, flying across the table and into a surprised diner's lap.

BUYING TIPS: Bamboo skewers are sold in packages of one hundred (small sizes in packages up to three hundred); metal models are usually sold in sets of four or six. Food tends to rotate on the round skewers, so look for flat or square ones.

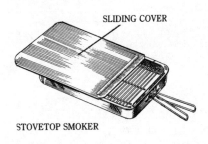

SLIDING COVER

STOVETOP SMOKER

STOVETOP SMOKER

ALSO KNOWN AS: Smoker cooker, smoke and poach, indoor hot smoker

DESCRIPTION: Stainless-steel tray with sliding cover, interior rack, and drip tay, sold with small containers of finely ground wood (mesquite, hickory, oak, or maple) called *smoke dust,* 15 by 11 by 3½ inches. A long wire handle extends from one end.

USE: Smoking and poaching quickly and simply on any heat source, including a conventional stovetop or oven.

USE TIPS: Sprinkle the smoke dust in the bottom of the tray. Some cooks add some moisture.

BUYING TIPS: Look for a heavier model that seals shut well. Doubles as a regular roaster, poacher, or steamer.

CHAPTER 10

Electric Cookers

About Electric Cookers

Included here are a number of very handy items that permit you to cook or serve without the benefit of a kitchen stove. Some are merely electric versions of a regular item, like the electric skillet. Others are unique. Most allow more control than flame-heated models.

Note that for cleaning, these are not immersible unless noted otherwise by the manufacturer. Many have component parts that can be removed, permitting the part with food contact to go into water or even the dishwasher. Look for items that can be washed easily.

BREAD MACHINE

ALSO KNOWN AS: Bread bakery

DESCRIPTION: Plastic-housed box, about 9 by 13 by 14 inches or more, which contains a computer-run combination mixer and oven, usually in a cylindrical shape. The lid may be flat or domed. All the bread ingredients are dumped into the container, which automatically mixes and kneads, rises the dough twice, shapes it, and then bakes it. Raw dough may be removed for hand-shaping rolls and bagels and the like. Simpler machines usually have a 1-pound loaf capacity (2 cups of flour) but others make up to 1½-pound loaves of certain breads. Dough is ready in about two hours; most breads are baked from start to finish in about four hours. May be sold with bread mixes and recipes.

USE: Baking bread automatically with little human intervention. Programmable computer allows for bread to be finished baking at the moment desired for serving.

USE TIPS: Experiment to find a recipe that works for you. The automation does not completely eliminate the need for judgment on the cook's part.

BUYING TIPS: Can be very expensive, with some of the fancier machines listing for well over four hundred dollars. Shop around, and if price is a problem, look for a simpler machine.

BUFFET RANGE

BUFFET RANGE

ALSO KNOWN AS: Portable burner

DESCRIPTION: Electric heating elements, or burners, in a decorative stand. Seven hundred and fifty–1,000 watts is a typical size, though one double-burner model has one of each. Heating elements usually lift up for easy cleaning.

USE: Maintaining cooking vessel at high heat for cooking or serving while on a buffet table.

USE TIPS: Monitor your pots carefully as it is easy to burn an almost-empty one.

CROCK POT

CROCK POT

ALSO KNOWN AS: Slow cooker, crockery cooker

DESCRIPTION: Insulated, electric pot, several quarts in capacity, which sits on a countertop. Controls vary with manufacturer but generally include a range of hotness. A very small version of this is the *hot pot*, which has usually no more than a 4-cup capacity. A more recent innovation is a two-part model made of a hot plate (with an attractive polyester shell) that may double as a griddle and a nonstick-coated aluminum cooking vessel with a porcelain exterior that sits on top. The vessels have a 2½- to 6-quart capacity and the larger one has a glass top that doubles as a 1½-quart serving dish. May be supplied with a roasting rack. Certain models are powerful enough to steam and fry food as well as slow cook them.

USE: Slow cooking of stews and soups, as well as serving same while maintaining heat. This and the two-part model can be used for serving at buffets when food must be kept warm for a long time. The hot pot is used to heat hot water in short periods of time, not for cooking.

USE TIPS: Overcooking is a problem if you leave the food to cook while you go to work. Be sure to calculate proper cooking times and don't expect miracles if you leave something for eight hours that needs only five, or vice versa. Double-check your recipe if it calls for slow cooking of raw eggs, meat, poultry, or fish: Harmful bacteria might grow in this warm, moist environment. Thermostatic settings are limited to "low to high" ranges, but recipes may specify exact temperatures—experiment for the right setting.

BUYING TIPS: This is a very useful item, but at one time it was thought to be the answer to everything, which it is not.

DEEP FRYER

ALSO KNOWN AS: Covered deep-fat fryer

DESCRIPTION: Tall, deep pot with a hinged top and an electronic control panel on the side. May have a plastic base or top with an interior of stainless or nonstick-coated steel or aluminum. The top may contain a replaceable charcoal filter, and most come with a built-in stainless-steel wire basket. Others are supplied only with a slotted spoon or scoop for removing the food from the oil. About 10 inches high by 11 inches wide; 4-cup oil capacity is normal (will be large enough for about 2 pounds of potatoes). Small models that hold only 2 cups of oil are available, intended for cooking two servings of any recipe, and large ones are made up to 2½-quarts capacity. Most have covers that snap on for airtight storage of the oil in the refrigerator without removing it from the appliance. Twelve hundred or 1,400 watts is an average power.

USE: Convenient, electric, thermostatically controlled, deep-fat frying. Thermostats maintain the fat at the correct temperature—375°F for most foods, lower for fish.

USE TIPS: If you fry frequently, this will speed up or eliminate the cleanup time because there is no spattered grease, and no odor.

BUYING TIPS: Look for the model with the most accessories: timers, automatic lowering and raising of basket, multiple thermostat settings, oil cleaner (allows some reuse of oil). More convenient and safer than using a pot over a gas flame.

DEEP FRYER

EGG BOILER

ALSO KNOWN AS: Automatic egg cooker

DESCRIPTION: Round, plastic, domed device that sits on a countertop. Capacity is seven or eight eggs, for hard cooking, sitting upright in a rack, or poaching four, in a special insert with indentations for each egg. Automatic shutoff and timed cooking cycles; 600 watts.

USE: Automatic cooking of eggs in boiling water to any desired level of doneness: soft, medium, or hard.

BUYING TIPS: Elaborate solution to a simple problem.

ELECTRIC CREPE PAN

ELECTRIC CREPE PAN

DESCRIPTION: Sort of an inverted frying pan, this has a slightly domed, nonstick surface that mushrooms over the metal and plastic base, with a long handle and thermostatic controls. 7½ inches in diameter.

USE: Making a crepe in forty-five seconds. The pan's surface is dipped into crepe batter and then turned upright for cooking; it is flipped over once again to drop the crepe onto a plate or stack of other crepes.

USE TIPS: Experiment to get your batter just the right consistency.

BUYING TIPS: Look for one that comes with a recipe book.

ELECTRIC FONDUE POT

DESCRIPTION: Small, enamel-clad pot on stand, with thermostatic control. Usually supplied with fondue forks. Inside the pot is a ring with fork slots.

USE: Serving any version of fondue: Savoyard (cheese), Bourguignon (oil), or Chinese (boullion).

USE TIPS: Follow recipes closely for success.

ELECTRIC FRY PAN

ALSO KNOWN AS: Electric skillet

DESCRIPTION: Rectangular or square, usually nonstick-coated, aluminum skillet ranging from a foot to 15 inches square or long, with thermostatic controls and low feet. On some models the cooking pan is detachable for cleaning. Exterior of some models is surrounded by polyester and stays cool during use. Controls on some models are removable to allow the cooking vessel to be washed.

USE: Sautéing where no stove is available. Decorative-styled models can be used for serving at a buffet.

BUYING TIPS: Look for a good-looking model for buffet or tabletop use. Nice to have, good gift item.

ELECTRIC GRIDDLE

DESCRIPTION: Flat, nonstick cooking surface with very low edge and up to 1,470 watts of power. Square or rectangular, from about a foot on either side, to 11 by 18, to 12 by 21 inches.

USE: Cooking food with little fat or liquid, such as grilled sandwiches or pancakes.

ELECTRIC WOK

DESCRIPTION: Traditional shape of a *wok* (see page 155) but with feet and thermostatic controls. Shallow, round pan, usually made of cast, nonstick aluminum, often with a 5- or even 6½-quart capacity; 17 or 24 inches in diameter. Some models have as much as 1,600 watts of power.

USE: Stir frying and steaming oriental style in the absence of a stove.

BUYING TIPS: Look for a removable heat probe; this allows for immersible cleaning.

FOOD DEHYDRATOR

DESCRIPTION: Boxy or cylindrical plastic item with small electric fan and thermostatically controlled heating element. An 8-inch-high, 13-inch-diameter dehydrator has about a 3½-square-foot capacity, with food on each of several trays; an 8-inch-high square model with five trays can dry almost 8 square feet of food. Supplied with a tight-fitting lid or door.

USE: Drying fruit and vegetables.

USE TIPS: Excellent for making nutritious snack foods such as banana chips and yogurt drops. Follow directions closely as to preparation and the addition of preservative chemicals.

IMMERSION HEATER

IMMERSION HEATER

ALSO KNOWN AS: Hot water heater

DESCRIPTION: Small metal coil, about an inch in diameter, with about a 3-inch-long "tail," connected to a regular power cord a few feet long. May be sold with a current converter for use abroad, and with a small cup in a travel bag.

USE: Rapid heating of one cup of water at a time, such as for instant coffee or soup, or tea. The coil is immersed in the water for just a few minutes.

USE TIPS: Do not ever plug in when the coil is not immersed in water. Though this is a handy item for travelers, be sure to check with hotel management before plugging in—it may drain too much current. And overseas, you need a current converter.

BUYING TIPS: Look for one with a current converter if you are planning to use this overseas. Most do not last very long, unfortunately.

MARINATOR

ALSO KNOWN AS: Marinizer

DESCRIPTION: Foot-deep, plastic appliance with a large, deep plate covered by a removable clear dome cover. A small electric motor mounted on the side evacuates the air in the chamber, creating a void in the food that the marinade fills.

USE: Automatically marinating and tenderizing all kinds of food in under three minutes.

BUYING TIPS: Definitely an improvement in time over the traditional process, but at a price—this costs close to two hundred dollars.

RICE COOKER

RICE COOKER

ALSO KNOWN AS: Food steamer and rice cooker

DESCRIPTION: Large, cylindrical or oval metal, electric cooker, designed to sit on a countertop, with a cover and a timer. Some models switch between rice cooking and steaming of other foods and have separate trays, racks, baskets, and high, domed lids for this purpose. Two and one fourth- to 4-quart capacity is typical (2 to 24 cooked cups of rice). Controls should allow for regular rice in fifteen minutes and automatically keep it warm when done, and inner cooking pot should remove for cleaning. A *compact electric steamer* is only 6 inches wide and 5 inches deep. Microwave version is just a plastic sphere that goes into the microwave oven.

USE: Cooking rice conveniently and to the point of producing nicely separated grains. Special steamer/rice-cooker models are well suited to steaming shellfish or vegetables as well as making rice.

USE TIPS: Experiment and check the quantity of water and time to use with different varieties of rice; long grain, short grain, Basmati, brown, wild, etc. Arborio rice, for risotto, is best cooked on the stovetop.

BUYING TIPS: This item is found in many modern Asian households. It eliminates the guesswork of cooking a staple food item, and above all eliminates the need to constantly watch the pot on a stovetop. Check combination steamer/rice-cooker models to see if they can handle fat before steaming meat, such as hot dogs. Look for models with a *steamer plate* for leftovers or fish and vegetables.

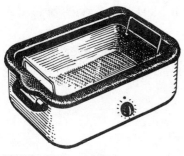

ROASTER OVEN

ROASTER OVEN

DESCRIPTION: Large, deep, rectangular pan that fits into a deep container with a thermostatic heating element. Eighteen-quart capacity. 1,440 watts is typical power. 16½ by 11½ inches.

USE: Baking, roasting, or broiling meat, poultry, or bread.

USE TIPS: Experiment to find the cut of meat and recipe that yields best results.

BUYING TIPS: Useful as an "extra" oven if yours is overused, or in a space with no kitchen.

SANDWICH IRON

ALSO KNOWN AS: Sandwich maker, sandwich press, sandwich toaster, sandwich grill

DESCRIPTION: Thermostatically controlled, clamshell-type iron with scalloped or plain compartments on both top and bottom. Made in single and double sizes, with either two or four sections, or sandwich halves. Most are lined with a nonstick material. Some are designed to cut ("crimp and seal") between sections very cleanly.

USE: Toasting filled sandwiches as well as cooking light items like eggs, pancakes, cornbread, or even miniature pizzas.

USE TIPS: Don't overfill your sandwiches.

BUYING TIPS: Look for rugged plastic housing a deep, nonstick interior. Some models have a convenient cord storage within the housing, which makes for neater use. Models that seal neatly around the edge make a neater-looking sandwich and prevent spillage. Handy item.

SELF-STIRRING PAN

DESCRIPTION: 1½-pint tall, cylindrical, nonstick aluminum pan with its own built-in stirring wand attached to a center post. Comes with a base that contains a thermostatically controlled, electric heating element.

USE: Constant and gentle stirring of sauces and cream soups that must be heated gently, such as hollandaise sauce.

BUYING TIPS: Gift item. Popular in France, land of the sauce.

SELF-STIRRING PAN

TOASTER

DESCRIPTION: Rectangular cube with slots on top into which are inserted bread items to be vertically toasted by electric heating elements within. Models range in number of slices done at once and thickness of slices; typical small models make two slices of traditional American packaged bread at a time. Others have slots that make up to four pieces of toast, and some, at up to 2 inches wide, can take bagels and croissants; a 10½-inch-long slot can handle even half a hero loaf. Some have slots of two different widths and others are infinitely adjustable and self-centering. Most are designed to sit on a countertop but under-the-cabinet models are also available. Advanced electronics are influencing design more and more, with some programmable microchip-operated toasters on the market and more accurate controls overall. One such improvement is a heat/moisture sensor that automatically compensates for bread freshness to obtain even browning. Another can be set for toasting frozen pastries just right. Now available with side panels that do not get hot.

USE: Toasting bread and bakery items.

USE TIPS: Never stick a metal utensil, such as a knife, into a toaster to remove a jammed piece of bread, or you could receive a bad shock. Unplug the toaster and use a pair of wooden *toaster tongs* (see page 135) instead.

BUYING TIPS: Higher wattage (over 1,000) makes for shorter toasting time. Look for an easy-to-clean crumb tray, heavy-duty heating elements, automatic switchoff, variable levels of toasting, and easy-to-use controls. Models designed to maintain a cool exterior are a great convenience, especially in homes with small children. Largely replaced in popularlity by the more versatile *toaster oven* (see next entry).

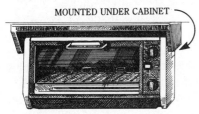

MOUNTED UNDER CABINET

TOASTER OVEN

TOASTER OVEN

ALSO KNOWN AS: Toaster-oven-broiler

DESCRIPTION: Rectangular metal cube with front door that folds down. Contains one wire rack. Typical outside dimensions are about 9 by 15 inches, but larger ones are as much as 17 inches long (.5 cubic feet interior space) and can hold a 2½-quart casserole or a 9-inch cake—and six slices of toast. At the extreme, one manufacturer offers an oven-broiler with a .9-cubic-foot interior large enough to cook a 10-pound turkey. Controls range from nonexistent to top-browning, multiple shades of toast, self-cleaning, interior light, and broiler venting. Some can be mounted under a cabinet to save counter space.

USE: Quick, light cooking, generally confined to reheating leftovers and making toast.

USE TIPS: Ideally suited to warming rolls and other bread items. Experiment with broiling, baking, and top-browning.

BUYING TIPS: For some people, this substitutes for a real oven and certainly for the vertical *toaster* (see previous entry). Look for a model with an easily removed crumb tray.

TORTILLA PRESS AND IRON

DESCRIPTION: Sort of a smooth *waffle iron* (see next entry), this has a distinguishing feature other than its two hinged, smooth, flat, nonstick surfaces: the top plate heats up to 300°F for baking and the bottom plate to 450°F for browning. The process starts with the placement of a ball of tortilla dough on the lower plate. When closed, this flattens and cooks the tortilla. The whole iron is about 7 inches in diameter.

USE: Making tortillas with one tool.

BUYING TIPS: Replaces the *tortilla press* (see page 92) and *griddle* (see page 185). Allows for easier, more consistent cooking.

TORTILLA PRESS AND IRON

WAFFLE IRON

ALSO KNOWN AS: Waffler, waffle baker

DESCRIPTION: Rectangular or round, flat metal device with hinged lid. Inside is a mold, traditionally of a crenulated, quilted pattern (sometimes called a waffle pattern), often made of nonstick-coated steel. Others include Mickey Mouse and heart designs. Common sizes are two servings (about 5 by 5 or 5 by 7 inches) or four servings (either side by side in a square, or wedges of a circle). Thin batter is poured into the lower portion and the device is closed; heating elements are on both sides to cook the batter evenly. A deeper pattern is used for making Belgian waffles. Also available in a cast-aluminum, nonelectric version that is placed over a gas flame (see page 188). Some models come with interchangeable plates for waffles and sandwiches. Another version, an *ice-cream cone baker* or a *wafer grill*, makes a very thin

WAFFLE IRON

waffle pattern crust that can be rolled into the form of an ice-cream cone (plastic *cone form* supplied). A similar version, the *pizzelle*-international dessert and waffle baker, or *pizelle iron* (see page 254), has a reversible grid that makes regular, thick waffles on one side and thin cookies on the other. The cookies can also be formed into cones by wrapping them around a *pizzelle cone roller* (see page 254).

USE: Making waffles, a breakfast or dessert recipe made from plain batter.

USE TIPS: Coat nonstick metal surfaces with a spray of fat prior to use.

BUYING TIPS: Light or tone indicator of doneness is a great help, especially when entertaining. Look for a model that converts into a sandwich grilling iron, a grill, and a griddle. A good buy, considering the cost of a brunch at a restaurant.

YOGURT MAKER

YOGURT MAKER

DESCRIPTION: Long, narrow, plastic tray about 5 inches high with five cup-sized holes into which five glass jars fit. Thermostatically controlled.

USE: Making fresh yogurt.

USE TIPS: Add fresh fruit or preserves as you wish.

BUYING TIPS: Look for a model with a thermometer measuring spoon for accurate temperature control.

PART III

Beverage, Garnishing, and Serving Items

Coffee- and Tea-making and Serving Equipment

About Coffee- and Tea-making Equipment

It is interesting that one of the simplest things to make, a brewed beverage, is one that attracts endless discussions of techniques and equipment. Perhaps that is because coffee and tea are strong flavors, but it may also be due to the fact that because it is relatively easy to make, say, a pot of tea, it also relatively easy to do it well or poorly.

In any case, there are plenty of things available to help with this common task. Don't forget that as with much of food preparation, the quality of the final product is affected as much by the quality of the food—type and grind—as by the technique. And neither beverage is improved by reheating, so use an insulated, thermal carafe whenever possible. A final note—almost any of these items makes a good gift.

Coffee-making Equipment

About Coffee-making Equipment

All serious coffee drinkers seem to want only the best-quality coffee, but so many are unsure how to get it. While the choice of a more expensive coffee grind is certainly a good start, there is much more to brewing good coffee than beans. The choice of equipment is one, as outlined below. Different methods yield distinctively

299

different results, and the choice is due to personal taste. All vary somewhat on how they handle the temperature of the water, how they mix the water with the coffee, and how the grounds are separated from the brewed coffee. The rest is a question of convenience or cost.

However, some basic rules do apply to brewing: Use fresh-roasted coffee; grind it as close to use time as possible; store ground coffee in an absolutely airtight container in a freezer or refrigerator; use bottled or clean cold water that has run for a while; use more coffee or a more acidic blend when brewing with hard water; use hot but not boiling water at 200°F (wait a minute after boiling to pour water over grounds); use the grind specified by the manufacturer of your coffeemaker; and don't boil or reheat coffee.

CAPPUCCINO MAKER

DESCRIPTION: Cappuccino is a mixture of milk and espresso coffee, made frothy by the injection of steam. Usually this is done with a nozzle that comes out of the side of an *espresso machine* (see page 306) but it can also be made by small gadgets made just for this purpose.

TYPES: *Café steamer* (Also Known As *the poor man's cappuccino maker*): Bent copper tube with a cork on one end that fits into the spout of a teakettle; boiling water forces steam out of the nozzle for frothing milk or coffee. Very inexpensive.

Cappuccino machine (Also Known As *beverage steamer* or *beverage frother*): 7-inch-high, cylindrical, plastic-covered electric device with one small metal tube coming out of the side. The tube emits steam under pressure.

Twenty-second cappuccino maker: Battery-operated mixer with a short metal rod tipped by a wavy blade that froths coffee and milk quickly. Essentially just a small mixer that does not use steam.

USE: Frothing beverages such as cappuccino and hot chocolate as well as reheating soups, dessert drinks, and cooking scrambled eggs and vegetables—all by injection of steam.

USE TIPS: Leave plenty of room for expansion in your cup or pitcher: Steam can froth milk up to four times its original volume.

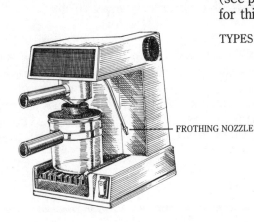

— FROTHING NOZZLE

CAPPUCCINO MACHINE

BUYING TIPS: Look for a model with variable steam intensity. Fancier electric models may be sold with video guide for cooking suggestions.

COFFEE FILTER

ALSO KNOWN AS: Coffee cone

DESCRIPTION: 1- to 10-cup-capacity paper, flat, wedge- or basket-shaped filters. A similar item is a *permanent filter,* a fine mesh, nylon or 23-carat gold-plated filter, supported by a plastic frame. Sizes are denominated by numbers (2, 4, or 6—specified on filter holder or drip coffeemaker), or by cup capacity. Gold filters are also made for brewing tea. Filters made from unbleached wood pulp are light brown in color, and perform as well as the more common white filters. Basket-shaped filters are popular with American automatic machines but cone-shaped filters are used more often in European and manual coffeemakers.

USE: Holding ground coffee in a holder for brewing in a *drip coffeemaker* (see page 304). Can also be used for tea.

USE TIPS: Paper filters are disposable, but the nylon and gold models are meant to be reused indefinitely and are usually dishwasher-safe. Wash immediately after use, and rinse very well. The gold filter imparts no taste to the coffee.

BUYING TIPS: Look for thick, strong, unbleached filters. Though the original box may suffice for most, if you want to keep a few filters handy, there is a small, wedge-shaped *plastic coffee filter holder* available. Use the nylon or very expensive gold filters, or ask for the natural brown-colored filters if environmental concerns matter to you. All the others are bleached to varying degrees with chemicals, especially chlorine, that may be harmful to the environment near the manufacturing plant or the place of final disposal of the used filter. Filters of either kind are safe to use.

COFFEE GRINDER

DESCRIPTION: Small, cylindrical, plastic-housed electric appliance with a removable cover that opens a space into which coffee beans are poured and in which a grinding blade is housed. Typical capacity is 2½ or 3 ounces ground coffee. The beans may descend into another chamber for grinding. Some have simple controls that you adjust to make fine or coarse grinds. Others have buttons you push as long as you want. A similar model is a *coffee mill,* which grinds the beans between two small millstones instead of breaking them apart with a stainless-steel blade, as in the grinder (note that some manufacturers call their grinder a mill). Capacity ranges up to enough beans for 40 cups. Features may include up to seven different grind settings and a timer to limit the volume of grinding. Some have an antistatic feature to reduce burning and sticking to the sides of the container. May be wall-mountable. Rarely found but also available is a hand-cranked, antique version, with a horizontal crank on top of a box with a little drawer or container for the fresh grindings.

USE: Grinding (or milling) coffee beans for immediate brewing. Also used for grinding peppercorns, spices, herbs, citrus rinds, and most nutmeats, depending on the brand.

USE TIPS: Brew immediately after grinding for maximum aroma and flavor. Coffee beans can be kept in the freezer to preserve freshness, and ground while still frozen. Experiment to find the coarseness that works for you, as too much milling may cause the grounds to make coffee with a bitter taste. Milling is less even, in general, than grinding. Most can also grind or chop other foods like nuts and grains.

BUYING TIPS: Look for more powerful, faster models for more efficient, cool grinding. Manufacturers of manual coffee grinders claim that less flavor is released in grinding than in milling (which pulverizes the beans), so more flavor is extracted in the brewing process, but mills ostensibly make a more even grain and don't heat up the beans. The difference, if any, is slight. Even small food-processors do a very good job. Take label claims for ounces needed per cup with skepticism—experiment to find what works for you.

COFFEE MEASURE

ALSO KNOWN AS: Coffee scoop

DESCRIPTION: Small plastic or metal, often stainless-steel, measuring spoon, ⅛-cup (6 teaspoons, or 30ml) capacity, usually flat-bottomed in style.

USE: Simply measure out as many spoonfuls of coffee as cups you are making. One-eighth cup of ground coffee usually makes one cup of coffee.

COFFEE MEASURE

USE TIPS: Accurate measuring of coffee grounds into most kinds of coffee maker is central to good-tasting coffee.

BUYING TIPS: Often supplied in large cans of ground coffee.

COFFEE MILL CLEANER BRUSH

ALSO KNOWN AS: Coffee grinder cleaner brush

DESCRIPTION: Round, wooden-handled, long-bristled brush about 6 inches long.

USE: Cleaning coffee bean dust from *coffee grinders* (see page 301).

COFFEE URN

DESCRIPTION: Large stainless-steel, polished aluminum, black plastic, decorative brass, or other metal container with a footed stand and a spigot coming out the bottom. Available in *drip* or *percolator* styles (see pages 304 and 309 respectively). Top lifts off for access to the filter basket or metal container where the coffee goes. Electric heating elements keeps water hot. Larger sizes have 55 to 101 cups capacity, but household models hold 12 to 42 cups.

USE: Serving large amounts of coffee and keeping it warm over a long period of time.

USE TIPS: Experiment prior to your dinner party to make sure you can brew coffee the way you want it.

BUYING TIPS: Look for models with a signal light, a lock-on cover (prevents spills), a nondrip faucet, and insulated handles. The drip method allows for more control over the strength of the coffee than the percolator method, which might get too strong if it continues to brew after it is done.

CUP WARMER

DESCRIPTION: Small, flat, plastic and metal electric device with a circular indentation and in most cases, a switch. A cup of coffee or tea sits in the indentation. A *mug-activated cup warmer* has no manual switch but switches on and off when a cup is placed on it or removed (and shuts off completely when unused for thirty minutes). One model is designed to work off of an automobile cigarette lighter; it also has a locking mechanism for the mug (which comes with its own spillproof top). A similar but larger item is the *decanter-activated warmer,* which holds a 12-cup decanter.

USE: Keeping a cup of coffee or tea warm.

USE TIPS: The decanter warmer effectively doubles the capacity of an automatic coffeemaker if you brew another pot after filling the decanter.

BUYING TIPS: Particularly suited as a gift to desk-bound drinkers. May be sold as a set with matching mug.

DRIP COFFEEMAKER

ALSO KNOWN AS: Filter drip coffeemaker, manual coffeemaker, café filtre (Fr.)

DESCRIPTION: Any of several designs consisting of a chamber for ground coffee over a chamber for the brewed coffee. Water is poured over the ground coffee.

TYPES: *Drip coffeepot* (Also Known As *double drip* or *French drip method coffeepot*): a 1- to 8-cup-capacity pot, usually round, with a cylindrical lid a few inches high. This cylinder has a perforated bottom, and the ground coffee is placed in it. The fancier types are usually French white porcelain, and the smaller, plainer ones of stainless steel. A white-speckled, blue enameled-steel pot is called a *coffee biggin* in the New Orleans area and Cajun country. Actually, the 1-cup model is not a pot, but rather just a coffee container that sits on top of a cup.

AUTOMATIC DRIP COFFEE MAKER

Electric, automatic drip coffeemaker: A three-chambered appliance, with a receptacle for cold water along the top and back side, a container for coffee grounds in a *filter* (see page 301) underneath the top part, and a glass serving container that sits on a hot plate. At least one brand offers a dual model for brewing two different types of coffee at the same time. Controls for quantity of cups to be brewed are on the side—1 to 12 cups is typical (1-cup models for office or travel that brew into a mug instead of a carafe are also made—one kind plugs into an automobile's cigarette lighter for power). Some models have microchip electronics that permit sophisticated timers to brew coffee up to twenty-four hours later (letting you program it at night to make fresh coffee the next morning), or to shut off the machine when it is empty or has not been used for more than five hours. Copper or aluminum disks and rings are sold to sit on the hot plate in order to avoid hot spots and scorched pot bottoms. Sophisticated thermostats maintain the same temperature over time, and other models have thermal carafes that maintain the heat by insulation. One even has a feature for impatient drinkers who can't wait the full seven minutes it takes to brew a pot—it stops the dripping while you sneak a cup. Some *espresso machines* (see next entry) can also brew drip coffee.

Hourglass: One-piece glass model made of two pyramidlike halves. The bottom is wide and holds the brewed coffee; the narrow-waist middle is covered with a wooden collar that serves as an insulated handle (or a plastic grip handle); and the top holds the coffee and filter. Pour hot water into the top. 2- to 13-cup capacity.

Neapolitan coffeemaker (Also Known As *Neapolitan flip*): Two-chambered plain, cylindrical copper or aluminum pot, with a small, separate area in one chamber (perforated on both sides) that is filled with ground coffee and screwed into place. The handles on the sides of the two chambers face opposite directions. Water is placed in the lower chamber and boiled; when it is boiling, the entire device is turned over so that the water drips through the coffee grounds and into the other chamber. The device is then unscrewed, and you have a small pot of coffee. The two opposite-facing handles are needed because of the bidirectional method of heating and then brewing. Usually made in small capacities of just a few cups.

Plain filter holder (Also Known As *coffee cone*): Plastic funnel-shaped device with small ridges on the inside and one or a few holes in the bottom designed for maximum steeping and saturation by water. The outside bottom has a large disk that allows it to sit on top of a cup, carafe, or a thermos for the brewed coffee, depending on the size. Holds *filters* for 1 to 10 cups (see page 301). Another version of this is a *one-cup tea* or *one-cup coffeemaker,* sold with or without a stand, which uses a permanent *gold filter* (see page 301).

HOURGLASS

PLAIN FILTER
HOLDER

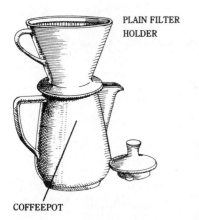

COFFEEPOT

USE: Brewing coffee by the single pass-through, drip method, which consists of pouring hot water over grounds in a basket or filter and letting it drip into the coffeepot. Electric model is for automatic and correct drip brewing, and in quantity. Filters trap bitter oils and sediments, brewing a particularly clear coffee not possible with the coffeemakers that use only perforated metal baskets.

USE TIPS: Measure your coffee and water carefully. Experiment until you have it down just right, and to see if you agree with the manufacturer's directions. Clean regularly, following the manufacturer's directions.

BUYING TIPS: One of the simplest and least expensive ways to make good, clear coffee. With the automatic model, look for a machine that can brew small pots as well as large ones. Even better ones can be programmed to start many hours after being filled with coffee and water, which is ideal for those people who require a fresh cup of coffee upon awakening (as well as those who want coffee after dinner without having to remember to make it). Another good feature is one that shuts the dripping off whenever the pot is removed for use. Check for convenient filling and cleaning, with swing-out filter baskets and the like. Look for a large, hook-shaped *coffeemaker brush* to be supplied. Excellent for those people who entertain a lot, or for small offices (dual version is great for those who need decaf along with the regular).

Look for easy-to-understand directions on the controls and an automatic model that brews with the hottest water possible and maintains that heat, perhaps with an insulated cone. Look also to see if it can be mounted underneath a shelf, or if cups can be stored on top of it. Carafes should be microwave safe. Above all, look for an automatic shutoff switch to avoid scorching empty carafes. Basket-type makers must have a water delivery that ensures thorough and even soaking of the coffee (cone-shaped types are designed with this in mind). Individual pots are ideal for a leisurely meal. Note that you must consume paper filters with this style, unless you get a permanent one (see page 301).

ESPRESSO COFFEEMAKER

ALSO KNOWN AS: Espresso machine

DESCRIPTION: Either of two styles of coffeemakers.

TYPES: *Electric espresso machine:* A squarish machine that is the little cousin of the kind found in café bars around the world. A boxy top part holds water and a few controls, including a water gauge (some machines hold enough for

STOVETOP ESPRESSO POT

4 cups, others as much as 35). A flat scoop with a handle holds the coffee grounds and snaps into place below the top part. On *espresso/cappuccino machines* a little tube for steam (for frothing milk and coffee for cappuccino) comes out from one side, and a drain area is on the bottom. Capacity of the water tank varies, but these machines usually brew one or two demitasse cups (1½ to 2 ounces each) at a time. Large, fancier models can brew 2 to 4 cups and may be combined with drip-brewing devices as well. Machines work either with pumps (hand or electric) or, as is more common with the smaller models, a boiler, or steam-pressure system, to bring the water through the coffee. Some have built-in coffee grinders and water filters.

Stovetop espresso pot: Small, two-part, cast-aluminum or stainless-steel pot with an hourglass shape and a handle on the top part only. The two halves screw together with a thick rubber gasket in the middle—water goes in the bottom half and the espresso grounds in an enclosed basket at the top. The hot water is forced by steam pressure through the coffee and into the top pot. Capacities are 1, 3, 6, 9, 12, and 14 cups. A smaller version replaces the top pot with a small tray where you put one or two espresso cups—a tube delivers the coffee through the grounds and directly into the cup.

USE: Making strong-brewed coffee espresso style, by forcing hot water through very finely ground coffee beans. The steam tube is for making cappuccino, with frothy milk. Machines make a cup in twenty seconds—very fast, hence the name.

USE TIPS: Most are geared to make 1½-ounce servings, but up to four at a time. Use lowfat milk for frothing—it works better than whole milk. Always try to keep some foam on the espresso, as it holds the most flavor.

BUYING TIPS: Electric machines with steamers cost more than those without. Look for one that has separate controls for the steam tube and the coffee. You may want to get extra rubber gaskets for the stovetop model. Test one to be sure it produces a slight foam on top of the coffee, called the "cream," where much flavor and aroma is concentrated. While there is much satisfaction to be gained from making your own cup of espresso on a fancy machine with all the attachments, some machines are too complicated and still yield the same results as the simple, manual models.

FRENCH PRESS COFFEE/TEA MAKER

FRENCH PRESS COFFEE/TEA MAKER

ALSO KNOWN AS: Cafetière, French press, coffee press, coffee/tea press, infusion coffee pot, plunge-filter coffeemaker, plunger coffeepot

DESCRIPTION: Usually made of 2mm-thick boro-silicate, heat-resistant glass with a stainless-, chrome- or silver-plated steel, nickel-plated brass, or plastic trim. This beermug-shaped pot, available in 3- to 12-cup capacities, has a plunger inside with a fine mesh metal filter on the bottom. Insulated handle is often made of a heatproof plastic. One plastic model has an extra large base for stability on picnic grounds or boats.

USE: Brewing small quantities of full-tasting coffee or tea quickly (three or four minutes is typical) by the direct-infusion method. The coffee (or tea leaves) and boiling water mix freely in the container, and then the plunger/filter is pushed down after several minutes of infusion, forcing the grounds to the bottom and making for strong, individually brewed coffee.

USE TIPS: Commonly used in French restaurants. Intended to be placed directly on the tabletop. Note whether your model is suitable for warming directly on the stovetop or not—most are not.

Use only boiling water. Coarse grinds are best. Clean filter regularly. Dishwasher-safe.

BUYING TIPS: If you are a serious coffee or tea drinker, this is a good buy. It enables you to make small amounts of regular coffee conveniently, avoid the consumption of paper filters, and avoid instant coffee altogether. Ostensibly leaves more oils and flavors, but produces fewer acids than drip or percolator methods. No need to replace filters. Expensive item.

HOT WATER DISPENSER

DESCRIPTION: 16-ounce-capacity hot water heater which sits on a countertop. Plastic, cylinder shape with an indentation for a cup.

USE: Heats one cup of water at a time, in ninety seconds.

BUYING TIPS: Only handy if you need small quantities of hot water repeatedly throughout the day.

MICROWAVE COFFEEMAKER

MICROWAVE COFFEEMAKER

DESCRIPTION: Plastic, two-part device consisting of a 10-ounce mug and a 5-inch-tall brewing part that looks like a taller mug with a funnel on top. The flat top has a hole that is covered by a removable piece that doubles as a coffee-measuring spoon. The inside holds a #4 paper *filter* (see page 301) in a plastic cone with a heat-sensitive valve that opens up when the coffee is brewed. The mug has a snap-on cover. A similar item is made for iced tea, the *microwave iced tea pot,* though it has a microwave-insulated mug for the ice cubes.

USE: Brewing fresh coffee or tea by the mugful in a microwave oven. Four minutes is normal brewing time.

BUYING TIPS: Regular coffeemakers are almost as fast and probably easier to use.

BASKET INSERT

SPREADER PLATE

STOVETOP PERCOLATOR POT

PERCOLATOR POT

ALSO KNOWN AS: Percolator

DESCRIPTION: Coffeepot with an insert consisting of a basket for coffee on top of a long narrow tube that leads from a disk on the bottom of the pot; a perforated *spreader plate* sits on top of the basket, just under the end of the tube. Water is boiled and forced up the tube so it can trickle back down through the coffee. Some models have controls to prevent the brewed coffee from repeatedly percolating through the grounds. Distinguished by the glass knob on top of the lid that allows you to see the coffee percolating and splashing into it. Made in two styles.

TYPES: *Automatic:* Self-contained stainless-steel, plastic, or glass pitcher or carafe with electric heating element on bottom. Brews and keeps coffee warm (at 170° to 180°F) automatically. 10-cups and larger capacity, limited by the design to be about the size of a pitcher that can sit on a tabletop. Also made in a 2- to 4-cup capacity as part of a travel kit.

    Stovetop: Stainless-steel pot with percolating insert, 2 to 12 cups is normal capacity. A small, nonelectric 4-cup glass model is made for use in microwave ovens.

USE: Brewing and serving coffee by the potful.

USE TIPS: Note that if you leave this going a while, the coffee might continue to percolate and get too strong. Clean insides carefully and often; many pots are sold with a V-shaped or long, narrow, *percolator brush,* also known as a *spout brush.*

BUYING TIPS: This is becoming a little old-fashioned, having been replaced by almost all the other automatic brewing machines for convenience and all other methods for quality. Glass models tend to make better coffee than metal ones, which some critics say impart a metallic taste to the coffee.

STEAMING PITCHER

ALSO KNOWN AS: Milk pan, frothing pitcher, milk warmer

DESCRIPTION: Typically a tall, cylindrical, stainless-steel pitcher, often with a straight wooden handle protruding directly out to one side, though handles that splay out toward a wide bottom are common as well. 16-ounce capacity. Capacity markings on side, with pouring lips.

USE: Holding milk for frothing with the steam nozzle on an espresso coffee machine, and serving same.

BUYING TIPS: Any container can hold milk for this purpose, but this has the ideal dimensions and shape.

TURKISH COFFEE PAN

ALSO KNOWN AS: Turkish coffeepot

DESCRIPTION: Very small pan, usually made of brass, called an *ibrik* in Turkish.

USE: Making thick, strong, Turkish-style coffee. Finely ground coffee is boiled with sugar and water three times.

USE TIPS: This requires both a technique and a taste acquired from experts.

BUYING TIPS: Decorative item for noncoffee drinkers.

VACUUM METHOD COFFEEMAKER

ALSO KNOWN AS: Vacuum coffeemaker

DESCRIPTION: Two large heat-resistant glass globes, nested one atop the other, with a glass tube leading from the upper globe

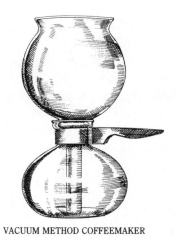

VACUUM METHOD COFFEEMAKER

down into the lower globe. An alcohol-burner heating stand is available as an accessory, as is a special, hook-shaped cleaning brush.

USE: Brewing coffee in a dramatic, fascinating, and effective manner. Water is heated in the lower globe, and most of it rises due to steam pressure, into the upper globe, mixing with the coffee. As it cools, it is sucked back down into the lower globe for serving (the "vacuum"). The grounds stay in the upper globe because the gasket acts as a filter.

USE TIPS: Clean thoroughly or the effect of the clear glass will be spoiled. Coarse grind works best.

BUYING TIPS: Convenience is sacrificed in favor of drama here. This brews a good cup of coffee but it takes time and much cleaning up.

Tea-making Equipment

About Tea-making Equipment

There doesn't seem to be as much variety in brewing methods for tea as there is for coffee, but that doesn't mean serious drinkers are any less adamant that their particular technique is the *only* way to brew tea. Virtually all tea is brewed by infusion, but choices can be made regarding water, time, temperature, and strength—and of course, the tea itself.

Note that a few items in the preceding section on coffeemaking items can also be used to brew or serve tea, notably the *cup warmer* (see page 311), the *French press coffeemaker* (see page 308), the *hot water dispenser* (see page 308), and even a *drip coffeemaker* (see page 304).

ICED TEA MAKER

AUTOMATIC TEA MACHINE

DESCRIPTION: A three-chambered electric device with a stainless-steel water reservoir with a heating element on top, a glass container with a tea infuser in the middle, and a glass serving container on the bottom. The bottom container sits on a hotplate. The automatic mechanism releases boiling water from the top and properly brewed tea from the middle; it is held at serving temperature (hot) in the bottom container.

USE: Controlled brewing of tea and provision of same for an infinite period of time at the proper serving temperature.

BUYING TIPS: This is far better than what you get with traditional methods when you are not paying attention, such as while you are working and want to have tea all day long—Either you boil dry your teakettle, overbrew your tea when you forget to remove your infuser or bag, or have to settle for cold tea after the first cup.

BREW BAG

ALSO KNOWN AS: Reusable tea bag

DESCRIPTION: Small, loosely woven cotton bag with a drawstring. A few inches long.

USE: Holding herbs or other plants for brewing tea.

USE TIPS: Also used for seasoning stews and soups (see *bouquet garni bag*, page 179) and even for brewing coffee, though it is smaller than bags designed expressly for that purpose.

BUYING TIPS: Ideal for brewing large quantities of tea if you wish to avoid cleaning loose tea leaves from the pot. Harder to clean than a *tea ball* (see opposite).

ICED TEA MAKER

ALSO KNOWN AS: Iced coffeemaker

DESCRIPTION: Foot-high electric device with large top and hollow middle, with flat stand. Comes with large glass pitcher with tight-fitting lid for refrigerator storage. Top compartment holds filter bag and water for brewing tea or coffee. Water-level indicator and shutoff controls are on side. Strength of brew is adjustable. A plastic, two-compartment model is made for use with microwave ovens.

USE: Automatic brewing of iced tea or coffee. Pitcher must be filled with ice cubes to cool the hot brew that is made by the machine.

USE TIPS: Experiment to see how much ice is needed to cool the brew without diluting it too much.

BUYING TIPS: It is unclear what advantage this has over brewing tea the usual way, other than that it is brewed automatically.

SPOUT PROTECTOR

SPOUT PROTECTOR

DESCRIPTION: Short rubber cylinder with one end cut on an angle. Fits over tip of spout of teapot.

USE: Protects porcelain teapot spouts from breakage, especially when being washed in the sink.

BUYING TIPS: Get a color that goes with your teapot.

TEA BAG HOLDER

TEABAG HOLDER

DESCRIPTION: A small, shallow dish, about 2 inches in diameter, available in a variety of designs, sizes, colors, and materials. Very common is a plastic or china dish in the shape of a teapot, often with the inscription "Let me hold the bag" on the inside flat space.

USE: Providing a resting spot for your used teabag when at table.

USE TIPS: Useful when serving mugs of tea.

BUYING TIPS: Often sold in sets of four. If you use cups and saucers, the saucer will serve the same purpose.

TEA BAG SQUEEZER

TEABAG SQUEEZER

DESCRIPTION: Small, stainless-steel tongs made from a V-shaped band of steel. The ends are perforated.

USE: Retrieving and squeezing the last tea out of a bag.

BUYING TIPS: Fancy item. Saves your fingers.

TEA BALL HOUSE

TEA BALL

ALSO KNOWN AS: Tea infuser, spice infuser, steeper

DESCRIPTION: Perforated, chrome-plated or stainless-steel, porcelain, or silver ball made of two halves that snap together, in the case of perforated metal, or slide together horizontally, if it is made of a stainless-steel fine mesh screen, with a small chain on one end that hooks on to the teapot handle. (The mesh model may also be known as a *multiuse ball* or a *mesh ball*). Never more than about 2 inches across, it may be spherical, cylindrical, or

SPRING TEA INFUSER

SNAP TEA INFUSER

even shaped like a little house or teapot. A small, bell-shaped, perforated steel model is called a *tea bell*. Some models come with a *tea ball holder,* a small saucer or tray of corresponding material for holding the used tea ball when wet. A small, flat version of the perforated steel ball is called a *tea clam*.

A spoon-shaped infuser, which may be known as a *tea infuser spoon,* comes in two designs: The *spring tea infuser,* which has a spring-loaded handle, or the *snap tea infuser,* which has a clamshell-type cover that snaps down in place. Both hold a tea-spoonful of leaves. A 5½-inch-diameter aluminum version is a *rice boiler,* for cooking rice.

USE: Brewing tea in teapots from loose tea leaves, as opposed to teabags. Teapots typically have a 4- to 6-cup capacity, while bags are for brewing 1 cup at a time. The spoon-shaped infuser is for brewing one cup at a time without a teapot.

USE TIPS: Always use water that has just reached boiling point in a teapot, but begin with fresh, cold water. Hot or reboiled water will taste flat and the tea won't blend well. Warm the teapot first. Don't fill the ball with too much tea because it expands when wet and will get compacted. A tea ball, especially the wire mesh multiuse ball, can also be used for bouquet garnis.

BUYING TIPS: It seems that the wire mesh may provide for quicker brewing than the perforated model, since the wire mesh is a bit more open, but in reality it is the type of tea itself that determines how brewing goes. Wire mesh balls usually are not as durable as the solid models, and more leaves get through them.

TEA COZY

DESCRIPTION: Quilted cotton or polyester dome, often just a plain arch but also in decorative and whimsical shapes, such as sitting cats. Available in many sizes, but when fully open, may stand a foot or more high and wide. Made in decorative patterns and colors, usually with a small ring on top for lifting.

USE: Keeping a teapot warm between servings.

BUYING TIPS: Common gift item.

TEAKETTLE

DESCRIPTION: Stovetop cookware in a variety of materials and shapes, including tin-lined copper, cast iron, enameled, stainless, or chromed steel, copper, and aluminum. Some are squat, others trim, and most have a whistling device that covers the spout. The common feature is a wide base and either a long, "swan neck" or short straight spout. The whistling device ranges from a simple hole that creates a whistle when steam rushes out to a multiple-toned harmonic production. Most have removable tops, but some are filled through the spout. May be artist- or designer-styled. Available in sizes ranging from approximately 1 quart to 2¾ quarts, with 2 quarts being typical. Particularly large kettles are sometimes called *humidifiers* because they may be left boiling slowly all day in order to humidify a house. Large electric models are available that merely plug into an outlet while sitting on a countertop—2 quarts is a standard capacity, and the better models have 1,500 watts of power.

USE: Boiling water for tea or cocoa. Not for brewing.

USE TIPS: Never boil dry. If you must lift the top to allow the water to pour, be careful not to let the steam burn your hand. Lift only a hair, enough to let some air enter. Scrub mineral deposits out routinely. Always start with fresh, cold water that has run out of the tap for a moment.

BUYING TIPS: Look for one with an insulated handle, and if possible, a dripless spout. Wide base makes for quicker heating. Aesthetics can play a big role in the choice of teakettles. Get something you love to look at, because this item is usually left on the stovetop. This item has found its way into museum gift shops, and prices can be very high. The electric kettle should have automatic boil switchoff and boil-dry prevention, as well as high-wattage for quick heating and the ability to whistle (or not) when ready. One model is designed to be completely disassembled and recycled when it is old and worn-out.

TEA MUG

DESCRIPTION: 10-ounce stoneware mug with a "wing" over the handle top. The wing is a slot about an inch deep into which a teabag can be drawn. The outside has dimples for your thumb.

USE: Squeezing and storing a teabag after brewing, as well as serving tea.

BUYING TIPS: Not for the faint-hearted who hate seeing used tea-bags sitting prominently in view.

INFUSER TEAPOT WITH WARMER STAND

TEAPOT

DESCRIPTION: Covered pot with a large handle and a spout of any imaginable design. Indeed, this is the subject of many folk and fine art attempts. More common are attempts at practical innovation, such as a 2-cup teapot that sits on top of a cup, keeping both warm; another is curved to fit around a cup. Materials range from the plainest of ceramic, porcelain, or glazed earthenware to the finest of silver or heat-resistant glass. Tops may lock on by design, but most don't. Sizes range from 2 cups to 12 cups, with 8 to 12 being average.

A specialized model, a *tea-infuser teapot* or *tea brewer,* comes with a separate or built-in perforated cylinder or basket called an *infuser, strainer,* or *sifter,* which holds the tea leaves. One model, sometimes called a *tea bell,* has a lever that raises the tea leaf container out of the water when the tea is brewed, storing it under the domed lid. Teapots may be sold with a candle-powered *warmer stand* as well, or as part of a *tea set,* with cups, saucers, and perhaps a cream pitcher and sugar bowl.

USE: Brewing and serving tea. Not intended for boiling water—use a *teakettle* (see page 315) for that.

USE TIPS: Gracefully keep your hand on the top while pouring. Clean tannins and other mineral deposits out periodically with a good scrubbing to avoid leaving a bitter taste in your tea. Baking soda is ideal for this. Some of the other common pointers for good tea brewing are: Use a clean teapot; use fresh, cold water; leave plenty of room in the ball or cylinder for the tea leaves to expand; put in 1 teaspoonful of tea leaves per cup, plus one for the pot; pour in the water as soon as it begins to boil, don't overboil; allow a good, long time for the tea to brew—five minutes is average.

BUYING TIPS: Ceramic and related materials are the best suited to this purpose; all others are merely decorative and may harm the taste of the brewed tea.

TEAPOT DRIP CATCHER

TEAPOT DRIP CATCHER

DESCRIPTION: Small, beaded brass chain with a large hook that hangs onto a teapot handle with a small, cylindrical piece of sponge at the opposite end. The chain is gathered in the middle by a small plastic butterfly that can be used to squeeze tea from the sponge. Attaches firmly over the top of a teapot from just under the lip of the spout to the handle on the other side, via the lid. The butterfly slides on the chain to tighten it against the lid.

USE: Absorbs drips from the tip of a spout and keeps the lid on snugly while the teapot is tipped for pouring.

USE TIPS: Note that the sponge is small and has a limited capacity.

BUYING TIPS: Pure convenience item.

DRIPLESS TEA STRAINER

TEA STRAINER

DESCRIPTION: Small, spoon-shaped and -sized tool. Small, fine wire mesh or finely perforated metal basket with a small hook on one side and handle on the other, or wings that fit over the edge of a teacup. Made of stainless or chrome-plated steel, silver, or wood and steel. A variation is the *dripless tea strainer*, a small cone-shaped strainer, no more than 2 inches across, that sits hinged on two small supports over a built-in saucer, all of stainless steel. Another version is a 2-inch-deep wicker basket with a long handle.

USE: Straining out loose, stray tea leaves when pouring fresh-brewed tea from a *teapot* (see opposite) and when neither a tea ball nor bag was used. The saucer of the dripless model is held to the side while pouring tea through the strainer; it catches drips from the wet leaves when set down on a table after use.

USE TIPS: Prior to pouring, pour a little cold water around the teapot to sink the floating leaves in order to reduce the amount that have to be strained out.

BUYING TIPS: This is an accessory to the traditional manner of brewing tea. Handy but considered unnecessary by many tea drinkers who are not bothered by a few loose leaves in their cups.

CHAPTER 12

Drink-making and Serving Tools

About Drink-making and Serving Equipment

There are many everyday kitchen items that are also commonly used in the bar area, and that creates a special challenge when it comes to classification. Many drink-related items have specialized names, but in fact these things have many more uses and are better known under their other names. For example, there is the *bar knife,* which is really a *fruit knife,* used to cut fruit into wedges for drinks. Some manufacturers call it a *fruit/bar knife,* further complicating the issue. All this is to say, please look in the other chapters to find items that you can't find but think might have been included here.

Storage Equipment

BOTTLE CAPPER

BOTTLE STOPPER

ALSO KNOWN AS: Reusable bottle cap

DESCRIPTION: A variety of gadgets that replace bottle caps or corks.

TYPES: *Bottle capper:* Plastic cap with hole in middle that screws onto a 1- or 2-liter soda bottle. The hole is sealed with a

BOTTLE STOPPER

gasketted stopper that is moved up or down by a large spring-loaded lever.

Bottle cork (Also Known as *stopper* or *wine cork*): Firm, narrow, tapered cork with plastic or wooden top.

Bottle stopper: Soft rubber cylinder with a hard plastic collar and a metal lever about 2 inches long on the top side. This handle pivots on hinges just above the collar; when pushed down, it expands the stopper and seals the bottle. Some are designed especially for 1- or 2-liter soda bottles, another, sometimes called a *wine stopper,* is designed especially for wine bottles.

Push-down bottle cap (Also Known As *two-way bottle cap*): Stainless-steel or aluminum cap made of flower-petal-like sections that fits snugly over the top of the bottle. A similar item is made of stiff plastic with a soft inner lining.

USE: Resealing bottles that have been opened.

USE TIPS: Be sure to reseal bottles carefully or you may lose the flavor or fizz.

BUYING TIPS: Usually sold in pairs. Fancy stopper may be sold with a drip ring (see page 337) as part of a *sommelier set.* These generally do a better job of sealing a bottle than the screw top provided by the manufacturer.

CAN CAP

ALSO KNOWN AS: Can cover

DESCRIPTION: Plastic disk, sometimes with a hinged door over an opening the size of the tap opening; another version just fits right in the tab opening.

USE: Resealing tab-opened cans; also keeps bees and wasps out.

USE TIPS: The can cap also affords a sanitary cap for drinking and has a small lip useful for lifting can tabs.

BUYING TIPS: Available in a variety of bright colors.

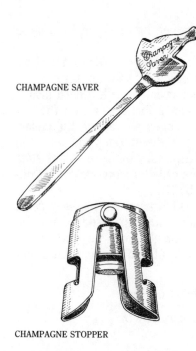

CHAMPAGNE SAVER

CHAMPAGNE SAVER

DESCRIPTION: Small, flattened stainless-steel spoon that has a decorative champagne bottle and bucket design in the place of the spoon bowl.

USE: Inserted handle-down into the neck of an opened, half-full champagne bottle to keep it fresh and bubbly for several days.

USE TIPS: Keep refrigerated.

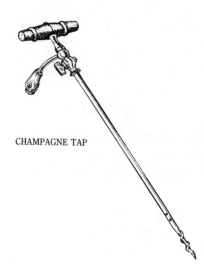

CHAMPAGNE STOPPER

CHAMPAGNE STOPPER

ALSO KNOWN AS: Champagne saver, champagne crown

DESCRIPTION: Stainless- or chrome-plated steel bottle top with hinged catches that grab underneath the lip of a champagne bottle. May have a lever that seals it tightly. One model, a *champagne opener/sealer,* has a sort of corkscrew built in to resist pressure as the cork is pulled.

USE: Recorking opened champagne.

USE TIPS: In the unlikely event you find yourself with leftover champagne, recork the bottle with this stopper as soon as possible and return it to the refrigerator. While it may be drinkable the next day, it is never as swell as the night before.

BUYING TIPS: Experts agree that fine champagne should be consumed by the bottleful during a relatively brief period. It is not intended to be a leftover refrigerator item.

CHAMPAGNE TAP

CHAMPAGNE TAP

DESCRIPTION: Chrome-plated hollow steel rod with a sharp, threaded tip (similar to a corkscrew's tip) and a short wooden T-handle, with a small faucet spout containing a thumbscrew just below the handle. Made either 7 or 13 inches long (the small size is for small bottles, or splits).

USE: Serving small quantities of champagne from an uncorked bottle. The tap is screwed through the cork and the champagne flows up the hollow rod through the faucet spout. The pressure in the bottle forces the champagne out when the thumbscrew is turned.

USE TIPS: Experiment to get the best results.

BUYING TIPS: Made in France and not widely distributed.

CORK SHARPENER

CORK SHARPENER

DESCRIPTION: Small plastic cylinder with blades inside, sold in various colors. About the size of a large cork.

USE: Sharpening used corks so that they can be used to recork bottles. Works like a giant pencil sharpener.

USE TIPS: Save your corks because they often split as they are sharpened. You may need extras.

BUYING TIPS: Easier to use than a knife.

PUMP CAP

DESCRIPTION: Small plastic cylinder with large screw-cap in middle. Screws onto 1-, 2-, and 3-liter soda bottles. Contains a short plunger with a T-cap that can be pushed down into the screw-cap.

USE: Pumped by hand five to twenty times to maintain pressure in carbonated beverage bottle, thereby slowing the rate of de-carbonation and maintaining the fizz.

BUYING TIPS: Better than the regular screw-top.

SODA TAP

DESCRIPTION: Pressure pump inserted into a 1- or 2-liter bottle of soda. All-plastic construction.

USE: Straw and siphon action dispense soda when button on siphon is pushed. Keeps soda carbonated by avoiding repeated opening of the screw-top.

USE TIPS: Kids love to play with this, but don't let them get carried away.

BUYING TIPS: Fun item that is convenient as well.

VACUUM WINE AIR REMOVER

VACUUM WINE AIR REMOVER

ALSO KNOWN AS: Wine preserver

DESCRIPTION: T-shaped giant syringe that plugs up a wine bottle. Most common kind is a two-part plastic device. A small rubber stopper goes into the neck of the opened bottle while a larger, syringelike part fits over it. The larger part has a T-shaped grip that you pull up to create a vacuum.

USE: Keeps opened wine fresh by completely removing the air from the bottle.

USE TIPS: Experiment—some wines respond better to this than others. Does not work on sparkling wines.

BUYING TIPS: May be sold with two or four reusable stoppers allowing you to have more than one bottle going at any time.

WINE BOTTLE TAG

DESCRIPTION: Small piece of thick paper with large hole in one end. Hole fits over wine bottleneck.

USE: Dating wine bottles in your wine cellar.

BUYING TIPS: Handy for collectors with large cellars. Sold in boxes of one hundred.

Mixing and Making Equipment

About Mixing and Making Equipment

The following items are very helpful to anyone who entertains often, as they will make it much easier to mix drinks and prepare ice in various forms. Most of them make good gift items, too.

COCKTAIL SHAKER

COCKTAIL SHAKER

DESCRIPTION: Tall stainless-steel or glass container, usually slightly tapered, with about a 16- to 32-ounce capacity. Some are supplied with two-part lids that obviate the need to be used with a *cocktail strainer* (see entry below). The lid base has a perforated center that is covered by a separate cap while shaking. A smaller, usually plastic, 1-cup or 15-ounce version is called a *mixer/shaker/blender* or a *shaker/mixer*, but is not intended for cocktails.

USE: Mixing fancy cocktails. The small mixer/shaker/blender is for mixing sauces, powdered diet drinks, or similar items.

USE TIPS: Shaking can be both invigorating and dramatic if you choose.

BUYING TIPS: Available in a range of materials and styles from inexpensive and utilitarian to fancy and decorative.

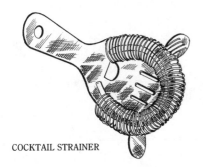

COCKTAIL STRAINER

COCKTAIL STRAINER

DESCRIPTION: Paddle-shaped, slotted, flat, stainless-steel tool with a coiled wire around the edge, sometimes just on one side.

USE: Straining cocktails from *cocktail shaker* (see entry above) into glass. The coiled wire keeps ice or fruit from entering the glass.

USE TIPS: Make sure that the paddle part covers your shaker to avoid spillage.

BUYING TIPS: Inexpensive, widely distributed item.

DOUBLE JIGGER

DOUBLE JIGGER

ALSO KNOWN AS: Jigger

DESCRIPTION: Two thimblelike metal cups, measuring large and small, combined in measures of, for example, 1 ounce and 1¼ ounces or ¾ ounce and 1 ounce, made of stainless steel, plastic, chrome, and sometimes silver, joined at the base in an hourglass shape. A jigger is a measuring device but there is no standard size, though some consider 1½ ounces a standard serving and 2 ounces a large one.

USE: Serving measured amounts of liquor.

USE TIPS: You've got to know which end is up.

BUYING TIPS: Note the capacities of each jigger.

ICE CRUSHER

ICE CRUSHER

ALSO KNOWN AS: Ice cracker, ice tapper, tap icer/cracker

DESCRIPTION: Heavy metal ball surrounded by a plastic holder with a long handle, usually made of plastic. Another version is similar to a large *garlic press* (see page 82): two levers hinged together that are squeezed down on a small square hopper at the hinge containing ice cubes. Finally, there is a boxy electric version that can handle over three freeze trays at a time and produce either coarse or fine textured ice.

USE: Crushing ice cubes for drinks or breaking up clumps of ice cubes that have frozen together.

USE TIPS: Do not pound on a soft wooden surface that you might dent.

BUYING TIPS: The electric version—or a *blender* (see page 70)—creates more even and finer results.

ICE CUBE TRAY

ALSO KNOWN AS: Cube tray

DESCRIPTION: Inch-deep plastic or aluminum rectangular tray with twelve to eighteen separate square or rectangular wells. Some models are available with round wells that have small cores in them to create hollow ice cubes. Plastic models are one unit while metal models have two parts, the metal dish in rectangular shape and the strips of metal to create the squares. The strips are attached to a lever that shifts them back and forth. Other variations are plastic trays that mold ice in the shape of golf balls, teddy bears, and so forth, and one that makes "cubettes"—seventy-five miniature cubes to a tray.

USE: Making ice cubes in home freezer units.

USE TIPS: If you'd like clear ice cubes, use warm or hot water. When removing the frozen tray, some cooks use gloves to prevent their fingers from sticking painfully to them.

BUYING TIPS: The plastic tray is a better bet all around. It's easier to get the cubes out (you just twist it or run hot water over it) and there's no danger of your fingers sticking to plastic the way they might to metal.

ICE PICK

DESCRIPTION: Thin metal spike about 3 to 6 inches long with a very sharp point and a short but wide wooden or plastic handle that may be steel-reinforced.

USE: Breaking apart small ice blocks or ice cubes that have melted together and been refrozen, or for chipping ice off of a large ice block. The wide and steel-reinforced heel of the handle can be used to hammer the ice or be struck by a hammer, chisel-style.

USE TIPS: If this is used in hammer and chisel fashion, be careful not to hit your thumb. If you are "stabbing" at a block, be absolutely certain that your other hand is safely removed from danger—the pick can easily slip or go through very fast and puncture your hand. Be very, very careful, especially if you are not used to this tool. It is very dangerous.

BUYING TIPS: Be sure the tip of the handle is reinforced, since it will be taking the brunt of the hammer blows.

ICE SHAVER

SIPHON BOTTLE

ICE SHAVER

DESCRIPTION: Plastic machine about a foot tall with a hand crank on top (electric models are available for professionals) and a wide container immediately under the crank. These are held by the back wall over a gap into which a bowl may fit.

USE: Shaving ice cubes into snowy consistency for mixing with drinks such as daiquiris or desserts such as snow cones.

USE TIPS: Syrups and drinks are absorbed very quickly by the shaved ice.

SIPHON BOTTLE

ALSO KNOWN AS: Soda siphon, seltzer bottle

DESCRIPTION: All-metal or glass bottle about 14 inches high and of about 1-liter capacity with metal mesh cover. Top is solid metal or plastic cone with three things pointing out at angles from it: a trigger lever, a short gas nozzle, and a long seltzer nozzle. Sold with carbon dioxide (CO_2) chargers, small metal pressurized cartridges that are screwed down onto the gas nozzle with a separate metal piece that fits over them (the nozzle punctures the tip of the charger, releasing the gas instantly into the bottle). One brand now offers a model that makes seltzer in 1-liter, reusable plastic bottles.

USE: Making and dispensing carbonated water under pressure. Model used with refillable bottles is like having a seltzer factory at home (otherwise, you are limited to one siphon bottle at a time).

USE TIPS: Filling the water above or below the normal line will affect the size of your bubbles, as does the temperature of the water. The problem is that not everyone agrees as to *how* it affects either one. It is a matter of taste.

BUYING TIPS: Good gift item.

Drink Serving Equipment

BOTTLE POURER

BRANDY WARMER SET

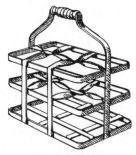

CELLAR CADDY

BOTTLE POURER

ALSO KNOWN AS: Drip stopper/pourer

DESCRIPTION: Small plastic or stainless- or chrome-plated steel stopper with a short spout, sometimes with a cap. The cork-sized stopper is hollow and usually has a soft fluted plastic or cork collar. A tiny air shaft allows air to enter the bottle as it is poured, and some models channel drips back into the bottle through it.

USE: Allows accurate and clean pouring of liquor or other bar beverages without having to recork after each use.

USE TIPS: Commonly used by professional bartenders.

BUYING TIPS: Usually sold in pairs. Helpful if you are pouring lots of drinks, such as for a large party.

BRANDY WARMER SET

DESCRIPTION: Silver or stainless-steel wire rack that holds a *brandy snifter* (see page 353) over a small *warmer candle* (see page 394). Usually decorative in style.

USE: Warming brandy to increase its aroma.

USE TIPS: Warm it only slightly.

BUYING TIPS: Great gift item.

CELLAR CADDY

ALSO KNOWN AS: Bottle carrier

DESCRIPTION: Six-bottle rack with carrying handle, made of decorative metal strapping.

USE: Carrying a large meal's wine selections upstairs from the cellar, or for creating a limited, portable bar in a small home.

USE TIPS: May also be used for water or other bottles.

CHAMPAGNE BOTTLE OPENER

ALSO KNOWN AS: Champagne star

DESCRIPTION: Small, four-bladed device that looks like a round claw. The blades fit into the notches left in the cork by the wire cage. Once pushed onto the cork and twisted slightly, it provides a good grip while the pressure pushes the cork out into your hand. Another version is a *champagne pliers,* which look like regular, curved-jaw pliers with a cap or loop on top to hold the cork; one type actually pries the cork up for you without twisting.

USE: Controlled opening of champagne bottles.

USE TIPS: Pay attention—some corks are under considerable pressure.

BUYING TIPS: Very handy for people who have trouble gripping champagne corks. The type that lifts the cork is easiest to use.

COASTERS

DESCRIPTION: Flat, decorative disks or squares, about 3 inches in diameter, made of wood, plastic, natural fiber, marble, cardboard, or paper. Marble or wood ones may have cork insets. A deep coaster with a rim, often of porcelain or marble, is called a *wine bottle holder* or a *wine coaster.*

USE: Absorbing or collecting moisture from cool or dripping glasses or wine bottles in order to protect the surface they are sitting on.

USE TIPS: Cheaper and more practical than using disposable napkins. The cardboard or fiber kind with beer labels imprinted may get soaked through and stop providing protection, though.

BUYING TIPS: Usually sold in sets of four or more.

CORK RETRIEVER

DESCRIPTION: Long wire shaft with wooden T-handle. A little disk or split wire is on the end of the shaft.

USE: Retrieving broken or fallen corks from within a wine bottle.

USE TIPS: Don't fish for corks in front of the guests at a fancy dinner party. Do it in the pantry. Better yet, open another bottle and do it later.

CORKSCREW

ALSO KNOWN AS: Cork puller, wine opener

DESCRIPTION: Short brass, stainless- or chrome-plated steel wire spiral (or twin spirals) with a variety of handle designs in plastic, wood, brass, or steel.

TYPES: *Air pump:* Giant syringe with the needle at a right angle to the pump cylinder, or an oblong, soft pump that you squeeze. Needle is inserted through the cork and air pumped into the bottle, forcing the cork out. Another version pops the cork out with pressurized gas from a cartridge, eliminating the need to pump.

Automatic decorker: Palm-sized plastic globe with a corkscrew spiral emerging from the bottom. The globe contains gears and a collar that fits over the top of the bottle. Usually made of plastic but variations on the design are available made of wood. Continuous twisting pulls cork out.

Cork puller (Also Known As *trouble-free cork puller* or *two-prong cork puller*): Two parallel, flat metal blades about ¼-inch wide, splayed apart at one end, with an oblong open handle at the other end. One blade is about 3 inches long, and the other about 2 inches. Comes with a flat plastic case for the blades. The longer blade is inserted between the cork and the bottleneck first, then the other blade, and then the tool is wiggled down gently. Once all the way down, pull up gently. The inside edge of the handle may have a small flat area that can be used as a bottle opener (put the prongs in the plastic case when using this feature).

Leverpull: Large, complex-looking item that may be the simplest and quickest tool, with two horizontal handles forming a clamp for the bottleneck and one vertical lever. After the device is clamped onto the bottle, the lever is brought down, forcing a corkscrew wire through the cork. When the lever is raised, the cork is pulled out. Made of high-tech composite material with a nonstick-coated stainless-steel screw. A larger, brass version of this is the *professional corkpuller,* designed to be clamped to the edge of a bar or countertop.

Plain corkscrew (Also Known As *power corkscrew*): The simplest model, just a steel coil screw and a T-handle,

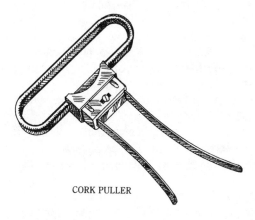

CORK PULLER

usually wood or plastic. The screw is twisted down into the cork and then the handle is pulled straight out with sheer force. Handle may be anything from a plain dowel to a beautiful, varnished piece of grapevine root. Often found as an accessory on folding pocket knives. The expanding *zigzag* version gives some leverage when you pull, but it is still a straight pull up.

Self-pulling corkscrew: Two versions. One is a T-shaped model, called a *bell corkscrew,* with a short wooden handle across the top of a 5-inch steel shaft with a spiral, screwpoint end. In the middle of the shaft is a small, loosely fitting, bell-shaped piece of steel that sits on the top of the bottle. As the corkscrew is turned the cork is pulled up the shaft by the screw and into the bell, almost completely removing it from the bottle. A small tug removes it the rest of the way. The other version, the *automatic corkscrew,* has two long, solid prongs or legs and a collar that fits over the bottle top and a screw that goes all the way up to the handle. The prongs have notches in them that make them fit tight at the bottle top. The cork moves right up and out as the T-handle on top is twisted. No pulling is necessary. A pocket model has a long handle that you can spin around instead of the T-handle.

Travel corkscrew (Also Known As *picnic corkscrew, pocket corkscrew, twin spiral corkscrew*): Comes in two parts. Has a case that fits over the spiral that is removed and inserted in the base to form a T-handle. Light and small. Usually made of plastic but also of wood and chrome.

Waiter's corkscrew (Also Known As *sommelier's corkscrew, waiter's wine opener,* or *pocket corkscrew*): Sort of a hybrid of the above two types, this is essentially a pocketknife with a corkscrew for the main blade and a small knife folding out of one end, plus a large bottle cap lifter folding over the other end. This lifter serves also as a base for a fulcrum when hooked on the rim of the bottle and the end of the main lever is lifted up to pull the cork out. Invariably made of stainless steel. Light and smallish. Also available designed for lefties.

Winged corkscrew (Also Known As *wing corkscrew*): The most complicated in appearance. The spiral is inside a sort of cage formed by two small shafts holding a cupped ring at the bottom that is usually lined in plastic (this fits

SELF-PULLING CORKSCREW

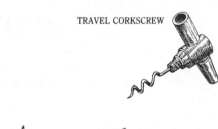

TRAVEL CORKSCREW

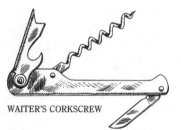

WAITER'S CORKSCREW

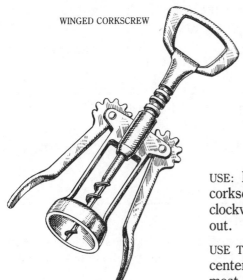

WINGED CORKSCREW

over the bottle top). Two handles come out from the middle of the device where they are attached by a pivot point and large gears; a ringed shaft emerges upward from in between these gears. The levers are up as the screw enters the cork; pushing them down easily removes the cork. The end of the shaft usually has a bottle cap lifter—an open, oblong loop with a small tab on the inside. Often made of solid brass but also of stainless or chrome-plated steel or plastic. Large and heavy if made of metal. Also available designed for left-handed use.

USE: Removing corks from wine bottles. In every case, the corkscrew must be inserted into the cork by twisting, usually clockwise. Each type then is worked differently to pull the cork out.

USE TIPS: Make sure the spiral's tip is entered securely in the center of the cork before pulling. The waiter's model takes the most skill but can be used the most quickly. The automatic decorker takes the least skill. Old and dried-out corks are the hardest to remove without damaging them; the cork puller is ideally suited for this job. If your screw does not enter the cork easily, try twisting it counterclockwise.

BUYING TIPS: Terrific gift. Quality and price ranges available to fit all budgets.

CRYSTAL WINE THERMOMETER

DESCRIPTION: Wide bronze or stainless-steel sheet formed into an incomplete ring that fits around a wine bottle. The outside contains a band with temperature markings on it that correspond to various types of wine.

USE: Serving wine at precisely the right temperature.

BUYING TIPS: Inexpensive gadget of dubious necessity.

DECANTER

ALSO KNOWN AS: Carafe

DESCRIPTION: Large glass or ceramic container, usually squash- or bottle-shaped, with a fitted stopper. Ranges in size from 8 or 10 ounces to a liter. Fine models intended for serving hearty

Burgundy wines have horizontal aspect to allow greater air contact with the wine.

USE: Serving wine or other beverages at a meal. Designed to be left on the table.

USE TIPS: Pour wine slowly from the bottle and do not upend it—keep the dregs in the bottle, not the carafe. This process is known as "decanting."

BUYING TIPS: Beautiful, cut-crystal models are traditional and make good gifts.

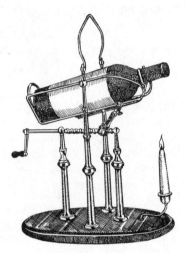

DECANTING CRADLE

DECANTING CRADLE

DESCRIPTION: Brass construction that suspends a wine bottle at various angles determined by a small crank. Base has a candlestick as well.

USE: Gentle, slow, precise, and dramatic pouring of very, very fine wines. The candle allows you to appreciate the color of the wine as it is poured.

USE TIPS: Not intended for bargain table wines.

BUYING TIPS: For those who always seek dramatic gimmicks.

DECANTING FUNNEL

DESCRIPTION: Heavy, silver-plated steel funnel with fine mesh screen inside.

USE: Filling decanter (see page 331) with old wine. The screen filters out bits of cork or dregs of wine.

USE TIPS: Pour slowly to minimize solids that need to be filtered out.

FLASK

DESCRIPTION: Pocket-sized, unbreakable bottle made of metal or plastic, with screw-on top. Usually shaped with a slight curve. Much variety in design. Metal models can be quite fancy, sold with leather pouches.

FLASK

FOIL CUTTER

USE: Personal liquor supply, usually carried in a coat pocket or a suitcase for emergency use. Top doubles as a small glass or jigger for measuring.

USE TIPS: Not quite as popular as they were during Prohibition, these are occasionally seen at sports stadiums, on the slopes, or at skating rinks, filled with brandy for warmth. Primary use is for travelers.

BUYING TIPS: Excellent gift material, if a little anachronistic. Available in a large array of materials and prices ranging up to very expensive, decorative silver models.

FOIL CUTTER

DESCRIPTION: Small, plastic, horseshoe-shaped items with a small blade inside. Fits over wine bottle top.

USE: Cuts and removes foil cap from wine bottles with a simple twisting motion.

USE TIPS: Safer and surer than using a knife.

BUYING TIPS: Inexpensive item, often included with more expensive *corkscrews* (see page 329).

ICE BALLS

DESCRIPTION: Plastic balls, or heart or animal-shapes, filled with a refreezable liquid, usually brightly colored water.

USE: Chilling drinks. A colorful substitute for ice cubes, and they won't dilute your drink.

USE TIPS: These may seem a simple frivolity, but they're actually quite practical. Kids love them, and they're especially appreciated by those people who don't feel comfortable using tap water for anything or don't want their drinks diluted by melting ice.

BUYING TIPS: Good gift item, particularly for those folks who use expensive, imported bottled water in their drinks. It would be foolish for them to dilute such beverages with ice cubes made from local tap water.

ICE BUCKET

ALSO KNOWN AS: Wine cooler, wine chiller, wine bucket

DESCRIPTION: Plastic, terra-cotta, marble, glass (24 percent lead crystal), chrome-plated, or silver-plated steel bucket that holds a wine bottle with ice and water, or if it is a terra-cotta or a double-walled, insulated model, sometimes called an *iceless chiller*, it holds just a wine bottle. Some are made with table-high stands; a *wine cooler holder* hangs from the side of a table. Finer models have small handles and may be monogrammed. Usually no smaller than 6 by 7 inches. One stainless-steel model holds four curved, plastic, refreezable cooling inserts that fit into the sides of the cooler.

USE: Keeping a wine or champagne bottle chilled after it is opened. Designed to be used on the table, or in a tableside stand. Some should be prechilled.

USE TIPS: Marble chillers can hold a bottle of wine to within one degree of its original temperature for an hour if they are properly prechilled. The model which takes cooling inserts can chill a bottle in thirty minutes and maintain that temperature for five hours, although that amount of time should not be necessary if the wine is any good—you'll drink it by then.

BUYING TIPS: Available in very fancy, decorative models. Good gift item.

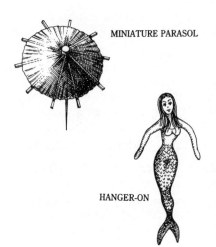

MINIATURE PARASOL

HANGER-ON

MINIATURE PARASOL

DESCRIPTION: Paper umbrella only a few inches long, made in various colors. Another item with a similar use is a *hanger-on*, a small plastic mermaid, monkey, donkey, flamingo, or giraffe.

USE: A decorative touch for tropical drinks, especially Mai-Tais.

USE TIPS: Avoid toying with these during an important discussion with a companion. It is distracting and considered especially disrespectful to repeatedly open and close one of these while someone is pouring their heart out to you.

BUYING TIPS: It is not necessary that these be very well constructed since they are usually used only once or twice. It's okay to go for the cheapest.

SODA BOTTLE HANDLE

SODA BOTTLE HANDLE

ALSO KNOWN AS: Easy-pour handle, two-liter bottle holder

DESCRIPTION: C-shaped, stiff plastic handle with angled loop at one end. Fits under the collar of 2-liter plastic soda bottles. One model actually has a locking, sealing cap that replaces the twist-off bottle cap. It also provides leverage for opening new bottles more easily. Another attaches with straps to the body of the bottle. Most are trigger-activated.

USE: Provides sure and sturdy grip for these large, soft bottles.

BUYING TIPS: Excellent idea for anyone with small or arthritic hands—these bottles are hard to grip because they are soft.

STIRRER STRAW

ALSO KNOWN AS: Stirrer

DESCRIPTION: Thin plastic tubes, about 3 to 4 inches high and only about ⅛ inch in diameter. Double-barrelled model is common. Some stirrers are just solid plastic rods about 5 inches long.

USE: Stirring bar drinks. Can also be used for sipping.

USE TIPS: For thick drinks, and for kids, use a plain *straw* (see next entry).

BUYING TIPS: Inexpensive item sold in packages of one hundred.

STRAW

DESCRIPTION: Paper or plastic hollow tube about ¼-inch wide and about 8 inches long. Available in solid or flexible styles, plain or patterned. Some specialized models exist: One, called a *cool straw,* has a small, decorative, water-filled plastic figure in the middle of the straw that, when frozen, ostensibly cools the beverage as it passes through it; another has a flavor-impregnated strip built in, which imparts a chocolate or strawberry flavor to the beverage as it passes through.

USE: For sucking liquids from a glass directly into the mouth.

USE TIPS: Although considered by most to be a kids' item, it's really just a fun and efficient way for anyone to drink a soda or milkshake. The flexible kind are also helpful for the bedridden. Do not keep sucking after the drink is gone from the glass, making an annoying and obnoxious noise that anyone with half-decent manners or a proper upbringing knows to avoid.

BUYING TIPS: The cool straw is not known to be very effective, although it is entertaining for some of us. Not considered a trendy gift.

TASTING GLASS

INAO WINE GLASS

JURY TASTING GLASS

ALSO KNOWN AS: Wine-tasting glass

DESCRIPTION: Either of two styles of a piece of fine crystal stemware.

TYPES: *INAO Wine Glass:* INAO, the International Standard Organization, sanctioned this short-stemmed design as the official tool for wine tasting. The rim is especially smooth. 8-ounce capacity. Good for all wines.

    Jury tasting glass: Stemless, squash-shaped glass with depressions for fingers and a narrow opening. Good for all wines and spirits.

USE: Serious wine tasting.

USE TIPS: Some people spit out the wine after tasting to avoid getting too intoxicated to make an accurate judgment. Swish wine around your mouth in order to run it over all your taste buds.

BUYING TIPS: Any glass will do, but these are specifically designed to show off a variety of wines' aroma and color.

VODKA TUBE GLASS

DESCRIPTION: Short, narrow tube with an enlarged bottom section. 2-ounce capacity. Usually sold with a large, open ice tub.

USE: Serving ice-cold vodka.

USE TIPS: Bury glass bottoms in crushed ice.

BUYING TIPS: Gift item.

WINE DRIP COLLAR

ALSO KNOWN AS: Wine drip stopper, drip ring, wine bottle collar

DESCRIPTION: Plastic or fancy silver-plated or pewter ring, about ½-inch thick and 2 inches across, lined with felt or other absorbent material. Fancy model may be sold with a *stopper* (see page 319) as part of a *sommelier set.*

USE: Slipped over the neck of a wine bottle prior to pouring in order to absorb any drips that may occur as wine is served.

BUYING TIPS: The elegant model is a fine gift. Need may be obviated by quick pouring or rubbing a bit of butter around the top of the bottle. Can be replaced by a handy napkin, too.

WINE DRIP COLLAR

WINE GLASS PLATE CLIP

ALSO KNOWN AS: Clip-on wineglass holder

DESCRIPTION: Small plastic device with prongs that slide onto a plate edge and hold a small, split, cupped ring that extends out from the plate. A wine glass sits neatly in the ring; the stem slides in and out of the opening.

USE: At stand-up buffets, holds your glass on your plate, freeing one hand for other uses, such as eating, while standing.

USE TIPS: Works with either red or white wine glasses, but check the width of your stems for compatibility with the clip prior to use.

BUYING TIPS: Not a widely distributed item.

WINE GLASS PLATE CLIP

WINE PRESERVATION AND SERVICE SYSTEM

DESCRIPTION: Modular system consisting of a pressurized canister of nitrogen, a regulator that sits on top of the canister, a stopper/dispenser with a spout and a pushbutton, and plastic tubing connecting the dispenser with the regulator. Pressurized nitrogen replaces oxygen in the bottle, both preserving the wine and forcing the desired amount out when the button is pushed.

USE: Preserving leftover wine in a bottle and serving pump-style when the button is pushed.

USE TIPS: Best used with fine wines.

BUYING TIPS: Decorative covers for the canister are available, along with convenient storage trays for the bottles connected to it.

CHAPTER 13

Garnishing Items

About Garnishing Utensils

Though most people don't consider garnishes part of an everyday meal, they are certainly part of most dishes prepared for entertaining. With only a few tools you can create decorative food. Most are sold as part of a *garnishing set* and are relatively easy to use (indeed, most are just types of knives). What is hard to do is to use them the first time. Garnished food definitely dresses up a meal.

One thing that is confusing is the tendency of manufacturers to call any knifelike tool a *garnishing* or *garnish knife.* They are sorted out in this chapter according to their function, but there is a lot of overlap nonetheless.

BUTTER CURLER

BUTTER CURLER

DESCRIPTION: Small, question-mark-shaped tool with a slightly corrugated stainless steel blade and a wooden handle. Also made entirely of wood.

USE: Cutting curls of butter from sticks.

USE TIPS: Keep the butter cold and the tool warm and wet. Unsalted butter works best. Keep curls on ice.

BUYING TIPS: Often sold as part of a *garnishing set.*

BUTTER MOLD

ALSO KNOWN AS: Butter pat press

DESCRIPTION: Small, bell-shaped wooden tool with short mushroom-shaped plunger/handle. Inside the round part is a flat, 1-inch-diameter, circular, decorative, shallow mold that is attached to the plunger.

USE: Molding butter pats, usually with a simple flower design, one at a time.

USE TIPS: Use heavily salted butter. Virtually impossible to use successfully on modern, store-bought butter without thoroughly chilling in ice water first.

BUYING TIPS: Excellent as a decorative or gift item. Not a serious cooking tool.

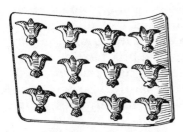
BUTTER MOLD SHEET

BUTTER MOLD SHEET

ALSO KNOWN AS: Butter mold

DESCRIPTION: Thick, flexible, plastic sheet with twelve decorative indentations about ½-inch deep and an inch or so across. Designs are wide ranging, including a round swirl, fleur de lis, sea shell, acorn, daisy, Santa face, happy face, and turkey, among others. Also available as a hollow wooden block a few inches long.

USE: Molding butter into decorative shapes for serving.

USE TIPS: Chill thoroughly prior to demolding.

BUYING TIPS: Inexpensive item.

BUTTER PADDLE

BUTTER PADDLE

DESCRIPTION: An 8½-inch-long flat, wooden paddle a few inches wide, with thin slots on one side. Sold in pairs.

USE: Rolling balls of butter for decorative serving. Paddles form balls with grooved imprint.

USE TIPS: Use cold butter and add a little chopped parsley for effect.

CHOP FRILL

CHOP FRILL/CHICKEN FRILL

ALSO KNOWN AS: Turkey leg frill

DESCRIPTION: Small paper cylinder, about an inch long, smooth on one end and frilly on the other.

USE: Decorating the ends of chops and legs, whether plain pork chops, a crown roast, or a roasted bird. Adds a touch of elegance, and also helps keep your fingers clean.

USE TIPS: Do not put in oven.

BUYING TIPS: Usually sold in bags of one-hundred.

CURL CUTTER

DESCRIPTION: Electric or manual appliance with heavy base and clear plastic cylinder that fits on top, with two different cutting blades. The blade remains fixed and the food is turned against it.

USE: Cutting potatoes and other vegetables into curls or spirals.

USE TIPS: Curls are an excellent form for deep frying. Spirals are more suited to garnishes or eating raw.

BUYING TIPS: Look for a model that comes apart easily for cleaning and stores conveniently with the base fitting inside the work bowl.

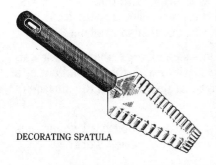

DECORATING SPATULA

DECORATING SPATULA

DESCRIPTION: Small, flat-bladed tool with a plastic handle. Blade is a truncated triangle with sharp, fluted edges. Each side has a different size of wave.

USE: Decorating butter, soft cheese, frosted cakes, and hors d'oeuvres by dragging the blade lightly along the surface of these soft foods. Also makes wavy slices of fruits and vegetables.

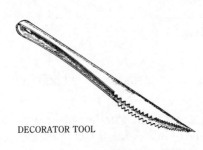

DECORATOR TOOL

DECORATOR TOOL

ALSO KNOWN AS: Garnish knife, V-shaped melon cutter

DESCRIPTION: Hand-sized knife with V-shaped blade, sharp on both sides; both sides come to a common point. Usually made of stainless steel and available in regular and "giant" sizes. The edges of some models have various sizes of jagged teeth, and because the knife is stamped from one piece of steel, there is not a separate handle. A U-shaped version may be called a *corer* because it can be used to core apples and other fruits.

USE: Carving fruit and vegetables for decorative pieces.

USE TIPS: Plunging the knife repeatedly into the side of a melon, one cut right next to another in a line around the middle, produces a jagged edge on each of the two halves.

BUYING TIPS: Often sold as part of a *garnishing set*.

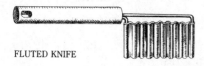

FLUTED KNIFE

FLUTED KNIFE

ALSO KNOWN AS: Decorator knife, decorating knife, deco-cut garnisher, garnishing knife, crinkled chip cutter, gaufrette knife, crinkle-edged cutter

DESCRIPTION: Hand-sized knife with a wide, corrugated blade a few inches long. Usually the blade is a separate piece of steel 2½ inches long held to the handle by a frame. One model, called a *multi "V"*, or a *wave-cut*, has a wide blade with three sets of V's, though a 6-inch-wide version sometimes called a *garnish chopper*, with a handle directly above the blade, is also available.

USE: Cutting small zigzag-shaped slices of vegetables. For a waffle or gaufrette cut, a slice is cut twice, with the second cut at a right angle to the first. May also be dragged across the surface of a block of butter for a decorative effect.

USE TIPS: This knife is not very sharp. Parboil hard vegetables like carrots and beets prior to cutting for easier work.

BUYING TIPS: Often sold as part of a *garnishing set*.

FLUTING KNIFE

ALSO KNOWN AS: Fluter, flex knife, slim jim

DESCRIPTION: Small, extremely sharp short-bladed knife. The plain, tapered, flexible blade is usually about 2 inches long. Basically a very short and narrow *paring knife* (see page 18). Sometimes made in a short, triangular shape.

USE: Carving various designs, such as fluted edges, into fruit or vegetables.

USE TIPS: Use wherever extreme control is necessary in detail work.

BUYING TIPS: One of the most versatile and useful garnishing tools.

FOOD PICK

ALSO KNOWN AS: Toothpick (incorrect), food pic

DESCRIPTION: Tiny plastic or wooden stick with pointed end, of many different designs.

PARTY FRILL PICK

TYPES: *Cheese pick:* Straight, sturdy plastic pick about 3 inches long. May have arrow tip.

Party fork (Also Known As *cheese fork* or *cocktail fork*): Miniature, two-pronged fork, made of lightweight plastic or stamped metal and a wooden or plastic handle, available in many colors.

Party frill pick: Wooden pick with colorful cellophane ribbons attached to the top.

Sword pick: Miniature plastic sword, complete with handle grip.

USE: Serving bite-sized pieces of food or holding food together in an attractive way. Often bite-sized cubes of cheese or sausage are served on a buffet platter with the picks stuck in them. The picks may also be presented in a separate container for use by the guests.

USE TIPS: These types are not very effective as toothpicks, but toothpicks can be used for all the purposes listed above, and they can be baked.

BUYING TIPS: Usually sold in packages of large quantities, such as seventy-two.

GARNISH KNIFE

DESCRIPTION: The shortest of all knives, this blade looks more like a wide hook. It is about an inch long and almost as wide.

USE: Cutting small pieces of vegetables and other food where total control is necessary.

USE TIPS: Some chefs use this for making turned vegetables, an old-fashioned technique of carving carrots or other similar vegetables into oblong shapes.

BUYING TIPS: Most people can do with a short *paring knife* (see page 18).

ICE CARVING CHISELS

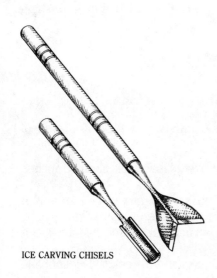

DESCRIPTION: Similar to wood carving chisels, these are almost always sold as a set of four to seven chisels. Shapes included are flat, called "straight" (available narrow to wide), curved gouge, and V-shape. May include a pointed knife with a very narrow, thick blade. A conical *gouge sharpening stone* is available as an accessory.

USE: Sculpting large blocks of ice for decoration.

USE TIPS: Be very careful—flying chips can hurt unprotected eyes and chisels can easily slip.

BUYING TIPS: Definitely for the serious entertainer only. One alternative is to use a rare novelty item, a plastic ice mold, which is filled with water and then frozen.

ICE CARVING CHISELS

ICE CARVING SAW

DESCRIPTION: A 17- to 30-inch-long saw with enormous teeth and a straight or pistol grip handle. Stainless steel blade.

USE: Carving sections of large blocks of ice.

BUYING TIPS: A rare, more professional item that may be fun to try for a very festive occasion.

ICE CARVING SAW

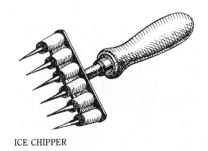

ICE CHIPPER

ICE CHIPPER

DESCRIPTION: Hand-sized, wide, forklike tool with wooden handle and six short steel spikes in a flat iron base. 7¾ to 9 inches long.

USE: Chipping large blocks of ice for sculptures.

USE TIPS: Keep your unoccupied hand safely away.

BUYING TIPS: Considered a professional item. Smaller but less accurate alternative to the *ice carving saw* (see previous entry).

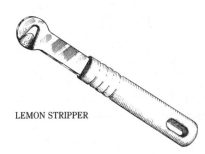

LEMON STRIPPER

LEMON STRIPPER

ALSO KNOWN AS: Citrus stripper, channel knife, lemon twister, lemon peeler, lemon decorator, decorator, stripper, canelle knife

DESCRIPTION: Small hand tool with very short blade, only an inch or so long, which has a hole in the center and a small arched part to one side of that hole. The edge of the arch next to the hole is sharp, but the outside edges of the blade are not. Made of stainless steel, often with plastic handle. Available in a combination model called a *zester/stripper*. A zester is a similar but slightly different tool described on page 118. A *mushroom fluter* is the same as a lemon stripper but with the arched cutting edge on the end, not the side.

USE: Cutting small strips of, or canelle grooves in, citrus fruit skin, usually lemons or oranges. Typical use of strips is for garnishing drinks, platters, pies, or cakes. Mostly used for obtaining two or more strips of lemon or orange at a time for use as a drink garnish, but also for notching cucumbers or citrus fruits prior to slicing to create a scalloped edge effect. This technique is referred to as *canelling*.

USE TIPS: The depth of the cut includes the bitter part of the skin; do not use in place of zests, which are cut with a *lemon zester* and do not include the bitter, white layer. Pull the stripper towards you very slowly and you will have more control.

BUYING TIPS: Handy if combined with a *lemon zester* (see page 118) in one tool, that is, with five small holes at the tip of the blade. Look for a model with a strong handle that can be put in the dishwasher.

LEMON WEDGE BAG

ALSO KNOWN AS: Lemon wedge cover, lemon bag

DESCRIPTION: Small, white cotton bag, about the size of a lemon wedge, with a tiny elastic at its opening. A *lemon cover,* or *lemon wrap,* is a plain square of material that must be tied.

USE: Protects diners from flying lemon seeds and errant squirting juice squeezed by particularly energetic guests at fancy dinners. Juice passes through wide mesh of bag.

USE TIPS: Note whether the manufacturer claims that the bags are washable or not. They can be rinsed, in any case.

BUYING TIPS: Intended for use at formal dinners.

MELON BALLER

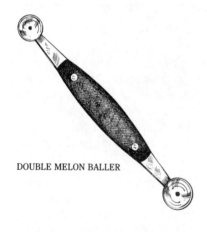

DOUBLE MELON BALLER

ALSO KNOWN AS: Melon/potato baller, food baller, vegetable scoop potato baller, melon-ball scoop, Parisian spoon, melon-ball cutter

DESCRIPTION: Hand-sized tool with a small bowl usually about the diameter of a quarter on the end; a *double melon baller* has a smaller ball on the other end as well. Actually, bowl sizes range from about $\frac{3}{8}$ to 1 inch. If it has only a small bowl, it is called a *mini-baller,* while a model with just the regular size may be called a *single baller.* Another version is the *scalloped,* or *scallop baller,* or *fluted baller,* which produces melon balls with scalloped edges. It is available also in a plain oval model. The bowl should have a small hole in the center. Typically made of stainless steel with a nylon, wood, or plastic handle.

USE: Cutting small balls of melon, such as cantaloupe or watermelon, for fruit cocktail or decorative displays. Also used on vegetables, mostly potatoes; flat, fluted ends are for butter.

BUYING TIPS: Look for a solid, sharp-edged tool. Larger models are of more use than smaller ones.

RADISH PRESS

RADISH PRESS

ALSO KNOWN AS: Radish decorator, radish rose maker

DESCRIPTION: Either of two types of cutting devices. One is a stainless steel tonglike tool, hinged at one end, with a ring at the other end of one arm that has eight ½-inch-deep cutting blades in a circle with a core at the center. The end of the other arm has a spoonlike crevice for holding a radish. The other type is a small plastic disk with the same size circle of cutting blades and core, about 3 inches in diameter. A modified version of this one is a small plastic disk with a core made of a cutting blade pointing out, all in plastic.

USE: Rapid cutting of radishes into decorative roses, or rosettes.

SPIRAL SLICER

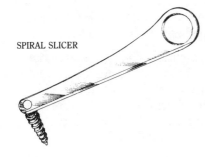

SPIRAL SLICER

ALSO KNOWN AS: Spiral cut, spiral cutter, radish slicer, radish cutter

DESCRIPTION: Plastic screw with wide threads, about an inch or so long, with a 6-inch-long handle at a 90-degree angle that pivots around the blunt end of the screw. The handle usually ends with a finger hole, and one edge is knife sharp. Some makes come with a spike for more control over holding the screw in place.

USE: Cutting spirals from fruits and vegetables. The screw penetrates the food, and the handle cuts it into a thin spiral as the whole thing is spun around and "through" the food.

USE TIPS: Practice in order to get the feel for this.

BUYING TIPS: Usually sold as part of a *garnishing set*. This is one of those gadgets that works so brilliantly in the hands of a skilled demonstrator in a department store but somehow becomes difficult to use by the time you get it home. Not a handy item.

TALLOW AND BUTTER SCULPTING TOOLS

DESCRIPTION: Set of four or six, 6-inch-long tools, usually made of hand-forged, high-carbon steel, with variously shaped tips on both ends of tools in some cases, or wooden handles in others. Shapes include loops, points, and serrated points or curves. May be sold with a short-bladed, double-edged modeling knife.

USE: Sculpting tallow or butter for display.

USE TIPS: Keep the sculpture very cold.

BUYING TIPS: Mainly a professional item.

TALLOW AND BUTTER SCULPTING TOOLS

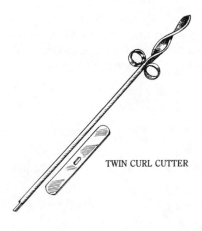

TWIN CURL CUTTER

TWIN CURL CUTTER

ALSO KNOWN AS: Curl cutter

DESCRIPTION: A 6-inch-long aluminum spike with one pointed and twisted end and one flattened end, with two small, ½-inch diameter rings spot-welded about 1½ inches from the sharp, twisted end. One edge of each ring is sharpened. Supplied with a 2½-inch-long, flat, ½-inch wide handle with a small slot in the middle. The handle slides onto the flattened end of the spike to form a T.

USE: Cutting fruit and vegetable curls. The spike is twisted through the food until it can be pulled out, leaving a core that is made of two curls. Once the core is gently twisted out and the curls separated, they can be intertwined with curls from other fruits or vegetables of a contrasting color. The handle is removed so that the spike can be pulled through the food.

USE TIPS: Do not pull the curls or they will break. Twist gently counterclockwise. Red beets and white turnips make great contrasting colors for candy cane decor. The twin-curl cutter leaves a large, empty core behind, suitable for stuffing and baking in another recipe altogether.

BUYING TIPS: Usually sold as part of a *garnishing set*.

V-CUT

V-CUT

ALSO KNOWN AS: V-shaped melon cutter, V-shaped cutter

DESCRIPTION: Hand-sized knife with a blade curved in the shape of a V; also made in U-shape, known as a *U-cut*. Stainless steel, usually with a plastic handle. Similar to the *decorator tool* (see page 342) but without the giant serrations. Available in a "giant" size as well, which is about an inch deeper.

USE: Cutting zigzag edges along the halves of a melon or other fruits and vegetables.

BUYING TIPS: May be sold as part of *garnishing set*.

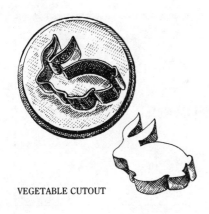

VEGETABLE CUTOUT

VEGETABLE CUTOUT

ALSO KNOWN AS: Cutout, deco cut, garnishing cutter

DESCRIPTION: Set of small, round plastic forms with high ridges in the shape of rabbits, crabs, fish, hearts, flowers, leaves, and stars. Each form has a base and mold. Another version looks like a *cookie cutter* (see page 234) and is made of metal. Also available is a *garnish cutter,* in which five are mounted on a disk. An *hors d'oeuvre/bread cutter* is a larger, deeper, thicker version. An *aspic cutter* is a smaller version, and a *truffle cutter* is sometimes made in a similar version.

USE: Cutting small pieces of vegetables such as carrots, beets, or green peppers into decorative and animal shapes. Smaller version cuts aspic or truffles.

USE TIPS: May also be used on pastry dough or fruit.

Tableware and Serving Equipment

About Tableware and Serving Equipment

The items described here are divided into two simple groups. The first consists of items used at individual place settings, and the second, called tabletop, consists of those items used on the table for serving all the diners. Some of these items are also found elsewhere in the book, such as gratin dishes, because they are used for cooking as well as for serving. If you can't find something that you think should be here, please check the index.

Some more decorative or furnishing items are not included at all, because what is listed here is generally on the basic side and relates directly to cooking and serving of food in the house. Items of this sort that are not included are things like candlesticks and picnic baskets.

Determining the right name to list was sometimes difficult, because professionals often call dishes by the item they usually hold, like "soups" for soup bowls, or "iced teas" for iced tea goblets. The name finally chosen is the one that most people understand.

Basic Place Settings

There are four basic items that anyone needs to eat and serve food. Because there is much variety among them and one must shop for them often, here is some useful information to help you make an informed purchase.

BOWL

DESCRIPTION: The bowl was probably one of the first tableware items ever made, and though it is usually made of china, or porcelain, bowls in fact are made of all materials: wood, terra-cotta, stoneware, plastic, or pewter, just to name a few. Anything can be eaten out of a bowl, if you want, but for our purposes, we are considering here bowls used for serving food at a well-set table. In this case, there is still plenty of variety, as follows:

GRAPEFRUIT
BOWL

ORIENTAL
SOUP BOWL

TYPES: *Grapefruit bowl:* Small bowl with textured bumps on the inside. Bumps help keep a grapefruit half from slipping.

Lotus bowl: Small bowl with pointed leaves for sides, resembling a lotus leaf. Similar to the oriental soup bowl (below) and used for soup or sauces.

Oriental soup bowl (Also Known As *Chinese soup bowl* or *rice bowl*): Relatively shallow, about 5 by 2 inches, with a high base.

Pasta bowl: Large, wide, shallow earthenware bowl, either in the individual size (8¼-inch diameter and 26-ounce capacity) or a serving size (12-inch diameter and 2-quart capacity).

Salad bowl: Both a small side dish about 6 inches wide for individual servings and a large one, about a foot wide, for holding a whole tossed salad. Usually sold as sets. Made of woven wood encased in plastic, as well as the usual materials, and found in square and flower shapes.

Soup/cereal bowl: Shallow, wide bowl about 5½ inches in diameter on the average. Ten or 11 ounces is a typical capacity, but they range from 8 ounces to 16 ounces. May be used for morning *café au lait,* too.

USE: Serving food at a well-set table.

USE TIPS: Check to see if wooden bowls are dishwasher safe—otherwise wash by hand and dry quickly to avoid damage.

BUYING TIPS: This is a guide to the more traditional uses and styles of bowls—in everyday use, anything goes.

COFFEE CUP

ALSO KNOWN AS: Teacup

DESCRIPTION: Small porcelain, pottery, or plastic container with small loop handle on the side. Six ounces is common capacity, but

8 to 10 ounces is not unusual. A *mug* is a deeper version that is cylindrical instead of bowl-shaped, and holds 8 to 13 ounces. Available in a wide range of styles and qualities from the very cheapest to the finest, gold-decorated models.

USE: Drinking hot coffee, tea, or chocolate.

USE TIPS: Always use saucers with cups, but not with mugs, for which *coasters* (see page 328) are more appropriate.

BUYING TIPS: Usually sold in sets of two, four, six, or eight, and so on, with saucers and often plates or entire dinnerware sets.

FLATWARE

ALSO KNOWN AS: Utensils

DESCRIPTION: Small hand utensils used in table settings. Though often any kind of flatware is called *silverware,* that item means literally any ware made of silver, whether sterling or silver-plated. In common usage silverware refers specifically to a *knife, fork, teaspoon,* and *soupspoon* used in everyday eating. Other flatware would include some serving items, such as a *sugar spoon, serving spoon, pierced serving spoon, salad fork, fish fork, fish knife,* and *butter knife.* Made of plastic, wood, pewter, silver, stainless steel, or aluminum in many styles, ranging from the plainest and cheapest disposable items to quality pieces considered to be fine and valuable art.

USE: Eating in a traditional, Western European style.

USE TIPS: Raise the food to your mouth; do not bend over toward the food. Tip the soupspoon into your mouth—do not slurp the soup out of it. Remove the food from a fork or spoon with your lips, not your teeth.

BUYING TIPS: Although all fine flatware used to be made exclusively of silver, now it is possible to substitute top-notch, beautiful stainless steel at a more reasonable price.

GLASSWARE

ALSO KNOWN AS: Glasses

DESCRIPTION: Any one of myriad designs of glass, plastic, metal, or wood, stemmed or stemless (*tumbler*), decorative or plain, which play on the basic design of a cylinder with one closed end.

Listed below are some of the traditional types, which are described in fairly standard but by no means rigid terms. Many specialized types of glasses are made, some with names of specific drinks, such as a *Margarita glass*, but all really fall into the general groups defined by the basic designs cited here.

Many are decorated with cuts, facets, or color trim. Thin, high-quality glasses are often made of lead crystal, which is hand-blown glass with up to 24 percent lead oxide added for brilliance and clarity. These glasses should ring when struck lightly with a fingertip. The less expensive models are usually machine made and have seems or edges to show it. Tempered glass has been treated to resist thermal or physical shock.

There are three basic groups of glasses: tumblers, stemware, and miscellaneous. The term *tumbler* is used to describe any plain, sturdy drinking glass that is basically cylindrical in design and that may be used for all beverages, including wine, in informal circumstances. *Stemware* refers to any glass with a foot, or stem, usually elegant in design and use. (A *goblet* is a glass that usually has a shorter stem and a less elegant appearance and is used just for water, but the term is used broadly (and correctly) to denote any kind of footed or stemmed glass.) *Miscellaneous glasses* commonly used for serving alcoholic drinks are sometimes sold as a *bar set* with as many as eighteen pieces of three different models, such as beer mugs or shot glasses.

TYPES: *Beer mug* (Also Known As *beer stein*): Large, heavy, solid glass with thick bottom and handle along one side large enough to grip with your entire hand. Cylindrical, either straight or with a slight taper in toward the top. Twelve to 17 ounces is a typical capacity range.

Beverage: Term for average-sized, cylindrical glass used chiefly for serving informally. Typical glass is tall, holding 8 to 12 ounces. Available in insulated plastic (double-walled) and anodized and brightly colored aluminum, as well as numerous glass designs. Typically used for water, milk, juice, or soda. Most common and useful model.

Brandy (Also Known As *cognac, brandy snifter,* or just plain *snifter*): Squat, bulbous, almost spherical footed glass, often of very fine quality. For serving fine brandy or cognac—drinks for which the aroma is everything—the shape is intended to enhance your ability to smell the liquor. About 5½ to 12 ounces is typical, though much larger ones are made as a gimmick. Servings are only 1 to 2 ounces. Also excellent for floral arrangements or other decorative uses (in larger sizes).

BEVERAGE GLASS

BRANDY GLASS

CHAMPAGNE FLUTE

COCKTAIL GLASS

CORDIAL GLASS

IRISH COFFEE GLASS

DOUBLE OLD-FASHIONED GLASS

Champagne coupe (Also Known As *sherbert glass* or *shrimp cocktail glass*): Shallow, wide, stemmed glass. Very difficult to drink out of or carry without spilling and decried by connoisseurs as ruinous to champagne bubbles. Most of the bouquet of fine champagne escapes the large surface unappreciated. A *coupette* has a wide, flared top, and is often used to serve Margaritas.

Champagne flute (Also Known As *toasting glass*): As much as 10 inches tall, with a slender, open, almost vertical-sided shape for the classic model. Depth of glass allows champagne bubbles to be visible as they rise to the surface, and concentrates the bouquet at the top. *Hollow stem* is fanciest construction, which is trumpet-shaped and may be called a *champagne trumpet.* Five to 8 ounces is a typical capacity. May also have a slightly inward curved, tulip shape.

Cocktail (Also Known As *martini*): Usually a 6-inch-high, 5-inch-wide, shallow, cone-shaped piece of stemware. Five-ounce capacity is normal but extra-large models are common.

Cordial: Small footed glass, typically with only 2½-ounce capacity. Antique cut and colored glass cordials are often found in private homes. For serving liqueurs, sherry, or port.

Footed water: Larger and heavier than similar wine glasses.

Highball: Tall, narrow glass in a cylinder shape, with 8- to 17-ounce capacity, although some manufacturers call their larger model a *Collins,* or *Tom Collins.* Very useful glass.

Hurricane: Eight and one-half-inch-tall goblet with flared top and bulbous bottom. Capacity as much as 22 ounces.

Iced Tea (Also Known As *cooler*): Particularly large glass, either a straight, tall cylinder or else a footed goblet. Sixteen ounces is a typical capacity, but often a cooler is a larger version, with as much as 24-ounce capacity. Made large to hold lots of ice.

Irish coffee: Footed, conical, or straight cylinder, with a coffee-cup-like handle. Typical capacity is 8½ ounces.

Juice: Small, usually tall and narrow glass. Typical capacity 6 ounces.

On-the-Rocks (Also Known As *rocks* or *Old-Fashioned glass*): Short and wide—about the same dimension both ways. Average capacity is 10½ ounces. A *Double Old-*

PILSNER GLASS

ALL-PURPOSE WINE

BALLOON GLASS

TULIP GLASS

Fashioned glass (Also Known As *DOF*) is a bit larger, at 12 or 13 ounces. Usually plain tumbler style, but also footed. Very common, useful model.

Pilsner: Tall, conical, hourglass, or flared, footed glass of about 13-ounce capacity. Stem is less than an inch long, or just a wide foot. Used for serving beer.

Port/Sherry: Narrow and footed, like a small champagne flute, typically holding 3¾ ounces.

Shot (Also Known As *whiskey*): Very slightly flared, short glass with a heavy base. The inside is quite flared. ½- to 2-ounce capacity (1½ or 2 ounces is considered standard by some), often with amount markings on inside. A *shooter* is a taller version, usually with 2-ounce capacity.

Wine: Wineglasses are made in all shapes, sizes, and color combinations, though all are footed. Interpretation of terms varies considerably from brand to brand and expert to expert, and manufacturers unfortunately use names like "wine," "Beaujolais," "red," and "white" interchangeably to the point of total confusion. Generally, red wines are served in larger, cupped glasses and white wines in smaller, narrower glasses (some white wines, such as Rhine wines from Alsace, have their own glass). However, some names are applied more often to certain shapes than others, as follows:

All-purpose: Common, quintessential, cup shaped, with 8 to 9½ ounces the most common capacity. Available from 6 to 16½ ounces.

Balloon: Spherical wineglass of any size. The largest (16 to 22 ounces), most spherical model is used for Burgundy wines and is often called a *Burgundy;* the largest version of all is called a *magnum.* Intended to be filled only about half way in order to enhance the bouquet, or aroma, of the wine.

Straight-sided: Though red wines are usually served in all-purpose glasses, some people prefer to use a smaller, short, straight-sided model, often called a *claret* glass for Bordeaux (claret is a British term for Bordeaux wines)—6½ to 8½ ounces is common.

Tulip: A flared rim atop a bell-shaped body, suitable for all kinds of wine and even champagne (8-ounce size). Available in a wide range of sizes, usually from 8 to 16 ounces.

USE: Serving beverages.

USE TIPS: Fine crystal is delicate and should not be cleaned in dishwashers. Some fine glass will crack if a hot drink is poured into it. Any kind of wine or drink can be served in any kind of glass, but using one that is traditionally designed for the specific beverage enhances the enjoyment of that drink's particular characteristics, notably the bouquet, or fragrance. And in fancier social situations, not doing so is distracting. Wine tastes better in larger glasses, generally. Some lead seepage may occur in closed lead crystal decanters used to store beverages for very long periods of time.

BUYING TIPS: Thin, hand-blown crystal is definitely worth the expense over plain, thick, heavier machine-made glass when it comes to wine or cognac glasses.

PLATE

DESCRIPTION: Round, flat, thin item with slightly angled edge. Lip varies from about ½-inch wide to 1½ inches wide (generally wider on the fancier versions). Made of porcelain (china), wood, precious metals, pewter, or plastic. Diameter tends to dictate what it might be used for, though of course all sizes are interchangeable in informal settings.

TYPES: *Bread plate:* Relatively rare, about 5 inches in diameter.
Dinner plate: About 9½ or 10 inches in diameter.
Salad/dessert plate: About 6 to 8 inches in diameter, or half-moon shaped.
Soup plate: Shallow bowl with large flange, about 9 inches in diameter with 12-ounce capacity; also used for pasta or cereal.

USE: Serving food that is eaten with utensils.

BUYING TIPS: Invariably sold in sets and in quantities ranging from disposable to museum-collectible, with prices to match. Look for those sold from *open stock,* meaning you can replace individual items from a set.

Specialized Place Settings

About Specialized Place Settings

Part of the fun of cooking is entertaining or just eating in large groups, as well as trying a variety of foods. Here are some items which can help you enjoy many particular foods, dishes, or serving styles.

ARTICHOKE PLATE

ARTICHOKE PLATE

DESCRIPTION: Small china plate with deep embossed depressions in a shape suggestive of artichoke leaves, with a large plain depression on one side and a circular one in the center.

USE: Serving artichokes; the center is for holding the artichoke and the depression on the left is for holding melted butter.

BUYING TIPS: This is nice, but any plate and small container of butter will do fine.

ASPARAGUS PLATE

DESCRIPTION: Long, narrow china dish with several textured indentations lengthwise and a plain indentation at one end.

USE: Serving hot asparagus. The long indentations hold a few spears nicely, and the plain indentation at the end is for holding melted butter or hollandaise sauce.

AVOCADO/POTATO DISH

ALSO KNOWN AS: Avocado dish

DESCRIPTION: Small, deep, elongated, oval porcelain dish, pointed at one end.

USE: Serving avocado halves or baked potatoes in an individual dish shaped just right to hold them.

SERRATED CUTTING EDGE

BUFFET FORK

BUFFET FORK

DESCRIPTION: Hybrid fork, designed to incorporate the bowl of a spoon and the cutting edge of a knife. Fine stainless steel.

USE: Eating single-handedly at a buffet.

USE TIPS: Do not serve food that is hard to cut at a buffet, even with this utensil available.

BUYING TIPS: Good gift item.

CAFE ROYALE SPOON

CAFE ROYALE SPOON

DESCRIPTION: Silver-plated spoon with decorative fluted pattern and two hooks at 120-degree angles to the handle. Hooks and handle allow spoon to rest over a coffee cup.

USE: Making *café royale* by placing a sugar cube and cognac in the spoon over a cup of hot coffee and igniting the cognac. When the flame dies out, the cognac/sugar mixture is poured into the coffee.

BUYING TIPS: Very limited use.

CERAMIC SOUP CROCK

CERAMIC SOUP CROCK

ALSO KNOWN AS: Serving crock, French onion soup crock

DESCRIPTION: Deep bowl, with a thick, integral handle protruding from one side, and a cover—all made of ceramic material.

USE: Cooking and serving hot soup or serving cold dips. Cover can be used for storage in refrigerator.

USE TIPS: May be placed over a candle on a warming stand.

BUYING TIPS: Not all bowls can be placed in the oven or under the broiler or even on a warmer, as this one can, making it excellent for French onion soup.

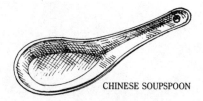

CHINESE SOUPSPOON

CHINESE SOUPSPOON

DESCRIPTION: Porcelain or plastic, oblong, flat-bottomed bowl with a curved handle several inches long. Traditional Chinese design.

USE: Eating soup.

USE TIPS: Heavy porcelain models double as a regular spoon rest.

CHOPSTICKS

DESCRIPTION: Straight, round, or square, tapered wood sticks, from 8 to 10 inches long and about ⅜- to ¼-inch thick. Made from a variety of materials, the most popular of which is Northern White Ash. Rare and beautiful ones can be found carved out of ivory or made of exquisite lacquerware. Some, usually the disposable models, are partially joined at one end and must be broken apart for use. May be sold in a set with porcelain *chopstick rests,* either small bars a few inches long or a small, shallow dish with a fish motif, similar to a *fish bone/sauce dish* (see page 362). Chinese-style, plain chopsticks have blunt ends, while Japanese-style chopsticks are often very fancy, tapered lacquerware. *Cooking and serving chopsticks* (see page 127) are much larger and thicker.

USE: Eating off a plate or out of a bowl. Used in place of knives and forks by peoples throughout the world.

USE TIPS: Learning to hold chopsticks is not hard. Find the right teacher and give yourself a chance. Pretend you are picking up a butterfly wing—don't grip them too firmly.

BUYING TIPS: Available in a wide range of prices and styles, from plain to extraordinarily fancy.

CORN DISH

ALSO KNOWN AS: Corn plate, corn tray

DESCRIPTION: Long, shallow dish with a corn pattern. Available in microwave-safe ceramics, wood, or plastic.

USE: Microwaving, serving, or buttering individual ears of corn.

USE TIPS: The curve of the dish holds any extra melted butter that drips off your corn. The ear can be rolled in this butter.

BUYING TIPS: Often sold in sets of four.

CORN DISH

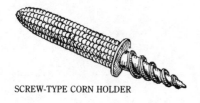

SCREW-TYPE CORN HOLDER

PRONG-TYPE
CORN HOLDER

CORN HOLDERS

ALSO KNOWN AS: Corn picks, corn cob holders

DESCRIPTION: Finger-sized plastic, wooden, or ceramic handles with steel prongs or wide plastic screws (also known as *screw type corn holders,* or *corn screws*) on one end. Available in many different designs, among which there are several classics, such as *Mickey Mouse.* Similar models incorporate the likenesses of dachshunds or alligators split in half. Others include a *miniature corn cob,* the most common design, which is almost always in yellow plastic. If this is made of plastic in one-piece construction, then it is microwave safe.

USE: Holding hot, buttered ears of corn without burning or buttering your fingers.

BUYING TIPS: Usually sold in sets of four or six pairs. Check the package carefully to see if "set" refers to pairs or individual pieces.

CRAB IMPERIAL DISH

CRAB IMPERIAL DISH

DESCRIPTION: Small, oblong porcelain dish in the shape of a crab body minus the claws.

USE: Serving Crab Imperial, a creamed and baked recipe.

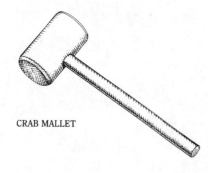

CRAB MALLET

CRAB MALLET

DESCRIPTION: Round-headed mallet made of hardwood, aluminum, or steel, about 2 inches in length and about 1½ inches in diameter, with a short dowel handle.

USE: Cracking the shells of crabs and lobsters.

USE TIPS: Pound lightly to avoid smashing the shell into the flesh of the crab. Not necessary on soft-shelled crabs. Nutcrackers work better on lobster claws. Popular at informal crab feasts when crabs are "picked" and eaten on paper-covered tables and making a mess is part of the fun.

BUYING TIPS: Buy one or two extras, as they tend to be accidentally thrown away along with the shells and newspapers.

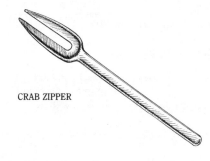

CRAB ZIPPER

CRAB ZIPPER

DESCRIPTION: Small, plastic forklike tool with two rounded, thick, curved tines and a straight handle. The inside edges of the tines are sharp.

USE: Opening up crab shells to extract the meat.

BUYING TIPS: Inexpensive item worth trying.

DEMITASSE SPOON

ALSO KNOWN AS: Espresso spoon

DESCRIPTION: Smallest spoon, made of stainless steel, enameled metal, silver, or even ceramic.

USE: Serving coffee—usually espresso—in *demitasse cups and saucers* (see page 362).

USE TIPS: Intended for stirring only, not for sipping.

BUYING TIPS: Usually sold in sets of four.

EGG CUP

EGG CUP

DESCRIPTION: Small, footed or square-based cup, just about egg-sized, available in many materials, including wood, plastic, porcelain, and metal. Another version is a plastic saucer with an egg cup molded into the center.

USE: Holding soft boiled eggs steady while you eat them right out of the shell.

USE TIPS: Cut the top off with an *egg topper* (see page 35), a scissorlike tool designed just for this purpose.

BUYING TIPS: Often sold in pairs.

EGG SPOON

DESCRIPTION: Small, narrow-bowled spoon with normal handle. Made out of stainless steel or other metals.

USE: Eating soft-boiled eggs from the shell after the top of the shell has been removed.

BUYING TIPS: Doubles as a baby-feeding spoon.

ESPRESSO CUP

ESPRESSO CUP

ALSO KNOWN AS: Demitasse, demitasse cup

DESCRIPTION: Small coffee cup, often no more than 2¼ inches in diameter and sometimes less; about 2-ounce capacity. Usually has vertical sides. Often sold in sets of two or six, called an *espresso set* or *demitasse set*.

USE: Serving espresso coffee.

USE TIPS: Not commonly used for any other beverage than espresso.

BUYING TIPS: Sets are sold with saucers and sometimes *demitasse spoons* (see page 361) as well.

FISH BONE/SAUCE DISH

FISH BONE/SAUCE DISH

ALSO KNOWN AS: Fishbone/lemon dish

DESCRIPTION: Small, shallow, porcelain dish in the shape of a fish.

USE: Holding fish bones as they are removed by diner, or holding a small amount of soy sauce for dipping sushi, or holding used lemon wedges.

BUYING TIPS: Nice addition if you serve much seafood.

FONDUE FORK

DESCRIPTION: Long, narrow, two-pronged fork made of stainless steel with plastic or wooden handle, usually a fine one such as rosewood. As much as a foot long.

USE: Eating fondue by dipping pieces of French bread, meat, or fruit into a *fondue pot* (see page 381).

BUYING TIPS: Sold in sets of as many as twelve forks.

FONDUE FORK

FONDUE PLATE

DESCRIPTION: Medium-sized compartmented china plate, usually with several small compartments and one larger one.

USE: Serving the pieces of beef and various sauces that go with fondue bourguignon.

USE TIPS: Place the meat in the larger compartment.

BUYING TIPS: Good gift item.

FOOTED DESSERT DISH

DESCRIPTION: Small, tulip-shaped, footed dish, usually of glass but also of other materials. Fluted, cut, or stamped decorative edges with normal sides. Various designs are found.

TYPES: *Ice cream:* Large, deep, full bowl design, often made of stainless steel, 3 inches wide.
　　　Parfait dish: Usually tall and narrow.
　　　Sherbert: Smaller, wider model with 4½-ounce capacity.
　　　Sundae (Also Known As *compote*): Taller, 11-ounce model with wide, tulip or stamped decorative edge. Often made of stainless steel or glass.

USE: Serving desserts of mixed fruit and ice cream with whipped cream.

USE TIPS: Only some kinds of glass can be used for frozen parfaits—test carefully before filling and freezing.

BUYING TIPS: Welcome addition to most tableware collections.

GRAPEFRUIT SPOON

DESCRIPTION: Small pointed spoon, about the size of a typical teaspoon, with serrated edges.

USE: Cutting the membranes of grapefruit while eating same.

USE TIPS: Not as efficient as cutting each section beforehand with a *grapefruit knife* (see page 26).

BUYING TIPS: Made in many exotic, decorative styles, particularly tropical.

CRANK

HAND-CRANKED PASTA FORK

HAND-CRANKED PASTA FORK

DESCRIPTION: Regular-sized fork, but with a round plastic shaft and a small crank handle at one end. Rotating the small handle with one hand while holding the shaft with the other causes the tines to rotate.

USE: Twirling spaghetti or other pasta around the tines in order to make a neat mouthful.

USE TIPS: Crank slowly, especially if you have a lot of sauce on your pasta.

BUYING TIPS: Not an essential piece of equipment, but an unusual one.

ICE CREAM SODA SPOON

ALSO KNOWN AS: Iced-tea spoon

DESCRIPTION: Long and narrow stainless-steel spoon.

USE: Designed for stirring and eating from tall glasses with iced tea, ice cream sodas, or any tall drink.

INDIVIDUAL SAUCE POT

DESCRIPTION: Stainless steel cup about 2 inches high and across, slightly flared at the top.

USE: Serving individual portions of cocktail sauce or melted butter.

BUYING TIPS: Very useful item.

LOBSTER AND CRAB PICK

LOBSTER AND CRAB PICK

ALSO KNOWN AS: Lobster fork

DESCRIPTION: Very slim, two-pronged fork on one end with a flat, spoonlike shape on the other end. About 8 inches long, available in plastic or stainless steel. A rare alternative is *lobster prongs,* a pair of long-nosed pliers made of highly polished, chrome-plated steel.

USE: For digging meat out of the crevices of crabs and lobsters.

BUYING TIPS: May be sold in a *seafood set* with lobster shears (see page 48) or *nutcrackers* (see page 366). Very helpful utensil.

LOBSTER BIB

DESCRIPTION: Short cloth or disposable paper or plastic garment that ties around the neck and covers the diner down to his or her waist. Invariably has a picture of a lobster printed on it.

USE: Protects your shirtfront while eating lobsters, which tends to be a messy operation.

USE TIPS: Everybody feels foolish in these bibs, but they really do serve their purpose well.

BUYING TIPS: Sold in sets of as few as four, but also in bulk.

LOBSTER CRACKER

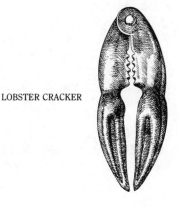

LOBSTER CRACKER

DESCRIPTION: Similar to a *nutcracker* (see page 366), this unique item is made from two levers designed to look like lobster claws that are hinged together at one end. Near the hinge the inside edges are jagged. Red aluminum, almost 6 inches long and 2¼ inches across.

USE: Cracking lobster claws.

USE TIPS: Make sure the claw is placed securely in the cracker or else it might shoot out as you squeeze. "Shedders" (thin and soft-shelled lobsters) may release a lot of water when cracked, so be careful and work over a bucket.

BUYING TIPS: Lever-style nutcrackers usually suffice.

MARROW SPOON

MARROW SPOON

ALSO KNOWN AS: Marrow scoop

DESCRIPTION: Particularly long and narrow, knifelike spoon, with a long handle. Often available in silver-plated steel.

USE: Removing the marrow from cooked bones.

BUYING TIPS: As some connoisseurs consider marrow a rare delicacy, this is considered a fancy item.

NUTCRACKER

ALSO KNOWN AS: Nut and lobster cracker, dual cracker

DESCRIPTION: Two kinds are distinctly different.

TYPES: *Lever:* The traditional, standard style. Usually made of stainless or chrome-plated steel, but also available in gold plate. Two levers, each at least 4 inches long, are connected at top by a hinge, often with a 1-inch-wide spring. The arms have a corrugated pattern or teeth on the inside, toward the hinge, although on the reversible model the indentations are on both sides. If there are two slightly scalloped sections (for large and small nuts or shells) it may be called a *dual cracker.* The indentations closest to the hinge are for smaller nuts. The spring device allows the nutcracker to stand at rest in an open position.

Screw or ratchet type (Also Known As *double wooden nutcracker*): One model is a small wooden cup with a large screw through one side. The blunt-ended screw is twisted down upon the nut, which is held in place by the bowl. Another one is a large metal oblong with a squeeze handle that comes off to one end. The handle activates a ratchet mechanism, which pushes a bar against a nut in the circle.

USE: For cracking nuts or shellfish.

USE TIPS: Be sure to cover the nut or shell being cracked with your hand to prevent debris from flying. Some lobster claws, especially those of softer-shelled *shedders* (thin and soft-shelled lobsters), hold tremendous amounts of water, so crack these over a deep plate or pot.

BUYING TIPS: May be sold as a set with six *nut picks* (see page 384).

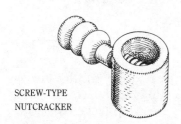

SCREW-TYPE
NUTCRACKER

OYSTER FORK

DESCRIPTION: Short, wide, cupped, three- or four-pronged, stainless steel fork, usually with a slight decorative feel to it.

USE: Eating oysters on the half-shell.

USE TIPS: Pierce the oyster with the fork so it does not slide off. Raise it to your mouth, leaving the shell on the plate.

OYSTER PLATE

DESCRIPTION: Stainless steel or ceramic plate with six or eight shallow, wedge-shaped depressions. A small, round depression is in the middle.

USE: Serving oysters on the half-shell; the central depression holds a small individual *sauce pot* (see page 364) or the cocktail sauce itself.

BUYING TIPS: Not an essential item; oysters can be served on any plate, often on a bed of crushed ice.

PAPER PLATE HOLDERS

DESCRIPTION: Woven wicker plate with thick rim, large enough to hold a paper plate that is snapped into it.

USE: Adding stiffness and weight to paper plates for use outdoors.

USE TIPS: Good alternative to plastic plates, but you must have enough plates for everyone.

SEAFOOD FORK

DESCRIPTION: Very small, narrow fork with two or three prongs. Made of stainless steel or silver.

USE: For extracting meat from shellfish.

BUYING TIPS: Very good item to have if you ever serve shellfish.

SNAIL FORK

DESCRIPTION: Very small, narrow, two-pronged fork, usually made of stainless steel. Prongs are very long.

USE: Removing cooked snails from shells.

SNAIL PLATE

ALSO KNOWN AS: Escargot plate

DESCRIPTION: Ceramic or stainless steel plate of two distinct designs. The ceramic plate (called a *baker-server*) is actually a small

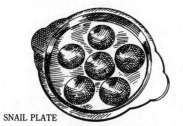

SNAIL PLATE

pan, with a handle and a top surface that has six deep, round, indentations. The snails are cooked in these indentations with butter, garlic, and herbs. The stainless steel plate has either six snail-shaped depressions or shallow round depressions and a wide lip, and holds ceramic snail shells (see below) or the original, real shells, in which the snails are cooked.

USE: Baking and/or serving snails. The ceramic plate is for both, while the stainless plate is just for serving.

USE TIPS: Alert your guests in advance that you plan to serve this delicacy. Not everyone is a taker.

BUYING TIPS: Very helpful item.

SNAIL SHELL

ALSO KNOWN AS: Snail holder

DESCRIPTION: Ceramic piece in the shape of a snail shell; usually brown.

USE: Cooking and serving snails. The snails are removed from their natural shells and placed in these holders, along with butter, garlic, and seasoning.

USE TIPS: These ceramic shells are placed on a special stainless steel plate with snail-shaped or shallow, round indentations, called a *snail plate* (see above entry).

BUYING TIPS: Wash and save for future use; buy tins of snails without the shells next time.

STEAK KNIFE

DESCRIPTION: Small or medium-sized knife with a pointed, usually serrated stainless-steel blade at least 2½ inches long and a wooden, plastic, or bone handle. Handles are usually decorative, such as rosewood or molded plastic that simulates marble, horn, or other natural and fine materials. Must be extremely sharp.

USE: Cutting steak on the dinner plate.

USE TIPS: Do not sharpen serrated edges.

BUYING TIPS: Usually sold in sets of two, four, six, or eight. Narrow serrations are better than the scalloped kind.

YOGURT SPOON

YOGURT SPOON

DESCRIPTION: Stainless-steel spoon with squared-off end and a shallow bowl. A totally similar spoon is called an *ice cream spoon* by one manufacturer.

USE: Designed specifically for scooping out every last bit of yogurt (frozen or otherwise) or ice cream from a container.

USE TIPS: Keep one at the office if you are a yogurt eater.

BUYING TIPS: Any teaspoon will suffice for most people.

Tabletop

About Tabletop Items

Tabletop is the term used for all those items which are not part of an individual place setting but, like salt and pepper shakers, are instead shared by the diners at a table. There is a seemingly endless array of both traditional and innovative items to choose from. They range from strictly utilitarian convenience items for everyday use to fancy items for serving at formal dinner parties or buffets.

ASPARAGUS TONGS

DESCRIPTION: Large, scissorlike utensil with one flat lever, often a rounded triangle, and one curved fork lever. Commonly made of silver as a fancy serving tool.

USE: Serving asparagus or other soft foods.

BUYING TIPS: Good gift item.

BAGEL SET

DESCRIPTION: Set of three items, including a wooden or plastic stick standing on a round base, an open-top wooden box with slits down two ends and curved top sides, and a small knife. *Bagel holder* often refers to a bagel-sized plastic sandwich which can contain a bagel and serves as a slicing guide.

USE: Slicing and serving bagels. The box holds a bagel on its edge while you slice through the guiding slots with the knife provided; the bagels can then be served from the stack held on the little stick.

USE TIPS: Do not cut bagels much in advance—they taste best if cut just prior to serving. Serrated-edged knives cut bagels better than plain-edged models.

BUYING TIPS: This is a safer way to cut bagels than without a guide, if that is a problem for you.

BOBECHE

ALSO KNOWN AS: Candle drip catcher

DESCRIPTION: Small glass, brass, or silver-colored metal saucer with large hole in center. Dinner candle fits through hole and saucer sits at the base of the candlestick.

USE: Catches drips from candles and prevents damage to tablecloth.

BUYING TIPS: Inexpensive item. Some candlesticks are designed to eliminate the need for a bobèche.

BOWL COVER

ALSO KNOWN AS: Bowl bonnet

DESCRIPTION: Round cloth or plastic with elastic hem, sold in a variety of sizes from about ½ foot to well over a foot in diameter. Cloth is usually a decorative print.

USE: Covers bowls of outdoor buffet or picnic food tightly to keep flies out and moisture in. Used to store same in the refrigerator to maintain freshness and flavor.

BUYING TIPS: Usually sold in sets of various sizes, such as 6 to 17 inches in diameter; try to buy one at a time to fit the bowls you generally put out. If considering plastic, be sure to get a thick one (heavy gauge has lower numbers—4 is about right). Clear plastic allows you to see what is in the bowl, but decorative patterns look better.

BREAD BASKET

DESCRIPTION: Traditionally made of woven wicker and lined with a linen towel or napkin. Round or square, but also made in a long, narrow version called a *French bread basket,* for those long French loaves.

USE: Serving bread at the table.

USE TIPS: Cover with a napkin during use if you wish to keep bread warm.

BUYING TIPS: Very useful item.

BREAD WARMER

ALSO KNOWN AS: Bun warmer

DESCRIPTION: Terra-cotta or marble disk about ½ foot in diameter and ½ inch thick. Also available in rectangular shape for long bread baskets.

USE: Heat in oven at 350°F, and then place in bottom of bread basket (see previous entry) to keep bread or rolls warm.

BUYING TIPS: Good gift item.

BUTTER CUP/SALT CUP

ALSO KNOWN AS: Butter chip, beurrier/salière (Fr.)

DESCRIPTION: Very small, shallow, earthenware cup.

USE: Serving butter (molded down flat into the cup) or salt (with a miniature spoon).

USE TIPS: For informal dinner parties.

BUYING TIPS: Not widely distributed but worth a search.

CORN BUTTER SPREADER

BUTTER SPREADER

BUTTER SPREADER

ALSO KNOWN AS: Corn butter spreader

DESCRIPTION: Small square hopper with handle. The bottom of the hopper has a grid and is curved convexly to fit an ear of corn. A lever controls the hopper cover, which presses down on a cube of butter placed in the hopper. A larger model, known as a *stick butter spreader,* holds an entire stick of butter (the *half stick butter spreader* holds half a stick). It has a flat end instead of a cob-curved end. The term *butter spreader* is also used for a 6½-inch-long, flat, wooden tool with a wide end. Some have a small container for salt built into the handle.

USE: Applying butter evenly and cleanly to hot corn cobs or, in the case of the flat-ended models, to baking pans.

BUYING TIPS: Very handy gadget that addresses a common problem.

BUTTER TRAY

ALSO KNOWN AS: Butter dish

DESCRIPTION: Small, long, narrow covered dish generally designed to hold a quarter-pound stick of butter. Typical overall dimensions are 8 inches long by 4 by 2½ inches. Made of all dishware materials, such as plastic, porcelain, wood, or any metal.

USE: Serving butter on the tabletop and storing it (covered) in the refrigerator.

BUYING TIPS: Basic models are supplied with refrigerators.

BUTTER WARMER

ALSO KNOWN AS: Butter melter

DESCRIPTION: One of a variety of designs of containers of melted butter.

TYPES: *Butter melter* (Also Known As *butter warmer*): Small saucepan, about 3 inches wide and 2 inches deep, usually of decorative style, that may have a pouring spout on one side. Often made of beautiful tin-lined copper, but also

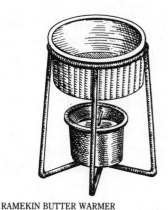

RAMEKIN BUTTER WARMER

found in thin stainless steel or aluminum. May come with small stand that holds a *warmer candle* (see page 394).

Butter warmer: Small ceramic *ramekin* (see page 243) sold with its own miniature stand and *warmer candle* (see page 394).

Ceramic butter warmer (Also Known As *sauce and gravy warmer*): Wide bowl with a built-in handle that fits on a wire stand over a *warmer candle* (see page 394).

USE: Making and serving melted butter to go with seafood that is dipped into it.

USE TIPS: Always heat butter carefully so as not to burn it. The thinner pans burn easily, too.

BUYING TIPS: Look for a pan with a pouring lip on it. You don't need a special pan just for butter, but it does help to use a small one, as it is harder to scorch it.

CAKE SERVER

ALSO KNOWN AS: Pie server, cake/pie server, pizza/pastry server, server, cake knife, pie and cake server

DESCRIPTION: Relatively small triangular blade that angles up slightly to a short handle held so the blade is horizontal. Often made of stainless steel, and typically available with a decorative handle. Available in fancy silver or acrylic versions too. Some manufacturers made a narrower version for cakes and a wider version for pies and pastry. One side may be sharp, and if so, it may be called a *slicer/server* or a *cake cutter and server*. Many variations.

CAKE/PIZZA PUSHER/SERVER

CAKE SERVER/SLICER

TYPES: *Cake/pizza pusher/server:* Standard flat triangular blade, but with a vertical paddle attached to a lever parallel to the handle. When the lever is squeezed, the paddle moves forward along a slot in the blade to push the slice off the blade.

Cake server: Combination of the flat blade and a wide, slotted blade that comes down against it, scissorlike, to hold the piece of cake.

Cake server/slicer: Completely different from the others. No flat blade, but instead a vertically walled triangle with a handle along the base. The cake slice stays inside the server when it is turned on its side.

PASTRY TONGS

Pastry tongs: Small, metal tongs made from one U-shaped stamped piece of stainless-steel band, with wide tips, or else a scissor design with extra wide, slotted tips. A small version of the first type is *candy tongs,* and of the second type, *truffle tongs.*

Pizza slice server: Robust, plain server with a wooden handle.

Serving knife: Knife with a flat, wide, triangular blade that is used vertically, like a regular knife, but that is wide enough to support a piece of pastry for serving when turned horizontally.

USE: Cutting and serving individual pieces of pies, cakes, pastries, and tarts, as well as any other food.

USE TIPS: Try not to cut a piece larger than the blade is wide, or else the edges may fall off, depending on the crust and filling. Test one piece before serving a crumbly or runny pie or tart at a dinner party. An alternative is the *bake-in pie-lifter* (see page 245). Very important item.

CAKE SERVING TRAY

DESCRIPTION: Sturdy plastic or stamped lightweight glass, stainless steel, silver, or porcelain platter in a variety of sizes, either round or rectangular. Edges are raised and decorative. A *cake base* is a heavy cardboard alternative.

USE: Serving decorated cakes. Raised rims keep cake from sliding off.

USE TIPS: Use a tray that fits the cake to avoid slippage.

BUYING TIPS: A large mirror serves in a pinch for larger cakes.

CALL BELL

DESCRIPTION: Low, round, inverted metal cup with a solid base and a small button on top. When the button is pushed briskly, the bell rings. A *tea bell* is a similar item but has the traditional straight handle and bell shape.

USE: Summoning servers to serve more of something or to clear the table and serve the next course. The tea bell is also used to summon your guests into a separate room when tea is served.

USE TIPS: Ring twice, briskly, but no more.

CARVING STAND

CARVING STAND

DESCRIPTION: 6-inch-high chrome-plated steel wire stand, made of two horizontal rings and three vertical legs in a decorative style

USE: Holding ham or leg of lamb for dramatic effect as well as convenience while slicing.

USE TIPS: Practice before attempting this in front of guests.

BUYING TIPS: Good gift item.

CAVIAR BOWL

DESCRIPTION: Serving bowl made of two parts, an outer bowl which contains ice, and a smaller bowl which is suspended over the outer bowl. The design is generally decorative and quite fancy, with an appropriate choice of materials: silver plate, nickel-plated brass, fine glass. Inner bowl can be removed and the outer bowl used for serving warm dishes, too.

USE: Serving caviar "on ice."

USE TIPS: Use only fine caviar with such a fancy item.

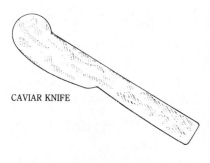

CAVIAR KNIFE

CAVIAR KNIFE

DESCRIPTION: Flat, one-piece knife with a bulbous tip, usually made of the fanciest materials, such as mother-of-pearl. About 5 inches long.

USE: Preparing individual servings of caviar.

USE TIPS: When spreading caviar, do it ever so gently so as not to crush any eggs.

BUYING TIPS: Expensive, fine item, often sold with a caviar spoon (see next entry).

CAVIAR SPOON

DESCRIPTION: Shallow, short, flat-handled spoon, typically made of mother-of-pearl. About 5 inches long. Squarish, with rounded corners.

USE: Serving caviar.

BUYING TIPS: Extraordinarily expensive. Metal is not used because it affects the taste of caviar or is stained by it.

CHAFING DISH

DESCRIPTION: Large (as much as 3 quart) sauté pan with cover that fits into another pan filled with water. The lower pan sits on legs over a *warmer candle* (see page 394) or container for canned fuel. Generally made of decorative materials, such as copper, brass, enameled steel, and carved wood. On some models the top sauté pan can be used without the water pan—for cooking a dessert a brief time.

USE: Maintaining food at serving temperature at buffets.

USE TIPS: Don't let the water evaporate away completely.

BUYING TIPS: Look for model where each pan can be used separately and conventionally.

CHEESE AND BUTTER SERVER/STORER

CHEESE AND BUTTER SERVER/STORER

DESCRIPTION: Small glass or plastic dish with integral cylinder and dome cover. The cylinder is about an inch or two high and is filled with butter, cheese, or pâté. A similar model, called a *party server,* has an extra wide plate with compartments that hold crackers or raw vegetables surrounding the domed center area that holds the cheese or pâté.

USE: Serving and storing butter, cheese, or pâté in the same container. The cover keeps food fresh in the refrigerator.

BUYING TIPS: Good gift item for people who entertain a lot.

CHEESE CLEAVER

CHEESE CLEAVER

ALSO KNOWN AS: Mini cheese cleaver

DESCRIPTION: Miniature version of *butcher cleaver* (see page 11). About 8 inches in maximum total length, with a blade of no more than 4 inches. Stainless steel or brass with wood or plastic handle. Usually considered a decorative item.

USE: Cutting firm and semifirm blocks of cheese as appetizers or after dinner for individual servings on crackers or small pieces of bread. Meant to be used on the buffet table.

USE TIPS: Best if used on a wooden cutting board.

BUYING TIPS: Available in a wide range of prices.

CHEESE MARKER

DESCRIPTION: Small, plastic flag, often a square, with a point extending from the center, pennant-shaped. Either blank or with the words, "This cheese is _____" (imprinted).

USE: Stuck in blocks of cheese for identification at parties.

USE TIPS: The ink you use to write the type of cheese should be washable so you can reuse the markers.

BUYING TIPS: Often sold in sets of four. Not for use at formal parties.

CHEESE PLANE

CHEESE PLANE

ALSO KNOWN AS: Cheese slicer (Incorrect: see page 378), cheese shaver

DESCRIPTION: Small, hand-sized utensil with a flat, triangular-shaped blade with a rounded tip and a slot toward the handle end. The slot actually is part of the blade curved down about ⅛ inch and it has a sharpened edge. Usually made of stainless steel. Handles range from simple wood to decorative plastic.

USE: Slicing harder cheeses very thinly. The plane is dragged along the surface of the cheese.

USE TIPS: Some cheeses respond better to this kind of slicing than others. Be sure to test your cheese before using this slicer at a party. Can be used for peeling asparagus, too.

BUYING TIPS: Available in a wide range of prices and styles.

CHEESE SHAKER

DESCRIPTION: Small glass or plastic jar with perforated or mesh screw-on lid. Large holes are preferable.

USE: Shaking grated parmesan or romano cheese onto an individual serving. Those with large holes can also be used for dried hot pepper flakes; those with smaller holes are more suitable for flour, sugar, salt, or spices.

USE TIPS: Decorative styles can also be used for keeping baking soda in the refrigerator or potpourri in the bathroom.

BUYING TIPS: Larger holes are preferable.

CHEESE SLICER

CHEESE SLICER

ALSO KNOWN AS: Deluxe cheese cutter, adjustable cheese slicer

DESCRIPTION: A paddle-shaped, 4½-inch-wide tool with a taut wire and small roller bar at the wide end. The roller bar is adjustable in terms of distance from the wire over a range of about a quarter inch. A refined version of the great French invention, the *wire butter cutter,* which is nothing more than a piece of wire about a foot long with small wooden handles on each end, used for cutting chunks of butter off large mounds.

USE: Cutting slices from blocks of firm or semifirm cheese. Use one hand to hold the slicer and one to hold the block of cheese steady.

USE TIPS: Adjust the roller bar to change the thickness of the slice. Let the roller rest on the cheese to give you uniform and smooth cuts.

BUYING TIPS: Replacement *cheese wire* is available when your wire breaks.

CHINESE SERVER

ALSO KNOWN AS: Oriental server

DESCRIPTION: Footed stainless-steel dish with cover, usually about 7½ inches in diameter.

USE: Serving hot Chinese dishes on the table.

USE TIPS: Some dishes are best left uncovered so they don't self-steam, such as those with cashews.

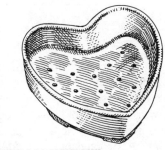

COEUR A LA CREME DISH

COEUR A LA CREME DISH

DESCRIPTION: Heart-shaped porcelain dish, either 4 or 7 inches both ways, with a perforated bottom and sides about an inch or so high.

USE: Serving a very creamy, moist French cream cheese dessert of the same name. The perforations drain off excess moisture.

USE TIPS: Place on another dish to catch any moisture that leaks through. Usually made from cottage and/or cream cheese with sour or whipped cream. Serve with strawberries, fruit sauce, or a special jelly.

BUYING TIPS: Traditional design is made of wicker, not china.

CORN BUTTER BRUSH

DESCRIPTION: Extremely small plastic brush made of a flat handle and a row of bristles about ½-inch wide.

USE: Applying butter meticulously to a cob of corn, or any other use where a small, sanitary brush is called for.

USE TIPS: Can also be used as a *pastry brush* (see page 250).

BUYING TIPS: Most people will find this more trouble than it is worth. Any brush will do.

CORNICHON TONGS

ALSO KNOWN AS: Pickle tongs

DESCRIPTION: Small wooden tongs with rounded shafts and curved, gripper ends. Spring loaded. Also found in a metal, scissorlike version with very narrow tips.

USE: Fishing small pickles out of serving vessels.

BUYING TIPS: Fancy models make nice gifts.

CRUMB SWEEPER

CRUMB SWEEPER

ALSO KNOWN AS: Crumber, hand-held sweeper, table sweeper

DESCRIPTION: Hand-sized, rectangular plastic box with a nylon-bristle roller brush and wheels that extend slightly out one side. Brush is attached to wheels that turn the brush as it moves over tabletop, much as a carpet sweeper works. Available in a variety of colors. Another, simpler version is simply a concave strip of aluminum, known as a *table crumber*. Also available is a *table vacuum*, literally a miniature vacuum cleaner.

USE: Sweeps up crumbs and ashes from a tablecloth-covered tabletop.

USE TIPS: Only really effective when used on tablecloth that won't pull when you sweep over it. Make sure the cloth is firmly anchored before using.

BUYING TIPS: Generally used only by waiters in fine restaurants.

DOILIE

DESCRIPTION: Round, heart-shaped, or rectangular paper or foil item, available from 5 to 12 inches in diameter or up to 12 by 18 inches. Invariably has a lace pattern around the edges, either embossed or perforated, with a scalloped edge. Available in plain white, red, or Christmas patterns. Best quality ones are made of grease-resistant, plasticized paper. Cardboard version is available for professionals. Very, very rarely found in linen.

USE: Placed under a cake or tart for decorative serving.

BUYING TIPS: Sold in packages of twelve or more to a box.

FLATWARE CADDY

FLATWARE CADDY

DESCRIPTION: Small, elaborately decorated, A-shaped metal stand, about 5 inches wide at the base and about 3 inches deep.

USE: Holding neat stacks of flatware for easy access at buffets.

BUYING TIPS: Good gift item for people who entertain a lot.

FONDUE POT

DESCRIPTION: A stainless or ceramic pot, usually of decorative quality and about 2-quart capacity. Usually sold as part of a *fondue set,* including a burner stand for a heat source of some sort, *fondue forks* (see page 362), and a tray to go underneath the other items. Also available in an electric version (see page 288).

USE: Serving fondue, the melted-cheese dish into which you dip pieces of French bread.

BUYING TIPS: Good gift item.

GRAVY BOAT

ALSO KNOWN AS: Sauce boat, gravy server

DESCRIPTION: Oblong china or stainless dish, deep and with a pouring spout on one end and often a handle on the other. May be made with a saucerlike bottom plate attached, or on a large foot. The model with a tall, narrow foot may be called a *dressing server.* The larger variety may go by the impressive name *gravy yacht.* A *fat and lean gravy boat* has spouts that pour off either the fat (on top) or the lean sauce (from the bottom), similar to the *gravy separator* (see page 110).

USE: Serving gravy, sauces, or salad dressing.

BUYING TIPS: Try to find a small ladle to go with the boat. Some boats are sold with a matching ladle.

HONEY DIPPER

HONEY DIPPER

ALSO KNOWN AS: Honey server, honey twirl

DESCRIPTION: Small sphere composed of several disks of graduating size, each disk separated slightly—about ⅛ inch—from the ones on either side of it; generally has a slim handle about 6 inches long. Made of either plastic or wood.

USE: For lifting a small dose of honey from a *honey pot* (see next entry) or other jar.

USE TIPS: Twirl slowly to hold a glob of honey neatly. Some people feel this is not any neater than using a spoon, but may even be messier. Leave the dipper in the honey pot.

BUYING TIPS: Inexpensive, handy item.

HONEY POT

HONEY POT

ALSO KNOWN AS: Honey jar

DESCRIPTION: Small ceramic jar, usually done in an artsy style, with a loose-fitting lid. May have a slot in the lid that allows a *honey dipper* (see previous entry) to protrude. Popular designs include a honey bear or a beehive.

USE: Storing and serving honey at the table.

USE TIPS: Soak in hot water periodically to liquify crystallized honey.

HORS D'OEUVRE DISH

DESCRIPTION: Shallow, rectangular, glass dish, 6½ by 3¼ inches, and about 1½ inches high. Stackable, decorative design.

USE: Serving hors d'oeuvres of all kinds.

BUYING TIPS: Usually sold in sets of four or six.

HOSTESS SERVER

DESCRIPTION: Double-tiered display made of two plates, one large and one small, connected by a wire rod that goes through the middle of both plates and ends in a small handle. The effect is to hold the small plate about 6 inches over the larger, bottom plate.

USE: Display and serving of small pastries at a buffet.

ICE CUBE SPOON

ALSO KNOWN AS: Ice cube server

DESCRIPTION: Stainless-steel spoon with large, shallow bowl that is perforated with a decorative leaf design.

USE: Serving one or two ice cubes at a time.

USE TIPS: An elegant item for intimate settings. Use with a steady hand or else the cubes will slide off.

KETCHUP AND MUSTARD DISPENSER

ALSO KNOWN AS: Squeeze bottle

DESCRIPTION: Soft, plastic, squeezable container, about 8-ounce capacity (hand-sized), with long nozzle and cap attached to base of top by a strip of plastic. Available in red and yellow.

USE: For keeping ketchup and mustard in handy containers. Red is for ketchup, yellow is for mustard.

USE TIPS: The ketchup one is especially handy since it eliminates the slow drip of ketchup out of a glass bottle. These are also a bit neater when kids are involved. Do not ever, repeat: ever, put ketchup in yellow containers and mustard in red ones. That is an inviolable rule.

BUYING TIPS: Ketchup and mustard are sometimes sold in squeeze bottles.

KETCHUP PUMP

DESCRIPTION: Small plastic pump made of a small plunger, a cap that screws onto a ketchup bottle, and a long tube that goes down into the ketchup.

USE: Dispensing ketchup from a bottle cleanly and easily by pressing a button.

BUYING TIPS: An alternative to the dispensers noted in the previous entry.

KETCHUP PUMP

MUSTARD JAR

DESCRIPTION: Small canister-type pot with a loose-fitting top which has a notch that allows a serving stick (a miniature spoon) to protrude. Found in porcelain, glass with a metal holder, plastic, and wood. Sometimes sold with a tiny plastic or wooden *mustard spoon,* with a bowl-shaped end.

USE: Serving Dijon-style mustard on the tabletop.

BUYING TIPS: Good item to have.

NAPKIN HOLDER

DESCRIPTION: Usually a flat, rectangular base with two uprights—solid side walls or posts—on each long side. Another version is flat, with a light bar across the napkins. Can be made of wood, plastic, metal (usually chrome-plated), or ceramic. Also available is a plastic *napkin dispenser* that mounts underneath a cabinet or tabletop. It is an enclosed box except for a small opening on one end from which napkins are extracted.

USE: Holds napkins upright and handy on or near the dining table.

BUYING TIPS: This is a popular folk-art item.

NUT PICK

DESCRIPTION: Thin, metal rod, about 7 inches in length, with a curved, pointed tip. Commonly made of chrome-plated steel but also available in fine metals such as silver as well as plastic. Often made with a decorative pattern.

USE: Extracting the meat from nuts.

USE TIPS: Can also be used with shellfish.

BUYING TIPS: May be sold as part of a set with a *nutcracker* (see page 366).

OIL AND VINEGAR CRUETS

DESCRIPTION: Small glass, pottery, or porcelain pitcher with tiny spouts and narrow tops, usually fitted with stoppers if the spouts are wide.

USE: Serving and storing oil and vinegar at the table.

OIL AND VINEGAR MIXER/POURER

DESCRIPTION: Large plastic pitcher with flat top and handle assembly. The inside is divided into two sections. The top has a knob which can be turned to set the mix of oil and vinegar. Comes with a plastic coaster to collect drips.

USE: Mixing oil and vinegar as they are poured out of the same spout.

USE TIPS: Experiment to find the right setting prior to pouring onto your salad.

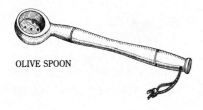

OLIVE SPOON

OLIVE SPOON

DESCRIPTION: Small wooden spoon with a spherical, perforated, deep bowl. Handle is usually round and carved with a decorative effect.

USE: Fishing olives out of serving dishes one at a time.

PARMESAN CHEESE HOLDER

DESCRIPTION: Silver-plated steel tongs made from a very wide, U-shaped piece of steel, with sharp points on the inside to hold a block of cheese and a screw that goes through both ends, which, when turned, squeezes a piece of cheese between them.

USE: Holding a chunk of parmesan cheese for grating at the table.

USE TIPS: For use with an equally fancy, silver-plated *grater* (see page 115).

BUYING TIPS: Relatively fancy, frivolous item.

PEDESTAL STAND

ALSO KNOWN AS: Cake stand

DESCRIPTION: Large, round plate with a wide pedestal foot, usually made of decorative porcelain or glass. Often sold with a glass or clear plastic dome cover, called a *cake dome*. Available in a revolving Lazy Susan version, too.

USE: Serving and displaying cake, pie, fruit, or pastry in a festive manner.

BUYING TIPS: Very useful item. Glass cake domes are hard to find in large sizes.

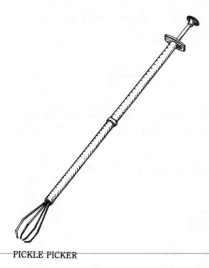

PICKLE PICKER

PICKLE PICK

ALSO KNOWN AS: Pickle fork, olive and pickle fork

DESCRIPTION: Short wooden handle with long, narrow, two-pronged fork. A more elaborate version, a *pickle picker,* is similar to a long, narrow hypodermic needle with an expandable claw that opens and closes with movement of the plunger. Another version of this is a solid plastic, U-shaped pincher which holds pickles by spring tension in the prongs. It is plunged into the jar and forced onto a large pickle.

USE: Reaching pickles in jars when your fingers can't.

USE TIPS: Works on olives as well, and the pickle picker is also good for use on ice cubes.

BUYING TIPS: More certain than a fork.

PITCHER

ALSO KNOWN AS: Beverage server

DESCRIPTION: Squat or plain cylinder or square of various designs and materials with a pouring spout and a large handle. Capacity ranges from 8 ounces (about 4 inches high) to 72 ounces. Larger ones are made, though, up to 2 gallons in capacity. Commonly made of ceramic but also of glass and plastic. One model is of square design and comes with a tight-fitting lid that allows it to be stored on its side; the lid contains a tap that provides for use from the horizontal position on the refrigerator shelf. Also found is a plastic, insulated pitcher, usually large, such as 2-quart capacity. Some have tight-fitting tops which can be turned to strain, pour, or close the spout. One make of a *Sangria pitcher* (which can be of any size or shape) has a large tube inside it that holds a number of ice cubes, thereby keeping the sangria cold without diluting it. One of the more specialized designs is the *cow creamer or pitcher,* used only for serving cream or milk. Another is the *frothing pitcher,* a 12- or 24-ounce stainless-steel pitcher with a horizontal handle, for making cappuccino.

COW CREAMER

USE: Serving beverages.

USE TIPS: Most pitchers have a spout which holds back most of the ice when pouring. However, many of these pitchers can be poured from the side if you want the ice to go into the glasses as you serve. This is usually done in informal restaurants. It is considered more elegant to place ice in a glass prior to pouring in order to prevent the splashing and noise created by cubes falling from a pitcher.

BUYING TIPS: Square pitchers use refrigerator space more efficiently than round ones.

PLATE WARMER

DESCRIPTION: Electric heating pads contained within a foldable fabric with foot-square sections. Folded zigzag style to envelope ten dinner plates.

USE: Warms plates to 160°F in 20 minutes.

BUYING TIPS: Excellent touch for dinner parties. Typical gift item.

PLATTER

DESCRIPTION: Extremely large, oval, porcelain or earthenware plate, typically 17 by 22 inches, with a large rim.

USE: Serving a large piece of meat, such as a turkey, roast, etc., or other foods set out in a decorative display.

USE TIPS: Check to see if platter is ovenproof.

BUYING TIPS: Available in a wide range of styles and prices. A "must" to have.

SALT

PEPPER

SALT AND PEPPER SET

SALT AND PEPPER SET

ALSO KNOWN AS: Salt shaker, pepper shaker

DESCRIPTION: Two containers, one for salt, one for pepper. Usually the pepper shaker has fewer or smaller holes than the salt shaker. Some are color coded: white for salt, black for pepper. Also made in a combined model with plastic tops that snap close; some are designed to make them *moisture-proof shakers*. Available in an extremely wide range of designs from cheap and simple to folk art to elaborate cut glass and silver. Some popular designs include: hot and cold water faucets, hens, tomatoes, lobster claws, eggs, and little people.

USE: Shaking salt or pepper onto an individual serving. Snap-tops are necessary for traveling models such as those used for picnics or camping.

USE TIPS: A few grains of rice in the salt shaker will absorb humidity and keep the salt flowing freely. Make sure that the tops are screwed on securely before placing shakers on the table.

BUYING TIPS: Some sets include a *pepper mill* (see page 121) instead of a pepper shaker. Get two sets: one for cooking and one for the table.

SALT MILL

DESCRIPTION: Typically a round, wooden or plastic, hand-sized item with a small thumbscrew at the top. The hollow inside holds coarse granules of sea or kosher salt. The grinding mechanism on the bottom is made of stainless steel or nylon.

USE: Grinding coarse or kosher salt onto salad and cooked dishes.

BUYING TIPS: Not an essential piece of kitchen equipment.

SANDWICH SERVER

DESCRIPTION: Round-bladed turner. Available in stainless steel with teak handle, as well as other more decorative materials.

USE: Lifting and serving small sandwiches at parties.

BUYING TIPS: Small tongs (see page 134) make a simpler alternative.

SERVING FORK

ALSO KNOWN AS: Serve fork

DESCRIPTION: Wide, large, stainless steel or silver fork with two, three, or four decorative tines and a decorative shape, sometimes that of a leaf. A flat, wide version is a *cold meat fork*.

USE: Serving cooked food from serving bowls or platters. A cold meat fork is for serving slices of cold meat.

BUYING TIPS: Often sold as a set with other serving implements.

SERVING TRAY

ALSO KNOWN AS: Waiter's and buffet tray

DESCRIPTION: Available in a variety of sizes, shapes, and materials, from the finest sterling silver to disposable foil. Typically oval or rectangular, about 19 inches long by about 14 inches wide, with a wide, shallow, curved edge. Smaller trays are specialized: *relish* or *dip tray* (10 by 5 inches); *bread tray* (oval, 13 by 7½ inches); *cocktail tray* (oval, 14 by 9½ inches).

USE: Transporting or making a nice presentation of hors d'oeuvres, petits fours, drinks, etc.

USE TIPS: Don't try carrying a full tray above your head unless you are experienced. Also, don't let others help themselves from the tray you're carrying; an unexpected shift in the weight you have carefully balanced may send the contents into someone's lap.

SIZZLE PLATTER

DESCRIPTION: Shallow, oval, heavy-duty cast aluminum platter, about 8 by 13½ inches, supplied with a heat-resistant, plastic tray that it fits into snugly. Sold in sets of four, but a 10- by 15-inch buffet platter is offered as well.

USE: Serving hot steaks with lots of sizzle.

USE TIPS: Coat with oil and preheat in oven prior to putting in broiler with steak for cooking.

SOUP TUREEN

DESCRIPTION: Large, squat, bulbous container of at least several quarts. Supplied with a domed lid. Usually decorative in design. Often sold with a matching platter.

USE: Serving soup from the tabletop.

BUYING TIPS: Good item to have; also good gift item.

SOY SAUCE SERVER

SOY SAUCE SERVER

ALSO KNOWN AS: Soy sauce pot, sauce dish, sauce/condiment dish

DESCRIPTION: Either of two designs: a small pot, usually with indentations on each side for better gripping between thumb and forefinger; or a small, shallow, footed dish about 2 inches across. This dish is often in the shape of a fish.

USE: Serving soy sauce on the table; the dish is used when serving sushi and sashimi as an individual serving alongside the fish, which is dipped into the soy sauce. The fish dish is also used for serving other sauces and as a *fish bone dish* (see page 362).

SPREADER

SPREADER

ALSO KNOWN AS: Palette knife, sandwich spreader, flexible French spreader, sandwich spatula

DESCRIPTION: Short but very wide-bladed knife with rounded tip and often with one serrated edge. Available with a stainless-steel blade with ceramic, wooden, or colorful plastic handles, as well as an all-ceramic construction. Another version sometimes referred to as a *cheese knife* is a teardrop-shaped blade with one sharp edge and a round handle. A miniature version known as a *cheese spreader, cocktail spreader,* or *party spreader* is only about 3½ inches long and less than an inch wide; it is also known as a *cheese knife* and an *hors d'oeuvre knife*. Actually, the term *palette knife* is a misnomer; that term more accurately describes a long, narrow *icing spatula* (see page 260 in pastry chapter).

USE: Spreading dips, pâtés, and soft cheeses on bread or crackers when serving appetizers. Also handy for spreading soft food on bread for sandwiches.

BUYING TIPS: Small ones are sold in quantities on the order of twelve or forty-eight.

SUGAR AND CREAMER

DESCRIPTION: Set of two porcelain, silver, or pottery containers, a small pitcher, and a small canister with or without a loose-fitting top, often with a cutout for the sugar spoon.

USE: Serving granulated sugar and cream on the table.

USE TIPS: Many people use milk instead of cream.

BUYING TIPS: Important item.

SUGAR AND SWEETENER SERVER

DESCRIPTION: Shallow, rectangular, two-compartment dish, a few inches wide.

USE: Designed expressly for serving sugar and sugar-substitute packets.

BUYING TIPS: Considered more of a restaurant item.

SUGAR SHAKER

ALSO KNOWN AS: Sugar dispenser, sugar server

DESCRIPTION: Glass jar, 12 ounces or larger, with chrome-plated steel, screw-on top. The top has a small opening in it that is covered by a flap. A *sugar meter* is a variation that has a non-moving, conical, plastic, or metal top with an opening inside the tip.

USE: Storing and serving refined sugar.

BUYING TIPS: Considered an informal item.

SUGAR TONGS

DESCRIPTION: Short, stainless or chrome- or silver-plated steel tongs made from one U-shaped piece, with decorative aspect. Slightly cupped ends, usually with small claws.

USE: Picking up individual cubes of sugar.

USE TIPS: Do not drop cubes into coffee or tea from a great distance or you will cause an embarrassing splash.

SYRUP PITCHER

DESCRIPTION: Glass jar with screw-on plastic or metal (chrome-plated or stainless steel) top with a long trigger grip that extends down along the side. The trigger opens a small spout on the top. Another type, the *honey/syrup dispenser* has a trigger grip, but instead of a spout, it has an opening in its narrow, pointed bottom. It is conical in shape and sits in its own bowl filled with hot water to warm the syrup or honey in order to make it free flowing. Also offered in a lead crystal model.

USE: Serving syrup or honey at the table.

USE TIPS: Use with a saucer—almost all pitchers drip.

BUYING TIPS: Very handy item.

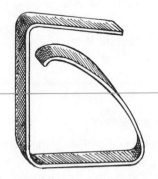

TABLECLOTH CLIP

TABLECLOTH CLIPS

ALSO KNOWN AS: Tablecloth holders

DESCRIPTION: Small, plastic, half-spiral spring with one straight side, about 2 inches in diameter overall. About ¾-inch wide. Also made of a triangular stainless-steel band of the same width. Another version is the tablecloth weight, a clothespinlike clip with a small, decorative weight hanging from it. Typically the weights are made of plastic-coated lead in the shape of apples and lemons.

USE: Holding picnic tablecloths in place on windy days. Place the clip over the tablecloth at the corner of the table. Flat side appears on top while the curved or larger side is hidden under the table.

USE TIPS: Very helpful item.

BUYING TIPS: Sold in sets of four.

THERMOS SERVER

ALSO KNOWN AS: Thermal server, thermos pitcher, vacuum bottle

DESCRIPTION: Insulated carafe, pitcher, or bottle made of glass, plastic, and/or metal. One-quart capacity is typical, but a wide range is available, some with wide mouths for serving soups and stews. The term *thermos* denotes a vacuum-insulated container; the inside container may be of glass, plastic, or stainless steel, while the outside may be of plastic or enameled steel or aluminum (*thermo* may only denote a foam-insulated container which insulates only for a few hours). Several dispensing tops are found which maintain temperature while being ready for service. One is a screw-on stopper which allows for pouring if it is not screwed on all the way. Another is a push-button which allows pouring in the "up" position only. And there is a pump model which dispenses upon pushing a large button.

USE: Maintaining temperature of both hot and cold liquids. Some models work effectively for as long as 18 hours.

USE TIPS: Excellent way to serve coffee or tea at mealtimes or in the office.

BUYING TIPS: Avoid glass bottles if rough transportation or handling is in store for you. Polished, untreated stainless steel is best, especially when made with advanced techniques that allow for a much smaller insulation area and overall size. An insulated drinking cup and permanent carrying handle are good features to seek out, too. And pour-through stoppers are a very convenient innovation. The most recent development features all-metal, unbreakable, well-designed small bottles that are so well insulated they can have thin walls.

TRIFLE BOWL

TRIFLE BOWL

ALSO KNOWN AS: Trifle

DESCRIPTION: Large, deep glass bowl on low pedestal, available in different sizes, ranging from an individual 4-ounce bowl to a party-size 50-ounce bowl and even a mammoth 124-ounce one.

USE: For the traditional British dessert made with fruit, sponge cake, custard, jam, and whipped cream. Striking display of the layers of this dessert are essential.

TRIVET

TRIVET

DESCRIPTION: Any design of a flat, protective material that looks appropriate on a dining table.

TYPES: *Cork trivet:* Round or square piece of cork, about ½-inch thick, ranging in size from 6 to 10 inches across. May be mounted on wood sheet.
 Expandable trivet and table mat: Wooden or chrome-plated steel slats connected by hinges. When expanded part way, they form a diamond pattern; when collapsed, a neat and small solid package.

USE: Protecting table surfaces from heavy or hot serving dishes.

USE TIPS: Expandable trivets still allow heat to reach the table.

BUYING TIPS: Style is strictly based on personal preference.

WARMER CANDLE

ALSO KNOWN AS: Chafing-dish candle

DESCRIPTION: Short, wide candle, about an inch in height, encased in an aluminum cup.

USE: Placed under warmers such as *chafing dishes* (see page 376) or in small *warmer stands* (see next entry) to keep food warm or butter melted.

USE TIPS: The aluminum casing should keep wax from dripping on the table, but be aware of the possibility nonetheless.

BUYING TIPS: Sold in packages of four but also available in larger quantities.

WARMER STAND

ALSO KNOWN AS: Food warmer

DESCRIPTION: Any of a number of designs that can hold *warmer candles* (see previous entry) and support a food dish. Two of the most common include either a crystal glass cup for one dish or a steel box with a grid that holds two candles and larger dishes. Sometimes a two-candle model is called a *plate warmer* and a one-candle model is called a *tea warmer*.

USE: Keeping food dishes warm on the tabletop.

USE TIPS: Remember to check the candles periodically in order to replace those that have burnt out.

WARMING TRAY

ALSO KNOWN AS: Hot tray

DESCRIPTION: Flat, large, rectangular electric tray made of various combinations of plastic, toughened glass, wood, metal, and stone. A 10- by 22-inch surface (average size) can hold two 1½-quart dishes and one 3-quart dish, all rectangular. Thermostatically controlled heating element keeps tray at predetermined temperature; on some models there is a hotter spot for soups or beverages. Most are just plugged in and turned on; a ceramic-covered model heats up to 250°F very quickly and then is unplugged. The heat is retained for about an hour. Some more elaborate models contain a deep serving unit that holds several serving dishes supplied with the tray.

A space-age version is a tempered glass *thermal dynamic tray,* or a *cordless hot tray,* that just reflects the heat (or cold) of a container placed upon it. Temperature loss is less than 9 degrees per hour. It is actually a form of ultraefficient insulation.

USE: Keeping serving containers of hot food warm when entertaining.

USE TIPS: Warmth can be deceptive—remove containers that are almost empty so the little food left does not burn.

BUYING TIPS: Measure your serving containers and see if they fit well on a tray before purchasing. Smaller models may only be able to hold one round dish. Note that some are quite handsome, with mahogany trim and the like. Very useful to have.

PART IV

Kitchen Accessories

Cleaning Tools

About Cleaning Tools

This chapter has two sections, both of which deal with cleaning tools that are used in the kitchen. The first deals only with those items used on food, the second with those items used on the cooking utensils. Excluded are those cleaning tools that belong more in the housewares department, as they are more often used in the rest of the house than in the kitchen. And as with the rest of the book, no supplies or consumable products are listed.

There are plenty of alternatives to all of these items, and often a specialized tool will suffice when used for something different; no one should hesitate to experiment here. Furthermore, many specialized items are not really necessary, they are just better. You can use almost any kind of brush to clean vegetables, for example. The point is to find what works for you.

Food Cleaning Tools

About Food Cleaning Tools

Though some people prefer specialized tools such as the ones described here, many other people make do with a plain rinse of running water. Any of these tools can be helpful, but none is essential.

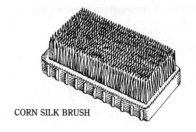

CORN SILK BRUSH

CORN SILK BRUSH

ALSO KNOWN AS: Corn desilking brush, corn brush

DESCRIPTION: Several different designs of a small brush. One is a small, rectangular, flat brush, made from one piece of plastic, with a thousand fine, soft plastic bristles about ½-inch long. It was originally designed as a surgeon's scrub brush, and is also sold labeled as a *carrot brush, celery brush, mushroom brush, potato brush,* and *asparagus brush*—all the same item. Also available with a wooden base and handle in a hairbrush design.

USE: Removing the silk from fresh corn ears, or soil from other vegetables.

USE TIPS: Brush in both the sideways and end-to-end directions to get gentle and firm effects.

BUYING TIPS: The all-plastic version can be easily washed in your dishwasher or just rinsed out, and can also be used for cleaning other small and delicate items. This specialized design is said to be more effective than any other for cornsilk. Any brush will do for firm vegetables other than mushrooms, for which a specialized design is available (see next entry).

MUSHROOM BRUSH

MUSHROOM BRUSH

ALSO KNOWN AS: Vegetable/mushroom brush

DESCRIPTION: Small brush, about 2 inches long, with delicate, very soft bristles about an inch long. Also available in the shape of a mushroom, with the bristles in place of the stem.

USE: Cleaning dirt off delicate mushrooms.

USE TIPS: Be gentle and work fast—mushrooms can't stand too much wetness or handling, as they absorb water rapidly and lose their flavor. Brush while dry, if possible.

BUYING TIPS: Inexpensive item designed to do this job well.

SALAD BASKET

SALAD BASKET

ALSO KNOWN AS: Metal spin-dryer, salad shaker

DESCRIPTION: Wire basket large enough to hold an entire head of lettuce, with long wire loop handles.

USE: Shaking freshly washed lettuce dry.

USE TIPS: This is most effective when swung vigorously outdoors. It is difficult to dry salad greens with a timid shake indoors, and besides, water will fly all over the kitchen, especially if you are enthusiastic about this.

BUYING TIPS: A low-cost alternative to the *salad spinner* (see next entry). Often hung on a wall in a visible place just for decoration.

SALAD SPINNER

SALAD SPINNER

ALSO KNOWN AS: Salad wash and dry, salad washer, salad dryer, plastic spin-dryer

DESCRIPTION: Large, solid plastic container—large enough to hold an entire head of lettuce—with a smaller basket container inside it. The basket spins on a point at the bottom when turned by a crank or a pull-cord on the top, and the water collects in the outer bowl. Some are designed to drain, though, and can be placed directly beneath the faucet. The crank is connected to the basket by a series of gears which cause the basket to spin at high speeds with little effort. The high speed causes water to fly off the food. Sizes are measured in quart capacity, typically 2 and 4 quart.

USE: Washes and dries all salad greens, most often lettuce for salads.

USE TIPS: Be sure to dry the outer container carefully prior to returning the spinner to a cabinet for storage.

BUYING TIPS: Make sure you have enough room to store this bulky item.

VEGETABLE BRUSH

VEGETABLE BRUSH

ALSO KNOWN AS: Potato scrubber, vegetable and dishwashing brush

DESCRIPTION: Hand-sized, plastic- or wooden-handled brush with a round head and short, tough bristles less than an inch long. Most have natural, tampico bristles, but many have softer nylon bristles. A wider, block-style version with shorter bristles and no handle is available, called a *potato/vegetable brush*.

USE: Cleaning dirt off freshly picked vegetables.

USE TIPS: Works well on dirty dishes, too.

BUYING TIPS: Very handy, versatile item. Stiff bristles make it ideal for this work.

WATER FILTER

DESCRIPTION: Either of two systems. One is a freestanding, electric machine that weighs over 10 pounds and is over a foot high. A gallon of water is poured into it. It is then brought almost to the boiling point and pumped through a granular active carbon filter. Two half-gallon decanters are supplied. The other system is a similar filter that attaches directly to your faucet and purifies the water as it flows through. Some models use an electro-chemical oxidation process in addition to carbon.

USE: Purifying water for drinking or cooking. Removes bacteria, viruses, contaminents, minerals insecticides, odors, and other pollutants, though not completely.

USE TIPS: Get advice from the health authorities in your area in regard to the contents of your water and the kind of filtration warranted.

BUYING TIPS: These are less expensive than buying bottled water. The best filters remove chalky hardness, chlorine, heavy metals (lead, mercury, and cadmium), rust, dust, and cloudiness. Look for change-filter reminder, tap shutoff, speed adjustability, double-action filters (ion exchange resin along with activated charcoal).

Cooking Utensil Cleaning Tools

BOTTLE BRUSH

BOTTLE BRUSH

DESCRIPTION: One- or 1½-inch-thick cylinder of nylon bristles woven into a twisted wire shaft with a plastic handle. A thicker version is the *jar and glass cleaner,* and a thinner version, no more than ½ inch thick, is the *spout brush.*

USE: Cleaning bottles, jars, glasses, and the spouts of pitchers.

USE TIPS: Pull out of tight containers slowly, as the bristles tend to spray water as they emerge.

BUYING TIPS: Inexpensive, handy solution to a common problem. Essential for baby bottles.

BOTTLE SCRAPER

DESCRIPTION: The longest, narrowest, stainless steel spoon made. Well over a foot long. Also available in plastic, in a long, rectangular configuration. A specialized model is the *mayo knife,* an almost foot-long plastic design with a specially offset, bevel-edged blade which is slightly indented at the tip.

USE: Removing the last bit of food from bottles, especially tall ketchup bottles.

BUYING TIPS: For the cook who must have everything.

BOTTLE SCRAPER

COUNTERTOP DISHWASHER

DESCRIPTION: Small, water-powered dishwasher with hose that connects to kitchen faucet. Circular rack with dome lid holds up to four place settings of dishes. About 20 inches in diameter and almost as high.

USE: Cleans and rinses without electricity. No drying cycle.

BUYING TIPS: Inexpensive and unsophisticated alternative to a built-in model.

DISH DRAINER

ALSO KNOWN AS: Dish rack

DESCRIPTION: Wood, vinyl-coated wire, or plastic construction made of an open framework with slots for holding dishes, glasses, and silverware. Available in a variety of colors. Folding models are also available. Usually sold with a drainboard (see page 404).

USE: Draining freshly rinsed dishes next to the sink. Folding dish racks are especially useful in small kitchens.

USE TIPS: Clean the underside periodically with a stiff scrub brush and strong soap.

BUYING TIPS: Sometimes a silverware holder is sold separately. This can be useful even if you have a dishwasher, for drying pots and pans or the occasional small item. A smaller alternative is the *over-the-sink drainer* (see opposite). Important item if you do not have a dishwasher.

DISH MOP

DESCRIPTION: Long wire handle with a spherical head made from pieces of cloth yarn. A similar item is a *sponge puff,* a ball of short pieces of sponge with a wooden handle.

USE: Gentle washing of dishes and utensils with warm, soapy water.

USE TIPS: Not intended for scrubbing.

DRAINBOARD

ALSO KNOWN AS: Draining board

DESCRIPTION: Wide, shallow-ridged, plastic sheet about 15 by 20 inches, with a pouring lip on one end and usually small feet or bumps on the bottom. Some models have larger bumps at the far end to tilt the board a bit toward the sink. Available in a variety of colors.

USE: Placed under dish racks (see page 403) to drain rinsewater into sink.

USE TIPS: Clean regularly or else there will be a buildup of gummy deposits. Place a small piece of wood or stone under the far end to tilt it up a bit more in order to increase drainage.

BUYING TIPS: Needed only if you do not have a dishwasher.

GLASS AND BOTTLE SPONGE

ALSO KNOWN AS: Bottle sponge, jar and glass sponge

DESCRIPTION: Cylindrically shaped foam rubber sponge about 4 inches long and 1½ inches wide, with a plastic or wooden handle.

USE: Cleaning inside glasses and bottles. Conforms to the shape of the bottle for efficient cleaning.

USE TIPS: Very handy, and it keeps your hand from getting stuck in a narrow-mouthed jar or bottle.

GLASS AND BOTTLE SPONGE

LATEX GLOVES

ALSO KNOWN AS: Rubber gloves

DESCRIPTION: Latex, one-size-fits-all gloves that reach to midarm. Available in a variety of colors. A special version of the standard glove is made of just the fingertips, *a half-rubber-glove*.

USE: Protecting hands during cleanup—hot water and detergent can chap some skin. The half-version is excellent for hard scrubbing jobs, especially for those who dislike wearing gloves.

USE TIPS: These gloves have no cushioning and pierce fairly easily, so they're inappropriate when heavy-duty protection is needed. Not to be confused with heavier gloves for use with painting or gardening chemicals.

ONION, GARLIC, AND FISH ODOR REMOVER

ALSO KNOWN AS: Cajun smart bar

DESCRIPTION: Small metal bar. Rub hands over bar under running water, as in using a bar of soap.

USE: Removes odors from your hands. Made of metal alloy that reacts with onion oil in a nonallergenic manner.

BUYING TIPS: Good, inexpensive gift item.

OVEN RACK CLEANER

DESCRIPTION: Two-inch-diameter disk with three sets of small pairs of teeth protruding, on the end of a 6-inch-long plastic handle. The pairs of teeth each house a small slot of a slightly different width.

USE: Scraping oven racks and barbecue grills. Slots in teeth are designed for various thicknesses of racks and grills.

BUYING TIP: Inexpensive, unique item that does its job well.

OVER-THE-SINK DRAINER

DESCRIPTION: Plastic or plastic-covered wire rack with grid that holds dishes. Small size fits over sinks up to 19 inches wide.

USE: Suspends over sink to drain wet dishes or food after washing.

USE TIPS: Doubles as a *colander* (see page 107) for rinsing large fruits and vegetables. Particularly helpful where counter space is at a premium.

BUYING TIPS: Smaller alternative to regular *dish drainer* (see page 403). Great for small kitchens.

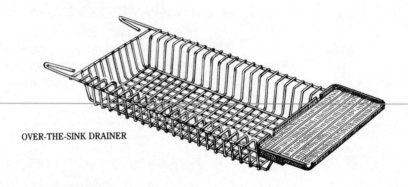

OVER-THE-SINK DRAINER

POP-UP SPONGE

DESCRIPTION: Dried, compressed, cellulose sponge, about an inch wide and a few inches long but only ¼-inch thick, that expands to hand size when moistened. Releases water very slowly. Can be found with the words "dishes" and "wipe up" printed on the side.

USE: Light cleaning jobs around the kitchen.

USE TIPS: These are great when storage space is tight, since they take up so little room when dry. Once wet, they will not reduce to the flat original size again, however. Rinse well after use with food.

BUYING TIPS: Cellulose is a natural substance, derived from wood pulp.

SCOURER

ALSO KNOWN AS: Scouring pad

DESCRIPTION: Copper or stainless steel spiral wire, gathered into a fist-sized ball. Also made of woven plastic.

USE: Scouring heavily encrusted food off cooking and eating utensils. This is your cleaning implement of last resort. Plastic is best for pans with delicate nonstick coating.

USE TIPS: Soak hard food before scouring. Note whether this scratches the finish on your pots and pans—test first, and be gentle. Caution: the metal wire has sharp edges.

BUYING TIPS: Every kitchen needs at least one of these. The plastic ones tend to last longer than some of the metal ones, and are easier on your hands, but only the metal ones can truly "cut" into seriously encrusted food.

SCOURING PAD HOLDER

SCOURING PAD HOLDER

ALSO KNOWN AS: Jewelry holder, soap pad holder

DESCRIPTION: Small plastic or ceramic piece, usually spherical, with one large opening on the upper part of one side or the top. Popular designs include an apple, frog, or duck, in which the animals have large open mouths. An assortment of fruit designs is also available.

USE: Holds soap pads, scouring pads, or small pieces of jewelry at the sink edge (many people remove their fancy jewelry while washing dishes).

USE TIPS: Pour out excess water to avoid undue rusting. Intended for only one at a time.

BUYING TIPS: Considered by many to be charming. Very handy.

SCRUBBER

ALSO KNOWN AS: All-purpose scrubber

DESCRIPTION: Nylon mat of varying degrees of coarseness and in either of two forms. Available as a plain, thin, rectangular, hand-sized *scrubber pad* or as the round tip of a long-handled utensil. A glove-shaped version is a *scouring mitt*. Some are rated Teflon® safe, meaning that they will not scratch that delicate nonstick coating material. Others are labeled light duty, heavy duty, and all-purpose. A hand-sized *power pot and pan scrubber* is available that is hooked up to the water faucet. The water comes through a hose to drive a turbine mechanism in the scrubber head, rotating a stiff nylon brush.

USE: Scrubbing small quantities of lightly encrusted food off cooking and eating utensils. Intended for everyday use.

USE TIPS: Most scratch polished metal unless labeled otherwise.

BUYING TIPS: Inexpensive item that wears out quickly.

SELF-SUDSING DISH SPONGE

DESCRIPTION: Small rectangular foam rubber sponge with a scrubber side. Plastic handle can be filled with detergent, which is released through the wet sponge as it is used. Sponge part is sold separately as a replacement part.

USE: General, light dish cleaning. The automatic detergent distribution saves you from having to reapply detergent to the sponge or to make a soapy water supply.

USE TIPS: Use sturdier items for encrusted food.

BUYING TIPS: This may increase your use of detergent.

SPONGE CLOTH

ALSO KNOWN AS: Sponge

DESCRIPTION: Hand-sized plastic sponge only about ¼-inch thick.

USE: Gentle washing of all utensils and surfaces.

USE TIPS: Not a sturdy item.

UTILITY BRUSH

ALSO KNOWN AS: Pot and pan brush, kitchen brush, dishwashing brush, dishwashing and vegetable brush, dish brush

DESCRIPTION: Round head about 1½ inches in diameter with stiff nylon or natural tampico bristles about 1 inch long. Handle of wood or plastic. A *sink and dish brush* has a rounded tip, with nylon bristles. An older version of this is the oval *sink and vegetable brush,* made with natural bristles woven into a wire loop with a wooden handle, and which resembles the *vegetable brush* (see page 401). Still another, called a *bassine brush,* combines brass bristles in the center with soft plastic bristles on the perimeter.

USE: Any kind of small cleanup job, but chiefly for scrubbing dishes or pots and pans. Not for heavy scouring.

USE TIPS: A great basic brush to have. Use a designated brush only for cleaning objects, and keep the similar-looking vegetable brush for vegetables only.

BUYING TIPS: Nylon bristles last longer than natural bristles. Some high-quality pots can scratch easily, so test first before using. Very useful to have.

CHAPTER 16

Storage and Convenience Items

About Storage and Convenience Items

There seems to be an infinite supply of innovative and traditional items for all aspects of kitchen storage and convenience. Included here are items that are as directly related to cooking as possible—those things a cook would actually use in the course of cooking and serving meals. You will not find those items that are more in the realm of furnishings or consumable supplies.

This is one area where competitiveness has spawned some very useful designs. It is worthwhile to look for items that fit your taste, space, and feel. There is no need to use something that is hard to open or too large for your shelves. Shop until you find the one that is just right for you.

Storage Items

About Storage Items

Many racks and hooks that normally would be screwed into a wall or cabinet door may be available with strong magnets that allow for instant installation on metal appliances.

BAG CLIP

BAG CLIP

ALSO KNOWN AS: Chip clip, freezer clip

DESCRIPTION: Looks like an extra-wide, spring-loaded clothespin. Opened by squeezing finger tip handles together. Plastic, available in many colors, and often imprinted with the rather unsurprising moniker "BAG CLIP." Also available printed with the words "cookies," "pretzels," "snacks," and "chips." Comes in miniature and large sizes. An extremely wide cat face design, called a *kitty cat bag clip,* and one shaped like a football, with an NFL team logo, are also available.

USE: Keeps bags of snack food closed and fresh.

BUYING TIPS: One of the most popular kitchen gadgets of all time.

BAG LOCK

BAG LOCK

ALSO KNOWN AS: Bag sealer

DESCRIPTION: Two plastic sticks, about half a foot long, hinged together at one end. One fits inside the other with a snap. Also designed as a small, plastic, U-shaped item that clips closed, somewhat like a badge pin. A "blade" of plastic fits into a track on the opposite side, creating a solid seal.

USE: Sealing plastic food bags for freezer or refrigerator storage.

BUYING TIPS: Saves having to buy expensive, specially designed bags. Allows reuse of plain bags.

BANANA TREE

DESCRIPTION: Small plastic column, topped by short arms that jut out in a T-shape, with a round base.

USE: Hanging bunches of bananas for easy ripening and longer freshness outside the refrigerator. Avoids bruising.

BUYING TIPS: Depending on your space, could be a good decorative item, bananas included.

CAN COVER

DESCRIPTION: In its simplest form this gadget is a plastic disk with a small ridge around the edge, the diameter of most 10- or 12-ounce food cans. Other models are more refined: Some have a reclosable pouring spout and others two pointed teeth, which pierce a can top when pushed down.

USE: Covering open cans of food.

USE TIPS: Particularly good for storing open cans of pet food.

BUYING TIPS: Often sold in grocery stores.

CANISTER

ALSO KNOWN AS: Storage jar

DESCRIPTION: Plastic, glass, ceramic, or metal cylindrical or tall rectangular container with lid that either fits on loosely, clamps down tightly, screws on, or squeezes on. Most are air tight, especially those with rubber gaskets. Usually sold in sets that include three to five small to large canisters; a large one might hold five pounds of flour. Many come with scoops as well. Some have knobs on the lid that contain a special material called *moisture absorber*, also available as an insert. One larger model that holds, say, 3 pounds of rice, has a measuring cup for a lid.

USE: Storage of staple foods in bulk, such as sugar or flour.

USE TIPS: Use the absolutely air-tight models for storing aromatic items like coffee or herbs, or to keep humidity away from rice. Saturated, ineffective moisture absorbers can be restored by heating them in a 250°F oven for 20 minutes.

BUYING TIPS: You can save much money and time by buying foods like cereals in bulk. Most canisters are almost airtight, especially plastic models, so don't worry about getting one with special clamps except for very delicate foods in very moist situations. Look for canisters that are easy to open and close, and plastic ones with molded-in grips. Square and rectangular designs use space more efficiently than round ones.

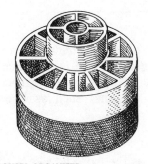

CAROUSEL ORGANIZER

CAROUSEL ORGANIZER

ALSO KNOWN AS: Gadget caddy, kitchen caddy, gadget organizer, utensil holder, tool holder

DESCRIPTION: Typically an 8-inch diameter, cylindrical, plastic device with concentric circles or tubes divided into two levels of compartments; also rectangular. Another common version is a plain cylindrical vase. Usually made in bright and designer colors. Sold with as many as twenty utensils. Made also of ceramic and sheet metal. Most models rotate on a ball-bearing base (called a *Lazy Susan*), but others just sit on the countertop; rectangular models can be hung on the wall.

USE: Holding quantities of cooking and preparation utensils, including those that don't fit in a drawer easily, in a convenient, quickly accessible way.

USE TIPS: Keep at a little distance from the stovetop to avoid melting the plastic or splattering the clean utensils while cooking.

BUYING TIPS: Holds up to two drawers' worth of utensils in the space of a dinner plate on your countertop, where they are much easier to reach.

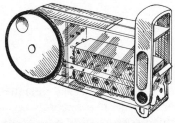

CHEESE SLICER AND STORAGE BOX

CHEESE SLICER AND STORAGE BOX

ALSO KNOWN AS: Cheese machine

DESCRIPTION: Clear plastic box, large enough to hold a good-sized brick of hard cheese, with a geared device at one end that pushes the brick toward the other, which has a guillotinelike cutter.

USE: Slicing and storing cheese in the same container.

USE TIPS: Always close after use to keep the cheese from drying out.

BUYING TIPS: Excellent idea for those who buy large blocks of plain cheese.

COOKIE JAR

COOKIE JAR

DESCRIPTION: Large jar, usually made of ceramic material, in decorative finish and shape. Loose-fitting lid sits on top. A 9-inch tall model can hold about a pound of large cookies. Also made in various imaginative and decorative designs, such as houses, barns, and even bears.

USE: Short-term storage of cookies.

USE TIPS: Not for long-term storage, as the loose lid allows air to circulate.

CRISPER

ALSO KNOWN AS: Celery crisper

DESCRIPTION: Unglazed terra-cotta cylinder, 4½ inches in diameter and 5½ inches high.

USE: Storing celery in the refrigerator for up to two weeks uncovered.

USE TIPS: Always keep a small quantity of water in the bottom—it will keep the celery moist.

DRAWER ORGANIZER

ALSO KNOWN AS: Flatware tray

DESCRIPTION: Plastic or plastic covered wire mesh tray designed to fit inside a kitchen drawer, generally with five sections separated by walls; sections may be shaped somewhat like forks and spoons in plastic models. Some models have a small sliding section that fits over the top, as well. Typically 11½ by 14 inches or 15 by 17 inches, and 2 or 3 inches deep.

USE: Holding various utensils in each section, such as forks, spoons, knives, soupspoons, and dessert or serving items.

USE TIPS: Clean regularly.

BUYING TIPS: No kitchen can be without one.

EXPANDING BREAD BOX

ALSO KNOWN AS: Expanding bread keeper, bread keeper

DESCRIPTION: Loaf-sized, two-piece, clear acrylic container with air vents. One side slides inside the other so that it reduces the box to the size of the remaining loaf.

USE: Keeps bread or pound cake fresh.

USE TIPS: A good substitute for plastic bags. Traditional sourdough bread is best kept in a paper bag or just cut-side down on the countertop—it needs the air.

BUYING TIPS: This is more efficient than the plain box of the old days. Good item to have.

GARLIC/MUSHROOM POT

ALSO KNOWN AS: Garlic pot, mushroom pot, mushroom keeper, garlic jar, garlic keeper, garlic storage jar

DESCRIPTION: Small pot or canister of unglazed terra-cotta or glazed ceramic, with large holes for ventilation, and a loose-fitting top. Often labeled, in the pottery, *garlic* or *mushrooms*. An *onion pot* is a larger version made for holding up to 3 pounds of onions.

USE: Proper storage of garlic cloves or unwashed mushrooms; ventilation reduces chance of rot or growth. Also useful for shallots and ginger root.

BUYING TIPS: Good way to store these foods.

GREASE CONTAINER

ALSO KNOWN AS: Oil strainer pot

DESCRIPTION: Small aluminum cylindrical container with a tight-fitting lid and a shallow strainer insert that fits over the base.

USE: Strains and stores cooking oil and grease for possible reuse or disposal, especially used deep-frying oil which is poured through the mesh to remove bits of food.

USE TIPS: Refrigerate or freeze fats for easy disposal as solids.

BUYING TIPS: It is generally not a good idea to reuse deep-frying oil. It accumulates food bits and moisture.

HANGING POT RACK

HANGING POT RACK

ALSO KNOWN AS: Ceiling rack

DESCRIPTION: Square, circular, or rectangular steel grid or frame available in a range of sizes but typically over 2 feet long, with removable "S" hooks and steel chains for hanging the grid from the ceiling. Usually painted black steel. Some models, called *crown* or *gourmet racks,* have arched steel strips instead of chains. One such model is a half-circle and can be wall mounted. Another version is a flat band that attaches to the wall, and there are corner racks, too. Some racks are made of wooden slats instead of steel, and have special, sliding hooks. All have either *S* or *J* hooks, on which to hang pots and pans from rings or from holes in their handles.

USE: Storage of large pots and pans. Commonly used items can hang and less often used items can be stored on top of the grid and fetched by climbing a ladder.

USE TIPS: Do not hang over a traffic area, but over a counter in order to avoid having to hang it so high you can't reach anything.

BUYING TIPS: Very handy and decorative item, but usually not inexpensive.

KETCHUP FUNNEL

ALSO KNOWN AS: Catsup funnel

DESCRIPTION: Long, narrow, plastic funnel that fits in the neck of a ketchup bottle.

USE: Transfering ketchup from an almost empty bottle to a fuller one. The upper bottle is left to sit upside down in the funnel for the time it takes the ketchup to make its way down and out.

LETTUCE CRISPER

DESCRIPTION: 7-inch diameter plastic bowl with a tight-fitting lid and small, perforated disk that sits just above the bottom of the bowl. The disk has a 2-inch spike in the middle.

USE: Storing lettuce in the refrigerator without letting it sit in water.

USE TIPS: Disk is removable so that bowl can be used to store anything.

BUYING TIPS: Handy item but one that takes up a fair amount of space in your refrigerator.

OIL CAN

OIL CAN

ALSO KNOWN AS: Cooking oil can, oil decanter

DESCRIPTION: Square, cylindrical, or conical stainless or tinned-steel can with narrow pouring spout, handle, and hinged lid or spout cover (on some models the spout is covered by a large lid that covers the whole container). Typically 1-pint capacity, though available in 1-quart capacity as well. Decorative designs for various types of oil may be found.

USE: Dispensing small amounts of oil without a mess, and storing oil protected from the damaging effects of light and air.

BUYING TIPS: Available in some highly decorative versions, as well as purely functional styles. Very helpful item.

OIL WELL

OIL WELL

ALSO KNOWN AS: Kitchen-oil spreader

DESCRIPTION: Short, round, soft bristled brush which fits inside a small plastic container.

USE: Greasing—applying a thin film of oil—to baking pans and sheets. Closed container helps preserve the oil on the brush and in the reservoir.

USE TIPS: Smell the brush periodically to be sure the oil has not become rancid.

ONION KEEPER

ONION KEEPER

DESCRIPTION: Two-piece glass item consisting of a saucer with an inch-high ring a few inches in diameter and a bell, or dome, cover that sits over it.

USE: Storing onions that have been partially used.

BUYING TIPS: Any closed container will do the job as well.

PRESERVING JAR

ALSO KNOWN AS: Mason jar

DESCRIPTION: Glass jar of various sizes, usually ½ pint, pint, and quart, with a two-part tight-sealing metal lid.

USE: Storing fruit and vegetable preserves put up in the home canning process.

USE TIPS: Follow recipes carefully in order to preserve food safely, primarily to avoid contamination.

RECYCLING BIN

ALSO KNOWN AS: Recycler box

DESCRIPTION: Wire frame, cardboard box, stackable modular plastic bin, metal or plastic rack for plastic bags, or any other container specifically designated for holding materials for recycling. Usually part of a two- or three-unit modular item. One corrugated cardboard box, 18½ by 12¾ by 24 inches, is designed to hold exactly 24 2-liter soda bottles or 135 aluminum beverage cans. Most are intended to be used with plastic bags as liners. Wooden cabinets are now made to hold a wire rack for three different bags; racks are enclosed by decorative cabinet. Stackable plastic bins—one for each category of material—may have drainage holes and labels for each material.

USE: Temporary storage of glass, metal, paper, or plastic for recycling.

USE TIPS: Rinse out all food from containers prior to storage in order to reduce the chance of attracting insects.

BUYING TIPS: Measure carefully to be sure of a convenient fit.

RIPENING BOWL

ALSO KNOWN AS: Ripener

DESCRIPTION: Spherical, clear plastic bowl with domed lid that has a teardrop-shaped depression in the top. 10 inches in diameter and 8 inches high.

USE: Storage of fruit that needs to be ripened a bit without causing brown spots or attracting fruit flies. Place in a cool area.

RIPENING BOWL

USE TIPS: Ostensibly, scientifically designed to be superior to paper bags by trapping the ethanol gas that the fruit emits. Intended for use on marginally underripe avocados, peaches, plums, pears, bananas, and tomatoes.

BUYING TIPS: Has only a very slight influence on ripening.

SINK CADDY

DESCRIPTION: Rectangular tray, about 4 by 8 inches, with compartments for sponges, bar soap, and small cleaning utensils. Many sizes, designs, and colors available; most often made of plastic.

USE: Organizing your kitchen sink area.

BUYING TIPS: Helpful item.

SLIDE-OUT TRAY

DESCRIPTION: Literally an extra, plastic drawer that sits in the bottom of a cabinet or on a shelf and has its own slides.

USE: Makes things stored in the back of a shelf easier to reach.

USE TIPS: Mount carefully so that once loaded, it does not tip forward.

SPICE RACK

HONEYCOMB SPICE RACK

DESCRIPTION: Any one of a number of designs in plastic or wood, supplied with empty, labeled plastic or glass jars. There is the *honeycomb rack* (ideal for wall mounting), with small plastic cubes set on an edge; the vertical *three-way rack,* in which the jars are presented on two or three indentations (used on a wall, on a counter, or in a drawer); and a *square carousel rack* (good for counter-top use), which holds four columns vertically on a rotating base. The most exotic one is an electric, motorized rack that rotates five jars out of twenty-two to the front at the touch of a button. Finally, small individual plastic shelves can be screwed or stuck onto walls or doors. Labels are available preprinted and sold separately.

USE: Holding small jars of spices and herbs.

USE TIPS: Keep spices in a cool place—not too close to the stove.

BUYING TIPS: If you are purchasing a rack to hold an assortment of previously bought spices, measure your spice jars to make sure they will all fit. Good item.

SPOON HOLDER

DESCRIPTION: Small, heat-resistant plastic block with short vertical and long horizontal slots. Clips onto the edge of a pot.

USE: Holding cooking spoons that will be used for stirring over the appropriate pot.

USE TIPS: Be careful not to heat up the handle with a high flame.

BUYING TIPS: Good idea—no spoon rest (see next entry) to clean up, and no hunting for the spoon.

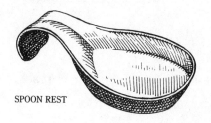

SPOON REST

SPOON REST

ALSO KNOWN AS: Spoon drip

DESCRIPTION: Shallow bowl or dish with a notch in one side—sort of an oversized spoon. Available in a variety of shapes, sizes, and colors, in wood, plastic, or ceramic. Also made as a flat, stamped piece of chrome-plated steel with three shallow indentations, and as a sort of oversized ladle with feet—a *ladle and spoon rest*.

USE: Resting cooking spoons and ladles, while still covered with food, on the stovetop. This is more easily cleaned up after cooking than the stovetop itself.

ARTICHOKE SPOON REST

USE TIPS: Handy to keep beside the stove for catching drips after spoon has been used. The oversized spoon design can also be used as a condiment server, or miscellaneous catch-all. The ladle rest has a high back which permits it to hold ladles upright.

BUYING TIPS: Good gift item, especially decorative types.

STORAGE RACKS

ALSO KNOWN AS: Kitchen organizers, cabinet organizers

DESCRIPTION: Plastic-coated steel wire, usually white, configured for various items and positions noted in the types below. Most have small loops for screws to be put through if screw-mounting them to a cabinet door or wall is required.

TYPES: *Dinnerware or chinaware storage rack:* Wide, bridge-shaped construction that holds stacked plates in the center and has hooks for hanging cups underneath, either directly under the plates in the narrower model or under wings on the outside for wider models. Sits on a cabinet shelf.

Garbage bag rack: About 9 inches across, 6 inches deep, and over a foot high, it holds 5-gallon vinyl garbage bags that are dispensed from a roll stored in the bottom. 1 gallon size also available. Designed to be mounted on the inside of an undersink cabinet door.

Ice tray caddy: Foot-long, U-shaped rack with brackets extending from each side toward the middle, on three levels. Holds three ice cube trays in the freezer.

Pan/tray organizer: Inverted U-shaped rack with five large, bent U-shaped brackets, each about 10 inches high and wide, forming wide slots. Designed to sit on a shelf and hold five large pans or trays.

Plate stand: Inverted U-shaped rack with at least four, 4-inch high, U-shaped brackets, depending on the length. Several plates are held vertically between each bracket. Designed to sit on a shelf.

Pot lid rack: Triangular, wall-mounted rack with six L-shaped brackets of graduated sizes extending out. The top one is very small and the bottom one very wide.

Refrigerator can dispenser: Plastic, sled-shaped rack that holds ten 12-ounce beverage cans on their sides, angled so that they roll toward the front and bottom where they can be removed one at a time.

Shelf rack: Plastic-coated wire racks that stack one atop another or slide in and out of one another. A solid plastic model is shaped like three small steps. A minimum of 14 or 15 inches wide, expanding up to 27 inches. Usually 5 or 6 inches high and about 8 inches deep.

Spice shelf: Long, narrow, wall-mounted, single-level rack for holding small spice containers.

Under-shelf shelf: A vinyl-coated wire shelf with long, U-shaped arms that hook over an existing shelf. Functions as a space-saving platter or tray holder.

Under-shelf stemware rack: Extra-shallow U-shaped brackets with slightly angled ends that screw-mount under shelves. Usually made in units of four slots 13¼ by

10½ inches. The rack is held about an inch from the bottom of the shelf, and the wide bottoms of stemware, like wineglasses, are slid into the slots. The glasses are stored upside down and thus do not collect dust in the bowls.

Wall or door rack: Narrow shelves, made in sets of two, three, or four, which mount on the insides of cabinet or kitchen doors, or go on the wall in a small area such as a closet, pantry, or hall as well as, of course, a kitchen wall. For storing jars and cans.

Wall grid: Rectangular or square grid with 1-inch squares, bent back around the edges so it stands about 1 inch off the wall. Supplied with mounting brackets for screwing into a wall and sold along with a wide array of accessories that hang from it: little hooks, big hooks, small baskets, shelves, and the like. Available in many colors and sizes, such as 12 by 18, 8 by 24, 5 by 24, and 24 by 36 inches. For hanging large utensils.

USE: Increasing storage space in the kitchen work area, cabinets, or appliances.

USE TIPS: Be extra careful when screw-mounting racks on the cabinet doors that you do not drill through the door; measure carefully and put a marker or a "stop" on your drill bit. Use the short screws supplied. Wall-mounting in plaster or hollow walls requires special screw anchors, which are available in any hardware store. Do not merely screw into plaster—the rack might pull out when fully loaded.

BUYING TIPS: Found in the housewares department of most hardware stores.

STRING BAG

ALSO KNOWN AS: French string bag, filoche bag

DESCRIPTION: Wide, loose mesh string bag with loop handles, about a foot square.

USE: Shopping for fresh food; when empty, stores well in a purse or pocket, yet is strong enough to expand and carry a heavy load.

BUYING TIPS: Saves trees, nonrenewable petroleum resources, and money. Traditionally used in Europe.

STRING BAG

THREE-TIER HANGING BASKET

DESCRIPTION: Set of three hanging baskets (small, medium, and large) strung together vertically with the smallest one on top. Made of lightweight wire mesh and chain.

USE: Storing food or small cooking items in the open air.

USE TIPS: Commonly used for potatoes, onions, and garlic. Though this is an attractive kitchen decoration, most other vegetables will last longer if they are chilled in the refrigerator.

BUYING TIPS: Good functional and decorative item.

TOOTHPICK HOLDER

DESCRIPTION: Small container with open top, available in a variety of shapes and materials, though usually made of ceramic or plastic. Most hold approximately one-hundred toothpicks.

USE: Holding a supply of toothpicks ready for easy access.

TWIST-TIE DISPENSER

DESCRIPTION: Plastic basket, about 4 inches across and an inch deep, which holds a reel of twist-tie material (small strand of wire imbedded in a ¼-inch-wide paper), with an offset part that contains a cutting edge.

USE: Dispensing twist-tie material to any length you desire.

USE TIPS: Very helpful if you do a lot of bagging of fresh food.

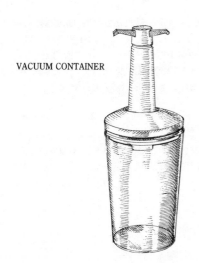

VACUUM CONTAINER

VACUUM CONTAINER

DESCRIPTION: Plastic container, usually clear, which is sold with a special top into which you can insert a vacuum-producing syringe. The syringelike handle is pulled, sucking out the air and temporarily sealing the container. Available in metric sizes, 500 to 1,000 cubic centiliters.

USE: Storage and increased preservation of fresh food over regular containers.

BUYING TIPS: Helpful on limited quantities of cooked foods.

VACUUM STORAGE BAG SEALER

ALSO KNOWN AS: Vacuum food sealer

DESCRIPTION: System composed of a machine and bags. The machine is a long, narrow device that voids plastic bags of air, then seals them. The bags are made from a roll of double laminated continuous film, either 8 or 10 inches wide and cut to fit. This plastic is impermeable to both air and moisture, and is heat resistant. Larger models of the machine have room for storing a roll of bag material, while smaller ones seal bags that are supplied separately.

USE: Vacuum-sealing bags of food for freezer storage and later cooking in a microwave oven or boiling water. Can also be used to keep nonfrozen food fresher longer.

USE TIPS: Cook up large quantities of your favorite recipes but pack them in bags of one serving each. Also suitable for long-term storage of important documents, jewelry, silverware, seeds and bulbs, and any other item that merits airtight and waterproof storage.

BUYING TIPS: Very convenient and practical item, depending on your cooking and eating style. Allows you to make a bag the same size as the food serving you are storing. Vacuum helps keep food fresh longer than that kept in regular plastic bags or containers.

VEGETABLE BAG

ALSO KNOWN AS: Salad crisper

DESCRIPTION: Terry cloth or 65/35 polyester/cotton bag with a cotton lining, ranging in size from 7 by 7 to 14 by 22 inches, with drawstring. One manufacturer gives names to each bag depending on its size, which denotes what vegetable it is intended to hold: potatoes, carrots, onions, etc. Some may have a plastic, sealable, lining bag.

USE: Wet or dry storage of vegetables or other foods.

USE TIPS: Can also be used for bread, wine, coffee, cheese, or fruit. Clean thoroughly after use.

WINE RACK

DESCRIPTION: Literally thousands of designs for this simple object abound. Elaborate brass or exotic wood racks have been made for years. More recently stackable, modular racks of a modern, efficient character have become common. They usually hold anywhere from a dozen to 4 dozen bottles per unit, and may be easily assembled or taken down. Wood, plastic, metal—all materials are used.

USE: Stores wine bottles horizontally, in a space-efficient manner. The horizontal position keeps wine against the cork, which in turn prevents it from shrinking.

USE TIPS: Place rack in an area that has constant moderate cool temperature and humidity, away from vibration, heat sources, and light. Sherry, Port, spirits, and liqueurs need not be kept horizontal nor, generally, do they improve with age, so only natural wine is kept in a wine rack. Arrange bottles by region and year.

BUYING TIPS: Good gift item, especially due to the wide range of designs available.

Convenience Items

ARM EXTENDER

ALSO KNOWN AS: Long-reach grabber

DESCRIPTION: Wooden or metal pole with wide tongs on one end and a lever handle at the other—about 5 feet long.

USE: Reaching for jars or boxes on high shelves or off the floor. Articles must be lightweight and easily grabbed by tongs.

USE TIPS: Also helpful for elderly or disabled persons.

BUYING TIPS: Very handy and inexpensive item.

ARM EXTENDER

BAG OPENER

ALSO KNOWN AS: Bag slitter, polybag cutter

DESCRIPTION: Small, U-shaped, finger-sized item with two round tips that squeeze together and a stainless-steel blade hidden inside. Some are equipped with a convenient magnet on the back for storage on a refrigerator door. Another version is wall mounted; a hook is open on the top side and a blade sits in the narrow opening.

USE: Slitting open plastic bags of snack foods or cutting string.

USE TIPS: Saves fingernails and teeth.

BUYING TIPS: If you have trouble opening snack food bags, and do so often, this is the gadget for you.

CAN AND BOTTLE OPENER

CAN AND BOTTLE OPENER

ALSO KNOWN AS: Can opener, can punch, can piercer, church key, can tapper, can tapper/bottle opener

DESCRIPTION: The familiar flat, ½-inch-wide stainless or chrome-plated steel, hand-sized device with two different ends: one is pointed while the other is blunt. Depending on the model, the blunt end may be flat and open or slightly arched. Both ends have little tabs on the handle side. The center part of the opener may be plain, with a magnet, or covered with wood or plastic.

A more specialized, simple version of this is the cast aluminum *wall bottle opener.* Small plastic versions of bottle openers for opening twist-off plastic or metal caps or regular pry-off bottle caps abound. (A device for opening food cans by cutting around the whole top is called a *twist can opener,* page 434.) There is much overlap in models that combine cutting with prying and lifting, but these are the basic types.

USE: Opening cans and bottles for drinking or pouring by piercing holes or prying lids off, not by cutting. The pointed end punches triangular holes in cans and the blunt end opens bottles by prying off tops.

USE TIPS: If a bottle top is on so solidly that it doesn't budge, just keep pulling the edge out a bit as you work your way around it. When you get near the starting point, it will just fall off. Watch out when opening pressurized cans—when you insert the pointed end of your opener some spray might come out. A second hole in a can top allows air to enter as you pour for a smoother flow.

BUYING TIPS: One of the most important basic and inexpensive items to have. Magnetic models are very convenient to keep at hand. Wall-mounted models, often seen in motel rooms, may be found with beverage brand names on them and older, antique ones can be considered collector's items.

CAN CRUSHER

CAN CRUSHER

DESCRIPTION: Either of two types are available. There is a fully automatic, boxlike electronic device about a foot high and deep, with a 12-ounce can-sized opening at the top. The other is a lever-based, slim, wall-mounted or countertop model that has a long arm.

USE: Crushing empty 12- and 16-ounce beverage cans into inch-high wafers for storage in a recycling bag. Saves space.

USE TIPS: Rinse out all cans prior to recycling.

BUYING TIPS: Automatic version is helpful to those with arthritis.

CAN TAB LIFTER

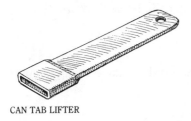

CAN TAB LIFTER

ALSO KNOWN AS: Tab can opener, tab grabber

DESCRIPTION: Small, flat, ½-inch wide plastic strip with small opening in one end.

USE: Lifting tabs on beverage cans.

USE TIPS: Helps avoid broken fingernails.

BUYING TIPS: Great cheap gift. Some *can caps* (see page 319) have a lip for this purpose. Effect can be duplicated by using a metal utensil. Not an essential kitchen tool.

CHINA STORAGE SET

DESCRIPTION: Quilted fabric bags in large rectangular and circular shapes with zippered lids.

USE: Dust-free storage of fine china. Usually holds service for 12.

USE TIPS: Label contents on outside of bag.

BUYING TIPS: Good idea for the meticulous housekeeper.

CLEAN AND DIRTY DISHWASHER MAGNET

CLEAN AND DIRTY DISHWASHER MAGNET

ALSO KNOWN AS: Magnetic dishwasher sign

DESCRIPTION: Large, flat, decorative magnet with plastic-coated image on each side. Depending on the make, this ranges from the words "dirty" and "clean" to one of a filthy little boy, and the other of a pristine little girl. Another version works only from one side but is turned upside down to show either word.

USE: Indicating if an automatic dishwasher has been run or not.

USE TIPS: Not of any help at all if used inconsistently.

COOKBOOK AND RECIPE EASEL

DESCRIPTION: Plastic, metal, or wooden device with various folds and crevices. Cookbook easels are about the size of a large cookbook. A *cookbook shield* is a clear, flexible plastic sheet with weighted ends that is placed over an open book.

USE: Holding cookbooks in place next to the prepartion area, and in the case of plastic-fronted models or the shield, protecting the book from food splatter.

USE TIPS: Bulky to store.

BUYING TIPS: This is also helpful if you don't have much counter space.

COUNTER SAVER

DESCRIPTION: Rectangular piece of tempered, heat-resistant, strengthened glass, with small rubber feet on the back. Either 12 by 15 inches or 16 by 20 inches, in a variety of decorative patterns and colors.

USE: Protecting a countertop from intense heat when a hot pot, pan, or casserole is placed on it.

USE TIPS: Can also be used for preparing raw fish or poultry so it is easier to clean up—the glass is nonabsorbent.

BUYING TIPS: Functions as a giant trivet. Other items, including large trivets or a pot holder, can fill the role of this item.

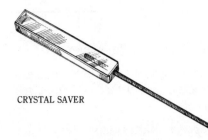

CRYSTAL SAVER

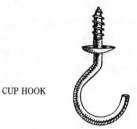

CUP HOOK

CRYSTAL SAVER

DESCRIPTION: Short, abrasive (microscopic diamonds) rod with a small handle.

USE: Rubbed lightly on chips in the edges of crystal glasses to smooth them out.

CUP HOOK

DESCRIPTION: Small question-mark-shaped hook with screw threads at one end and a shoulder, or plate, just above them. Available in several sizes and made of rubber-coated or painted metal or brass. A larger model is known as a *mug hook*. Safety models have snap lever to close the opening. Also available mounted on a bar in sets of four or more. Screws into underside of shelf.

USE: Hanging mugs and cups from under kitchen cabinets or shelves.

USE TIPS: Place where you are not likely to knock the hanging cups while reaching for something else. It saves space if you have limited room in your cabinets.

BUYING TIPS: The mug hook is slightly larger and more practical since it can hold more sizes of cups.

GARBAGE DISPOSAL STUFFER

ALSO KNOWN AS: Disposal plunger

DESCRIPTION: Blue or white plastic, round, T-shaped device with scalloped tip and sides. About 6 inches high and a few inches across.

USE: Stuffing food down a garbage disposal unit while it is running. Scalloped sides allow water to continue to enter the drain.

USE TIPS: Never use a small utensil for this job—you might drop it down the unit. It is OK to leave this item in place while the disposal is running.

JAR OPENER

ALSO KNOWN AS: Jar lid loosener, jar and bottle opener

DESCRIPTION: One of five designs for gripping lids that refuse to yield to pure hand force. An electric model that combines features of all of these is also available.

AUTOMATIC JAR AND BOTTLE OPENER

JAR AND BOTTLE WRENCH

JAR VISE

TYPES: *Automatic jar and bottle opener:* Battery-operated, under-the-shelf-mounted appliance that has a wide, open cone on the bottom. A sensor switch activates and turns the cone slowly when a jar top of up to 4 inches diameter is placed against it. The cone rotates very slowly but with three to five times the twisting power of the average human hand—you just hold the jar against it. Batteries last a year, on average.

Jar and bottle wrench (Also Known As *jar and bottle opener, adjustable jar wrench*): Heavy cast or steel wire levers about 8 inches long, connected by a hinge. The levers form a large circle at the hinge. A *universal* or *6-way jar and bottle opener* has several different sizes hinged together; both types work like large pliers. One version has an adjustable metal band loop and a 6-inch-long plastic handle. The loop is tightened against the lid by turning a knob on the handle. Still another version is a crescent-shaped, flat piece of plastic with teeth on an inside ridge and a small roller at one end. The opener is rotated until the jar cap is jammed between the roller and the teeth.

Jar vise (Also Known As *under-cabinet lid grip* or *under-counter jar opener*): Plastic triangle or plastic-mounted metal triangle with jagged inside edges, mounted under kitchen cabinet with screws. The jar lid is wedged into the slot and the jar rotated against it.

Rubber lid grip (Also Known As *rubber jar opener, rubber hand gripper, lid grip*): Floppy rubber disk, about 6 inches in diameter and about ⅛-inch thick, either round or shaped like a large hand. Another version is a corrugated cone shape. This simply provides a nonslipping grip for your hand.

Screw-top jar opener: 2- or 3-inch-long, inch-wide chrome-plated steel device with gears and tracks inside and a twist handle on top. When the handle is twisted, it opens and closes a set of jaws connected to the gears and tracks.

Twist-off bottle cap opener (Also Known As a *capscrew*): Faucet-handle-sized plastic ring with cone-shaped open interior.

USE: Gives you a grip on hard-to-open lids or caps; works on any size bottle or jar.

USE TIPS: Often just tapping the lid on a countertop or floor will make it easier to open.

BUYING TIPS: Any one of these is likely to be an extremely helpful item that takes up a minimum of space. Particularly helpful to those people who have trouble gripping things; the automatic model is best for people with the weakest grips.

KITCHEN TOWEL HOLDER

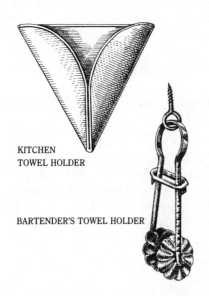

KITCHEN
TOWEL HOLDER

BARTENDER'S TOWEL HOLDER

DESCRIPTION: Any number of designs that keep kitchen towels at ready access. One of the most popular is a 1-inch-deep triangular plastic device, about 2 inches at its widest point, which has a Y-shaped slot. Another has a 1-inch-diameter, 1-inch-thick cap with an X-slot cut into the flexible plastic. Others include simple rings or loops of metal or plastic that are wall-mounted. Another type is the *bartender's towel holder,* a screw-mounted metal clip with two clamshell ends. A small metal slide keeps the ends gripping the towel.

USE: Convenient temporary storage of a single cloth towel at a time.

USE TIPS: Plug the towel in the slot with your finger.

MILK- AND JUICE-CARTON SPOUT

MILK AND JUICE SPOUT

DESCRIPTION: Either of two designs. One is a small, round plastic device, pointed and threaded on one half, with a plain, inch-long cylinder on the other half, that screws into the top of any size unopened coated paper carton of milk or juice. Supplied with a cap. The other, designed only for half-gallon cartons, is an inverted U-shaped plastic band 2 inches wide and 4 inches high that fits directly over the top of a carton. Two sharp prongs point down inside it, one making a small air hole and the other providing a pouring spout.

USE: Better, easier pouring and storage than with the fold-out spout.

USE TIPS: Pour from new, full cartons very carefully. Be sure to follow manufacturer's instructions for insertion.

BUYING TIPS: The screw-type spout does not allow air to enter as milk pours out, so it doesn't work very well. On either type, slightly imperfect insertion may cause some dripping.

OVEN MITT

ALSO KNOWN AS: Hot hand, hot mitt

DESCRIPTION: A thick, quilted piece of cotton material in the shape of a glove, any number of barnyard animals, or deep-sea creatures. Surface may be coated with a nonstick substance for easy cleaning, and is available in a range of colors and patterns from high-tech reflective aluminum to traditional checked patterns. Also made of specially treated leather. Glove versions come in three lengths: wrist, forearm, and elbow, or BBQ (13, 15, and 17 inches long).

USE: Holding hot ovenware, bakeware, and pan handles without burning your hands.

USE TIPS: Make sure you know the limits of your mitts. For especially hot dishes, such as a steel pan handle that has been in a hot oven, or for times when you might have to hold a dish for a while in order to serve the food, use additional protection, such as a dish towel or *pot holder* (see opposite). Never use wet—the heat will come right through and burn you.

BUYING TIPS: Get a good one—thin ones, or those designed with an area or break without insulation—are dangerous to use.

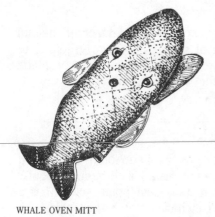

WHALE OVEN MITT

PAPER TOWEL HOLDER

DESCRIPTION: Device about a foot long designed to hold a roll of paper towels in either of two versions:

TYPES: *Freestanding:* Vertical spindle on a base, with a small vertical rod on the outside edge of the base. Usually made of nice-looking wood, but also available in an all-wire construction, marble, or as a small plastic disk with a short protrusion.

　　Wall-mounted: Metal, wood, or plastic bar with two holes for screw-mounting and two end pieces, or ears, at right angles that each have 1½-inch disks on their insides. Others may have fixed ears that hold a removable rod.

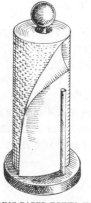

FREESTANDING PAPER TOWEL HOLDER

USE: Holding a roll of paper towels for easy dispensing.

USE TIPS: People tend to use too many paper towels. Make it a rule to use cloth for drying your hands and sponges for cleaning up most spills, and you'll conserve trees while reducing trash and saving money.

BUYING TIPS: The freestanding model can be a big help at picnics or when barbecuing on the patio.

POT HOLDER

ALSO KNOWN AS: Hot pad

DESCRIPTION: Square, quilted or woven cotton, insulated material in decorative colors or high-tech aluminum. Traditional checked patterns are common. Also made of leather. About 8 inches square is typical, but sizes range from 6 to 10 inches. Should have a loop for hanging from one corner. A *pan handler,* also known as a *pot handler* or *hot handle holder,* is a long, narrow, pocket version that slips over the hot metal handles of pans. This is made of thick rubber as well as the traditional quilted material.

USE: Protecting your hands when holding hot pots or pans.

USE TIPS: Never use holder if wet—the heat may be transferred through it to your hand.

BUYING TIPS: Common gift item. Look for especially thick ones made of durable material. An alternative to the *oven mitt* (see opposite).

REFRIGERATOR LINER

DESCRIPTION: Large, lightweight aluminum foil tray, 13¾ by 22 inches, with a narrow edge.

USE: Separating meat and dairy products in a refrigerator in order to follow Kosher guidelines.

BUYING TIPS: Specialized item not widely distributed.

REMOVABLE HOOK

DESCRIPTION: Small plastic or metal hook with a base that either contains a magnet or else is a suction cup, usually of clear plastic.

Both kinds come in small and larger sizes, but generally even the largest hook is no more than ½ inch deep.

USE: Commonly used to hang dish towels on refrigerators, but can be used to hang any lightweight item.

USE TIPS: The magnetic models don't hold much weight, so put them on the side of the refrigerator rather than the door—shutting the door could dislodge them.

BUYING TIPS: Commonly sold in sets of two to six.

SHAKER

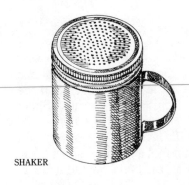

SHAKER

ALSO KNOWN AS: All-purpose shaker, all-purpose dredger, sugar dredger, sugar shaker, flour dredger, dredger

DESCRIPTION: Stainless steel or aluminum mug with perforated or mesh screw-on top. Available with either small or larger holes.

USE: Dispensing small quantities of flour, granulated or powdered sugar, cinnamon, salt, pepper, or other spices.

USE TIPS: Efficient way to put a little flour on meat prior to sautéing.

BUYING TIPS: Much easier, cleaner, and less wasteful to use than a hand-held strainer. Good item to have.

SINK MAT

DESCRIPTION: Flexible rubber grid about a foot square, usually sold as a set, including a pair for double sinks, a small "saddle" mat for the sink divider, and a larger one that serves as a drain board next to the sink.

USE: Creates a cushion lining for a kitchen sink, protecting glass and chinaware from accidental breakage.

USE TIPS: Clean often to prevent mold buildup. Most can be put in the dishwasher.

TWIST CAN OPENER

ALSO KNOWN AS: Can opener with cap lifter

DESCRIPTION: Two hand-sized levers with a hinge and a butterfly twist handle at one end; a gear drive and a cutting wheel are near

TWIST CAN OPENER

the hinge. Usually made of chrome-plated or stainless steel, though some are now made all of plastic; fancier steel models have large plastic-covered handles. Also made in a high-tech design compact version, without levers: An oblong cutting wheel is forced by movement down into the can. A *multiuse can opener,* also called *three-way can and bottle opener,* has a lever with one pointed can-piercing end and a blunt cap-lifting end; the more traditional design incorporates only the hooked cap-lifting device either at the end of one lever or somewhere near the hinge. Also available in a left-handed version and in a wall-mounted, crank-operated model that swings back flat to the wall when not in use (*swing-away* model). A very simple, 2-inch-long version uses prying instead of gears and long levers to cut through the lid, cutting about ½ inch every time you lift it up.

Electric can openers come in a variety of designs but all perform the same way: They squeeze the can edge between a cutting wheel and a gear. One kind cuts under the rim on the outside so that the cutting wheel does not touch the food. Another cuts in such a manner that the lid can be replaced on the can for short-term storage. Designed for wall or under-cabinet mounting, or countertop use. Many models incorporate other features as well, such as a knife sharpener, a bottle opener, a jar opener, and a bag opener. *Can and bottle openers* (see page 426) are similar.

USE: Opening cans by twisting and cutting through the top with a gear device and cutting wheel that are squeezed together, and opening bottles by lifting off caps. Multiple-use models can open cans by punching through as well, if they have the pointed lever end.

USE TIPS: Make sure the gear and cutting wheel are positioned securely before cranking away, and watch for a splat of the can's contents at the beginning and end of your work.

BUYING TIPS: Very common, traditional, and useful tool. Look for newer models that cut the rim in a way that lets you recap the can with its own lid, and leaves no sharp edges. Look also for a left-handed model if you need one. The knife sharpener in electric can openers is generally to be avoided, according to the knife manufacturers, because it is not made well enough to do a good job.

CHAPTER 17

Kitchen Kitsch

About Kitchen Kitsch

For some reason the kitchen is the focus of much fun, semifunctional, folkloric objets d'art, much of which can be considered as "kitsch" due to its extreme nature. Is there any way to explain why there are thousands of different refrigerator magnets, or why so many people must have a kitchen witch? Maybe it is just the innate need we have to express ourselves in archetypal fashion. In any case, it seems that kitsch items find their way into almost every kitchen, and that merits a look.

Noted below are items which are best known for their kitschy design. Some are often simply displayed just for art's sake, whatever that is. Following these items are utilitarian ones described elsewhere in this book that are often decorated, or even expressly designed, in kitschy styles.

Strictly Kitsch Items

CERAMIC WALL MOLDS

DESCRIPTION: Oval, square, round, or rectangular plaque in the shape of a deep plate, with a colorful relief decoration of fruits, flowers, or plants. One edge has a hanging hole provided.

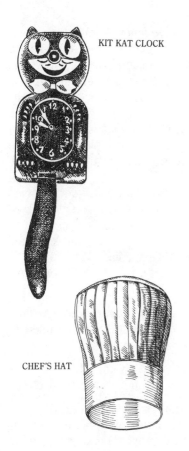

KIT KAT CLOCK

CHEF'S HAT

CHEF'S JACKET

USE: Kitchen decor with a food-related theme.

BUYING TIPS: Widely distributed but also considered a craft item.

KIT CAT CLOCK

DESCRIPTION: Wall-mounted electric clock, about a foot long, with a long flat tail that swings slowly back and forth, like a pendulum. Clock face is mounted on cat's body, and cat's eyes roll side to side at the same speed as the tail. Available in a variety of pastel colors, as well as the traditional black.

USE: Telling time and entertainment.

USE TIPS: This has been popular since the Depression.

BUYING TIPS: Every kitchen needs a good, friendly clock. This is one of the most traditional and the friendliest. Alternatives include clocks shaped like vegetables.

KITCHENWEAR

DESCRIPTION: Traditionally designed cotton, plastic, or paper clothing.

TYPES: *Apron:* Cotton or plastic sheet worn in front of the body with a bib and neck straps. Available in ankle or knee length; ankle-length model often called a *garçon model,* as it is favored by waiters in French cafés. Often decorated with a catchy phrase, such as "kiss the cook" or "I'm the boss, that's why," or a long involved humorous statement.

Chef's hat (Also Known As *toque* [Fr.]): Cotton, cotton blend, or paper hat, made of a wide headband and a large, stiff, pleated top that either rises straight up or is gathered loosely at the bottom. Big, important chefs are rumored to qualify for the hundred-pleat model, representing their knowledge of a hundred ways to cook an egg. The smallest sizes may have no pleats and are often intended for use by students; 9-, 10-, and 12-inch models are the norm. All are often called by their French names: The flat, low model is a *calotte,* the tall, classic model a *toque,* and the tallest straight model a *dodin-bouffant*

Chef's jacket: Cotton twill, double-breasted, boil-proof, military or tunic-collared shirt. White only. *Grand chef's,*

NECKERCHIEF

or *chief chef's, jackets* have twelve fancy, knotted, or hand-rolled buttons; vented arms; elegant styling; three-color collars; and are of the highest quality cotton, while the lower end of the line models may have only ten regular buttons or even a regular shirt front with four or six plain buttons.

Chef's pants (Also Known As *baker's trousers*): Heavy cotton or cotton blend trousers made in a black-and-white checked pattern. Also available in all white or black with grey pinstripe.

Clogs: Laceless slip-on shoes with thick wooden soles covered with nonskid rubber. Upper may be ventilated (perforated) leather.

Neckerchief: Large white or black-and-white checked cloth, 40 inches long on the longest edge, which is tied in a simple knot. Worn with a chef's jacket to absorb perspiration at the neck.

USE: Comfortable, utilitarian, traditional working clothing. Top-of-the-line quality and design hats and jackets are also used to impress the diners while strolling into the dining room.

USE TIPS: Bakers may prefer the all-white pants, while the dark ones are generally worn only by the grandest of grand chefs.

BUYING TIPS: While professional clothing is not considered essential in most home kitchens, it makes a welcome gift for serious cooks (it is quite handy and a pleasure to wear) and can be quite fun to have.

KITCHEN WITCH

KITCHEN WITCH

DESCRIPTION: Long-nosed, stringy-haired, babushka'd, broom-riding lady with a hanging string. It is 5 to 10 inches long.

USE: Brings good luck to your kitchen.

USE TIPS: Hang near a doorway. Dust regularly.

PICTURE TOAST

ALSO KNOWN AS: Toast marker

DESCRIPTION: Square plastic sheet, the size and shape of an average slice of bread, with cartoon characters or romantic messages formed by raised lines that are an integral part of the

PICTURE TOAST

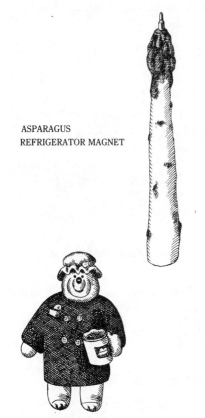

ASPARAGUS
REFRIGERATOR MAGNET

BEAR REFRIGERATOR MAGNET

plastic. Popular models include Minnie or Mickey Mouse, a smiling face, and a heart with "I Love You" written inside. Others say "This is your day" or "Good Morning." Some have magnets imbedded in the back for placement on an appliance door.

USE: Pressed into a slice of bread before toasting, the indentation stays lighter in color than the rest of the toast, and a readable message or picture is seen.

USE TIPS: Especially appreciated at sleepy breakfasttime. Don't press too hard or it will work as a cookie cutter, cutting right through the bread.

REFRIGERATOR MAGNET

ALSO KNOWN AS: Magnetic memo holder, memo holder

DESCRIPTION: Small plastic, ceramic, metal, cloth, or wood sculptures of various designs, which incorporate a small magnet. Favorite designs of plain magnets include foods, such as individual pieces of fruit, cheese, ice cream cones, balloons, dolls, or even fried eggs (also known as *breakfast magnets*), zoo and farm animals, and dinosaurs. Notable magnet designs also include four types of chewing gum packages, eight types of chocolate candy, nine types of canned soup, each of the United States, hamburgers, fruitcrate labels, crabs, fish, liquor bottles, Brillo cartons, teddy bears, cups of coffee, garbage cans, pancakes, dogs, cats, pigs, martinis, wineglasses (full), half-eaten muffins, tacos, Marilyn Monroe, Santa Claus, dolphins, beer cans, hundred dollar bills, peas, teeth, sardine cans (open), witty signs, each of the Three Stooges (Larry, Curly, and Mo), bottle caps, Ronald Reagan, whisks, pliers, hats, shoes, Mickey Mouse and other Disney characters, lobsters, vegetable oil bottles, traffic signs, combs, scissors, potato bags, corn cobs, giraffes, fat ladies, gingerbread folks, blackboards, knives and forks, flowerpots, irons, football helmets (with team insignia), cigarette lighters, tennis rackets, baseballs, caps, peanuts, hot peppers, fried chicken, starfish, all sorts of imaginary animals and other beings, telephones, wreathes, and rolling pins, just to name a few. Others have some other function as well, including small thermometers (in rainbow/balloon or butterfly styles), or clips for shopping lists.

USE: Decorating refrigerator doors and holding notes, snapshots, and works of art on same.

USE TIPS: Known to be especially suitable for holding artwork of small children or snapshots of new grandchildren.

BUYING TIPS: Suitable for artistic or emotional expression of all sorts.

WALL PLAQUE

ALSO KNOWN AS: Pennsylvania Dutch plaque

DESCRIPTION: Small wall plaque or trivet made of needlepoint, cross-stitch, wood, ceramic, or plastic, with decorative script declaring a warm and loving, homey phrase such as "No matter where I serve my guests, it seems they like my kitchen best."

USE: Adding warm, homey atmosphere to a kitchen.

USE TIPS: Do not use in a high-tech, Eurostyle kitchen.

BUYING TIPS: Popular in major tourist areas.

Kitschy Utensils Listed Elsewhere in This Book

CLEAN AND DIRTY
DISHWASHER MAGNET

Any kitchenware item can be kitschified. Listed below are relatively utilitarian items which are often found in kitschy style. Most are so decorative that one would tend to leave them out for display purposes even when not in use.

CHEESE SHAKER (page 377): The ceramic, mouse-shaped version is appropriate for the contents.

CLEAN AND DIRTY DISHWASHER MAGNET (page 428): Some versions of this get very imaginative and artsy, while others just use the two words, "clean" and "dirty," which would not qualify for inclusion here.

COOKIE JAR

COOKIE JAR (page 414): This item is usually done in styles that appeal to children, the prime consumers of cookies.

CORN DISH (page 359): Although there are other vegetable-themed dishes, this is a classic, which makes a nice display as well.

COW CREAMER

COW CREAMER (page 386): Why people accept a cow that disgorges milk through its mouth is hard to understand, but this is very popular.

HONEY POT

OVEN MITT

PIE BIRD

SALT AND
PEPPER SHAKERS

SCOURING PAD
HOLDER

ARTICHOKE SPOON REST

WIND-UP TIMER

TOPPER

CUTTING BOARD (page 50): Long wooden cutting boards are commonly decorated with scrollwork or phrases, often in foreign languages. Do not cut on a decorated side, as the paint may chip off.

HONEY POT (page 382): Although sugar bowls are not turned out in sugar cane or beet style, honey seems to strike the imagination and inspire more thematic designs. Available in a honey bear as well as a beehive style.

OVEN MITT (page 432): Found more often in decorative patterns and sometimes in quite inspired animal designs, this is something all cooks must have.

PIE BIRD (page 252): Though a plain funnel would suffice, and indeed is the traditional style, these are much more fun, especially when serving children.

PITCHER (page 386): Artists often take advantage of the large surface of pitchers to express themselves quite vigorously, and designs are not limited to decoration but include pitchers that are actually shaped artistically into birds and animals as well as those that are draped with leaves and fruit.

PLATE/BOWL (pages 356 and 351): Both leaves and fruit seem to form these imaginative decorative and functional items.

SALT AND PEPPER SHAKERS (page 387): Next to *refrigerator magnets* (see page 439) these items seem to be the most popular area for artists to stretch the limits of functionality in the name of art.

SCOURING PAD HOLDER (page 407): Form and function convene here in a generally humorous interpretation of small animals that can decorate the otherwise humdrum sink.

SPOON REST (page 420): While most people seem to choose a banal, plain version, there is plenty of room for creativity.

SPREADER (page 390): Rare is the plain-handled spreader, and luckily, the art form often fits the function very well, making for more comfortable handles than would exist if they were left plain.

TIMER (page 99): Offered in even the most chic and modern of stores, food and cooking-theme timers are quite common and every bit as functional as their plain counterparts.

TOPPERS (page 264): Any celebration that merits a large, decorated cake can be graced by one of these. The selection is large, so search until you find the one that suits your taste.

TRIVET

TRIVET (page 393): By their very nature some trivets are quite decorative, especially lacy, cast-iron ones. Very easy to hang.

UTENSIL HOLDER (page 413): This normally very plain, functional item is also very easy to decorate with embossed or painted designs, which make a nice contrast with their plain contents.

Cooktops, Ovens, and Ranges

Every kitchen needs more than utensils, of course. Large appliances are needed—definitely a refrigerator and freezer, and perhaps a dishwasher, a range hood, a garbage disposal unit (now called a *food waste disposer*), an instant hot water dispenser, and a trash compactor. But above all, every kitchen needs a cooktop, an oven, or a range of some sort that combines them, for the actual cooking.

Unfortunately for the uninitiated, some models offered are now so complex that they are called "cooking systems." It is no longer a case of just choosing between gas and electric or even between cheap and expensive. There is a wide and confusing range of products available, and here are a few guidelines that should enable you to make an intelligent choice that reflects your needs and preferences.

Common Terms

The following terms are used when describing all kinds of cooktops, ovens, and ranges.

CONDUCTION: Heat transferred by direct contact from heat source to cooking vessel.

CONVENTIONAL COOKTOP: One with individually visible, slightly raised gas or electric burners.

COOKTOP: The top surface of a stove in which the burners of any kind are held. May also contain a grill, a vent, a wok ring, or other accessories, as well as plain working or storage surface. Also refers to a self-contained unit that is mounted or dropped into a countertop.

COOKTOP/DOWNDRAFT EXTRACTOR: Ventilation system that is built into the cooktop alongside the burners or at the rear of the cooktop and sucks the smoke and odors down and into an exhaust duct. Some are always flush and some are flush in storage but pop up a few inches when working.

DROP-IN RANGE: Stove designed to fit into a counter with cabinets on either side and a platform underneath. Sold without side panels.

FREE-STANDING RANGE: Stove designed to stand independently of any counter or cabinets, but also next to them. Has finished side panels.

GAS: Natural gas is available through municipal supply or bottled LP (liquid propane) gas by

443

home delivery. LP gas delivers slightly less heating power to a gas burner.

GLASS SURFACE COOKTOP/ELECTRIC SMOOTHTOP: Smooth glass-ceramic surface with built-in electric burners underneath. (Described in more detail on page 447).

HOB: European name for a solid cooking element, whether gas or electric. Derived from an older term for a projection at the back or at the side of a large cooking fireplace used to keep things warm.

HOOD, EXHAUST HOOD, OR RANGE HOOD: Enameled-steel or stainless-steel tent or shelf situated over the stovetop, containing a vent fan and filter. Also called an *updraft ventilation system.* Hood either recirculates filtered air ("ductless hood") or sends it via an exhaust or ventilation duct to the outside ("ducted hood"). Generally a few inches wider and longer than the cooktop and mounted on the wall or ceiling. Most have a light incorporated in them, and some have dimmers. Air change and noise levels are rated by the Home Ventilating Institute. May have excess heat-sensitive controls that switch it automatically to maximum venting as needed.

OVEN: Insulated and heated compartment, usually with one to three racks for baking or roasting. Door is usually hinged at bottom but some are hinged on the side.

RADIATION: Heat transferred across air from a hot surface to the food or cooking vessel.

RANGE: Combination of cooktop with gas or electric burners and an oven; also called a stove.

SLIDE-IN RANGE: Range without side panels designed to fit snugly in a space between cabinets but on the floor.

STOVE: Combination of cooktop with gas or electric burners and an oven; also called a range. A stove may also be used solely as a heat source, i.e., a pot-bellied stove.

WALL OVEN: Also called a *built-in oven,* it fits into a spot made just for it in the kitchen wall. Must have a built-in exhaust fan. One main advantage of a wall oven is that it is easier to handle heavy dishes at that height.

About Cooktops

There are only two heat sources for most cooktops and ranges: natural gas or electricity (those that use wood, coal, or other fuels are not included here). However, how that fuel is converted into heat on the cooktop and used with your pots and pans is subject to much clever innovation.

Almost everyone will agree that the choice between gas and electricity is dictated by three things: budget, the availability of a gas or electric hookup, and personal preference.

Budget is simply a price study. Electric cooking is usually more expensive than gas, but that can change with utility rates. And though gas cooktops and ranges can be expensive, it is the electric ones that get all the high-tech innovations, so electric cooktops outsell gas models by a wide margin. The margin narrows considerably for ranges. As for energy source, cooks must use an electric stove if there is no gas hookup available, and must use gas if there is no heavy-duty, 220/240 volt electricity (ironically, some gas stoves require an electric hookup for the pilotless ignition and timers). However, one of the main elements of choice is personal preference—the kind of stove you learned to cook upon generally determines what kind you prefer later in life. As for details, see below.

Convertible or *modular cooktops* of both types are available, with modules for different styles of burners, grills, griddles, ventilators, rotisseries, deep-fryers, woks, extra large burners for stock pots or canners, poachers, or steamers, all of which you can insert or remove to suit your special needs or replace with updated, improved versions as they are made available (these are also available built-in on any kind of cooktop). Modules can be removed for easier cleaning, and some are designed expressly to be placed directly into a dishwasher without the heating element. The main advantage of modules for some people is the ability to mix gas and electric burners on a cooktop, thereby gaining the advantages of both.

All types of cooktops are made in 30- and 36-inch-wide models, with a depth of about 20 to 22 inches. Burners are arranged in a variety of ways, including a grand curve, a square, in-line, or an offset pattern. For each style described here, a description is followed by both positive and negative notes.

GAS COOKTOPS

Gas burners are now available in either of two types, *conventional* or *sealed,* and not much else. The conventional burner is an aluminum ring or cylinder that sits inside a large hole in the cooktop; a sealed burner has a solid porcelain coated cap and the burner element stem is sealed to the cooktop surface. The sealed design protects the burner from boilovers and keeps spills from going below the cooktop where it is so hard to clean in the conventional model; it also lends itself to more contemporary, slick designs (such as a tempered glass surface) and is now offered in several colors. This is the only functional difference, but a considerable one. Both types are supplied with removable cast-iron or porcelain-enameled cast-iron burner grates for pots and pans to sit upon (though sealed burner models are larger), and both make gas flames the same way. Sealed burner cooktops are slightly more expensive than the standard model and are available in higher-quality, better-looking models. Burners range from 6,000 to 12,000 BTU's capacity (the latter is considered a high-speed burner), but 9,000 is average.

Electronic ("pilotless" or "intermittent") ignitions are available now as an alternative to the constant-burning ("standing") pilot flame, and are considered energy-efficient as well as a safety feature. These cause the gas to ignite when the burner is turned on, as well as automatically reignite the burner should the flame be accidentally blown out. The lack of pilot flames helps keep the cooktop and kitchen cooler, too. For convenience, thermostatically controlled burners are available, as are click stops on burner control knobs for various preset flame sizes. Some of the best models have star-shaped burners rather than rings, for better heat distribution. Many of these features are now standard.

Gas cooking is popular because burner controls offer instant, infinite visual adjustment to heat, especially when turning it off and on (instant "off" is important to stop burning or boiling or cooking a delicate sauce; instant "on" is just a time element). Any kind of cookware may be used, including warped or poor quality cookware, as well as specialized items like woks and canners; it is especially easy to use with extra-large cooking vessels. Sealed burners eliminate a major and difficult cleaning problem. Gas burners are now incorporated into cooktops only 2 inches deep, allowing for creative design solutions such as placement above drawers—there is little heat generated below. Natural gas is usually much less expensive than electricity. You can cook with gas during a power outage. For what it's worth, professionals tend to go with gas.

On the negative side, gas stoves can only be installed where there is a gas supply (either municipal or bottled), and pilot lights, which must be left lit on some models, use small amounts of gas needlessly and can heat up a small kitchen. Some people fear explosions from gas that accumulates when a pilot goes out or a burner is turned on but not lit. Both these problems are eliminated by the electronic ignition feature. Finally, gas burners vary only slightly from brand to brand. If you want quite different, high-tech innovations, then gas is not what you want: Electric cooktops do vary tremendously and have all kinds of new technologically advanced designs.

ELECTRIC COOKTOPS

In general, electric cooktops are popular because they can be installed anywhere there is 220 volt/30 amp electricity and because, with the exception of coil burners, they are easily cleaned and lend themselves to innovative design solutions in the glass-ceramic models. In fact, vast choices are there for the consumer, especially in the high end of the model line. Electric burners are slightly better than gas at maintaining a steady, low heat for simmering and warming. Wattages generally indicate the same relative heat capacity no matter what kind of element is used. The only difference from element to element is the time it takes to heat up or cool down, and the type of heat generated, which is noted below.

On the negative side, most electric burners, especially the inexpensive models, are slow to heat up and slow to cool down, though the newer technology addresses this problem. Because most electric burners heat via conduction, cooking utensils must have perfectly flat bottoms in order to maximize contact with the heating element (heavier cookware works best), and must be within an inch or so of the size of the burner (some burners have two sizes built-in, and at least one model offers an oblong-shaped burner). Be sure to purchase a cooktop with a range of burner sizes starting at 6 inches in diameter and including at least one 9 inches in diameter. Most electric cooktops cannot be used for cooking with traditional woks (without flat bottoms) or canners unless a special concave or extra-large module designed for that purpose is installed. Some people find that designs which do not obviously show that a burner is hot are very dangerous, especially with inexperienced cooks or helpers. Most don't indicate how hot they are, either, whereas gas flame levels are easily visible. You can't cook during a power outage. And electricity usually costs much more than natural gas.

There is now a variety of types of electric burners and cooktops, and although not all are widely distributed, they are discussed here. The cooktop styles include two traditional types with burners on the cooktop and three newer types with burners underneath a smooth glass-ceramic surface, listed in order of popularity:

CONVENTIONAL COIL: For years, this flat, spiral coil, often called by a brand name, Calrod®, has been the standard for electric cooktops, and is generally the least expensive. Using electrical resistance wires, it heats both by conduction (where it touches the pot or pan) and by radiation (heating the air next to it), making it more forgiving than the following styles as far as uneven or oversized cookware is concerned. Small burners are rated from 900 to 1,500 watts, and larger, 8-inch burners at around 2,100 watts. Spillovers and cooking debris fall through the coils below the cooktop or into a drip bowl that must be removed to be cleaned (some are porcelain coated and can be cleaned in a self-clean oven). Removable elements and easily raised cooktops ease the cleaning task. This style of burner is slow to heat up and cool down, but faster than the solid element type, below.

SOLID ELEMENT: Solid, cast-iron disks sealed into the cooktop. The disk contains electric wires similar to the conventional coil burners, but being solid, presents a visually pleasing design, which is also easier to clean, as no food can drop below the cooktop. It may also be higher-rated, up to 2,600 watts. These are the only advantages. It is more expensive than the standard burner style and even some radiant styles described below. Cast-iron burners present an evenly heated surface that is the slowest to heat up and cool down in relation to the other types—they can be extremely slow, taking more than half an hour in some cases. These are sold with *thermostatically controlled* models (sometimes called *temp sensors*), which maintain a steady, preset temperature, as well as with *thermal limiters* (sometimes called *red dot elements* or *thermal protectors*), identified by a red dot in the center of the disk, which lowers the heat automatically if a pot boils dry or is too warped for proper contact with the burner element. Cast iron can rust and must be maintained, like cast-iron cookware, with periodic coatings of oil. These burners may heat up the surrounding cooktop somewhat, and heavy, flat cookware must be used.

GLASS-CERAMIC COOKTOPS

The following types of cooktops, also called *smoothtops,* are similar to one another in that electric elements are housed underneath a black glass-ceramic surface. Presently there is one principal manufacturer of this material, Ceran®, who developed this partly crystalline glass. When this style was first introduced in the 1960s by another manufacturer, all models used a type of opaque white glass that was largely unsatisfactory. This new material is translucent, allowing you to see if the element is hot or not, and ceramic, meaning it is tempered and impact resistant—you can pour ice water on a hot burner area without harming it. Burners under Ceran cooktops are equipped with thermal limiters to keep them from overheating the surface if a pot boils dry or is removed. Glass or ceramic cookware is less efficient to use than thick stainless or stainless-clad cookware on such a cooktop. Ceran is stain resistant and holds a decorative pattern permanently. It also heats more quickly and efficiently than the earlier material, and should not be confused with the plain tempered glass cooktop used on gas stoves.

This kind of cooktop lends itself particularly well to dramatic design solutions and high-tech innovations, many of which are European, and the flat surface can be used as a workspace when not being used for cooking. It is extraordinarily easy to clean because of being smooth, though routine cleaning calls for a nonabrasive paste of baking soda and water or a special cleaning cream supplied by the manufacturer; burnt-on food can be scraped off with a razor blade scraper (sugar or anything else that melts must be removed immediately or it will pit the surface). Smoothtops are generally 25 percent more efficient than conventional electric cooktops (on the other hand, they are more expensive). Because of all these characteristics, more than half of all electric cooktops sold in Europe are glass-ceramic, as are an increasing share of those sold in the United States.

HIGH-SPEED RADIANT GLASS-CERAMIC: Also called rapid-response or some similar term, the smooth, translucent, durable surface has cooking areas that glow red when they are too hot to touch, even when the unit is tuned off. This is by far the most common style of glass-ceramic cooktop burner. Radiants are designed to heat up more quickly than the traditional coils, using the same resistance wires which are in the air under the glass surface, not encased in flattened tubes or cast-iron disks. Three- to five-second response is considered excellent, and they can heat up fully in 10 to 15 seconds. A 6-inch burner typically is rated at 1,200 watts, an 8-inch at 1,700 watts, and a large 9-inch burner at 2,100 watts. Despite the name, these burners heat mainly by conduction, and flat-bottomed cookware is necessary. Generally the least expensive of the glass-ceramic cooktops.

QUARTZ-HALOGEN GLASS-CERAMIC: Similar to the above design, with which it is usually combined, this type has halogen-filled quartz lamp tubes encircled by electric resistance wires and gives off mostly efficient infrared radiation with only some heat by conduction. They glow instantly (called an "immediate [or instant] visual response" by manufacturers), glowing brighter as they get hotter and staying lit until the burner area is cool enough to touch. These usually have higher wattages (2,200 is typical) than the above electric styles, and when combined with a radiant element in the same burner, create a quick, hot, quickly adjusted burner. Most cooktops have one or two halogen burners, along with one or two regular burners. Generally more expensive than the above types.

MAGNETIC INDUCTION GLASS-CERAMIC: Perhaps the most high-tech and most expensive of the new cooktop styles (regular models are from a third more to twice as expensive than above styles; one extraordinary cooktop costs over $3,500), this style features the same smooth, durable, sleek glass-ceramic top or, in one case, burners imbedded in ceramic tiles or a granite surface, but the burners work in a radically different and 35 to 60 percent more efficient manner. Solid-state electronics use a high-frequency alternating current not to get hot but to create such a strong magnetic field that when a utensil made of a ferromagnetic material (iron, steel, nickel, or alloys—anything that reacts to a magnetic field) is placed on it, the utensil heats up immediately—and the cooktop stays relatively cool. Indeed, the surrounding material can be anything, such as butcher block, Formica®, Corian®, or stainless steel. The 1,800-watt burners have infinite range (recommended for canning), respond instantly to accurate controls, turn off automatically when the utensil is removed, and only use the energy required by a particular utensil. This design is exceptionally safe and energy-efficient, and because it doesn't get hot and burn spilled food, it is extra easy to clean. Induction is the electric cooking style closest to gas in terms of rapid response and control (it is 50 percent more efficient), though you must change your habits in order to use it: The utensils must be magnetic-reactant (no glass, ceramic, copper, or aluminum, even aluminum-clad) and larger than 4 inches in diameter (a dropped spoon will not get cooked); they must have food in them first; they must be heated slowly at first to prevent overheating; and they should be heavy, but they can be uneven. Controls are often designed to be the fanciest, high-tech style, such as one that uses a touch-sensitive,

illuminated, moving bar graph. This is available from only a few manufacturers.

About Ovens

Though a familiar term and common appliance, there are in fact quite a few options to consider when purchasing an oven. Here are a few points of difference between the various common types. These ovens are usually sold as distinctly different units, but some are combined and at least one brand has a top-end model that combines all three and handles all oven functions. Combination models are the wave of the future and make terrific sense.

THERMAL/THERMAL RADIANT

This is the standard, classic way of baking or roasting, relying on dry heat generally radiated up from the bottom but in some more sophisticated models, from the sides as well. Electric ovens may have a heating element on top for more rapid and even cooking, and may be better at broiling. Both gas and electric ovens are now available in self-cleaning models that heat up so high the food waste is literally burned off. An alternative is a continuous-clean oven with an interior coating that resists stains. Oven racks must be cleaned separately. Four cubic feet is a very large oven capacity (over 24 inches wide, usually), 3 feet or so is average, and 2 cubic feet is more common for secondary ovens, such as proofing and warming ovens designed for extended periods of use at low heat (120°F).

CONVECTION

This is an oven with a fan that forces superheated air throughout the oven for quicker, more even baking, browning, and cooking no matter what level the food is on or how filled the racks are. The oven is found in three versions: Stand alone countertop, microwave combination, or regular thermal oven combination (it is also made in a nonelectric model, a *stovetop convection cooker,* which sits over a gas burner). The small electric countertop model, about 2 feet wide and 1½ feet deep, usually has a 1.2 cubic foot capacity—sufficient for a good-sized turkey. At least one model is made out of small, stackable, modular plastic elements and uses extra-hot, extra-fast circulated air to the extent that it rivals a microwave in speed with some foods. The standard model might be called a thermal *convected oven.* Convection ovens typically cut cooking times by 30 percent. They are also suitable for broiling and slow cooking, and with special racks, dehydration.

Convection ovens are very popular with professional bakers, who need an even distribution of heat when baking in quantity. They are very good for soufflés, too. They are especially good at sealing in the juices of meats. Because the air is moving so quickly, different foods cooked simultaneously tend not to pick up other, unwanted flavors, making this a common choice for caterers or those who entertain often. The convection system is often incorporated into a microwave oven to promote browning without loss of moisture or doneness. Convection cooking is ideal for foods requiring less than 20 minutes cooking time, such as bread items or cookies. Look for models with a rack or two. A small model is very useful as a second, or supplementary, energy-efficient oven. Check that the door seals the heat in—not all models do this well. The better-quality range and wall oven manufacturers offer the convection feature on most thermal models.

MICROWAVE

Unlike conventional ovens, a microwave oven cooks with moist heat, the moisture being supplied by the food itself. Microwaves bounce off the metal sides of the oven (usually lined with plastic) and set the food's molecules bouncing around so much that they generate heat within the food itself. Contrary to popular myth, this still means that food cooks from the outside in. The microwaves are either moved around by a fan or the food is rotated for even cooking. Some of the better models feature either a concealed radiant heat source or a built-in convection or thermal oven for browning and crisping with dry heat (large and fatty foods that cook for a long time will brown with microwaves alone). Microwave radiation does not ordinarily pose a health threat; there is, however, a problem with packaged food that may not cook evenly or that may allow some chemical migration from, say, the packaging to the food. Follow manufacturer's directions carefully to avoid all problems.

Sizes range from a ½-cubic-foot mini-model to a family-size 1.4 cubic feet; the mid-size models may offer much more than the mini-size models for only a slightly higher price. The current industry standard rates a low-power oven at 550 to 600 watts, and a high-power oven at 750 to 800 watts. Higher wattage means faster cooking. Cabinets may be designed for built-in, countertop, undercabinet, or over-the-cooktop installation.

Microwave ovens are handy in areas where a full kitchen is not possible, such as an office, and for those kitchens where much frozen or refrigerated food that must be defrosted or reheated is used. Make sure you have correct, microwave-safe cookware that is transparent to microwaves (microwave-safe) and can withstand the high heat of the food it holds (see note on page 200). Do not use Melamine plastic or any solid metal cooking container in a microwave. Read the manufacturer's directions very carefully, as they contain directions on cooking various types of foods and what kinds of utensils to avoid. *Not following these directions carefully can cause a serious accident.*

Microwave ovens are popular because they cook food quickly. This is not only a convenience, but it allows you to start with frozen food. Some claim it leaves more nutrients and flavor in certain foods. These ovens also stay cooler than conventional ovens, keeping the kitchen cool and eliminating a cause of burns to children. Avoid ovens with complicated control panels; five, or at the most ten, cooking levels are sufficient (one model gives you one hundred to choose from). Ignore claims for self-cleaning microwave ovens; most can't get hot enough, so you just have to wipe them out. Nonstick linings and rounded corners make this easier. Look for bottom-feed power systems for more even cooking, and sensors—either temperature or moisture—that automatically stop the cooking when the food is done (moisture sensors may be better). Other features to look for include automatic reheating of cooked food, multistage or multilevel cooking programs, automatic defrosting, and a "done" bell that rings only once. Over 80 percent of American households have a microwave oven.

About Buying a Range

A range, also called a *stove,* combines a cooktop and oven with any features that you might want, such as plain countertop, a mixture of gas and electric burners and ovens, grills, griddles, warming ovens, salamanders (small broilers), and so on. Now there are more choices of colors and surfaces, too: brushed stainless steel, black or white tempered glass (as well as the Ceran® electric cooktops), and porcelain-enameled steel in white, almond, black, and gray. Ranges are available in 20-, 21-, 24-, 27-, 30-, 36-, 40-, and 48-inch-wide models, though the latter two widths are only found in the professional category described below. Most are within an inch or so of 27 inches deep (check manufacturer's brochures for accurate dimensions and to see whether handles and hookups are included).

As for features, look for a self-cleaning oven, easy-to-read and accessible controls that, if they are on the back panel, are not blocked by cookpots and are vertical so they won't catch food debris, an easily cleaned glass-fronted control panel, storage drawers, easily changed lightbulbs, removable or easily propped up cooktops for easier cleaning, and a clear glass oven window. Compare oven and cooktop design carefully to find maximum capacity of large pots and casseroles. For large families or those who entertain often, double-oven models, called *over-and-under,* make sense. Some now mix both gas and electric burners on the stovetop. Downdraft ventilation is available on a wide array of models, too. You need to decide if you want controls on the back, side, or front. You might burn yourself reaching for controls in the back.

Then there are the ranges for serious cooks who don't want a professional model. Some of the best are adapted from professional ones especially for the home cook, featuring increased capacity and sturdiness. One unusual British range that is custom assembled and installed has as many as four ovens and seven cooking stations, comes in eight colors, works with either coal or gas, weighs as much as 1,100 pounds, and can cost close to $10,000. It has no knobs or controls and is left on continuously because it takes up to twenty-four hours to reach working temperatures. Each cooking station is maintained at a constant temperature.

PROFESSIONAL/COMMERCIAL RANGES

Serious, professional and semi-professional, well-to-do cooks often purchase commercial or professional ranges intended for the hard knocks of day-to-day restaurant use and install them in their homes. Now some manufacturers offer these models with the residential gas safety features required by law. They are also designed to fit into counter and cabinet spaces like regular consumer models. If you need and can afford one, these ranges are clearly superior to the regular models. For the many thousands of dollars they cost, they ought to be.

They are better insulated and sturdier (more stainless steel parts, making them more than twice as heavy as domestic models), and above all, they are larger: larger in dimensions (40 or 48 inches wide is normal, but 60-inch-wide models are available), larger in capacity (up to eight burners, 4-cubic-foot ovens up to 28 inches wide, with one model 35½ inches wide), larger and more accurate in heating ability. They are just simply more powerful. You can cook faster on a burner with a larger flame (15,000 BTU/hr vs. 9,000 on a normal range), which is definitely helpful when cooking many different things or when heating an extremely large stockpot. They are almost always offered in gas versions. You can simmer precisely, and you can definitely fit more cooking vessels on the cooktop (with its oversized, porcelain-coated cast-iron grates) or in the oven at the same time—a must for serious entertainers or caterers. They are often the focal point of a kitchen.

Some of the professional features are unique, such as a gas-infrared in-the-oven broiler. This cooks food quickly to sear it well and prevents smoking. Removable drip trays and other features make these ovens easier to clean. Controls work precisely to cook from a gentle simmer of a small saucepan to a roiling boil of a huge stockpot. Others may have a built-in range hood for which a large exhaust duct is necessary. Look for a model designed to keep front-panel control knobs cool despite their placement over the oven opening. Most have some feature to deflect the heat.

Perhaps the most noteworthy aspect of professional ranges vs. consumer models is the availability of accessories or specialized cooking arrangements. These ranges can come with large surface grills, waist-level broilers, warming and proofing ovens, and combination convection/thermal ovens. (It is a sign of advanced design and quality when a consumer model has these options.) Most wide models offer side-by-side ovens or hardwood cutting boards. The base may be closed off or have stainless-steel legs.

Mail-Order Catalog Guide

It is unfortunate that serious kitchenware stores are not found everywhere. They are wonderful stores to browse in and can be positively inspirational for your cooking repertoire—not only might you decide to try making a particular recipe because you came across the specialized utensil necessary for that dish, but you will find that many stores sponsor lively demonstrations or book signings with visiting professionals.

On the other hand, a small number of general and specialized mail order catalogs fill the gap left by this dearth of kitchenware stores—and they do so quite creatively. Most feature clear pictures and very readable copy, and some have a range of items that would be hard to stock in a small store (though they *are* listed in this book). Prices do not appear to vary tremendously from catalog to catalog except when expensive appliances are on sale. Quality is another thing. Research carefully before you buy.

Included here is what a recent survey found. By the way, this list is by no means exclusive, nor should a listing here be considered an endorsement.

BRIDGE KITCHENWARE
212-838-6746

214 East 52nd Street
New York, NY 10022
Fax 212-758-5387

Though the mail-order catalog is new, the Bridge store in midtown Manhattan has been a mecca for professional chefs for many years. They feature top-quality imported and domestic professional products, including some rare and esotoric items. Product descriptions in their 44-page catalog contain much useful information despite numerous misspellings. The group photos, though clear, are a little confusing to use. Intended to be an annual publication.

A COOK'S WARES
412-846-9490

211 37th Street
Beaver Falls, PA 15010-2103
Fax: 412-846-9562

46 pages of no-nonsense, brief copy in a simply designed newsprint catalog. Items are listed with small black-and-white line drawings and both retail and discount prices, as much as 50% off. Small selection of books. Only top-of-the-line consumer and professional items are in-

cluded. Published several times a year, this shows the mark of being a small and personal business

THE CHEF'S CATALOG
800-338-3232

3215 Commercial Avenue
Northbrook, IL 60062-1900
Fax: 705-480-8929

Probably the most complete and focused of the mail order catalogs, this successful operation concentrates on serious, high-quality cooking equipment and appliances with only a few pages of cleaning or storage items. Intended, in their words, for the "cooking enthusiast." Clean layout, clear pictures, and intelligent, brief, copy. One recent issue ran to 56 pages.

COLONIAL GARDEN KITCHENS
800-752-5552

340 Poplar Street
Hanover, PA 17333-0066

A small-format, inexpensive gadget-oriented catalog almost 100 pages long, CGK includes a lot of nonfood-related items, mostly for clothing care and storage. Oriented to the homemaker rather than the serious cook, but with many very handy items. Seasonal plus special sales.

COMMERCIAL CULINARY
800-999-4949

P.O. Box 30010
Alexandria, VA 22310
Fax: 703-550-8034

38 pages of clear, brief copy with a simple black-and-white layout on good-quality newsprint, this is one of the most straightforward catalogs. It features professional utensils and appliances as well as replacement parts at discounted prices.

COMMUNITY KITCHENS
800-535-9901

P.O. Box 2311
Baton Rouge, LA 70821-2311
Fax: 800-321-7539

Without a doubt this is the most appetizing catalog to look at, thanks primarily to well-reproduced top-notch food photography, but also to a generous, full-size, sophisticated layout. Food products occupy almost as much space as cooking equipment, which is usually shown in use. Features high-quality, serious cookware and gift-type accessories. Only 45 pages long. Monthly.

CRATE AND BARREL
800-323-5461

P.O. Box 9059
Wheeling, IL 60090-9059
Fax: 708-215-0482

Generously laid out and well-written catalog with only a very limited number of quality kitchenware items (it is mostly tableware) which represent a minor sampling of products available in the large stores of this chain. Good prices all year long.

FIGIS COOK'S SHOPPE
715-341-1363

3200 South Maple Avenue
Marshfield, WI 54449

Small, limited selection of gadgets and food items mixed in with a small group of utensils and appliances. Published on major holidays.

THE GRILL LOVER'S CATALOG
800-252-8248

P.O. Box 1300
Columbus, GA 31993-2499
Fax: 404-571-6088

A very nicely done catalog limited to indoor and outdoor barbecue equipment, sauces, and supplies. Published by a major manufacturer of grills, it features non-competitive equipment of other manufacturers as well. Bi-monthly.

J. B. PRINCE COMPANY
212-302-8611

29 West 38th Street
New York, NY 10018
Fax: 212-819-9147

Straightforward and plain presentation of the finest professional tools from all over the world with a concentration on dessert-making equipment and fancy or unusual display items—no cookware. Also includes an extensive book section as well as a separate 47-page catalog of books aimed at the professional. 96 pages long.

LAMALLE OF NEW YORK
212-242-0750

36 West 25th Street
New York, NY 10010
Fax: 212-645-2996

Though primarily directed toward trade or professional clients, this friendly, informal import company also takes orders from knowledgeable individuals looking for even the most obscure French item. They are especially strong in wooden and wire tools, pastry molds, and copper cookware.

THE MICROWAVE TIMES
800-328-2846

Box 1271
Burnsville, MN 55337-0271

The smallest of all the catalogs, this 5-page flyer concentrates on equipment intended for microwave use and books on microwave cooking. Bi-monthly.

POTTERY BARN
800-922-5507

Mail Order Department
P.O. Box 7044
San Francisco, CA 94120-7044
Fax: 415-421-5153

This short, large-format catalog is beautiful to look at. It features both fancy and utilitarian tableware, with only the occasional cooking utensil. Monthly.

SIGNATURES
714-943-2021

19465 Brennan Avenue.
Perris, CA 92379
and

STARCREST
714-657-2793

19465 Brennan Avenue.
Perris, CA 92379

These are not catalogs per se but rather envelopes of 1-page flyers featuring pricey gadgets and accessories among a greater quantity of cleaning gadgets, storage items, jewelry, and home furnishings presented in a hard-sell manner. They appear to be similar in everything but company name and phone number. Published every few weeks.

WILLIAM GLEN
800-842-3322

2651 El Paseo Lane
Town & Country Village
Sacramento, CA 95821
Fax: 916-482-3562

Glossy, gorgeous color layout of beautiful, high-quality equipment and fancy tableware, with a more straightforward black-and-white insert for basic tools. Not a wide selection, but a helpful one, with several food products included. 38 pages; published twice a year.

WILLIAMS-SONOMA
800-541-2233

Mail Order Department
P.O. Box 7456
San Francisco, CA 94120-7456
Fax: 415-421-5153

At 80 small-format pages, this features an intense layout with beautifully staged and printed photos. Top-quality, serious cookware, appliances, and serving equipment (including fine china and crystal) are featured here, with the occasional gadget, ornament, or cleaning tool as well as some food items. Monthly.

WILTON ENTERPRISES
800-772-7111, ext. 320

2240 West 75th Street
Woodridge, IL 60517

194 pages of cake decorating and baking equipment, Wilton's "Yearbook" (as they call their catalog) includes detailed instructions for creating the dozens of elaborate theme cakes shown in lavishly reproduced color photos. Every small decorating tool is included here, along with basic cake pans and molds.

THE WINE ENTHUSIAST
800-356-8466

P.O. Box 39
Pleasantville, NY 10570-0039
Fax: 800-833-8466

Perhaps the most specialized of catalogs listed here, this includes wine storage systems and accessories ranging from the simplest classic item to the most high-tech, as well as glasses, decanters, and even fine art prints of Burgundy. Bi-monthly.

THE WOODEN SPOON
800-431-2207

Route 145, Heritage Park
P.O. Box 931
Clinton, CT 06413-0931
Fax: 203-669-4401

A very wide selection of utensils and gadgets for all cooks, this 48-page, small-format catalog has very few non-cooking items. The pages are a bit crowded but the copy is very well written. Seasonal.

Index